The Tempter's Voice

THE TEMPTER'S VOICE

Language and the Fall in Medieval Literature

Eric Jager

Cornell University Press

Ithaca and London

Copyright © 1993 by Cornell University

All rights reserved. Except for brief quotations in a review, this book, or parts thereof, must not be reproduced in any form without permission in writing from the publisher. For information, address Cornell University Press, Sage House, 512 East State Street, Ithaca, New York 14850.

First published 1993 by Cornell University Press.

International Standard Book Number 0-8014-2753-3 (cloth)
International Standard Book Number 0-8014-8036-1 (paper)
Library of Congress Catalog Card Number 93-11811

Printed in the United States of America

Librarians: Library of Congress cataloging information appears on the last page of the book.

⊗ The paper in this book meets the minimum requirements of the American National Standard for Information Sciences—Permanence of Paper for Printed Library Materials, ANSI Z39.48-1984.

Excerpts from the following works reprinted by permission:
The Ancrene Riwle: The Corpus MS.: Ancrene Wisse, translated by Mary B. Salu. © 1955 by Burns & Oates, Ltd.
Avitus, *The Fall of Man*, edited by Daniel J. Nodes, pp. 18–48, by permission of the publisher. © 1985 by the Pontifical Institute of Mediaeval Studies, Toronto.
Larry D. Benson (Editor), *The Riverside Chaucer*, Third Edition. Copyright © 1987 by Houghton Mifflin Company. Used with permission.
The Celestial Cycle: The Theme of Paradise Lost in World Literature, with Translations of the Major Analogues by Watson Kirkconnell. © 1952, University of Toronto Press.
Confessions of St. Augustine by St. Augustine, translated by Rex Warner. Copyright © 1963 by Rex Warner, renewed 1991 by F. C. Warner. Introduction copyright © 1963, renewed 1991 by Vernon J. Bourke. Used by permission of New American Library, a division of Penguin Books USA Inc.
Early English Christian Poetry Translated into Alliterative Verse, edited and translated by Charles W. Kennedy. © 1952, Oxford University Press.
"Langue d'Amour" by Laurie Anderson. © 1984 Difficult Music (BMI).
The Literal Meaning of Genesis, vol. 2. John Hammond Taylor, S.J., translator, Ancient Christian Writers series, no. 42. © 1982 by Rev. Johannes Quasten, Rev. Walter J. Burghardt, S.J., Thomas Comerford Lawler. Used by permission of Paulist Press.
Saint Ambrose: Hexameron, Paradise, and Cain and Abel, translated by John J. Savage; and *Saint Augustine on Genesis*, translated by Roland J. Teske; Fathers of the Church series, nos. 42 and 84. © 1961, 1991, Catholic University Press of America.
St. Augustine: On Christian Doctrine. Translated by D. W. Robertson, Jr. Copyright © 1958 by Macmillan Publishing Company; and from *John Milton: The Complete Poems and Major Prose*, edited by Merritt Y. Hughes. Copyright © 1985 by Macmillan Publishing Company. © 1957 by Odyssey Press. Reprinted with the permission of Macmillan Publishing Company, Inc.

To my father
And in memory of my mother

[Adam] signifies in Greek the whole world, for there are four letters, A, D, A, and M. But as the Greeks speak, the four quarters of the world have these initial letters. . . . Adam therefore has been scattered over the whole world. He was in one place, and fell, and as though broken small he filled the whole world; but the mercy of God gathered together the fragments from every side, and forged them by the fire of love, and made one what was broken.

—ST. AUGUSTINE

CONTENTS

ILLUSTRATIONS

ACKNOWLEDGMENTS

I AM GRATEFUL to many people for helping me in the course of writing this book. For its early progress I am indebted to Thomas Toon, Thomas Garbáty, Macklin Smith, Ralph Williams, and Charles Witke of the University of Michigan, and also to the late James Downer, whose wisdom and hospitality are remembered by so many. For more recent help, I am grateful to many Columbia colleagues: first, those who generously read sections of the book in draft—David Damrosch, Joan Ferrante, Robert Hanning, David Kastan, Howard Schless, Edward Tayler, and David Yerkes; and, second, those who endured parts of it in colloquia or who offered useful suggestions—Peter Awn, Christopher Baswell, Renate Blumenfeld-Kosinski, Caroline Bynum, Ann Douglas, Kathy Eden, Kathryn Gravdal, Patricia Grieve, John McGee, Sandra Prior, James Shapiro, Victoria Silver, George Stade, and Robert Stein. Several fine research assistants—Betsy Beckmann, Sarah Kelen, and James Cain—tracked down elusive materials in the Columbia libraries and, along with the other graduate students in my seminar (Autumn 1991), contributed valuably to my thinking about this book.

Beyond Columbia, many friends, colleagues, and correspondents have offered advice and help: Edward Baker, Carol Bradof, Susan Burchmore, George Cooper, Kimberly Devlin, Marsha Dutton, Edward Ericson, Allen Frantzen, James Hala, John Lofty, Michael Martin, Vincent McCarren, Pat Moloney, Paul Remley, and John Vickrey. I especially thank Peter Brown and Lee Patterson for their helpful comments on a version of Chapter 2 delivered in a talk at Princeton, and to my host on that occasion, William Chester Jordan.

At Cornell University Press, Bernhard Kendler patiently guided this book into print, and Carol Betsch shepherded it through its production. The readers for the press—Sherron Knopp of Williams College and Ann W. Astell of Purdue University—gave perceptive critiques that enabled me to improve the argument in many ways, large and small. Victoria Haire capably edited the manuscript.

Archival assistance was provided by Julian Conway of the Department of Manuscripts at the British Library; Robert Melzak of the Index of Christian Art at Princeton University; and Robert E. Lewis, editor-in-chief of the *Middle English Dictionary*, who kindly allowed me to consult unpublished material. For photography or photo permissions, I am grateful to Lawrence Alphonse of the Department of Manuscripts at the British Library; Mary Clapinson of the Bodleian Library; Charles E. Pierce, Jr. (director), Inga Dupont, and H. George Fletcher of the Pierpont Morgan Library; George Lonsdorf of the Cloisters; Annette Weir of Art Resource; D. D. Schroeder; and E. Peter Schroeder. Brian Fleishman provided crucial assistance in printing out the revised manuscript. Special thanks go to Laurie Anderson for permission to quote from one of her songs in the Epilogue.

My last and most important personal acknowledgment is to my wife, Peg, who has supported my work on this project for years with her wise counsel and unfailing goodwill. In addition to offering many useful suggestions along the way, she helped crucially with the index. My debt to her is infinite.

This book received generous financial support from various sources. It was first sponsored by a Carrye and Abraham Hart Fellowship from the Department of English at the University of Michigan and a Horace H. Rackham Predoctoral Fellowship from the graduate school. Columbia University gave support through summer fellowships from the Council for Research in the Humanities, and especially through a combined Chamberlain Fellowship and Junior Faculty Developmental Leave, which provided a full year of leave from teaching. The university also helped defray photo and permissions fees.

Parts of this book were presented as lectures and conference papers at Iowa State University (1986), Western Michigan University (1987), Princeton (1991), and Columbia (1991). Sections of Chapter 4 appeared as articles in *Neophilologus* 72 (1988): 434–48 and 75 (1991): 279–90, and *English Studies* 71 (1990): 307–21, whose editors kindly have granted permission to use this material.

ERIC JAGER

New York, New York

ABBREVIATIONS

ACW	Ancient Christian Writers (ed. Johannes Quasten et al.)
AM	*Annuale Mediaevale*
A-S	Anglo-Saxon
AS	*Augustinian Studies*
ASE	*Anglo-Saxon England*
ASPR	*The Anglo-Saxon Poetic Records*
AW	*Ancrene Wisse*
BL	British Library
B-T	Joseph Bosworth and T. Northcote Toller, eds., *An Anglo-Saxon Dictionary* and *Supplement*
CCSL	*Corpus Christianorum, series latina*
CHB	*The Cambridge History of the Bible*
DOE	*Dictionary of Old English*
EETS	Early English Text Society (OS = Original Series)
ES	*English Studies*
FOC	Fathers of the Church (ed. Roy Deferrari et al.)
IE	Indo-European
JEGP	*Journal of English and Germanic Philology*
JHI	*Journal of the History of Ideas*
KJV	King James Version (Bible)
LCL	Loeb Classical Library
LOF	A Library of Fathers of the Holy Catholic Church
LXX	Septuagint (Bible)
MAE	*Medium Aevum*
ME	Middle English
MED	*Middle English Dictionary*
MGH	Monumenta Germaniae Historica
MLLM	*Mediae Latinitatis Lexicon Minus*
MLN	*Modern Language Notes*
MLQ	*Modern Language Quarterly*

MS(S).	Manuscript(s)
N&Q	*Notes & Queries*
NLH	*New Literary History*
NM	*Neuphilologische Mitteilungen*
NPNF	A Select Library of the Nicene and Post-Nicene Fathers of the Christian Church (ed. Philip Schaff)
OCT	Oxford Classical Texts
OE	Old English
OED	*Oxford English Dictionary*
OF	Old French
OL	Old Latin (Bible)
OLD	*Oxford Latin Dictionary*
OP	Old Provençal
OS	Old Saxon
OTP	*The Old Testament Pseudepigrapha*
PL	*Patrologia Latina* (ed. Jacques-Paul Migne)
PLL	*Papers on Language and Literature*
PMLA	*Publications of the Modern Language Association of America*
PQ	*Philological Quarterly*
REA	*Revue des études augustiniennes*
RES	*Review of English Studies*
RSV	Revised Standard Version (Bible)
TLL	*Thesaurus Linguae Latinae*
vr(r).	variant(s)
Vulg.	Vulgate (Bible)

Abbreviations for Patristic Writings
(Works are by Augustine unless indicated otherwise.)

Cat	*De catechizandis rudibus*
Civ	*De civitate Dei*
Conf	*Confessiones*
Doc	*De doctrina Christiana*
Dom	*De sermone Domini in monte*
Enar	*Enarrationes in Psalmos*
Ench	*Enchiridion*
GenL	*De Genesi ad litteram*
GenM	*De Genesi contra Manichaeos*

Lib	*De libero arbitrio*
Mag	*De magistro*
Nup	*De nuptiis et concupiscentia*
Ord	*De ordine*
Par	*De Paradiso* (Ambrose)
Sol	*Soliloquia*
Spir	*De spiritu et littera*
Trin	*De Trinitate*
Ver	*De vera religione*

NOTE ON BIBLICAL CITATIONS

FREESTANDING biblical quotations are from the Revised Standard Version, unless noted otherwise; citations from the Psalms follow the Vulgate numeration. Biblical passages appearing in quoted sources are reproduced as quoted, unless a note indicates otherwise. On the versions of the Bible used by patristic and medieval exegetes, see the Introduction. For the various editions of the Bible quoted in this book, see the Bibliography (s.v. Bible).

The Tempter's Voice

INTRODUCTION

The Serpent asked the first question in the world.
—*The Venerable Bede*

THE STORY OF Adam, Eve, and the Serpent is one of the oldest and most enduring myths of Western culture. Since ancient times the third chapter of Genesis has seen countless interpretations and has served numerous ideological ends. During the first four Christian centuries, and for another ten medieval centuries, European civilization found—or founded—in the "Fall," among other things, a powerful myth about language. Patristic ideas about language and the Fall, and the lively medieval response to these ideas in learned and popular writings, form the subject of this book. My aim is to explore how biblical commentators, moralists, and poets used the Fall to address practical and theoretical problems of language relating to literature, knowledge, power, society, and eros.

In making Genesis 3 central to Christian theology, patristic authorities such as Augustine turned the Fall into not only a prime example for social and moral issues of the day but also a kind of primal scene for language, a garden of signs having far-reaching significance for discourse in the church and society.[1] Medieval authors further developed the Garden as a ground for language theory and a stage for practical problems of language. There were other biblical stories about language, of course, most notably the confusion of tongues at Babel (Gen. 11). However, while Babel was important to medieval language theory, this later crisis of the word, this "second Fall," did not emerge as a major literary topos until after the Renaissance, with the decline of Latin as a "universal" language and

---

1. On the Fall as a paradigm for moral and social issues in the early church, see Elaine Pagels, *Adam, Eve, and the Serpent* (New York, 1988); and Peter Brown, *The Body and Society: Men, Women, and Sexual Renunciation in Early Christianity* (New York, 1988).

the beginnings of comparative philology.[2] For the Middle Ages, problems of language had their prime representation at the Tree rather than at the Tower, that later, man-made sign and center of transgression.

As a key episode in Genesis, the biblical book of origins, the myth of the Fall furnished patristic and medieval culture with major elements of its Christian anthropology.[3] In this scheme of things, the Fall functioned as a "myth" both in Mircea Eliade's sense of the term—a primeval story explaining the origin and nature of things—and in Roland Barthes's sense—a fiction whose narrative and symbols could be manipulated to benefit those having (or seeking) power, authority, or legitimacy.[4] Not only was the medieval myth of the Fall an inherited story or a prior text that profoundly shaped thought and society by exerting the power of the past over the perception of the present; it was also an imaginative construct or projection of medieval culture itself, which wrote its own historical reality into the mutable narrative details and symbolic values of this myth. In short, much as the ancient myths of Greek tragedy both shaped and mirrored the sensibility of classical Athens, the myth of the Fall helped to create medieval culture and in turn was substantially created by it.

Medieval culture used the Fall as a myth about language for three discursive domains in particular: doctrine, hermeneutics, and eloquence.

In the first place, interpreters saw the Fall as centering on a challenge to God's teaching or precept about the Tree of Knowledge, with a resulting subversion of established tradition and authority in Paradise. Though today the Serpent might seem to represent an enlightened critical or scientific spirit, and Eve a legitimate feminist

2. George Steiner, *After Babel: Aspects of Language and Translation* (London, 1975), p. 59, describes Babel as "a second Fall" in treating mainly postmedieval forms of the myth (see pp. 61–73). On Babel in the Middle Ages, see Jesse M. Gellrich, *The Idea of the Book in the Middle Ages: Language Theory, Mythology, and Fiction* (Ithaca, N.Y., 1985), pp. 98–101, with references.

3. Robert J. O'Connell, *Art and the Christian Intelligence in St. Augustine* (Cambridge, Mass., 1978), refers to Genesis as "the ancient world's classic locus for the Christian anthropology" (p. 53). See also R. Howard Bloch, *Etymologies and Genealogies: A Literary Anthropology of the French Middle Ages* (Chicago, 1983), chap. 1, esp. pp. 34–53; and Stephen G. Nichols, "An Intellectual Anthropology of Marriage in the Middle Ages," in *The New Medievalism*, ed. Marina S. Brownlee, Kevin Brownlee, and Stephen G. Nichols (Baltimore, 1991), pp. 70–95.

4. Mircea Eliade, *Myth and Reality*, trans. Willard R. Trask (New York, 1963). Roland Barthes, *Mythologies*, trans. Annette Lavers (New York, 1972).

challenge to male power structures and discourse, the patristic and medieval interpreters who defined the traditional myth saw matters otherwise.[5] For them the Fall was rather a crisis of dissemination that had seriously compromised teaching, text, and tradition as embodied in God's precept about the Tree. As Augustine put it, the truth had been passed down "from the Lord through the man to the woman" and then was disrupted by falsehood transmitted "from the Devil through the woman to the man."[6] The Fall was thus the archetypal crisis of knowledge, authority, and hierarchy, and what had happened in the school of Paradise had weighty import for the whole culture of discourse, not only in the church and institutions of learning but also in society and the domestic sphere.

Second, the Serpent's question about God's command, and the ensuing discussion about the meaning of God's word and the significance of the forbidden fruit, suggested that the Fall was also centrally concerned with signs, texts, and problems of interpretation. Again, the Serpent might well be seen as having applied a revealing hermeneutic of suspicion to the received text of God's word, and Adam and Eve as having learned the "true" meaning of that divine text. Patristic and medieval tradition, however, instead condemned the tempter as a false interpreter, and Adam and Eve as misguided exegetes who mistook the meaning of God's word and committed the original sin of sign abuse by eating and enjoying the fruit rather than respecting its higher significance. According to Dante, the first humans were exiled from the Garden not for "the tasting of the tree" but for "the transgression of the sign."[7] Besides a paradigm for the art of interpretation, the Fall was considered the genesis of scriptural hermeneutics itself, having made necessary a written supplement to God's original spoken word, as well as the veiling of God's truth in scriptural allegory. Such notions about writing, hermeneutics, and the Fall profoundly affected attitudes

---

5. E.g., the Serpent's critical spirit was recognized by Bede, *In Pentateuchum commentarii*, Genesis 3, *PL* 91:212, as quoted above in the epigraph to this Introduction ("*Cur praecepit vobis Dominus, et reliqua. Haec prima interrogatio in hoc mundo fuisse dicitur*"). Gnostic exegetes, "heretics" to the church, anticipated "modern" views by reversing most of the patristic values assigned to the myth; see below, Chapter 1.1.

6. *GenL* 11.34.45; *PL* 34:245–486; trans. John H. Taylor, *The Literal Meaning of Genesis*, ACW, nos. 41–42 (New York, 1982).

7. Dante, *Paradiso* 26.115–17 ("*il trapassar del segno*"); *The Divine Comedy*, ed., trans., and comm. Charles S. Singleton, 3 vols. in 6 pts. (Princeton, 1970–75). Trans. from Richard A. Shoaf, *Milton, Poet of Duality: A Study of Semiosis in the Poetry and the Prose* (New Haven, 1985), p. 33.

toward language in the mixed oral and manuscript culture of the Middle Ages.

Finally, eloquence had played a key role in the temptation leading to the Fall. Eve had been seduced by the Serpent's crafty words, and she in turn (the text hinted, and interpreters assumed) had imitated her tempter by similarly seducing Adam with "some persuasive words"—as Augustine put it, giving license to generations of poets.[8] The common belief that the Devil had spoken *through* the Serpent, using that creature as a kind of ventriloquist's puppet, enhanced the Fall as a scene for not only rhetoric but also fiction, theater, and performance in general. And by allegorizing the fig leaves as emblems for the tendency of fallen humans to "cover" their faults with words, as Adam and Eve did in offering excuses to God after their sin, medieval culture extended the Fall even farther as a paradigm for rhetorical artifice. As such, the Fall posed a set of theoretical problems for the whole art of rhetoric inherited from classical ("pagan") culture. On a more practical level, the Fall was the original scenario for verbal seduction, whether as practiced by heretics urging their false doctrines on the faithful, or by men and women deceiving or manipulating each other in the sexual politics of society and the home. With its femme fatale and phallic Serpent, the Fall as a rhetorical scenario raised especially troublesome questions about eloquence and gender, about the feminine allure or masculine thrust of the tempter's voice in general.[9]

While the story of the Fall profoundly shaped medieval notions about language, medieval culture used the Garden as a representational ground for its own more local ideas about language, expressing these through explications or retellings of the Fall in a wide variety of literary forms. The main repositories of medieval ideas about language and the Fall were books written in scholarly Latin, but the Fall's broader significance for the lives of medieval people is most vividly reflected in the vernacular literature on Genesis 3 that began appearing as early as the eighth century and had grown into a flourishing garden of letters by the late Middle Ages. This abundant vernacular literature on Genesis 3, though often underwritten by patristic (or scholastic) tradition, translates many ideas about language and the Fall into more accessible terms for a much larger audience—both clergy and laity, nobles and commoners, men and

8. *GenL* 11.30.39.

9. Although the Serpent often has a woman's face in medieval tradition, patristic and medieval authors also exploit the other, phallic, side of the Serpent.

women. Vernacular poets, playwrights, moralists (and artists) were the agents of this dissemination.

By the time of Charlemagne (ca. 800), monastic poets in Anglo-Saxon England were adapting the Fall to the alliterative idiom of native heroic poems such as *Beowulf*, appropriating "pagan" poetry for Christian use, replacing oral tradition with a scriptural one, and—in what was yet a missionary era in England—thereby warning about the dangers of false teaching, tales, and traditions. By the twelfth century, clerics were turning the Fall into liturgical drama for the spiritual instruction of the populace and also to treat important issues in domestic and feudal politics. By the thirteenth century, moral treatises written for laywomen in England and France were using the Fall as a cautionary tale about the rhetoric of seduction as well as to address various domestic and social problems centering on discourse between the sexes. And by the fourteenth century, lay poets such as Dante and Chaucer were using the Fall to deal with issues of language specifically in terms of reading and writing, terms that reflected the growth of literacy and book culture among the middle and upper classes.

With respect to language, then, the Fall's significance gradually expanded from the concerns of ecclesiastical or monastic life to include a broader audience defined by lay literacy and vernacular literature. And as vernacular writings invested the Fall with significance for an ever-larger cultural sphere, interpretations of Genesis 3 increasingly addressed the whole order of medieval society itself. Indeed, as the Fall was retold in the developing vernacular languages, in new genres, and for diverse audiences and purposes, it more and more came to reflect medieval Europe's own reading of itself.

Although the Fall's status as a major paradigm for medieval culture may seem obvious from the period's literature and art, only during the last few decades or so has the Fall come to enjoy an important place in medieval literary scholarship. And even during this time the study of the Fall as such has fluctuated greatly, having been introduced in the 1950s on a historicist basis, then widely rejected by scholars and critics on New Critical and other grounds, and only quite recently revived on fresh theoretical foundations—namely, structuralist, poststructuralist, and feminist.

By the mid-twentieth century, historians of medieval literary theory such as Charles Sears Baldwin and pioneers in medieval comparative literature such as Erich Auerbach and Ernst Robert Curtius had established the importance of Augustine's theories of language for medieval rhetoric, poetics, and the arts of language in general.[10] In 1951, D. W. Robertson, Jr., published a subsequently famous—or notorious—manifesto, "The Doctrine of Charity in Mediaeval Literary Gardens," which argued that Augustine's doctrine of the Fall and Redemption ("charity") furnished a major interpretive paradigm—indeed, the only legitimate one—for understanding medieval literature, whether saints' legends or courtly romances, sermons or fabliaux.[11] Further articles followed, and a decade later Robertson's monumental treatise, *A Preface to Chaucer*, extended and refined his original thesis.[12] During the fifties and sixties, Robertson and other exegetical (or "patristic") critics applied their methodology to a wide variety of medieval literary texts.[13]

This new brand of historicism engendered strong objections from many scholars and critics, within as well as beyond the field of medieval studies, in part because of its inherent methodological problems, in part because it dismissed modern (post-Romantic) hermeneutics as "sentimental" or even "solipsistic," and not a little because many found the diet itself bland, distasteful, or too austere; surely medieval literature offered more than just spiritual "fruit."[14] Curiously, exegetical critics missed one of their own best moves in

---

10. Charles S. Baldwin, *Medieval Rhetoric and Poetic to 1400: Interpreted from Representative Works* (New York, 1928), chap. 2. Erich Auerbach, "Sermo humilis" (orig., 1941), trans. Ralph Manheim, in *Literary Language and Its Public in Late Latin Antiquity and in the Middle Ages* (New York, 1965), pp. 25–81. Ernst Robert Curtius, *European Literature and the Latin Middle Ages* (orig. 1948), trans. Willard R. Trask (Princeton, 1953), pp. 73–74, and passim.

11. D. W. Robertson, Jr., "The Doctrine of Charity in Mediaeval Literary Gardens: A Topical Approach through Symbolism and Allegory," in *Essays in Medieval Culture* (Princeton, 1980), pp. 21–50 (orig. pub. *Speculum* 26 [1951]: 24–49).

12. D. W. Robertson, Jr., *A Preface to Chaucer: Studies in Medieval Perspectives* (Princeton, 1962), esp. pp. 65–113. For Robertson bibliography, see *Essays in Medieval Culture*, pp. 383–84.

13. Principally, Bernard F. Huppé; see his *Doctrine and Poetry: Augustine's Influence on Old English Poetry* (Albany, 1959). See also Donald R. Howard, *The Three Temptations: Medieval Man in Search of the World* (Princeton, 1966); John V. Fleming, *The Roman de la Rose: A Study in Allegory and Iconography* (Princeton, 1969); and Brian O. Murdoch, *The Recapitulated Fall: A Comparative Study in Mediaeval Literature* (Amsterdam, 1974).

14. For a critique, see E. Talbot Donaldson, "Patristic Exegesis in the Criticism of Medieval Literature: The Opposition," (orig. pub. 1960), in *Speaking of Chaucer* (New York, 1970), pp. 134–53. Recent assessments include Lee Patterson, *Negotiating the Past: The Historical Understanding of Medieval Literature* (Madison, Wis., 1987), pp. 3–39; and Carolyn Dinshaw, *Chaucer's Sexual Poetics* (Madison, Wis., 1989), pp. 31–39 (with list of other critiques, p. 208, n. 3).

underestimating the crucial role of language in Genesis 3, the studious medieval attention to this role, and the resulting implications for language, literature, and culture in general. Robertson, for example, in analyzing medieval versions of the Fall, tended to emphasize the visual attraction of the forbidden fruit while discounting the Serpent's tempting words, an important verbal prelude to the Fall—full of semiotic, rhetorical, and poetical interest—that for obvious reasons interested medieval authors at least as much as visual stimulation did.[15] Despite its excesses and defects, however, exegetical criticism performed a valuable service in drawing attention to the truly important (though hardly all-explaining) place of the Fall as a medieval paradigm. And even where it aroused only negative reactions, it helped to stir some medievalists out of their slumbers in the garden's shade.

The patristic critics aside, medieval theories about the Fall received more attention during the 1960s and early 1970s from philosophers and intellectual historians than from literary critics.[16] Doubtless this neglect reflected many critics' lingering distaste for anything smacking of "fruit and chaff" or "charity." During the same period, however, several influential critics and theorists drew attention to the Fall as a crucial myth about language in Western culture. For example, Paul Ricoeur (1960) and Kenneth Burke (1961) produced modern commentaries on the Fall as a paradigm for rhetoric, hermeneutics, and the like.[17] Michel Foucault (1966) noted the important place accorded to Adam's "reading" of Nature in early modern thought.[18] And, in a development that was to have major theoretical

15. E.g., *Preface to Chaucer*, pp. 72, 80. The earlier "Doctrine of Charity" also stresses the role of *visio* at the expense of verbal prompting in Genesis 3 and other, typologically related narratives.

16. E.g., Ulrich Duchrow, "*Signum* und *superbia* beim jungen Augustin (386–390)," *REA* 7 (1961): 369–72; Joseph A. Mazzeo, "St. Augustine's Rhetoric of Silence," *JHI* 23 (1962): 175–96; Peter Brown, *Augustine of Hippo: A Biography* (Berkeley, 1967), pp. 261–62 (with refs.); Marcia L. Colish, *The Mirror of Language: A Study in the Medieval Theory of Knowledge* (1968; rev. ed., Lincoln, Nebr., 1983), pp. 32–33, 176, 212–13; B. Darrell Jackson, "The Theory of Signs in St. Augustine's *De Doctrina Christiana*," in R. A. Markus, ed., *Augustine: A Collection of Critical Essays* (New York, 1972), p. 113 (orig pub. *REA* 15 [1969]: 9–49); O'Connell, *Art and the Christian Intelligence*, pp. 70–83, and passim.

17. Paul Ricoeur, *La Symbolique du mal* (Paris, 1960), pt. 2, chap. 3; trans. Emerson Buchanan, *The Symbolism of Evil* (Boston, 1969), pp. 232–78 ("The 'Adamic Myth' and the 'Eschatological' Vision of History"). Kenneth Burke, *The Rhetoric of Religion: Studies in Logology* (Boston, 1961), pp. 172–272.

18. Michel Foucault, *The Order of Things: An Archaeology of the Human Sci-

consequences, Jacques Derrida (1967) traced modern "logocentric" notions about language—about signs and subjectivity, speech and writing—to a Christian myth of the Fall within which the Middle Ages had reinscribed the Neoplatonism inherited from antiquity: "the age of the sign is essentially theological" and "the sign is always a sign of the Fall."[19] Finally, Genesis 1–3 had begun to attract new analysis and revisionist readings by feminist critics, especially regarding Eve as a representational site for women in the troubled interpretive history of the Fall myth.[20]

By the mid-1970s, and increasingly throughout the 1980s, further developments related to these theoretical trends began to be felt within the domain of medieval literary study itself. In particular, Augustine's theories about language, including the crucial role of the Fall in these theories, began to attract new interest because of their important continuities—and contrasts—with key issues of recent critical theory. It was discovered that Augustine's theories anticipated major themes in structuralist and poststructuralist thought, such as the structure of the sign, the polysemy of the textual signifier, the link between language and desire, and the dynamics of readerly response to texts. The year 1975 seems to have been the *annus mirabilis* for Augustine and critical theory, for it marked the appearance of articles, in a range of scholarly journals, on Augustine, Saussure, and sign theory; on Augustine, Derrida, and writing; and on Augustine, Petrarch, and poetic indeterminacy.[21] During the late seventies, and throughout the eighties, new critical perspectives on medieval culture increasingly looked to Augustine's theories about

---

ences (orig., *Les Mots et les choses*, 1966; trans. 1971; rpt. New York, 1973), pp. 38–39. For a critique, see Anne Ferry, *The Art of Naming* (Chicago, 1988), pp. 15–16, 27–28.

19. Jacques Derrida, *Of Grammatology*, trans. Gayatri C. Spivak (Baltimore, 1976), pp. 14, 283; on the myth of the Fall, see esp. pp. 10–18, 280–95.

20. The manifesto was Phyllis Trible, "Depatriarchalizing in Biblical Interpretation," *Journal of the American Academy of Religion* 41 (1973): 30–48. See references to Trible et al. in Carol Meyers, *Discovering Eve: Ancient Israelite Women in Context* (New York, 1988), pp. 78–79, with notes and bibliography. See also John A. Phillips, *Eve: The History of an Idea* (San Francisco, 1984); and Gregory A. Robbins, ed., *Genesis 1–3 in the History of Exegesis: Intrigue in the Garden* (Lewiston, N.Y., 1988).

21. I.e., Louis G. Kelly, "Saint Augustine and Saussurean Linguistics," *AS* 6 (1975): 45–64; Margaret W. Ferguson, "Saint Augustine's Region of Unlikeness: The Crossing of Exile and Language," *Georgia Review* 29 (1975): 842–64 (esp. 858–59, 863); and John Freccero, "The Fig Tree and the Laurel: Petrarch's Poetics," *Diacritics* 5 (1975): 34–40. See also the earlier discussion by Stanley E. Fish, *Self-Consuming Artifacts: The Experience of Seventeenth-Century Literature* (Berkeley, 1972), pp. 21–43 ("Augustine: Words as Signs").

language and the Fall. Literary scholars who have led this enterprise include R. Howard Bloch, Carolyn Dinshaw, Neil Forsyth, John Freccero, Jesse Gellrich, Giuseppe Mazzotta, Stephen Nichols, R. A. Shoaf, and Eugene Vance.[22]

Following the lead of these and other scholars, I attempt in this book to supplement (in small but, I hope, useful ways) the study of the Fall as a central medieval myth about language, particularly about doctrine, hermeneutics, and eloquence. Although I cover a fairly wide and diverse field of materials—in terms of historical period, linguistic medium, and literary genre—the volume is not meant to be a comprehensive survey of medieval literature on the Fall or even of medieval literature dealing specifically with the Fall as a myth for language (which alone is a vast field).[23] Rather, the focus is on the formative period of the learned (Latin) tradition about language and the Fall and its continuation in a select but representative series of later and more popular (vernacular) writings. My purpose is to show not only the continuity of this myth from Augustine to the late medieval period (and even beyond) but also how this myth was adapted by writers to suit diverse historical conditions, cultural aims, languages, literary genres, and audiences.

While it is true that certain features of Genesis 3—especially its speeches, with their overtones of persuasion, interpretation, or instruction—were apt for representing ideas about language, it was what medieval authors and readers brought to that text, both from learned tradition and from their own lives and historical surroundings, that enabled them to find such richness there for language. That this exotic Mesopotamian tale of Adam, Eve, and the Serpent was inherited by the Middle Ages at all, and that it became a major

22. Studies by these and other critics are cited throughout this book. For an orientation, however, the following may be consulted: Eugene Vance, *Mervelous Signals: Poetics and Sign Theory in the Middle Ages* (Lincoln, Nebr., 1986), chaps. 1, 2, and 7 (rpts. of earlier essays); Bloch, *Etymologies and Genealogies*, chap. 1; Nichols, "An Intellectual Anthropology"; Freccero, "The Fig Tree and the Laurel"; Giuseppe Mazzotta, *Dante, Poet of the Desert: History and Allegory in the Divine Comedy* (Princeton, 1979), chap. 1; Gellrich, *The Idea of the Book*, pp. 149–57; and Dinshaw, *Chaucer's Sexual Poetics*, intro. See also Julian N. Wasserman and Lois Roney, eds., *Sign, Sentence, Discourse: Language in Medieval Thought and Literature* (Syracuse, N.Y., 1989), essays by R. A. Shoaf, Glenn C. Arbery, and Phillip Pulsiano.

23. A survey of the patristic and medieval literature of the Fall appears in John M. Evans, *Paradise Lost and the Genesis Tradition* (Oxford, 1968), chaps. 3–7, with primary and secondary bibliography. See also Robert Couffignal, *Le Drame de l'Éden: Le récit de la Genèse et sa fortune littéraire* (Toulouse, 1980).

verbal paradigm, reflected many other historical contingencies as well. The text of Genesis 3 (itself a chapter unit fixed in medieval times) was shaped by a process of transmission fraught with linguistic and scribal variables, and more contingent yet was its interpretation, massively shaped by the patristic concept of the "Fall" and numerous other theological notions.[24] In the Middle Ages both the text and its accumulated commentary often had a monolithic appearance, especially as embodied in the Latin Bible with its built-in gloss (a running commentary on the text). Both text and gloss, however, comprised material from very diverse sources in early and late antiquity.[25]

To begin with, the version of Genesis 3 used by most patristic exegetes in the western (Latin) church, and later by some medieval exegetes as well, was a linguistic palimpsest—a Latin translation from a Greek version of the Hebrew original. This Old Latin version, based on the Septuagint, the Greek Old Testament produced by Hellenized Jews in the third century B.C., was favored by Augustine and other western exegetes even after Jerome's Vulgate Old Testament (based directly on the Hebrew) became available around 400 A.D. Some of the conclusions reached by patristic authors about language and the Fall arose from peculiarities in the linguistic texture of the Old Latin version, which was venerated in the belief that it shared in the divine inspiration ascribed to the Septuagint.[26] This is one of several important ways in which, through either text or commentary, Jewish tradition shaped the patristic, and hence medieval, understanding of Genesis 3.

A second point relates to the scriptural canon. Genesis 3 occurs in the very oldest strand of the biblical literature, which was woven together with other strands over the centuries to form a series of ever-larger sacred scriptural canons, first the Pentateuch (the Torah or Law), eventually the complete Hebrew Bible, and still later the Christian Bible as defined by patristic authors and the medieval

24. The "Fall" (Latin *casus*, *lapsus*, or *ruina*) was only one of several metaphors used by patristic authors for the primal human transgression, but it became dominant through Augustine's influence. See Norman P. Williams, *The Ideas of the Fall and of Original Sin: A Historical and Critical Study* (London, 1927); on terminology, see lecture 4, esp. pp. 302–3.

25. For background on text, canon, and commentary, see *CHB*, ed. P. R. Ackroyd, C. F. Evans, et al., 3 vols. (Cambridge, 1963–70), esp. vols. 1–2.

26. Actually a variety of Old Latin versions existed; see *Vetus latina: Die Reste der altlateinischen Bibel*, vol. 2 (Genesis), ed. Bonifatius Fischer (Freiburg, 1951), 56–78 (Gen. 3). On the texts used by Augustine, and therefore perpetuated by medieval quotation from his works, see *CHB* 1:544–47.

church.[27] As the canon changed over time and from one religious tradition to another, Genesis 3 became subject to new interpretations, not simply because of accompanying changes in exegesis and theology but because Scripture, progressively enlarging, acquired new internal complexities. As a primal episode in the history of humankind, Genesis 3 was used to explicate other parts of Scripture; reciprocally, other passages were invoked to explain the many contradictions and gaps in Genesis 3 and to harmonize it with the rest of Scripture.[28]

Besides the text, and its scriptural context, there was extrinsic commentary on Genesis 3. Though the teachings about Genesis 3 that became fixed as doctrine by about the sixth century in the Latin church were predominantly Augustinian, and though Augustine's exegesis was profoundly original, his ideas in general, and those about language and the Fall in particular, reflected a diversity of sources in patristic, Jewish, and classical tradition. Augustine's exegesis was directly indebted to his teacher Ambrose and other (mainly Latin) exegetes, whereas Ambrose himself had drawn on Greek patristic exegetes such as Origen and Basil, as well as Philo of Alexandria, a Hellenistic Jew. Certain Augustinian ideas and motifs about language and the Fall can also be traced to other Jewish commentary and the Old Testament apocrypha and pseudepigrapha. In addition, Augustine's exegesis is heavily indebted to the classical tradition of language theory inherited by learned Christian culture, including (though not always directly) Plato, Aristotle, the Stoics, the Homeric allegorizers, and Neoplatonists like Plotinus.

Classical culture provided not only specific philosophical and hermeneutical vantage points from which to read Genesis 3 but also, in the Graeco-Roman tradition of the language arts, poetic and rhetorical models for analyzing and imaginatively reworking the story. For example, exegetes used technical rhetorical terms to explicate

27. Most modern biblical scholars accept some form of the documentary hypothesis, which distinguishes various literary strands or traditions ("documents") in the Pentateuch. Genesis 3 occurs in the so-called J (Yahwist) document, usually dated ca. 950 B.C. On textual criticism of the Old Testament, see *CHB* 1:67–113. On the literary character of Genesis 3 in its "documentary" context, see Evans, *Paradise Lost and the Genesis Tradition*, pp. 11–14. For a new translation of Genesis 3, and the novel suggestion that this story (with the rest of "J") may have been authored by a woman, see David Rosenberg, trans., and Harold Bloom, comm., *The Book of J* (New York, 1990).

28. For a superb study of the accretions of scriptural text, commentary, and myth around Genesis 3 from remote antiquity to Augustine, see Neil Forsyth, *The Old Enemy: Satan and the Combat Myth* (Princeton, 1987).

Genesis 3, particularly its speeches, at the same time assessing the arts of rhetoric and poetry in terms of the Fall's moral consequences for language. Christian-Latin poets combined both these tendencies in poems on the Fall that used classical verse forms and poetical devices even as they raised the problem of "fallen" language. For Christian authors, the myth of the Fall thus became a focal point for assessing and appropriating the classical heritage. Indeed, however diverse his actual historical sources, Augustine turned the Fall into the ultimate mythical expression, totalizing and self-contained, for ideas about language in general.

Rather than being grounded on history, philology, myth, or metaphor as generally defined by modern textual scholars and literary critics, patristic and medieval interpretations of Scripture were predicated on signifying relations held to be created by God and discovered through grace to the human understanding.[29] The divine Author of Scripture had laden his word with several kinds of significance—the "letter" of the text had various "senses"—and the capacity of this polysemous text to generate significations often was limited by little more than the imagination of exegetes and what Augustine called the rule of "charity."[30]

Although a relatively terse narrative, Genesis 3 was analyzed, explained, amplified, and allegorized in its every detail to yield its divine and (often) hidden riches. Patristic and medieval exegetes in fact required a good deal of poetic license to produce what Frank Kermode has termed their "indefinite multiplication of spiritual readings."[31] As Erich Auerbach remarks of Augustine's mature biblical commentary in the *City of God* (book 14 of which is devoted to the Fall), "there is visible a constant endeavor to fill in the lacunae of the Biblical account, to supplement it by other passages from the Bible and by original considerations, to establish a continuous connection of events, and in general to give the highest measure of rational plausibility to an intrinsically irrational interpretation."[32] However logical its apparent method or tone, then, patristic and medieval commentary on Genesis 3 is never without its quantum of "irrationality." Patristic and medieval ideas about Genesis 3, be-

29. For theoretical background, see Gellrich, *The Idea of the Book*, chap. 3.

30. See *Doc* 3.10.14–16; ed. H.J. Vogels, *Florilegium patristicum* 24 (1930): 1–103; trans. D. W. Robertson, Jr., *On Christian Doctrine* (Indianapolis, 1958).

31. Frank Kermode, *The Genesis of Secrecy: On the Interpretation of Narrative* (Cambridge, Mass., 1979), p. 37.

32. Erich Auerbach, *Mimesis: The Representation of Reality in Western Literature*, trans. Willard R. Trask (Princeton, 1953), p. 75.

ginning with the Pauline literature, often strike the modern reader as eisegesis rather than exegesis, as a reading of things *into* the text rather than out of it. Not that modern readings of Genesis 3 are inherently any more rational or plausible than patristic or medieval ones, for every age has placed its peculiar constructions on this text. Indeed, many modern interpretations incorporate notions inherited from ancient or medieval tradition, to the point that these readings, or "misreadings," have themselves been virtually canonized.[33] The reasons that biblical interpreters of one age or another have tended to find this or that sense in the text are to be sought mainly in the cultural milieu. And *why* patristic and medieval authors read Genesis 3 as they did is as much a subject of this book as *how* in fact they did read it.

Convinced of the text's divine inspiration, Augustine saw reflected in Scripture what has been called a "single symbolic system" of meaning and interpretation, although Augustinian exegesis actually comprised several distinct (and separately originating) modes of reading that were not really codified as a "system" until the scholastic era.[34] A brief explanation of these various modes of exegesis will help set the terms for discussion in this volume.

The most basic mode of reading Genesis 3 (after Augustine) is *historical* (or "literal") exegesis, which treats the Fall itself as an actual event occurring as "recorded" and Adam and Eve as real physical (and fully psychological) persons. Historical exegesis dwells on the nature, cause, and interrelations of the external events of the Fall and on their underlying psychological motives. Of special interest are the speeches in the Garden, which are read as actual, audible exchanges having deep moral and psychological significance. In short, historical exegesis treats Genesis 3 as virtually a transcript of real—and profoundly significant—events.

For Augustine and the tradition after him, the historical Fall is in turn the basis for various *allegorical* modes of reading Genesis 3, which interpret the characters, events, and imagery of the Fall in terms of other figurative gardens, including not only the soul, the church, and the heavenly Paradise but also the "garden" of marriage and of the feudal demesne. For my purposes in this book, the two most important kinds of allegorical exegesis are *typology* and *tropology*.

33. Meyers, *Discovering Eve*, p. 78, with a list of traditional "misreadings."
34. Forsyth, *The Old Enemy*, p. 425. On patristic and medieval exegesis, see *CHB* 2:155–219; and Henri de Lubac, *Exégèse médiévale: Les quatres sens de l'Écriture*, 4 vols. (Paris, 1959–64).

Typology, a patristic mode of reading the Jewish Scriptures as a foreshadowing or prophecy of events in the Christian era, turned Genesis 3 into a paradigm initially for the life of the church.[35] First applied to Genesis 3 by the Apostle Paul, typological exegesis in its primary form treats Adam as a figure (or "type") for Christ, Eve as a figure for the church, and the Serpent as a figure for heretics, false teachers, and the archenemy Satan.[36] By suggesting that the Fall figuratively recurs whenever false teaching wins out over true, typology turns Genesis 3 into a continually renewable moral exemplum for the ongoing life of the church in its battles over doctrine, interpretation, and the like. A further typology that contrasted Eve and Mary, stressing the different fruit of their wombs—the seductive Serpent's word *versus* the redemptive divine Word—greatly enriched the Fall as an originary scene for language in medieval culture.

A secondary form of Fall typology applied the sexual politics of Paradise—the original marriage triangle comprising Adam, Eve, and the Serpent—to the social and domestic spheres, treating the Fall as the original seduction scenario. Medieval moralists used the Fall to warn the vulnerable "daughters of Eve" (whose chastity might be tested by eloquent male seducers modeled on the Serpent) and the "sons of Adam" (as potential victims of feminine wiles modeled after Eve's). This secondary, domestic form of Fall typology turned the original story into a widely adaptable paradigm for manners and morals in the everyday life of the Middle Ages.

Tropology, the second of these two main allegorical modes, offers a related but technically distinct application of Genesis 3 to the moral life of the individual, being concerned specifically with the soul, the inner life, or what might be called "moral psychology." Appearing first in Philo and elsewhere in Jewish tradition, the tropological reading of Genesis 3 was brought into Latin exegesis by Ambrose.[37] As used by Augustine, and hence later patristic and medieval tradition, it interprets Adam, Eve, and the Serpent as emblems

35. On typology in general, see Erich Auerbach, "Figura," trans. Ralph Manheim, in *Scenes from the Drama of European Literature: Six Essays* (1959; rpt. Gloucester, Mass., 1973), pp. 9–76; and James S. Preus, *From Shadow to Promise: Old Testament Interpretation from Augustine to Young Luther* (Cambridge, Mass., 1969), pt. 1.

36. E.g., Rom. 5.14, 2 Cor. 11.2–4. For Paul on Genesis 3, see Forsyth, *The Old Enemy*, chap. 14. Gal. 4.24 expressly mentions scriptural allegory.

37. Philo of Alexandria, *Legum allegoria* 2.18.71–73; ed. and trans. G. H. Whitaker, *Allegorical Interpretation of Genesis 2–3*, in *Philo*, vol. 1 (London, 1929), pp. 140–473; see *CHB* 1:379–83, 435–38. Cf. the Syriac *Apocalypse of Baruch* 54.19, as cited by Forsyth, *The Old Enemy*, p. 216.

for the faculties of reason, appetite, and the senses, respectively. On this model, an internal "fall" occurs in the individual sinner whenever reason (Adam) "consents" to the "delight" of appetite (Eve) toward some illicit pleasure of the senses (the Serpent). Through tropology, the external dynamics of the first sin became the model for the internal dynamics of *all* sin.

To sum up, these various modes of interpreting Genesis 3 extended the Fall's significance to a wide variety of situations involving language in the church, society, and the life of the individual. Whereas historical exegesis dwells on the external and internal events of the Fall in the Garden of Eden, typology deals with the Fall as reenacted (primarily) in the church or (secondarily) within society or the household, and, finally, tropology concerns the Fall as recapitulated in the soul.

The question naturally arises, How were patristic ideas about Genesis 3, and specifically about language and the Fall, transmitted to the vernacular (and also Latin) literary tradition of the Middle Ages? In the early Middle Ages, patristic writings were to be found only in the monastic libraries, though by the thirteenth century, with the rise of the universities, they achieved wider availability through the *pecia* system of secular book reproduction—the medieval bookstore or copying center.[38]

Patristic ideas about the Fall were also disseminated by later commentators who incorporated the writings of earlier exegetes, often verbatim, into their own treatises. In matters of doctrine and scriptural exegesis, authority was more important than "originality," and the tradition of citing the *auctores*—especially Augustine—was practiced by a long line of later commentators on Genesis 3: Isidore of Seville, Gregory the Great, the Venerable Bede, Alcuin of York, Hrabanus Maurus, Bernard of Clairvaux, Hugh of St. Victor, Peter Lombard, Bonaventura, and Thomas Aquinas, to name only some of the more important authorities.

Finally, there were the great medieval glossed Bibles. By the twelfth century or so, many key patristic ideas about language and the Fall had been incorporated into Scripture itself in the form of

38. On patristic curriculum authors, see Curtius, *European Literature*, pp. 48–54. On monastic libraries and scriptoria, see M. L. W. Laistner, *Thought and Letters in Western Europe, A.D. 500 to 900*, rev. ed. (1957; rpt. Ithaca, N.Y., 1966), chap. 9. On secular book reproduction in the later Middle Ages, see Graham Pollard, "The Pecia System in the Medieval Universities," in *Medieval Scribes, Manuscripts, and Libraries: Essays Presented to N. R. Ker*, ed. M. B. Parkes and Andrew G. Watson (London, 1978), pp. 145–61.

the "Ordinary Gloss" (*Glossa ordinaria*), so called for its inclusion of patristic commonplaces on given passages of Scripture.[39] A glance at almost any page of a medieval glossed Bible reveals how the gloss had literally accumulated "around" the text, massively "supplementing" it (to use Auerbach's phrase) by pressing significance upon it from all sides (fig. 1). A complete glossed Bible, with its high proportion of gloss to text, usually ran to many folio volumes. In a typical glossed Bible, within the twenty pages or more required to accommodate Genesis 3 and its voluminous glosses, often only a single verse or just part of a verse appears on a page, surrounded by its multiple senses, a rich abundance of spiritual "fruit" among the scriptural "leaves." Typically the page is thick with glosses from Augustine, among others, and specifically his views on the Serpent as a false teacher, or Eve as a misguided exegete, or Adam as one persuaded by feminine wiles.[40] Thus, by the High Middle Ages, many crucial patristic ideas about language and the Fall had become virtually part of holy writ.

Evidence for the role of the Fall as a myth about language in medieval culture appears not just in literary tradition but in visual art as well, including the manuscript drawings or illuminations known mainly to monks, the richly decorated prayer books commissioned by wealthy patrons, and the scenes of the Fall widely depicted in the window glass and sculptural programs of medieval churches, the so-called Bible of the poor. The medieval iconography of Genesis 3 is a vast area which I do not pretend to survey here, but I cite occasional examples to show how themes and motifs involving language, although most suited to discursive treatment, are reflected in medieval art of the Fall.[41]

39. See Beryl Smalley, *The Study of the Bible in the Middle Ages* (1952; rpt. Notre Dame, 1964), pp. 46–66; *CHB* 2:204–9; and Christopher F. R. de Hamel, *Glossed Books of the Bible and the Origins of the Paris Booktrade* (Woodbridge, Suffolk, 1984).

40. E.g., in a typical thirteenth-century Bible that I have examined at the British Library (MS. Royal 3 C.ii), the gloss on Gen. 3.4–5 (fol. 25v) contains several key notions from Augustine's literal commentary on the Fall (*GenL*): (1) that Satan used the Serpent as a vocal instrument (*velut organo*); (2) that the Serpent's words prompted Eve's desire for the fruit; (3) that Eve mistook the meaning of God's command; and (4) that Eve perhaps spoke "persuasive words" to Adam.

41. On the Fall in medieval painting and sculpture, see Louis Réau, *Iconographie de l'art Chrétien*, vol. 2, pt. 1 (Paris, 1956), pp. 75–93. On Fall typology in medieval art, see Gertrud Schiller, *Iconography of Christian Art*, trans. Janet Seligman, vol. 2 (Greenwich, Conn., 1972), pp. 130–36 (with plates). On the Fall in manuscript art and other media, see Bernard S. Levy, ed., *The Bible in the Middle Ages: Its Influence on Literature and Art* (Binghamton, N.Y., 1992).

As a study of a tradition in its patristic origins and medieval development, this book has two parts.

Part One is arranged topically, with separate chapters on the Fall as a paradigm for doctrine, hermeneutics, and eloquence, though with some attention to chronology within the chapters. Here I rely mainly on a triumvirate of important and representative figures: Ambrose of Milan (333–97), who was the first to offer a detailed reading of the Fall as a crisis of language; Augustine of Hippo (354–430), clearly the most influential authority among Latin exegetes and the one most responsible for turning the Fall into an expression of language theory; and (a less-familiar name) Avitus of Vienne (ca. 450–518), the first Latin poet to treat Genesis 3 at any substantial length, with psychological subtlety, and with detailed attention to the role and significance of language in the Fall. Likewise a bishop in the church, Avitus was widely read in the Middle Ages and was a major influence on vernacular poetry about Genesis 3.

In Part Two, which deals with the medieval reception, use, and transformation of patristic ideas about language and the Fall, I proceed less by topic and more by chronology, author, and work. The focus of each chapter is on a vernacular work (in one case, two works) that articulates a certain problem (or set of problems) having to do with language and the Fall within a distinct historical environment for a specific audience: namely, Anglo-Saxon poetry of the ninth century; French and English moral literature for women from about 1200 on; and late medieval poetry written for the increasingly literate middle and upper classes. I stress the continuing influence of the Latin tradition on vernacular literature by referring to important figures in the transmission of patristic ideas about the Fall to the authors and works under consideration—figures such as the Venerable Bede, Alcuin of York, Bernard of Clairvaux, Peter Lombard, and Bonaventura.

Although this book is meant to be read as a sequence of argument and exposition, each chapter is to some extent an independent unit which may be read on its own. As a kind of vade mecum into the garden, or forest, of patristic and medieval ideas about language and the Fall, a brief sketch of each chapter follows.

In Chapter 1, I discuss how patristic culture developed Genesis 3 into a paradigm of true and false teaching, or doctrine and heresy, and an archetypal crisis of authority and hierarchy. In treating the Garden as a kind of school, with God as the true Teacher, the Serpent ("Satan") as a false teacher, and Adam and Eve as misguided pupils

or catechumens, patristic authors read into the Fall their own preoc-
cupations with doctrinal purity, the scriptural canon, and church
polity. At the same time, they set the terms for applying the politics
of language and learning in Paradise to the religious, social, and
domestic spheres at large—to the authority of lord over vassal, of
priest over communicant, of husband over wife, and of man over
woman generally.

I turn in Chapter 2 to an examination of the Fall as a patristic
model for the abuse of verbal signs and of signs in general, and hence
as a totalizing myth for sign theory, writing, and hermeneutics.
Augustine in particular saw the Fall as entailing Adam's catastrophic
loss of a direct knowledge of divine truth; as both history and allegory, this crisis represented the original cause of error and ambiguity in the realm of signs, the impetus for God's revelation in
Scripture, and a paradigm of exegesis that warned the descendants
of Adam and Eve, as readers and listeners, not to similarly abuse
God's written word. The sign theory and scriptural hermeneutic thus
invested in the Fall became in turn the basis for a broader literary
hermeneutic in the Middle Ages that similarly held the Fall to be
the origin and paradigm of misreading and miswriting.

In Chapter 3, I deal with the patristic notion of the Fall as the
archetypal abuse of eloquence, and as such its grave implications
for the arts of rhetoric and poetry in particular. Ambrose and Augustine analyzed the rhetorical strategies pertaining to the Temptation, and the psychology of persuasion involved in both of its stages
(Serpent-Eve, Eve-Adam), whereas Avitus dramatized in his poem
the crucial role of rhetorical artifice in the Fall. In treating the Fall
as a rhetorical episode, patristic authors wrestled with the problem
of taming eloquence to serve the Truth in preaching and poetry. At
the same time, in the social and domestic spheres, they turned the
Fall into a paradigm for sexually charged temptation scenarios.

In Chapter 4, I take up the Anglo-Saxon poetic tradition of the
Fall, examining the dramatized version of Genesis 3 in the Old
English poem *Genesis B* (9th c.). Although indebted to the biblical
poetics of Latin poets such as Avitus, *Genesis B* adapts the Fall to
the Germanic heroic style, treating it specifically from the viewpoint
of Carolingian monastic culture. The notion of the manuscript
book's superiority to oral tradition and memory, a widely shared
monastic attitude articulated by Alcuin, among others, seems to
underlie the poem's treatment of the Fall as a tragedy of oral culture
wherein Adam and Eve are fooled into accepting a false oral tradition
from a Tempter claiming to carry word from God. Indeed, the poem's

sole manuscript source, a codex of biblical poems marked for oral reading (ca. 1000 A.D.), explicitly attests to a clerical notion of writing, both human and divine, that opposes itself to the "fallen" oral tradition of the pagan and preliterate past.

I move beyond the walls of the monastery in Chapter 5 to show how the Fall was adapted into a cautionary tale for women in both anchorhold and household after about the year 1200 and how the Garden thus became a representational ground for class, gender, and other concerns in the later medieval period. Here Bernard of Clairvaux's psychosexual reading of the Fall offers a vantage point for our examining how the myth was transformed into vivid seduction scenarios in two widely read vernacular works written by men for an audience of literate women: *Ancrene Wisse* (ca. 1225), a rule for female religious recluses known as anchoresses; and *Le Livre du Chevalier* (1371–72), a "courtesy book" containing biblical stories and other exempla to teach manners and morals to young noblewomen. Transposing Eve's story into contemporary terms, the authors of both books dwell on how desire operates in the female psyche when exposed to temptation in the form of seductive masculine eloquence. They interpret Genesis 3 in terms of either the spiritual values of the ascetic life or the material values of the feudal aristocracy, asserting control over the bodies, mental life, and conversation of women, and thus illuminating key aspects of social, domestic, and religious life in the later Middle Ages.

In Chapter 6, I broaden the study further by examining Chaucer's fabliau version of the Fall in the *Merchant's Tale*, a satire of Augustinian semiotics in which a squire (the Serpent) seduces the young wife (Eve) of an old knight (Adam), the lovers using secret signs and letters to arrange their tryst in a pear tree. The mediation of desire through letters reflects Augustine's notion of "fallen" writing as well as the medieval penchant for figuring the world and human experience through textual metaphors. At the same time, like Dante's own version of literary seduction in the story of Paolo and Francesca, Chaucer's tale reflects the rising literacy of the laity in the late Middle Ages and the increasingly personal and private significance of reading and writing. In the dramatic context of the *Canterbury Tales*, which includes not only the tale's unreliable narrator but also the poet's own concluding "Retraction," this dark comedy of eros circles back on itself to raise critical problems about reading, writing, and the Fall.

Part One

Augustine's Garden

Chapter 1

The School of Paradise

The command came from the Lord through the man
to the woman, but sin came from the Devil
through the woman to the man.
—*Augustine*

DURING THE EARLY centuries of the Christian era, patristic authors inaugurated a view of the Fall as the original crisis of knowledge, tradition, and authority by interpreting Genesis 2–3 as a paradigm for doctrine and teaching, among other things. Treating Paradise as an allegorical figure for the church, particularly in its educational role, patristic authors interpreted the Fall according to their special concerns with doctrinal purity, the scriptural canon, and church polity. On the patristic view, Adam and Eve had failed to follow the divine Teacher's precept (*praeceptum*, "advice, teaching") about the Tree of Knowledge, instead following the tempter's false teaching.[1] In so doing, the first humans had also violated the "proper" order of teaching in the Garden, typically imagined as a hierarchy of instruction in which God held authority over Adam, and Adam over Eve. Furthermore, the first couple had either corrupted or neglected

1. *Oxford Latin Dictionary* (hereafter *OLD*), ed. P. G. W. Glare (Oxford, 1982), s.v. *praeceptum* 1. This nominal form, common in patristic references to God's speech about the Tree, does not actually appear in either the OL or Vulg., but the verb used of God's "command" in Genesis 2–3, *praecipere*, has equivalent overtones; see *OLD*, s.v. *praecipio* 5b ("to give instruction in, teach, propound"). Cf. *disciplina* ("instruction, teaching," etc.) as applied to God's command (e.g., Augustine, *Ver* 45.83; ed. Klaus-Detlef Daur, *CCSL* 32:169–260; trans. John H.S. Burleigh, *Of True Religion*, in *Augustine: Earlier Writings* [Philadelphia, 1953], pp. 218–83). For a typical scholastic analysis of God's command as doctrine or teaching, see Hugh of St. Victor, *De sacramentis christianae fidei* 1.6.7; *PL* 176:173–618; trans. Roy J. Deferrari, *On the Sacraments of the Christian Faith* (Cambridge, Mass., 1951).

God's word as entrusted to them at the outset, a lapse viewed as a dangerous precedent for tampering with Scripture itself. In sum, the Fall served patristic authors as a model for many of the problems of dissemination—doctrine, authority, and textual integrity—that confronted the church throughout its first few centuries.

1. The Hierarchy of Eden

The historical church had been founded on a tradition of teaching that descended from Christ through the apostles to the various apostolic churches throughout the Mediterranean world. By the late fourth century the institutional church, on the model of the Roman imperium, was evolving into a hierarchy of authorities, including pope, bishops, and priests. All these authorities were in some sense responsible for spreading true doctrine among believers and guarding against the heresies that continually rose up within and against the church to threaten the purity of doctrine itself as well as the integrity of the institution that taught it.[2] Doctrinal purity and ecclesiastical authority were inextricably joined, for publicized doubts or questions could soon turn into controversy, controversy into schism, and schism into disaster. Avitus, as an important bishop in southern Gaul, evoked the sanctity of this ecclesiastical hierarchy when, amid the controversies of his own day, he wrote, "If you doubt the pope, the whole episcopate, and not merely a single bishop, will totter."[3]

An early precedent for applying the Fall as a paradigm to the problems of authority and teaching in the Church appeared in the writings of Paul.[4] Writing to the Christians at Corinth, Paul uses Genesis 3 as a typology for the conflict between doctrine and heresy, comparing the Serpent to false teachers or preachers, Eve to the

2. A useful introduction to early church history is Henry Chadwick, *The Early Church*, The Pelican History of the Church, vol. 1 (Harmondsworth, 1967). On doctrinal history, see John N. D. Kelly, *Early Christian Doctrines*, 5th ed. (New York, 1978); and Jaroslav Pelikan, *The Christian Tradition: A History of the Development of Doctrine*, 5 vols. (Chicago, 1971–89).

3. Avitus, *Epistola* 31; in *PL* 59:198–290, 381–86 (col. 249); as quoted and trans. in Fulbert Cayré, *Manual of Patrology and History of Theology*, trans. H. Howitt, vol. 2 (Paris, 1935), p. 210.

4. Although the corpus of writings considered authentic to Paul has been much reduced by modern biblical scholarship, patristic and medieval tradition accepted the now canonical epistles as being authoritatively his; hence, for convenience, throughout this book I refer to the epistles as his. Besides the Pauline passages on Genesis 3 cited here, see Rom. 16.20; 1 Cor. 15.22, 45; Eph. 5.31.

church, and Adam to Christ: "I feel a divine jealousy for you, for I betrothed you to Christ to present you as a pure bride to her one husband. But I am afraid that as the serpent deceived Eve by his cunning, your thoughts will be led astray from a sincere and pure devotion to Christ" (2 Cor. 11.2–3). He goes on to cite false preachers (v. 4) and false apostles (*pseudoapostoli*, vv. 13–14), likening them to Satan, who "disguises himself as an angel of light."[5]

The marital metaphor that frames this comparison helped to shape the Fall into an archetype for sexual temptation and seduction, but Paul's stress falls on matters of teaching and the corporate body of believers. In another important passage Paul similarly evokes a Fall typology to establish a "proper" order of instruction within the church, an order that allows only men to teach or to govern: "I permit no woman to teach [*docere*] or to have authority [*dominari*] over men; she is to keep silent. For Adam was formed first, then Eve; and Adam was not deceived, but the woman was deceived and became a transgressor" (1 Tim. 2.12–14).

These passages profoundly influenced the patristic use of the Fall as a model for teaching and authority as well as for gender relations. In their own more extensive commentaries on Genesis 3, patristic authors were quick to develop Paul's notion that the Fall had been mainly Eve's fault and that Adam, and hence men in general, possessed greater authority, rationality, and even "likeness" to God. "Read this way," notes Elaine Pagels, the story "proves woman's natural weakness and gullibility."[6]

Although these Pauline texts clearly shaped the basic patristic view of the Fall as a crisis of instruction, the emergence of God as the Teacher, of Adam as his assistant, and of Eve in a tertiary role also reflected the influence of an important early challenge to the Pauline model. The Gnostics—a collective name for various heretical sects—likewise invoked Genesis 3 as a paradigm for doctrinal matters, but most Gnostic interpretations reversed the polarities of original story, allegorizing it *not* as a calamitous fall but instead as a kind of step upward for humanity.[7] On the Gnostic view, moreover, Eve emerged in a positive light, for she represented a spiritual principle that taught the soul or psyche (Adam) a higher wisdom or knowledge (*gnosis*): "Gnostic authors loved to tell, with many var-

5. On false teachers or preachers in the guise of angels, see also Gal. 1.8.

6. Pagels, *Adam, Eve, and the Serpent,* p. 24.

7. On Gnosticism, see Kelly, *Early Christian Doctrines,* pp. 22–28. On Gnostic readings of Genesis 3 in particular, see Forsyth, *The Old Enemy,* pp. 330–32; and Pagels, *Adam, Eve, and the Serpent,* chap. 3.

iations, the story of Eve, that elusive spiritual intelligence: how she first emerged within Adam and awakened him, the soul, to awareness of its spiritual nature; how she encountered resistance, was misunderstood, attacked, and mistaken for what she was not."[8] Gnostic texts typically characterize the Serpent as Eve's teacher, often under the title of "Instructor." Gnostic accounts of Genesis 3 thus completely invert the Pauline values assigned to its characters and events, turning these values into expressions of "heretical" doctrine and the whole story into a model for teaching the same.

Not surprisingly, Gnostic interpretations of Genesis 3 scandalized orthodox patristic exegetes, not only because they seemed perversely to switch the roles of God and the Serpent but also because they inverted the Pauline and patristic ideal of male authority and female receptivity.[9] The patristic values placed on the various characters in Genesis 3, with respect to teaching and authority, may in fact be seen as a strategy for upholding Genesis 3 along Pauline lines as a story about threats to *orthodox* doctrinal teaching. At the same time, however, the patristic reading also reflected certain conditions prevailing in the institutional church. Like the apostolic succession from which it claimed authority, church office was limited exclusively to men, and the church's model for the transmission of knowledge was strictly patrilineal. The exclusively male ecclesiastical hierarchy had no place for female teachers, and neither did the patristic reading of Genesis 3. As patristic authors saw it, Eve merely usurped the role of "teacher" that properly belonged to Adam and, ultimately, to God.

The patristic notion of Paradise as a kind of school drew on the classical ideal of the garden as a place of philosophical dialogue and retreat.[10] But this notion relied mainly on Christian allegories of Paradise as a figure for either the church or the soul as a site of instruction. The Paradise/church allegory had been established already by the end of the second century, and Augustine evoked it specifically in connection with the doctrinal threat represented by heretics.[11] Augustine, following Ambrose, also allegorized Paradise as the individual soul; and, in an image that he popularized, Christ was the "inner Teacher."[12] Following the gospel parables of vineyard

8. This and the following quotations are taken from Pagels, *Adam, Eve, and the Serpent*, pp. 66–69.

9. See Pagels, *Adam, Eve, and the Serpent*, p. 77.

10. *OLD*, s.v. hortulus 3, hortus 3. See Brown, *Augustine of Hippo*, chap. 11.

11. *GenL* 11.25.32.

12. Paradise/soul: Ambrose, *Par* 3.12; *PL* 14:275–314; trans. John J. Savage, *Par-*

and field, which figure God's word as "seed" that bears "fruit," patristic authors used agricultural imagery to enhance Paradise as a figurative place of instruction, either individual (the soul) or collective (the church).[13] Medieval art of the Fall often depicts God holding a book as he "teaches" his command to Adam or to both humans; the symbolic book represents God's teaching, among other things, either as originally spoken or as later embodied in Scripture (fig. 2).

Patristic exegetes promoted Genesis 3 as a story about doctrine and heresy, and upheld their models of ecclesiastical authority, by equating the Fall with the overthrow of a specific hierarchy of teaching. By patristic consensus, political and verbal authority in Paradise had been structured according to a three-tier hierarchy, namely, God/Adam/Eve; and this original order had been subverted by another, competing discursive structure, namely, Serpent/Eve/Adam. According to the patristic account, Adam was properly God's subordinate, just as Eve was his, and the Fall resulted from an inversion of authority instigated by the Serpent.

Patristic authors derived this scheme of things from the fact that God's precept (Gen. 2.16–17) comes before the creation of Eve (vv. 21–22), which they took to imply that Eve did not learn of the command directly from God but *through Adam*. This interpretation—or interpolation—clearly was meant to compensate for the textual datum seized upon by Gnostic allegorists, namely, that Adam received the fruit (and hence "knowledge") *through Eve*. The patristic stress on hierarchical divisions between God and the humans, and between man and woman, allows that in some sense a fall is built into the political and discursive structure of Paradise, or at least that it is foreshadowed by these divisions.[14] But patristic exegetes did not see the

---

adise, in *Saint Ambrose: Hexameron, Paradise, and Cain and Abel*, FOC, no. 42 (New York, 1961), 285–356; and Augustine, *GenM* 2.3.4 and passim; *PL* 34:173–220; trans. Roland J. Teske, *Two Books on Genesis against the Manichees*, in *Saint Augustine on Genesis*, FOC, no. 84 (Washington, 1991), pp. 45–141. Inner Teacher: Augustine, *Mag* 11.38; ed. Klaus-Detlef Daur, *CCSL* 29:139–203; trans. John H. S. Burleigh, *The Teacher*, in *Augustine: Earlier Writings* (Philadelphia, 1953), pp. 64–101; and *Conf* 11.8; ed. Martinus Skutella, rev. H. Juergens and W. Schaub, *Confessionum libri xiii* (Stuttgart, 1981); trans. Rex Warner, *The Confessions of St. Augustine* (New York, 1963).

13. Augustine's own monastery in Hippo was "a 'seminary' in the true sense of the word: a 'seed-bed' from which [his] protégés were 'planted out' as bishops in the leading towns of Numidia" (Brown, *Augustine of Hippo*, p. 143, noting *GenL* 8.8.16, on Adam and Eve as gardeners).

14. Burke, *The Rhetoric of Religion*, p. 203, speaks of a "proto-fall" implicit in the created divisions. David Damrosch, *The Narrative Covenant: Transformations*

2. God (with book) instructing Adam about the Tree of Knowledge. Eve is significantly absent. Stone carving, 13th c.: Chartres Cathedral, north portal, central bay, right side. Foto Marburg / Art Resource, New York.

Fall as being in any way the logical outcome of the order of things in the Garden; rather, the crucial fault line appeared with Eve's rebellion from God's word as handed down to her.

Ambrose is the first Latin exegete to elaborate on the original hierarchy of Eden and its implications for the Fall. Ambrose describes Adam—but never Eve—as one who "used to talk with God" in Paradise and as God's "conversational intimate."[15] Furthermore,

---

of *Genre in the Growth of Biblical Literature* (New York, 1987), pp. 137–43, discusses the "separation of Adam and Eve from God" (p. 138) on the basis of divisive hierarchies that are in place well before the Serpent's entrance. See also Vance, *Mervelous Signals,* chap. 7 (on "vertical" vs. "horizontal" discourse in *Le Jeu d'Adam*).

15. *Epistola* 45.13, 16; *PL* 16:1144 ("primus ille homo, qui cum Deo loquebatur

Ambrose states: "[The Devil] did not accost the man who had in [God's] presence received the heavenly command. He accosted her *who had learned of it from her husband and who had not received from God the command which was to be observed*. There is no statement that God spoke to the woman. We know that he spoke to Adam. Hence we must conclude that the command was communicated through Adam to the woman."[16] The contention that Eve had "learned" (*didicerat*) the command from Adam echoes Paul's model of teaching in the church, and just two paragraphs later (12.56) Ambrose cites one of Paul's dicta on the subject ("Adam was not deceived, but the woman was").[17]

Going further than his episcopal teacher, Augustine appeals not only to narrative sequence but also to grammar to support his contention that God addressed his precept to Adam alone and hence that Eve had a merely *indirect* knowledge of the precept. In the Old Latin Bible used by Augustine, God's speech about the Tree contains mostly plural verb forms, implying a plural audience.[18] (These plural forms, mistranslated from the Greek Septuagint, were corrected back to singular forms in Jerome's Vulgate version.) So Augustine was faced with the problem that God seemed to have addressed his command to a plural audience, that is, to *both* Adam and Eve. Noting the grammar of the text, Augustine at first allows that God may in fact have spoken to both humans: "Here the verb is in the plural, presumably because God is addressing both of them" (*GenL* 8.17.36). But then—citing another Pauline dictum on women and learning—Augustine entirely removes Eve from the original scene of instruction: "Another explanation could be that, since God knew He was going to make the woman for the man, He thus gave His command with observance of the proper order [*ordinatissime*] so that the command of the Lord would come through the man to the woman. This is the rule that St. Paul urges in the church: 'If they would learn

---

in paradiso positus"; "confabulator assiduus"); in *PL* 16:849–1286; selections trans. Mary M. Beyenka, *Saint Ambrose, Letters*, FOC, no. 26 (New York, 1954).

16. *Par* 12.54 (emphasis added).

17. Ambrose cites this text also at *Par* 4.24, 10.47.

18. In Augustine's OL version, only the first of four verbs has the singular form: "You may eat [*edes*] of every tree that is in Paradise; but of the tree of the knowledge of good and evil you shall not eat [*non manducabitis*]. In the day that you eat [*ederitis*] of it you shall die [*moriemini*]" (Gen. 2.16–17, text and trans. in Taylor, *The Literal Meaning of Genesis*, vol. 2 [ACW, no. 42], p. 329; on ancient textual vrr. in these verses, see p. 260, n. 89).

anything, let them ask their husbands at home [1 Cor. 14.35]' "
(GenL 8.17.36).

In using this second Pauline statement about men, women,
and teaching to uphold the supposedly proper order (ordo) of teaching in Paradise, Augustine reveals that a sense of male superiority,
and not simply rhetorical and narrative analysis, is driving his
conviction that Adam was intellectually and verbally "closer" to
God than Eve was. Elsewhere Augustine cites Paul's main dictum
on the subject ("Adam was formed first, then Eve; and Adam was
not deceived, but the woman was") to support this view that God
delivered the command to Adam alone and that Adam in turn was
to have instructed Eve: "Perhaps the woman had not yet received
the gift of the knowledge of God, but under the direction and
tutelage of her husband she was to acquire it gradually" (GenL
11.42.58).

While Augustine's politics of Paradise enforces a particular hierarchy of gender with respect to God's word—man first, woman
second—it also suggests a certain narrative outline for the whole
course of the Fall. In a passage about another order, namely, the
order in which God questioned the humans after their sin, Augustine
shapes the Fall into a tragic plot that hinges on the reversal of the
entire moral, intellectual, and verbal order of the Garden: "There is
surely some special meaning in the fact that just as the command
was given to the man, and through him transmitted to the woman,
so the man is questioned first. For the command came from the
Lord through the man to the woman, but sin came from the Devil
through the woman to the man."[19]

What was earlier just "another explanation" of the primal teaching scene has now become a certitude. Ever the rhetorician, Augustine here uses parallelism and antithesis to emplot Genesis 2–3 in
terms of a tripartite sequence of obedience and instruction ("from
the Lord through the man to the woman") and then its antithesis,
a tripartite sequence of sin and error ("from the Devil through the
woman to the man"). Like the scriptural narrative itself ("Now [au-
tem] the Serpent was more subtle"), Augustine's summary of the
Fall turns on the pivotal word autem ("but, however"), which marks
the division between the two orders of truth and falsehood.[20] Augustine's syntax stresses the paired opposition of not only truth/

19. GenL 11.34.45 ("Praeceptum enim a Domino per virum usque ad feminam,
peccatum autem a diabolo per feminam usque ad virum").

20. Autem appears in the OL version of Genesis 3.1 cited by Augustine (e.g.,
GenL 11.1.1).

falsehood but also man/woman so as to define the subversion of a certain "original" hierarchy.

The patristic notion of an instructional hierarchy in Eden had far-reaching consequences for the literary tradition of Genesis 3. For one thing, it helped reinforce the paired notions of "rational" man and "appetitive" woman that were applied to Adam and Eve as representatives of their sexes, as well as the notions of "masculine" reason and "feminine" appetite in the usual tropology of the Fall.[21] The patristic notion of "proper order," as Augustine calls it, maintained Adam's intellectual superiority to Eve and his nearer likeness to God, ideas that became commonplaces during the Middle Ages and thereafter, as attested by Milton, among others—"Hee for God only, shee for God in him."[22]

2. Dissemination and the Fall

In treating the Fall as a paradigm of instruction, Ambrose and Augustine are interested in both the external and internal (psychological) processes involved in the transmission—and transgression—of God's precept. As they deal with these matters, they each put forward influential ideas about language, knowledge, and tradition. But whereas Ambrose focuses on the integrity of the precept itself, Augustine stresses the role of memory in retaining and observing the precept.

Ambrose holds that during Eve's conversation with the Serpent the precept was corrupted through its faulty repetition by *both* speakers. First of all, while pretending to quote the text of God's command—"to give utterance to the words of God"—the Serpent inserted a falsehood (*mendacium*) by asking Eve whether God had forbidden them to eat of *any* tree (*Par* 12.56). Although Eve, in replying, correctly rehearsed the command's specificity to the Tree of Knowledge, she herself then corrupted it by adding another condition, that is, "neither shall you touch it" (v. 3). From this analysis Ambrose concludes: "There was nothing inexact about the command itself. The error lay in the report [*in relatione*] of the command."[23]

21. On the tropology, see below, Chapter 2.4.

22. John Milton, *Paradise Lost* 4.299; *John Milton: Complete Poems and Major Prose*, ed. Merritt Y. Hughes (Indianapolis, 1957).

23. *Par* 12.56. Damrosch, *The Narrative Covenant*, pp. 141–42, notes the "surprise" occasioned in antiquity (e.g., the Talmud) by Eve's memory lapse regarding

Speaking like a textual critic, Ambrose goes on to stress that any change in God's word corrupts it. Eve's example is a lesson about the need to preserve God's word in its "simple, original form." The present passage teaches (*docet*) us as much itself: "We realize [lit. "learn," *discimus*] that we ought not to make any addition to a command even by way of instruction. Any addition or qualification of a command is in the nature of a falsification. The simple, original form of a command should be preserved" (*Par* 12.56). Citing the biblical warning to those who tamper with Scripture (Rev. 22.18–19), Ambrose adds, "If this is true [of John's revelation], how much truer is it that nothing should be taken away from the commands laid down by God!" Ambrose thus equates God's spoken word, as received by Eve, with Scripture itself (which, after all, contains a "record" of that divine utterance). Although Eve's exchange with the Serpent is an oral one, Ambrose treats it as tantamount to a written text susceptible to errors in the course of transmission.[24] In so doing, he reflects the church's concern with the integrity of scriptural tradition, particularly a notion of textual purity that eventually would be embodied, institutionally, in the medieval scriptorium.[25]

In his analysis of the Eve-Serpent exchange, Ambrose of course recognizes that if Eve was in error and if she learned of the precept through Adam, Adam may have passed along to Eve an erroneous knowledge thereof. Defending his assumption that Adam conveyed the command to Eve in its "simple, original form" (*pura enim et simplex mandati forma*), and that it was she who (following the Serpent) introduced error, Ambrose emphatically rejects this conjecture:

> Many believe that this was Adam's fault—not the woman's. They reason that Adam in his desire to make her more cautious had said to the woman that God had given the additional instruction: "Nei-

---

God's "simple prohibition"; in ancient literature, "long speeches are routinely repeated word for word."

24. Tertullian (fl. ca. 200), *De anima* 16, PL 2:646–752, had said much the same of heretics, "claiming that they *interpolant* (corrupt, adulterate) the Scriptures" (Jeffrey B. Russell, *Satan: The Early Christian Tradition* [Ithaca, N.Y., 1981], p. 95n).

25. See Cassiodorus, *Institutiones* 1.30; ed. Roger A. B. Mynors, *Cassiodori Senatoris Institutiones* (Oxford, 1937); trans. Leslie W. Jones, *An Introduction to Divine and Human Readings* (1946; rpt. New York, 1969). In addition, see Alcuin, as cited below, Chapter 4.1; and writing tropes cited in Chapter 6.1. During the Middle Ages the term "document" (*documentum*, from *docere*, "to teach") came to have the sense of teaching or truth as embodied in writing; see *Mediae Latinitatis Lexicon Minus*, ed. J. F. Niermeyer (Leiden, 1976), s.v.

ther shall you touch it." We know that it was not Eve, but Adam, who received the command from God, because the woman had not yet been created. Scripture does not reveal the exact words that Adam used when he disclosed to her the nature and content of the command. At all events, we understand that the substance of the command was given to the woman by the man. (*Par* 12.56)

Significantly, Ambrose here acknowledges that there is no scriptural basis for ascertaining the "exact words" (*ipsa verba*) in which Adam conveyed the command to Eve. To maintain his view that Adam preserved the command correctly and that Eve altered it, Ambrose resorts to an assumption about the "substance" (*seriem*) of the command. Adam's actual words being unknown, Ambrose nonetheless assumes that they were adequate to the command's "nature and content" (*formam seriemque*).

Defending his notion of the command's descent through a male/female hierarchy, Ambrose admits that "there may appear to be an element of uncertainty in deciding which of the two [humans] was guilty," but, following Paul, he concludes that "the woman is responsible for the man's error and not vice-versa. Hence Paul says: 'Adam was not deceived, but the woman was deceived and was in sin' " (*Par* 12.56). The repeated appeal to Paul's authority shows that Genesis 3 as a whole, with its gaps and inconsistencies, is not as "simple" for Ambrose as God's command itself. Ambrose illustrates here how exegetes attempting to "fill in the lacunae" in the scriptural narrative inevitably drew attention to the gaps in the text.[26] Like Paul, Ambrose endeavors to make his interpretation seem a "logical" derivation from Scripture, but certain assumptions—Adam's rightful authority over Eve, Adam's transmission of the command to her in its "purity"—very clearly shape the constructions placed on the text.

Augustine probes much farther than his mentor into the problem of how God's precept was disseminated in Paradise, dealing with a wide range of questions concerning the origin, semantics, and epistemology of language there. Consistent with patristic tradition in general, Augustine holds that Adam spoke Hebrew and that the inception of human language lay with Adam's naming of the animals (and, later, Eve). These notions raise hermeneutical issues that will be taken up later in this book; here, two points should be stressed.[27]

26. Auerbach, *Mimesis*, p. 75, as quoted more fully above, Introduction.
27. Adam as namer, *GenL* 9.12.20 (animals), 9.19.36 (Eve). Adam's Hebrew id-

First, human language was an originally male prerogative that belonged to woman only by extension. Eve, as yet uncreated, was excluded from the inaugural moment of human language, the naming of the animals. In Augustine's own metaphor, Eve, created from Adam's side, was "grafted" onto the Adamic trunk (*GenL* 9.16.29); likewise she was grafted onto the trunk of Adamic language. Furthermore, as soon as Eve was created, Adam conferred a name on her as well. By a "natural" order, then, Adam was the namer, Eve the named. Linguistic roles thus divided the first couple from the start, with man as the implied subject of language and woman as its object.

Second, the Hebrew idiom shared by God and Adam in the first speech acts of human history was identical with the language of Scripture. In *The City of God* (16.11), Augustine explicitly asserts that the language of Adam, the *Ursprache*, survived the confusion of tongues at Babel to become eventually the language of Scripture. This equation reinforces the perceived link, and the continuity, between God's written word and the word of God pronounced in the Garden.

Although Adam founded a language (*lingua*) and was the first to give names, Augustine maintains that both humans were taught to speak (*loqui*) by God. As beings not born but made, Adam and Eve did not learn "to understand [one] another speaking... by growing up among those who do or by studying under a teacher" (*GenL* 8.16.35)—that is, through the laborious social or educational process experienced by their descendants and described by Augustine in the early chapters of the *Confessions*.[28] Rather, they were taught to speak by God himself: "Certainly [it was] no problem for God to teach men to speak whom He had made in such a way that they could learn this art from others in case there were others present from whom they might learn."

But this argument still left unanswered a crucial question of epistemology. How were the first humans, as inexperienced users of language, able to grasp the terms of God's command? As Augustine puts it, "How could man... understand [*intelligere*] what was said to him about the tree of the knowledge of good and evil when he was completely ignorant of the meaning of evil?" (*GenL*

---

iom, *GenL* 9.12.20, and *Civ* 16.11; ed. and trans. George E. McCracken et al., *The City of God against the Pagans*, 7 vols., LCL (London, 1957–72).

28. See *Conf* 1.6–20, as discussed below, Chapter 2.5.

8.16.34).[29] This question about prelapsarian language and knowledge reflects the general problem of verbal epistemology that Augustine considers at length in *Of the Teacher*, where he is concerned to define the relation of signs to the knowledge of things themselves. Augustine's answer to his own question has to do with the system of differences that structure both the created world and the conventions of human language.

According to Augustine, words do not by themselves teach or convey knowledge but merely *remind* persons of things already known to them through the intellect or learned through sense-experience (*Mag* 12.39). Clearly relying on this idea in his commentary on Genesis, Augustine surmises that God was able to teach or impart to Adam and Eve an understanding of "evil" and "death" through the principle of contraries, as based on sense-experience:

> Most unknown things are understood from their contraries which are known.... So, in perceiving the life within him, a man might take precautions against its opposite, that is, the privation of life (which we call death).... It does not matter what syllables make up its name.... And whatever word may be used to designate the same thing in any other language, the mind perceives a sign in the spoken word, and at the sound it recognizes what it would think even without the sign....
>
> To the first man and woman, therefore, life was already sweet, and undoubtedly they tried to avoid losing it. When God instructed them in this matter, whatever sounds or other means He used, they were able to understand. (*GenL* 8.16.34)

The attempt to explain how God's word impinged on the human understanding in the Garden of Eden is in turn part of Augustine's larger attempt to reconstruct the mental experience of humans before the Fall, an effort related to his overarching theology of the word, or what Marcia Colish calls the "verbal theory of the knowledge of God" that informs his writings throughout.[30] In using this theory to account for man's primal knowledge, Augustine appeals

29. Ambrose, *Par* 8.40, had raised this problem without really addressing it: "Man...had a mental conception of evil [*opinionem accepit mali*], inasmuch as he was enjoined to abstain from evil."
30. Colish, *The Mirror of Language*, p. 7.

not only to the principle of contraries but also to the key role of memory.[31]

Augustine explains in his treatise *On the Trinity* that both the sensible word and the concept it signifies are subject to a tripartite mental process of memory, intellect, and will, a process replicating the image of the Trinity in the human soul (*Trin* 13.20.26). The profound influence of this logocentric epistemology on learned medieval culture can hardly be overstated, for it converts the notion of humans as creatures made in God's image (Gen. 1.26) into specifically *verbal* terms, stressing that the soul is a repository of God's word.

Some practical consequences of this epistemology appear in Augustine's lengthy meditation on consciousness in book 10 of the *Confessions*. There he stresses that knowledge, and the exchange of knowledge, depend on traces left by words in the memory, traces that comprise both the sensible and conceptual aspects of language. For example, feelings or ideas such as "sorrow" and "fear" exist apart from language, but "we could not talk about them at all, unless we could find within our memory not only the sounds of the words (according to images impressed upon it by the senses of the body) but also concepts of the things themselves."[32] Although words themselves cannot *teach* things to the soul, as Augustine stresses in *Of the Teacher*, they constitute the crucial material and conceptual forms in which knowledge is embodied within the memory, which is the soul's repository of experience.

These ideas about memory, knowledge, and learning underlie Augustine's commentary on how Adam and Eve receive, retain, and respond intellectually to God's word as embodied in the command. Describing the relative ease of obeying that command, Augustine notes how readily it could be remembered: "This command, which forbade the eating of one kind of food where a great abundance of other kinds lay close at hand, was as easy to observe as it was brief to remember [*tam breve ad memoria retinendum*], especially since the will was not yet then opposed by desire."[33] Unlike Ambrose, then, Augustine does not fault Eve's differing version of the command or take this version as proof that she altered or corrupted it. Rather, Augustine cites Eve's repetition of God's command as evidence that she retained it, intact, in her memory: "No one would

31. On memory in Augustine's epistemology, see Colish, *The Mirror of Language*, pp. 36–38; and Vance, *Mervelous Signals*, pp. 35–38, 52–56.

32. *Conf* 10.14.

33. *Civ* 14.12.

be able to say that the woman had forgotten the command of God" (*GenL* 11.30.38). Continuing, Augustine stresses that memory is the key to Eve's knowledge of the command: "The sin is more evident when the command is retained in memory [*memoria retinetur*] and God as present in His command is despised. Thus, when the Psalmist said, 'Those who are mindful of His commandments,' it was necessary for him to add, 'in order to keep them' [Ps. 102.18]. For many people hold them in memory to despise them, and their transgression is the more serious in so far as forgetfulness does not excuse them." The crucial role that Augustine assigns here to memory reflects the verbal epistemology set forth in the treatise on the Trinity, where memory is the basis of verbal understanding and response: "[The will] unites those things which are held [*tenebantur*] in the memory with those things which are thence impressed on the mind's eye in conception, [and] completes, indeed, some kind of trinity, since itself is a third added to two others."[34] Augustine likens the memory specifically to the Father, the intellect to the Son, and the will to the Holy Spirit (15.23.43). Eugene Vance sums up the crucial role of memory in this verbal epistemology by stating, "To return to memory is to return to the Father."[35]

But Eve fails to return to the Father. By "despising" God's word, as Augustine puts it, she despises God himself, for he is consubstantial with his word, "present in his command" (*in illo Deus assistens praesensque*). Yet God as "present" in his word is the only presence of God that Eve, already once removed from his immediate presence through a teaching hierarchy, actually enjoys. Indeed, for Eve, the verbal "presence" of God is also his absence, since she is removed from him by precisely the distance of the precept. God's presence-and-absence through his word is crucial to medieval versions of the Fall, which often stress the sanctity (or vulnerability) of God's word as his only earthly trace and the tenuous "holding" power of the chain of memory, teaching, and tradition.

The last—and weakest—link in the chain, as defined by patristic authors, Eve puts even more distance between herself and God when, "despising" his word, she violates it and eats of the forbidden fruit. Augustine does not suggest that in doing so Eve realizes and fulfills a principle that is already implicit in her assigned position at the

34. *Trin* 13.20.26; ed. W. J. Mountain and Fr. Glorie, *CCSL* 50 (2 pts.); trans. Arthur W. Haddan and W. G. T. Shedd, *On the Holy Trinity*, NPNF, ser. 1, vol. 3 (1887; rpt. Grand Rapids, 1980), pp. 1–228.

35. Vance, *Mervelous Signals*, p. 52. See also Bloch, *Etymologies and Genealogies*, pp. 53–63.

end, or bottom, of things. Indeed, for patristic authors in general, as for the medieval exegetes that followed them, Eve's transgression represents nothing inevitable (though foreknown by God) and certainly no heroic rebellion (as it did, for example, to the Enlightenment interpreters who revived, after a fashion, the Gnostic reading).[36] Rather, Eve's "despising" God's word was viewed as a calamitous violation of the whole divinely instituted order of Paradise. After the Serpent, Eve was the first to challenge the "received text," the "tradition," or the "canon" as passed down to her, but orthodox exegetes scarcely admired Eve's daring.

3. The Teacher of Death

Eve's departure from God's teaching was prompted of course by the Serpent, whom patristic tradition associated with false doctrine or heresy, and with Satan himself. Paul's typology of the Fall had cast the Serpent in the role of a false teacher or preacher trying to "seduce" the church (Eve). Further support for the Serpent-Satan identification appeared in Revelation, with its repeated mention of "that ancient serpent [serpens antiquus], who is [called] the Devil and Satan" (12.9, 20.2). By about the end of the fourth century, patristic authors had virtually secured the Serpent's identification with Satan, the "father of lies" (John 8.44) and hence the fountainhead of false doctrine and the chief heresiarch.[37] The Serpent had long been a convenient emblem for rival discourse of any sort, as when Jerome, censuring Jovinian's writings in defense of marriage, wrote that he heard "the hissing of the old serpent; by counsel such as this, the dragon drove man from Paradise."[38] A contributing factor was no doubt the prominent role of serpents in classical myth and the alleged role of demons in the classical pantheon, which prompted patristic authors to identify the biblical Serpent with pagan teachings and the Fall in general with idolatry.[39] As Neil Forsyth has

36. See Phillips, Eve, pp. 80–81.

37. On the evolution of these ideas, see Forsyth, The Old Enemy, pp. 232–35, 252–56, 304–5, 377–78, 422–27. See also Russell, Satan, pp. 66–67, 78, 82.

38. Jerome, Contra Jovinianum 1.4, in PL 23:211–338; as cited and trans. in Pagels, Adam, Eve, and the Serpent, p. 93.

39. E.g., Clement of Alexandria, Exhortation to the Greeks 2.11–12; ed. and trans. G. W. Butterworth, in Clement of Alexandria, LCL (London, 1953). I am indebted to Ehren Fordyce for this reference. On the Devil, idolatry, and the Fall, see Michael Camille, The Gothic Idol: Ideology and Image-making in Medieval Art (Cambridge, 1989), pp. 58–61, citing Augustine, Civ 8.18.

stressed, however, "the main factor that drove the church toward the identification of serpent and Satan was the political struggle with heresy which occupied so much of the energy of the young church."[40]

Patristic authors before Augustine tended to equate the Serpent with Satan and heresy primarily on the basis of allegory. Thus Ambrose interprets the Serpent as a sign or emblem (*figura*) for the Devil, glossing its venom as false teaching disseminated by Satan, who "has vomited into this world what might be called poisonous [*venena*] wisdom."[41] Verbal "poison" was a topos in commentary on Genesis 3; for example, Josephus (1st c. A.D.) held that God punished the Serpent for its part in the transgression by replacing its native power of speech with poison.[42] Thereafter the Serpent's verbal "poison" emerged as a major image in patristic glosses on the Fall, particularly with respect to false teaching.

Following the pattern of Paul's seduction typology and using the traditional Serpent/Satan allegory, Ambrose elaborates on the Fall as a paradigm for false teaching within the church, likening Adam and Eve to young catechumens and the tempter to specific heretics in the church's recent past:

> Take the case of the Gentile who is eager for the faith. He becomes a catechumen and desires a greater fullness of doctrine to strengthen his faith. See to it that in his willingness to learn he is not exposed to false doctrine. Take care that he does not learn from Photinus or from Arius or from Sabellius. See that he does not hand himself over to teachers of this sort, who would attract him by their airs of authority, so that his untrained mind, impressed by the weight of such august prestige, will be unable to discriminate the right from the wrong. (*Par* 12.58)

Ambrose probably wrote his commentary on Genesis shortly after becoming bishop of Milan (in 374), and here he seems to speak in his episcopal capacity as one responsible for supervising the teaching

40. Forsyth, *The Old Enemy*, p. 304; on Augustine's interpretation of the Serpent, see Forsyth, pp. 422–28. Also useful (though it excludes *De paradiso*) is Michael P. McHugh, "Satan and Saint Ambrose," *Classical Folia* 26 (1972): 94–106.

41. *Par* 2.9 ("figure"); *Par* 12.55 ("poison"), quoting Matt. 12.34 ("You brood of vipers, how can you speak good things when you are evil?").

42. Josephus, *Jewish Antiquities* 1.50; ed. and trans. H. St. J. Thackeray et al., 7 vols., LCL (London, 1930). Verbal poison is a commonplace in classical and biblical literature (e.g., Ps. 140.3, Rom. 3.13, and quotations in *OLD*, s.v. *uenenum* 3b).

of doctrine in his diocese. All the "teachers" (*magistri*) named here and compared to the Serpent had been proscribed as heretics by the church during the last century or so.[43]

In the same passage, Ambrose offers examples (mainly from the New Testament) of texts construed in heterodox ways by these "teachers," and he advises that the catechumen read Scripture for himself rather than in the light of suspect authority (*auctoritas*): "[No] interpreter [should] stand in his way.... The catechumen first ought to reflect on the matter in his own mind, so as to discover the real meaning of these passages. He is influenced by the prestige of his teachers. It would have been more to his advantage if he had not investigated at all rather than have come upon such an instructor." Ambrose here glosses the Serpent as a figure or "type" for any heretical exegete (*interpres*), teacher (*magister*), or instructor (*doctor*) who might distort or corrupt God's teaching and use his prestige or authority to sway inexperienced believers.

Augustine further develops the Serpent/Satan identification. In his first commentary on Genesis he explains the Serpent as a figure for the Manichean heretics against whom he is writing the treatise itself.[44] Invoking a traditional gloss, Augustine writes that the Serpent "signifies" not only the Devil but also "the poisons of the heretics and especially of these Manichees and all those opposed to the Old Testament."[45] He then uses Paul's typology to incorporate details from the Temptation into a paradigm for the dissemination of heresy:

> Who more than [the heretics] utter the words, "You will be as gods"? In their proud vanity, trying to win others to that same pride, they assert that the soul is by nature that which God is....
> In general, all heretics deceive by the promise of knowledge and find fault with those whom they find believing in all simplicity.
> ...They do not heed the Apostle who says, "I fear lest, as the serpent seduced Eve by his cunning, so your minds are also being

43. Sabellius (3d c.) taught that the persons of the Trinity were merely diverse manifestations and not distinct realities (Modalism); Photinus (4th c.), bishop of Sirmium, spread Modalism and Adoptianism (a denial of Christ's divinity); Arius (d. 336?) taught that the Son was created rather than being coeternal with God the Father (Arianism).

44. A brief summary of Manicheanism appears in Kelly, *Early Christian Doctrines*, pp. 13–14; on Augustine, the Manichees, and Genesis 3 in particular, see Forsyth, *The Old Enemy*, pp. 421–28.

45. *GenM* 2.14.20 (*significat*), 2.25.38.

corrupted." I believe that these men were prefigured by that prophecy.[46]

By citing Genesis 3 as a "prophecy," Augustine turns the Temptation into a paradigm for all "heretical" assaults on church teachings, particularly on the "simple" believers who also worried Ambrose. As Forsyth remarks, the Temptation thus becomes "an archetype of the relation between truth and heresy, itself a continuing process."[47]

Augustine goes on to gloss the forbidden fruit as a figure for heresy: "Let [Adam] not receive from [Eve] the forbidden food, that is, the deceit of the heretics with their many promises of knowledge and the disclosure of the so-called secrets, by which their error is made more hidden so as better to deceive."[48] This gloss exemplifies the patristic effort not only to reclaim Genesis 3 from heretics like the Gnostics and Manichees, with their cult of secret knowledge, but also to *preempt* heterodox interpretations by asserting the text's intrinsic significance as a "prophetic" warning about such heretics and their teachings. In his later, literal commentary on Genesis, Augustine went beyond his predecessors, and even his own early exegesis, in identifying the Serpent as both a sign and instrument of Satan, a kind of mouthpiece used to deceive Eve. This ventriloquistic motif, which had profound rhetorical implications, shows the great lengths to which Augustine went in order to secure the Serpent's *historical*—and not just allegorical—identity with Satan and false doctrine.[49]

In his metrical version of Genesis 3, Avitus dramatizes his predecessors' notion of the Fall as the archetypal conflict between truth and heresy.[50] Specifically, Avitus casts the Serpent as a false teacher who rivals the teaching of the divine Teacher, leads Eve into error with his pretended authority, and incites her in turn to misteach Adam, thus inverting the whole divine order of instruction in Paradise.

46. *GenM* 2.25.38–2.26.39.
47. Forsyth, *The Old Enemy*, p. 426.
48. *GenM* 2.27.41 ("vetitum cibum, id est haereticorum fallaciam").
49. *GenL* 11.27.34 (the Devil used the Serpent "as an instrument [*velut organo*]") and *Civ* 14.11. See discussion below, Chapter 3.2. For background on Augustine's theories about the Devil, see Russell, *Satan*, chap. 7.
50. Of Avitus's poem in general, Evans, *Paradise Lost and the Genesis Tradition*, p. 137, states that "doctrine has been turned into poetry."

Following the second (Yahwist) creation account, Avitus puts Adam's creation before Eve's and makes him the sole audience to the divine speech that gives humans dominion over the earth (1.133–43), thus establishing Adam's role as God's earthly authority. Avitus departs from Ambrose and Augustine by placing Eve's creation prior to the speech about the Tree of Knowledge, having God pronounce the precept about the Tree to *both* humans, and even emphasizing the dual audience through grammatical hints in the speech itself.[51] But this speech also establishes a teaching hierarchy that presumes Adam's authority over Eve, as later becomes clear in the subversion of this authority posed by the Temptation.

Describing himself as the humans' "Teacher" (*Doctor*), God warns Adam and Eve not to try to learn (*discere*) the knowledge that is forbidden them:

> Let not rash worry press you to learn what your Teacher
> Prohibits you to know; better for the blessed not to know
> That which, in being sought, would harm them.[52]

The close of the scene underscores God's role as Teacher to the humans: "leaving them thus instructed [*instructos*] in that sacred place, / The glad Father bore himself away to heaven's starry vault."[53] Evident here are the patristic notions of God as Teacher and of an original paradisal order based on divine teaching. Although Avitus does not explicitly put Adam into the role of Eve's teacher, he equates the Fall with an overthrow of the initial and normative hierarchy of teaching in Paradise, for both the Serpent and Eve, in turn, usurp God's teacherly role.

Even before Satan disguises himself as the Serpent (on Augustine's model) in order to approach Eve, the poem describes him as a false teacher, one who "teaches [*docet*] wickedness" (2.58). Once disguised as the reptile and equipped with "poison" (*ueneno*, 2.141), the tempter approaches Eve and makes a long speech praising her

51. E.g., "These riches together shall provide your food [*uestros . . . cibos*] without end" (1.305–6).

52. Avitus, *Poematum de spiritalis historiae gestis* 1.313–15 ("nec uos forte praemat temeraria discere cura, / quod Doctor prohibet: melius nescire beatis / quod quaesisse nocet"); ed. Daniel J. Nodes, *Avitus, The Fall of Man* (Toronto, 1985), with some translations (often modified) from Watson Kirkconnell, comp. and trans., *The Celestial Cycle: The Theme of Paradise Lost in World Literature, with Translations of the Major Analogues* (1952; rpt. New York, 1967), pp. 3–18.

53. 1.324–25 ("At Pater instructos sacrata in sede relinquens / laetus in astrigeram caeli se sustulit aulam").

beauty, power, and fertility. He concludes by expressing a wish for a certain knowledge:

> As, nonetheless, free touch must be restrained
> From one delightful tree, I long to know
> Who with dread order has begrudged such gifts.[54]

In thus voicing a wish to know (*scire*) about the forbidden Tree, the tempter implicitly challenges God's earlier warning that it is better for Adam and Eve not to know (*nescire*), not to learn (*discere*), such things. Avitus summons poison again as a danger sign: "seductile Eve into her ears / Received the deadly poison [*uenenum*]."[55]

Apparently impressed by the show of knowledge in the Serpent's praise of her qualities and his allusions to creation at large, Eve rehearses God's precept and then disastrously invites the "most learned" (*doctissima*) Serpent, as she now calls her tempter, to explain God's word to her:

> the Creator, swearing with dread voice,
> Said that if harmful freedom broke His law,
> We should atone straightway for our offense
> With a certain "death." What He meant by death,
> Do thou willingly explain to me, most learned Serpent,
> Since it is a mystery to the untaught.[56]

Avitus here dramatizes some of the central concerns about teaching, heresy, and the Fall articulated by Ambrose and Augustine.

First of all, this moment recalls Ambrose's scenario of the novice whose "willingness to learn" may expose him to false doctrine, and who may "hand himself over to teachers" who "would attract him by their airs of authority." Besides elevating the Serpent to "learned" status, Eve describes herself as "untaught" (*rudis*), a claim contradicted by her earlier having been taught by God himself. Within the church the term *rudis* ("untaught, ignorant") was commonly applied

54. 2.157–60 ("Ut tamen una / contineat liber dulci super arbore tactus, / scire uelim; quis dira iubet, quis talia dona / inuidet et rebus ieiunia miscet opimis?").

55. 2.166–67 ("mortiferum seductilis Euua uenenum / auribus accipiens").

56. 2.178–82 ("si libertas temeraret noxia legem, / iurans terribili praedixit uoce Creator / quadam nos statim luituros "morte" reatum. / Quid uocitet mortem, tu nunc, doctissimae serpens, / pande libens, quoniam rudibus non cognita res est").

to catechumens.[57] In describing herself as "untaught" and in soliciting the Serpent's instruction, Eve improperly puts herself in the role of his student or catechumen—a subversion of the divine/human instructional order detailed earlier in the poem.

Eve's request for an explanation of "death" (*mors*) also calls to mind Augustine's verbal epistemology as applied to the Fall, particularly the question of "how the first man and woman were able to understand God when He named or threatened what they had not experienced" (*GenL* 8.16.35).[58] Possibly differing with Augustine, Avitus may here be implying that God's terms really did mystify the humans, or at least Eve. More likely, however, Avitus is suggesting, consistent with Augustine, that Eve understood God's precept well enough to "remember" and "observe" it but that the inquiring Serpent aroused her curiosity to know more.

In the narrative sequel to this scene, Avitus underlines the inversion of the teaching order brought about by Eve's ill-advised request: "At this the sly serpent and teacher [*magister*] of death / Eagerly instructs [*docet*] Eve to her ruin and speaks to her captivated ears."[59] The phrase "teacher of death" (*leti magister*) may glance slyly at *magister ludi* (lit. "master of the game"), a title applied to schoolmasters and tutors in the Roman grammar schools.[60] In any case, by characterizing the Serpent as a *magister*, a term also used by Ambrose in reference to the heretical teachers represented by the Serpent, Avitus clearly suggests that Eve has now enrolled herself in the Devil's school.

The Serpent's second speech to Eve leads her further down the garden path toward forbidden knowledge. The truth is embodied not in God's word, she now learns, but in the apple, described as a tasty vessel of divine secrets:

> this apple, which you fear to touch,
> As being a thing forbidden, will empower you
> To know whatever secrets the Father keeps from you.

57. As in the title of Augustine's treatise, *De catechizandis rudibus*; ed. I. B. Bauer, *CCSL* 46:115–78; trans. S. D. F. Salmond, *On the Catechising of the Uninstructed*, NPNF, ser. 1, vol. 3 (1887; rpt. Grand Rapids, 1980), pp. 282–314. For semantics, see *OLD*, s.v. *rudis* 5–7.

58. On the hermeneutical import of this scene, see below, Chapter 2.3.

59. 2.183–84 ("Callidus inde draco et leti tum sponte magister / interitum docet et captas sic fatur ad aures").

60. *OLD*, s.v. *magister* 8a–b (quots. w. *ludi*).

. . . . .

For when you shall have tasted the divine juice
With your mouth, at once your eyesight will be cleared,
Making you equal to the gods. . . .[61]

In order to know—again, *scire*—Eve must experience the taste (*sapor*) of the fruit, an implied contrast with the wisdom (*sapientia*) embodied in God's word. The Serpent further objectifies the offered knowledge by plucking "an apple from the fatal tree" to tempt Eve even more, but Avitus signals that the deadly agent is already within her, in the form of the Serpent's instructive/destructive discourse, the "poison [*uenenum*] of ambition [that] has crept in."[62] It "creeps" (*serpit*), a figurative extension of the Serpent itself.

The reversal of the original order of instruction continues in Eve's temptation of Adam. Eve, having eaten of the fruit, now ironically claims that she comes to her husband not in ignorance (*nescia*) but having been instructed (*docta*):

Take food, sweet husband, from the seed of life,
Whose potency, perhaps, will make you like the Thunderer
And equal to the gods. I do not give this gift
In ignorance, but duly instructed.[63]

Eve's pride in her new "learning" adds dramatic irony and an ominous tone to the scene, for it echoes her earlier flattery of the "learned" Serpent. Besides expressly likening herself to her new teacher, Eve, in claiming to teach Adam, *imitates* her own tempter, and this *imitatio* of both his message and his example perpetuates the false tradition of knowledge that now has been brought into being.[64] Through this comparison, Eve also implicitly denies (or

---

61. 2.196–97, 200–202 ("Namque hoc, quod uetitum formidas tangere, pomum / scire dabit quaecumque Pater secreta reponit . . . / Namque ubi diuinum libaueris ore saporem, / mox purgata tuo facient te lumina uisu / aequiperare deos").

62. 2.210 ("letali ex arbore malum"); 2.220–21 ("serpitque uenenum / ambitione nocens").

63. 2.242–45 ("Sume cibum dulcis uitali ex germine coniux, / quod similem summo faciet te forte Tonanti / numinibusque parem. Non hoc tibi nescia donum, / sed iam docta feram").

64. On the rhetorical implications of Eve's *imitatio*, see below, Chapter 3.3.

forgets) what she was taught by her divine Teacher and even that he ever instructed her at all.[65]

From a patristic viewpoint, it is especially ironic and tragic that Eve here asserts teacherly authority over Adam. Though Avitus, unlike Ambrose and Augustine, does not spell out a prelapsarian hierarchy in which the man taught the woman, Eve's claim now to be teaching Adam not only dramatizes the challenge being mounted against the authority of the divine *Doctor* but also may be meant to echo (and refute) the heretical notion that Eve conveyed true knowledge to Adam from the Serpent.[66] Eve's remarks a few lines later stress that the Fall involves a violation of man's authority over woman:

> ...it is a crime
> For a man's mind to hesitate to do
> What I, a woman did. You were afraid,
> Perhaps, to go before me in this matter.
> At least now follow me....[67]

Eve's talk of precedence and sequence suggests that in taking the initiative she has inverted the Pauline and generally patristic notion of proper order between the sexes ("Adam...first, then Eve"). On the patristic model, Adam is supposed to precede (*praecedere*) Eve in authority and virtue, but now he obeys her in sinful submission when told to follow (*consequere*).

Once precedence is violated, the other consequences of the Fall quickly follow. When Eve holds out to Adam "the dish of conquering death [*fercula mortis*]" (2.252), scarcely does he accept the "poison" (2.259) and experience its "taste" (*sapor*, 2.262) than he feels a new, sorrowful knowledge. As noted earlier, Augustine associated both the forbidden fruit and the Serpent's poison with heresy. Here Avitus blends these two central images to point up that Adam swallows

---

65. Claudius Marius Victor, *Alethia* 1.413, ed. P. F. Hovingh, *CCSL* 128:125–93, describes Eve as "learned [*docta*] in evil" as she goes to tempt Adam; cited in Evans, *Paradise Lost and the Genesis Tradition*, p. 125. In Avitus, Eve's touting her own "learning" adds dramatic irony.

66. Michael Roberts, "The Prologue to Avitus' *De spiritalis historiae gestis*: Christian Poetry and Poetic License," *Traditio* 36 (1980): 399–407, notes that Eve's false learning is also evident in that she "speaks [to Adam] like a pagan of a multiplicity of divinities," and that her words "recall those of the serpent in his speech of temptation to Eve (2.201–202)" (p. 405).

67. 2.247–49 ("mentem scelus est dubitasse uirilem, / quod mulier potui. Praecedere forte timebas, / saltim consequere atque animos attolle iacentes").

the lie and the false doctrine being "passed on" to him by Eve from the Serpent.

The Temptation closes with the triumphant Serpent exulting to the humans that "whatever was mine to know [*scire*] is now yours" and claiming that in having taught (*docui*) Adam and Eve he has also won possession of their souls:

> . . . let Him keep
> The body once created by Himself.
> The soul, which I have taught, is surely mine.
> Mine is the greater part. To your Creator
> You may owe much; but to your master, more.[68]

Satan's claim to authority over the humans as their "master" (*magister*) suggests that to teach or instruct the soul is to take possession of it. Avitus may be echoing Augustine's notion that to believe falsehood is to place oneself under Satan's authority and power (*Lib* 3.10.31). In any case, by claiming "the soul, which I have taught," the tempter usurps the role that Augustine assigns to the inner Teacher, Christ.[69] In the last book of his poem Avitus evokes Christ teaching in the temple (6.64) and thereby restoring the original order of instruction in the "paradise" of both the church and the soul. For now, however, the Teacher of Death seems to have prevailed over the divine Teacher.

In dramatizing how the Fall subverted doctrine and the order of instruction itself, Avitus stresses two other points established by earlier exegetes. As a corollary to their view of the Fall as a story about doctrine and authority, Ambrose and Augustine had maintained that the Fall itself was profoundly instructive as a moral *exemplum*. According to Ambrose, Scripture records the Temptation "so that we learn how we can escape [the Devil's] arts" and so that "thereby taught and instructed we may avoid these pitfalls."[70] Augustine concurs that the story of the Fall constitutes a lesson "for the instruction [*erudiendo*] of men" (*GenL* 11.28.35). Following his predecessors, Avitus points the moral of the Fall by appealing di-

---

68. 2.413, 419–21 ("Quicquid scire meum potuit, iam credite uestrum est. . . . / teneat, quod condidit ipsae; / quod docui meum est; maior mihi portio restat. / Multa creatori debetis, plura magistro").

69. *Mag* 11.38. Although Christ taught outwardly while on earth, "inwardly . . . is where the good and only master teaches all his disciples" (*Conf* 11.8).

70. *Par* 12.58 ("ut discamus quemadmodum artes ejus cavere possimus," "ut docti instructique caveamus"), trans. modified.

rectly to his audience right after Adam eats of the forbidden fruit: "blinder you will be, if not content / To know [*noscere*] alone the things a great Creator / Wished you to have known [*te nosse*]."[71] On a rhetorical level, the arresting second-person pronoun (*tu*) capitalizes on the poet's imaginative art by forcing the audience to be "present" at the dramatized scene of the Fall. On a theological level, this apostrophe invokes the typology and genealogy of original sin, the Augustinian doctrine that puts all of Adam's and Eve's descendants, *in germine*, at the instructive scene.

In treating the Fall as a cautionary tale about doctrine and heresy, teaching and authority, Avitus in turn assumes that Scripture is continuous with God's original, spoken word. Just as the divine Teacher taught Adam and Eve in the Garden, so he offers his lessons to their descendants in his Book. Augustine commonly speaks of how Scripture "teaches" (*praecipit*), and Ambrose likens God's original, spoken precept directly to Scripture: "With the Word of God before us . . . we seem to be listening to the very voice of the Lord, whereby some things are forbidden and other things are advised."[72] Avitus enforces the same continuity between God's spoken and written word, not only by making his audience "present" at the Fall through moral apostrophe but also by dramatizing Scripture in narrative and speeches, so that, in several senses of the phrase, "we seem to be listening to the very voice of the Lord." The drama of the Fall, recreated through the imaginative collaboration of poet and audience, thus becomes a powerful vehicle for instruction, as eventually realized even more fully on the medieval stage.

4. Conclusion

Patristic authors turned the conflict over God's precept in the Garden into a paradigm for central issues of doctrine, tradition, and authority in the church. They held that God had taught true doctrine to Adam, who in turn had conveyed it to Eve, only to have the whole hierarchy of Eden subverted by the false teaching of the Serpent. Developing various Pauline glosses on Genesis 3, exegetes treated the Fall as a typology for the perennial conflict between truth and heresy and for the rightful authority of men over women in the church and society. At the same time, Genesis 2 and 3 provided a

71. 2.267–68 ("Nunc mage cecus eris, cui iam non sufficit illud / noscere, quod tantus uoluit te nosse Creator").

72. Augustine, *Doc* 3.10.15, 3.16.24. Ambrose, *Par* 8.39. Cf. 2 Tim. 3.16.

model for the church as a tradition based on a divine word disseminated and preserved through memory, speech, and writing. In the Garden, Adam and Eve had failed in the face of tempting falsehood to "keep" God's word as delivered to them; in the church, the "seed" or "poison" of heresy and error likewise posed a constant threat to the purity and integrity of God's word as both a written text and a living presence.

Patristic glosses on the Fall as a paradigm for problems of doctrine, tradition, and authority profoundly shaped medieval interpretations of Genesis 3. In the first place, the notion that the Fall represented a conflict between doctrine and heresy furnished a model for the continual theological disputes of the Middle Ages. In the ninth-century English poem *Genesis B*, for example, Adam and Eve disastrously exchange God's teaching (*lar*, "lore") for that of Satan, a theme that reflects the church's continuing struggle against either heathen mythology or homegrown heresies. At the same time, this poem deals with the problem of what constitutes sacred "tradition" in a culture that is still mainly oral. As for the problem of gender and authority embodied by the Fall, it continued to show up in myriad forms but particularly in medieval moral treatises written by clerics for women, and which in the name of God claim Adamic authority over the unreliable "daughters of Eve." Such treatises draw heavily on the Fall as a seduction scenario, adapting Paul's typology from the ecclesiastical sphere to social and domestic life in order to provide cautionary tales warning women against male seducers. Late medieval poetry on the Fall, like Chaucer's, similarly stresses the crisis of authority and instruction in the Garden, though adapting these themes to freer literary forms such as the fabliau and to a more worldly audience. Whether rendered as a doctrinal drama, a cautionary tale, or a serio-comic fable, the Fall continues to reflect the problems of dissemination bequeathed by the "theology of seed" that runs through patristic glosses on Genesis 3. That is, because language is taken to embody or signify original sin and its consequences, medieval authors can shape the politics of Paradise into narratives about not just doctrine and heresy but also sexuality and the body, lineage and property, and even poetry itself.

Chapter 2

The Genesis of Hermeneutics

You clothed men with skins when by their sin they became
mortal. And so you have like a skin stretched out the
firmament of your book, that is, your words which so well
agree together and which, through the agency of mortal
men, you have placed above us.
—*Augustine*

PATRISTIC CULTURE bequeathed to the Middle Ages the notion that
the Fall had involved an abuse of signs, texts, and interpretation,
among other things, and that this crisis was exemplary for various
hermeneutical problems faced by fallen humans. Exegetes used the
Fall as a hermeneutical scene, both historical and allegorical, to
account for such matters as humankind's loss of an original vision
of the truth, its exile into a realm of ambiguous signs and interpretive
toil, its subsequent need for a written revelation, the cause for the
obscure "covering" of biblical allegory, and finally the interpretive
principles that would keep Adam's and Eve's descendants from abusing God's scriptural word and thus repeating the hermeneutical errors of their first parents.

As with the school of Paradise, the hermeneutics of the Fall was
largely invented by Augustine, who used Genesis 1–3 as an expres-
sive matrix for the theory of signs and scriptural exegesis that he
bequeathed to the Middle Ages. While Augustine's hermeneutical
theory had multiple sources in classical, Jewish, and earlier patristic
authors, including of course his teacher Ambrose, in both their development and expression Augustine's ideas reflected his own "pain-
ful meditations on the effects of the Fall."[1] Elaborated by later

---

1. Forsyth, *The Old Enemy*, p. 425. A good introduction to Augustine's sign
theory is Colish, *The Mirror of Language*, chap. 1. For a more technical treatment,

exegetes and dramatized by poets such as Avitus, Augustine's hermeneutics of the Fall in turn passed to the Middle Ages, where it widely influenced general sign theory, scriptural hermeneutics, and, eventually, a broader medieval theory of interpretation applying to vernacular texts as well.

1. Signs and the Fall

Augustine's scriptural hermeneutics rests on a theory of signs in which the Fall occupies a crucial place. Before the Fall, according to Augustine, the humans (or at least Adam) had enjoyed a direct knowledge of God through an "inner word"—an unmediated intellectual vision like that enjoyed by the angels themselves. With the Fall and the exile from Paradise, however, Adam and his descendants lost this vision and were banished into an alien realm where they had to seek knowledge indirectly through material signs apprehended by the bodily senses, signs being either things themselves, or images, or words. Adapting a Neoplatonic notion, Augustine held that after the Fall the material world had become a "region of unlikeness" where humans searched amid the opacity of things and the ambiguity of signs for a lost knowledge of the Creator.[2] The fallen material world "differs" or "others" the ineffable word of God as embodied in signs and words, particularly metaphor and allegory, which are forms of *alieniloquium* ("other-speech").[3] This notion—of the Fall as an exile from the unmediated divine word into a region of semiotic difference, deferral, and displacement—was fundamental to Augustine's sign theory and to the medieval hermeneutics of the Fall.

That the Fall had displaced the first humans not just geograph-

---

see Markus, ed., *Critical Essays*, pp. 59–147. The debt of Augustine's sign theory to the Fall is reflected in Freccero, "The Fig Tree and the Laurel"; Vance, *Mervelous Signals*, chaps. 1–2; Gellrich, *The Idea of the Book*, pp. 152–53; and Forsyth, *The Old Enemy*, chaps. 24–25.

2. Augustine, *Conf* 7.10, describes a "region of total unlikeness" (*regio dissimilitudinis*) where he can hear only God's distant "voice" calling to him. For references and discussion, see A. Solignac, comm., *Oeuvres de Saint Augustin: Les Confessions*, Bibliothèque augustinienne, 2d ser., vol. 13 (Paris, 1962), pp. 689–93; Ferguson, "Saint Augustine's Region of Unlikeness"; Vance, *Mervelous Signals*, pp. 23, 47, 190, 195; and Charles Dahlberg, *The Literature of Unlikeness* (Hanover, N.H., 1988).

3. "Allegoria est alieniloquium" (Isidore of Seville, *Etymologiae* 1.37.22; ed. W. M. Lindsay, 2 vols., OCT [Oxford, 1911]).

ically (from Paradise) but also semiotically (from an original, "natural" language) gave this event a "traumatic" significance in the history, and the collective memory, of the human race. Comparing Augustine's notion of the Fall as a crisis of signs to Freud's notion of infantile trauma as the formative hermeneutical moment, Peter Brown notes that both thinkers "assume that the proliferation of images is due to some precise event, to the development of some geological fault across a hitherto undivided consciousness: for Freud, it is the creation of an unconscious by repression; for Augustine, it is the outcome of the Fall."[4] Essentially, then, Augustine viewed the Fall as the primal scene for the human culture of signs: "The Fall had been, among many other things, a fall from direct knowledge into indirect knowledge through signs. The 'inner fountain' of awareness had dried up: Adam and Eve found that they could only communicate with one another by the clumsy artifice of language and gestures."[5]

The idea that before the Fall humans enjoyed a direct, unmediated knowledge of God is fundamental to Augustine's sign theory and hermeneutics, and to the whole medieval tradition that follows. In his first Genesis commentary, *De Genesi contra Manichaeos*, Augustine depicts God as "speaking" directly to Adam's soul, without external language, prior to the Fall: "God watered [the soul] by an interior spring, speaking to its intellect [*loquens in intellectum ejus*], so that it did not receive words from the outside."[6] Augustine also describes this special inner discourse as seeing "the face of truth," "the interior light of the truth," or "the inner light of knowledge," and also as dwelling in the "presence" or "sight" of God.[7] The first humans did not originally have bodies of "mortal flesh"; instead they had "heavenly bodies" transparent to mental or spiritual motions and hence capable of receiving this direct, unmediated knowledge from God or other spiritual beings: "Thoughts could [not] be hidden in those heavenly bodies, as they lie hidden in these [mortal] bodies."[8] Augmenting his other metaphors of water, light, and inner speech, Augustine cites gestures or facial expressions

4. Brown, *Augustine of Hippo*, p. 261.

5. On these and related semiotic points, see also Vance, *Mervelous Signals*, pp. 190–91.

6. *GenM* 2.4.5.

7. *GenM* 2.21.32 ("facies veritatis"); *GenM* 2.16.24 ("praesentia Dei," "lux illa interior veritatis," "conspectus Dei"); *GenM* 2.25.38 ("interioris sapientiae lux").

8. *GenM* 2.21.32 ("illis corporibus coelestibus"). See O'Connell, *Art and the Christian Intelligence*, pp. 53–54. On the mutation of the body with the Fall, see *GenM* 2.21.32.

as analogies for the "natural" language of Paradise that transcended bodily and temporal signs altogether: "Rather as some states of soul are apparent on the countenance, and especially in the eyes, so I think that in the clarity and simplicity of those heavenly bodies absolutely no states of the soul [were] hidden."

Augustine's statement that initially man "did not receive words from the outside" (*non extrinsecus verba exciperet*) has been taken to mean that before the Fall God did not address the humans through exterior speech at all and that the Fall itself precipitated humans into corporeal language.[9] But Augustine's literal-historical commentaries offer a different account of verbal signs before the Fall: "The Scripture narrative is such that we are led rather to assume that God spoke to man in Paradise as He spoke later to the patriarchs, such as Abraham and Moses, namely, under some corporeal form."[10] In his historical exegesis, Augustine evidently shifted away from his earlier view that Adam "did not receive words from the outside."[11] Augustine's historical exegesis similarly treats the other speeches in the Garden (the Serpent's words to Eve, Eve's alleged words to Adam, etc.) as audible linguistic exchanges. At the same time, however, Augustine's later exegesis continues to insist on a special inner word originally confided to the humans and lost with the Fall.[12] On Augustine's mature view, then, the first sin did not precipitate humans into signs or language per se; rather, in depriving them of the inner word, it restricted them solely to communication by external means. Augustine's revised view in turn became decisive for medieval tradition.

If the language of Paradise had been audible, corporeal, this necessarily raised certain questions about humans as linguistic beings as well as about the first human language itself, the *Ursprache*. In his literal commentary on Genesis, Augustine maintains that Adam, prior to the Fall, particularly when naming the animals (Gen. 2.20), used a specific language; that this language was the original language of humankind; and that elements of it may yet survive in the names of animals (*GenL* 9.12.20). In the *City of God*, Augustine makes

9. E.g., Jackson, "The Theory of Signs," in Markus, ed., *Critical Essays*, p. 113.

10. *GenL* 8.18.37 ("in aliqua specie corporali").

11. Cf. *GenL* 8.27.50 ("Why do we doubt that God spoke to [Adam] through some such creature in a language which he could understand?"); *GenL* 11.33.43; and *Trin* 2.10.17–18.

12. E.g., *GenL* 8.27.50 ("there should be no doubt that God moved Adam's mind in time in a mysterious and unaccountable manner"); *GenL* 11.33.43–44 also mentions the divine "light" and "face" that figure in his earlier commentary.

even more detailed and comprehensive claims about the *Ursprache*. Adam's language was Hebrew, thus removing any doubts about its survival. After the division of tongues at Babel, this "primitive language of the race" survived in the line of Heber (a fifth-generation descendant of Shem); hence its designation as Hebrew. Furthermore, as the language of the patriarchs and the prophets, the original Adamic language also became "the authoritative language of Scripture."[13] Thus, by a kind of *translatio linguae* that follows the lines of Old Testament genealogy, Augustine forges a continuity between the language of the Garden and the language of Scripture. Other patristic and medieval commentators follow similar lines of inquiry, although sometimes with different results.[14]

Besides investigating what language Adam spoke and understood, Augustine philosophizes on the significance of Adam's role as the first namer. Adam named the various animals on the basis of a rational ordering of their species or kinds: "When they had gathered before him and he had distinguished them according to their kinds [*generatim*], he gave them their names [*nomina*]" (*GenL* 9.12.20). By this account, reason first apprehends natural or inherent categories of being, and then language expresses them by means of its own corresponding categories. The same notion of "propriety" seems to underlie Augustine's account of Adam as the namer of Eve. Adam named his wife twice, once before the Fall, as "Woman" (Gen. 2.23), and once afterward, as "Eve" (Gen. 3.20). Although Adam's renaming of Eve after the Fall suggests a change in *her* status, Augustine maintains that in both cases Adam himself exercised an undiminished control of language; if before the Fall he was filled with a "spirit of prophecy" (*GenL* 9.19.36), in renaming woman afterward he was moved by a no less "marvelous inspiration" (*GenL* 11.38.51).

As R. Howard Bloch has suggested, Adam's role as the first namer furnished patristic and medieval culture with crucial questions about the adequacy of words to their referents, questions about

13. *Civ* 16.11; occasional citations (as here) from *The City of God*, trans. Marcus Dods et al. (New York, 1950), are noted.

14. E.g., Dante holds that Adam's language survived after Babel in the speech of the Israelites; see *De vulgari eloquentia* (ed. Aristide Marigo) 1.6.5; ed. Michele Barbi, *Opere di Dante*, vol. 6 (Florence, 1938); trans. Robert S. Haller, *On Eloquence in the Vernacular*, in *Literary Criticism of Dante Alighieri* (Lincoln, Nebr., 1973), pp. 3–60. In *Paradiso* 26.124–29, however, Adam states that his language disappeared even before Babel, as a result of natural change and human fallibility. For other patristic and medieval loci on these questions, see Bloch, *Etymologies and Genealogies*, pp. 37–44.

which Augustine himself is often ambivalent.[15] Augustine's uncertainty about the capacity of verbal signs to denote their referents probably reflects his assimilation of "widely divergent views about the nature of language in general," ranging from a Cratylism that posits a natural resemblance between word and thing, to a profound skepticism about words as arbitrary signs that infinitely mediate and defer knowledge or reality rather than making it present to the seeker.[16] On the one hand, Augustine holds that Adam used language both before and after the Fall in such a way that name and object, word and referent, were in perfect accord; Augustine makes no suggestion that Adam's power to name things declined or was compromised after the first sin. On the other hand, as already suggested, and as will be further explored in this chapter, Augustine treats corporeal language as an inherently limited medium for knowledge. Furthermore, he maintains that names and words themselves constitute signs of the Fall, as with the verb *mori* ("to die"), which, as a term denoting the consequences of original sin, "can no more be declined [*declinari*] by us in speech than can the act that it denotes in reality."[17] Later the mythographer Fulgentius (ca. 480–550) would suggest that the Fall actually altered the meaning of signs or symbols, beginning with Adam and Eve themselves: "Ah, nothing is safe from the wiles of the serpent, that the man who stood for the beginning of life should become the symbol of death for his posterity, and the woman who gave birth to the living should emerge as the destroyer of her own descendants!"[18]

15. See Bloch, *Etymologies and Genealogies*, chap. 1, passim, esp. pp. 35, 39–40. On Adam as namer, see also Damrosch, *The Narrative Covenant*, pp. 138–42.

16. Bloch, *Etymologies and Genealogies*, p. 47.

17. *Civ* 13.11. This passage is cited by Paula J. Carlson, "The Grammar of God: Grammatical Metaphor in *Piers Plowman* and *Pearl*" (Columbia Univ. diss., 1983), pp. 62–63. Cf. Augustine, *Enar* 95.15; ed. Eligius Dekkers and Johannes Fraipont, *CCSL* 38–40; trans. NPNF, ser. 1, vol. 8 (1887; rpt. Grand Rapids, 1980), pp. 474–75, as quoted above in the epigraph to this book (trans. modified).

18. Fulgentius, *De aetatibus mundi et hominis*, chap. 1; ed. R. Helm, *Fabii Planciadis Fulgentii opera* (Leipzig, 1898), pp. 129–79; trans. Leslie G. Whitbread, *On the Ages of the World and of Man*, in *Fulgentius the Mythographer* (Columbus, Ohio, 1971), pp. 177–231 (quotation is on p. 190). A kind of Cratylism invests many medieval commonplaces about language and the Fall. For example, newborn males were said to cry "A!" (as in "Adam"), and newborn females "E!" (as in "Eve"), to express the misery inherited from their first parents; and the famous palindrome "Eva"/"Ave," formed by Eve's Latin name and Gabriel's salutation to Mary (Luke 1.28), signified that the mother of Christ redemptively "reversed" Eve's failings as the mother of humanity. For examples of these and related tropes, see John M. Fyler,

On the whole, Neoplatonic tendencies led Augustine and other patristic authors to place severe ontological and epistemological limits on signs in general, including words.[19] Both the Platonic and Christian myths of the *logos* held signs to be symptoms of a primal catastrophe, whether this catastrophe was conceived as the soul's "fall" into the body or as humankind's fall into sin. Thus signs as representations were held to be inferior to what they signified—material things, mental ideas, or the highest intelligible realities. Accordingly, signs could never be adequate to the knowledge, either sensory or intellectual, that they purported to signify. Furthermore, signs were merely traces or vestiges of absent subjects, human or divine, and as such they could represent at best only a diminished—and at worst merely an illusory—presence. Jacques Derrida remarks on this essentially Augustinian legacy in its modern, secular manifestations: "The sign is always a sign of the Fall. Absence always relates to distancing from God."[20]

To sum up so far, then, Augustine's account of linguistic signs in the Garden had two major implications for patristic and medieval hermeneutics: first, that the humans had used signs *before* the Fall; and, second, that the function of signs had been profoundly altered by the Fall. Not that Adam's idiom changed with the Fall, for the *Ursprache* long outlived its first speaker; nor that words or names were any less fitting to their referents after the Fall, for Adam could rename Eve afterward with no less "marvelous inspiration." Rather, from the beginning Adam and Eve had to deal with signs—whether words or signifying things (e.g., the forbidden fruit)—but after the Fall they had to do so without the benefit of the inner word. This loss of the inner word did not introduce the problem of interpretation, which was already part of the created order; rather, it aggravated the difficulties of interpretation faced by humans after the Fall. To see the importance of this point, it is necessary to turn to Augustine's general theory of signs.

Under Augustine's broad definition, "a sign [*signum*] is a thing which causes us to think of something beyond the impression the thing

---

"Man, Men, and Women in Chaucer's Poetry," in *The Olde Daunce: Love, Friendship, Sex, and Marriage in the Medieval World*, ed. Robert R. Edwards and Stephen Spector (Albany, 1991), pp. 154–76 (esp. 160–62).

19. On Augustine's indebtedness to Plotinus concerning the Fall, knowledge, and the senses, see O'Connell, *Art and the Christian Intelligence*, pp. 70–76.

20. Derrida, *Of Grammatology*, p. 283.

itself makes upon the senses."[21] Signs, including words, are thus dual entities, consisting of both a material and an intelligible aspect—or, to use structuralist terms, a signifier and a signified.[22] The two aspects of the sign enable it to mediate between the bodily and intellectual realms, for "[there is no] other reason for signifying, or for giving signs, except for bringing forth and transferring to another mind the action of the mind in the person who makes the sign" (Doc 2.2.3). Augustine often refers to words as "vessels" for ideas, a trope suggesting that verbal signs should be mediating instruments rather than ends in themselves.[23]

Before the Fall, the two aspects of the sign were perfectly related to each other, the material sign serving as a transparent vehicle for what it signified. The Fall, however, had profoundly ruptured the sign. Broadly speaking, this rupture had to do with a subjection of the soul to the body, the mind to the senses. With the Fall, Adam lost his direct intellectual vision of God and came to depend for knowledge exclusively on sensory experience, a realm of ambiguity and confusion: "When man fell away from the unity of God the multitude of temporal forms was distributed among his carnal senses, and his sensibilities were multiplied by the changeful variety."[24] Without the inner "word," "light," or "fountain" of truth, fallen humans experienced a new, alarming slippage between signifier and signified. Signs, which belong to the realm of the body, partook of the ambiguity and opacity of things as they appeared to the fallen bodily senses.[25]

The Fall explained not only the condition of signs but also the condition of humans themselves as users of signs. Exiled from the Garden and from God's presence into a world containing only traces of an absent God, they now had to labor for the knowledge they had

21. Doc 2.1.1 ("signum est enim res praeter speciem, quam ingerit sensibus, aliud aliquid ex se faciens in cogitationem venire").

22. On the dual aspect of signs, see also Conf 10.14. Augustine's point is repeated by Dante, De vulgari eloquentia 1.3.2. On differences between Augustine and Saussure on signs, see Kelly, "Saint Augustine and Saussurean Linguistics."

23. E.g., Conf 1.16 (vasa), 5.6 (pocula).

24. Ver 21.41. On the turning of human reason toward the senses, including the ears and the province of the verbal arts, see also Ord 2.14.39–41; ed. W. M. Green, CCSL 29:87–137; trans. Robert P. Russell, Divine Providence and the Problem of Evil, FOC, no. 5 (New York, 1948), pp. 227–332.

25. "Now it is necessary that we be admonished about the truth through these eyes and these ears, and it is difficult to resist the phantasms which enter the soul through these senses, although truth's admonition also enters through them" (GenM 2.20.30).

lost with the Fall. At the most basic level, the labor of the Fall involved the learning of language itself. The fallen body, the "flesh," blocks or inhibits the free exchange of mind or spirit, and signs are necessary "for bringing forth and transferring" ideas and feelings from within the self. As noted earlier, Augustine held that God had taught speech to Adam and Eve in Paradise (*GenL* 8.16.35); after the Fall, however, humans, beginning as infants, laboriously have to learn signs and words for themselves.[26]

At a more advanced level, the Fall also subjects humans to the labor of interpretation in general. In his first commentary on Genesis, Augustine allegorizes the agricultural labors to which God cursed Adam (Gen. 3.17–19) as an emblem for the constant intellectual toil to which humans are doomed in the fallen world, where ambiguous signs and the deceptive senses bedevil every effort to discover the truth:

> Anyone born in this life has difficulty in discovering the truth because of the corruptible body.... These are the labors [*labores*] and sorrows which man has from the earth. The thorns and thistles are prickings of tortuous questions or thoughts concerned with providing for this life. Unless these are uprooted and cast forth from the field of God, they generally choke off the word [*verbum*], so that it does not bear fruit in man, as the Lord says in the gospel. (*GenM* 2.20.30)

The imagery of God's word as a plant or seed, borrowed from the gospel parables of the vineyard and the field, here enriches Augustine's figurative gloss on the agricultural imagery of Genesis 3, making that text an even more fertile ground for sign theory.[27] Elaborating his gloss, Augustine speaks of everyone's Adamic duty to cultivate (*colere*) God's word in the "field" of his own soul and thereby earn his spiritual "bread."[28]

For Augustine, the rupture of signification that occurred with the Fall also exaggerated the sign's material and temporal nature. Spoken words exist only momentarily as sound, since each successive syllable displaces the one before it, and "there could never be a complete sentence unless one word, as soon as the syllables [*partes*

---

26. On Augustine's account of his own language acquisition, see below, section 5.

27. Mark 4.18–19 is cited; cf. Matt. 13.18–23. Cf. Tertullian, *De anima* 16, on heretics "sowing" (*interpolans*) "weeds" in the field of God's word.

28. *GenM* 2.20.30 ("agrum istum interius"); cf. the "sterile plantations of sorrow" and "thorns" of desire in *Conf* 2.2.

suas] had been sounded, ceased to be in order to make room for the next" (*Conf* 4.10).[29] At the same time, words belong to the material order, the sensory realm, where they are produced and received by bodily means—mouth and ear, or hand and eye. The Fall enhanced the sensuousness of the sign by alienating it from its signification, so that even words of instruction or prayer must struggle free from the body as "signs proceeding from the mouth and sounding out aloud.... And the reason why these words have to be pronounced physically with the voice is the deep of this world and the blindness of the flesh because of which it is not possible to see thoughts, so that they have to be uttered audibly in our ears" (*Conf* 13.23). The temporal and material qualities of language thus exemplify for Augustine the nature of language as a fallen medium subject to time, to bodily decay, and to death—each syllable dying away to make room for the next, like the order of history and of earthly human life itself.

The same temporal and material qualities also betoken the incapacity of signs, particularly words, to convey or represent knowledge purely or completely. The inner word known to Adam before the Fall had been consubstantial with the divine Word (*Verbum*); and God's externally spoken word to Adam had been a perfect mirror of this inner word, a veritable divine "presence" in itself (*GenL* 11.30.38). After the transgression of God's precept, however, signs and words came to embody the refracted and confused state into which knowledge had fallen. In partaking of the bodily and temporal order of things, and in trying to convey concepts from one mind to another, language necessarily divides knowledge into discrete parts—syllables or letters—splitting the unitary signified among multiple signifiers. As a result, meaning always slips along the line of language; knowledge or truth is always dispersed or deferred over a succession of signs.

The slippage of the sign also affects the human attempt to grasp the whole significance of history, or of the cosmos. Although fallen humans can understand the parts of a poem in their totality, they cannot likewise comprehend the whole divinely authored poem of history: "There is no one who cannot easily hear a whole verse or even a whole poem; but there is no one who can grasp the whole order of the ages. Besides, we are not involved as parts in a poem, but for our sins we are made to be parts of the secular order.... The

---

29. See also *Ver* 22.42, and Vance, *Mervelous Signals*, chap. 2, "St. Augustine: Language as Temporality."

course of history is made up of our labours" (*Ver* 22.43). Human toil (*labor*) goes into the making of history, again as a result of Adam's curse, but to understand the whole order of the ages, to parse such a period, to scan such a poem—as yet incomplete—lies beyond the human grasp.[30]

In sum, Augustine perceived life after the Fall as a continual struggle in the confusing and often frustrating realm of signs. This is not to say that Augustine saw no possibility of transcending signs and the related consequences of the Fall. As we shall see, Augustine held that Christ's redemptive work on the Cross had partially restored the vision of God lost by Adam in the shadow of the Tree, and that humans would ultimately abandon signs altogether at the Resurrection, when the elect would regain Paradise and also the original unmediated vision of God.[31] Here all semiotic difference would vanish, and God, the ultimate Signified, would become present to humans without any mediating signifiers. Until then, however, humans possessed only traces of God in the form of signs that are inextricably part of the temporal and corporeal order of Creation itself.

2. Writing and the Fall

One especially important sign of the Fall was writing. For patristic authors, the Fall marked a transition from the spoken to the written—or, in modern terms, from "orality" to "literacy"—a distinction cutting across both divine and human discourse. Exegetes blurred this distinction when figuring God's spoken command about the Tree of Knowledge as a written text, but essentially they viewed the prelapsarian world as preliterate, too, and script as a phenomenon of the fallen world. The notion that humans had fallen into writing, so to speak, was crucial to patristic hermeneutics. Although Scripture provided fallen humanity with its main source of knowledge about God, patristic authors felt a profound ambivalence about writing. This ambivalence, like that about signs in general, was ultimately a Neoplatonic legacy, and patristic exegetes reinscribed it within the story of the Fall, largely through ingenious allegories that turned Genesis 3 into an originary scene for textuality.

A special link between writing and sin appears already in the

---

30. On history as a "poem," see also *Civ* 11.18.
31. See *Conf* 13.15, as discussed below, section 5.

Jewish apocrypha and pseudepigrapha that helped to shape, either directly or indirectly, patristic ideas about the Fall.[32] For example, in the book of *Jubilees* (2d c. B.C.) writing is associated with hidden or forbidden knowledge and an ability to evoke sinful responses in readers.[33] And, departing from an earlier tradition that Moses invented the alphabet, the *Vita Adae et Evae* (1st c. A.D.) suggests that writing was employed already by the very first humans and as a direct result of the Fall.[34] In the *Vita*, Adam and Eve recount the Fall to their children as an edifying oral tradition; but after Adam dies, Eve, foreseeing her own death, institutes a written tradition, telling her children, "Make now tablets of stone and other tablets of clay and write in them all my life and your father's which you have heard and seen from us."[35] Apart from the intriguing detail that here woman, not man, institutes the written tradition, this story suggests that the Fall, which results in death, therefore makes necessary a permanent (i.e., written) record of the past, including a record of the Fall itself.

Whatever the influence of such literary antecedents, the main source of the patristic ambivalence about writing was Neoplatonic doctrine. Plato had equated script with illusory representations in general, and hence, ultimately, with the death of the soul.[36] As a

---

32. On the pseudepigrapha and early patristic exegesis of the Fall, see Evans, *Paradise Lost and the Genesis Tradition*, chap. 2; and Forsyth, *The Old Enemy*, esp. chaps. 8–12.

33. *Jubilees* 8.2–4, in *The Old Testament Pseudepigrapha* (hereafter *OTP*), ed. James H. Charlesworth, 2 vols. (Garden City, N.Y., 1983–85), 2:71 ("[Cainan] found a writing which the ancestors engraved on stone. And he read what was in it. And he transcribed it. And he sinned because of what was in it"). See also 1 *Enoch* 69.9, *OTP* 1:48.

34. Moses as inventor of the alphabet (or "grammar") appears in a fragment attributed to Eupolemus (ante 1st c. B.C.) and preserved in Eusebius and Clement of Alexandria; see *OTP* 2:865 for references. Another ancient tradition held that Hebrew fell into disuse with the Fall, until revived by Abraham, in both speech and writing; see *Jubilees* 12.25–27, *OTP* 2:82.

35. *Vita Adae et Evae* 50.1, *OTP* 2:292. The two kinds of media, stone and clay, ensure the survival of the text no matter which punishment, flood or fire, God sends upon humans. On the *Vita* in literary tradition, see Forsyth, *The Old Enemy*, chap. 12; and Evans, *Paradise Lost and the Genesis Tradition*, pp. 55–58. Stephen G. Nichols, Jr., "Solomon's Wife: Deceit, Desire, and the Genealogy of Romance," in *Space, Time, Image, Sign: Essays on Literature and the Visual Arts*, ed. James A. W. Heffernan (New York, 1987), pp. 19–37, discussing the *Vita*, notes that Eve commissions the tablets and that earlier she "writes" and "reads" her story as embodied in her own footprints leading from the Garden (p. 21).

36. See esp. Plato, *Phaedrus* 274c–279c; trans. Lane Cooper et al., *The Collected*

mere image or copy of speech, writing was twice-removed from thought, the inner *logos*, and as such was even farther removed from the highest realities, the Forms or Ideas. For Plato, writing—by comparison with speech—signifies absence not presence, illusion not reality, *mimesis* not *logos*. In a further move, Plato annexed the metaphor of "inner writing" to denote a certain natural, interior, and universal discourse—a discourse anterior to language and approximating the *logos* itself.

Plato's deprecation of writing passed from Hellenistic Neoplatonism into early Christian tradition, principally through the apostle Paul. Paul's famous dictum that the letter "kills" whereas the spirit gives life (2 Cor. 3.6) adapts the Hellenistic suspicion of the letter to the Christian inheritance of Jewish law, associating the external written code with the body, sin, and death.[37] In the same passage, Paul adapts the Platonic metaphor of inner writing to Christian themes: "You are a letter from Christ delivered by us, written not with ink but with the Spirit of the living God, not on tablets of stone but on tablets of human hearts" (v. 3). Elsewhere Paul contrasts the external written law with a higher natural law that is inscribed within, "written on...hearts" (Rom. 2.15).[38] These phrases soon became commonplaces of patristic exegesis and found their way into commentary on Genesis 3 as a textual and hermeneutical scene.[39]

As various critics have suggested, Christian-Neoplatonic attitudes toward writing had profound consequences for the Middle Ages, as well as later times.[40] Typically, speech was associated with nature, life, spirit, and presence, whereas writing was linked with

---

Dialogues of Plato, Including the Letters, ed. Edith Hamilton and Huntington Cairns (1961; rpt. Princeton, 1963).

37. "Littera enim occidit, Spiritus autem vivificat." Paul's distinction has roots also in ancient legal and rhetorical theory; see Kathy Eden, "The Rhetorical Tradition and Augustinian Hermeneutics in *De doctrina christiana,*" *Rhetorica* 8 (1990): 45–63 (pp. 51–52, with references).

38. The figure of inner writing occurs also in the Hebrew scriptures (e.g., Prov. 3.3, 7.3; Jer. 17.1) but without a negative comparison to external writing.

39. Augustine, *Conf* 6.4, mentions that Ambrose often cited this verse in his sermons, with great consequence for Augustine's own biblical hermeneutics (e.g., *Doc* 3.5.9, and *De spiritu et littera; PL* 44:201–46; trans. Peter Holmes, *On the Spirit and the Letter,* NPNF, ser. 1, vol. 5 [1887; rpt. Grand Rapids, 1980], pp. 79–114). For discussion, see Robertson, *Preface to Chaucer,* pp. 292–303.

40. See Curtius, *European Literature,* chap. 16, "The Book as Symbol"; Derrida, *Of Grammatology,* pp. 10–18, "The Signifier and Truth"; and, for a useful analysis, Gellrich, *The Idea of the Book,* chap. 1.

artifice, death, matter, and absence. Furthermore, on a figurative level, speech usually was identified with a natural, interior "writing," as opposed to ordinary, external writing. According to Jacques Derrida, the Middle Ages perpetuated the notion of "a certain fallen writing," which is "perverse and artful" and "exiled in the exteriority of the body."[41] Derrida's imagery of Fall and Exile implies that patristic and medieval culture readily assimilated the inherited suspicion of writing into the biblical myth of a primeval catastrophe that had forced humans into the realm of external—and specifically written—signs. We can assess this biblical myth of writing and the Fall by turning now to some exemplary and influential patristic glosses.

Patristic authors held that God had originally "inscribed" his law upon Adam's heart; that the Fall had "erased" or otherwise compromised this interior law; and that God had compensated Adam's descendants for this loss by offering them an external written law. Ambrose is the first Latin exegete to combine these notions into a single account of the Fall as the origin of writing in general and of Scripture in particular: "Had [Adam] not broken the command and had he been obedient to the heavenly precepts, he would have preserved for his heirs the prerogative of nature and of innocence which was his from birth. But because the authority of the natural law was corrupted and blotted out [corrupta atque interlita] by disobedience, the written Law was determined necessary."[42] The external ("written") law thus was a supplement to an original, internal testament. If properly attended to, the law written or stamped (impressum) on human hearts enables believers to "hear" God's "voice" as Adam did: "We seem to be listening to the very voice of the Lord [vocem Domini], whereby some things are forbidden and other things are advised" (Par 8.39). Here inner inscription is equivalent with "voice," "breath," "spirit," and divine presence.

Augustine presents a similar argument: "Because men, desiring those things which are without, even from themselves have become exiles, they were given also a written law; not because it had not been written in hearts, but because you were a fugitive from your own

41. Derrida, Of Grammatology, pp. 15, 17. Cf. Derrida, Writing and Difference, ed. and trans. Alan Bass (Chicago, 1978), p. 68: "The difference between speech and writing is sin, the anger of God emerging from itself, lost immediacy, work outside the garden."

42. Epistola 73.5; PL 16:1252, trans. Mary M. Beyenka, Saint Ambrose, Letters, in FOC, no. 26 (New York, 1954), p. 465 (as letter no. 83).

heart. By him that is everywhere you are seized; and to yourself within, you are called back."[43] Again, the law "written in hearts" is commensurate with an inner "voice," a voice that is said to "call back" (*revocare*) the sinner in the paradise of the soul, as God called for Adam and Eve in the Garden after their sin. The external written law, as embodied principally in Scripture, is meant to lead humans back to the inner law of the heart, whether "spoken" or "written."[44]

In another move that was to have major importance for medieval hermeneutics, patristic exegetes also used the "leaves" and "fruit" of the Garden as textual and exegetical emblems. Specifically, the leaves represent the "letter" of the text, and the fruit stands for its "spirit."[45] A passage from Ambrose comparing the literalist reader of Scripture to Adam and Eve illustrates how the fruit/leaf allegory helped turn the Fall into a textual scene: "He frequently produces examples from holy Scripture, citing them as instances of how a just man may fall into sin, the sin of adultery.... He patches together examples for his purposes from the list of prophetical books of Scripture. He sees the leaves and ignores the fruit."[46] Augustine likewise uses the "leaves" and "fruit" of Genesis 3 as contrastive terms for the letter and spirit of Scripture. For example, comparing Scripture to a tree or garden, Augustine describes spiritually minded readers as birds seeking "fruit" among the "leaves" of the text: "[Your words] are shady gardens of fruit, and they see the fruit hidden under the leaves, and they flutter around it in joy, and, cheerfully chirping, they peer for it and pluck it."[47]

43. *Enar* 57.1; trans. *Expositions on the Book of Psalms*, 6 vols., LOF 24, 25, 30, 32, 37, 39 (Oxford, 1847–57), 30:97 (modified). Various allusions to the Garden follow in 57.1, 2.

44. Augustine elaborates and codifies the contrast between God's internal and external "writing" in *De spiritu et littera*, as discussed in Vance, *Mervelous Signals*, pp. 8–11. See also *Conf* 2.4, where Augustine prefaces his famous pear tree story with a reference to "a [divine] law written in men's hearts" (quoting Rom. 2.15); and *GenL* 8.27.50.

45. Augustine does not always equate the "letter" and "spirit" with the literal and figurative senses of Scripture, respectively. By "letter," Augustine generally means an *erroneous* fixation on the literal sense ("literalism"); the "spirit" of Scripture can reside in either literal or figurative passages, depending. Like taking figurative expressions literally (*Doc* 3.5.9), taking literal expressions figuratively (*Doc* 3.10.14) also threatens the "spirit" of the text. See further below, section 3; and Preus, *From Shadow to Promise*, chap. 1, esp. pp. 11–15.

46. *Par* 13.65.

47. *Conf* 12.28. Augustine does not explicitly mention "leaves" in this passage but implies them in "shady gardens of fruit" (*opaca frutecta*). For explicit wordplay on *folia* ("leaves, pages"), see *Nup* 2.17; ed. Charles F. Urba and Joseph Zycha, *Corpus*

"Fruit," of course, is a common biblical image for spiritual values. Besides Christ's parable of the "good" and the "bad" trees, each with its different "fruits" (Matt. 7.17–20), and Paul's gloss on "the fruit of the Spirit" (Gal. 5.22–23), the Christian scriptures use "fruit" (*fructus*) specifically to represent a proper or spiritual understanding of God's word: "He who hears the word and understands it ... bears fruit."[48]

The patristic gloss on the "leaves" of Genesis 3 has a more arcane origin in ancient etymologies that associated books with trees or plants.[49] From about 200 to 400 A.D., book format in the West changed as the roll or scroll was widely replaced by the codex, a format adopted most quickly in Christian circles, where it was used to "codify" the enlarged scriptural canon.[50] The term *codex* (or *caudex*), originally meaning the "trunk or stem of a tree," was extended to ancient "books" formed of waxed wooden tablets and eventually to books of parchment or papyrus "leaves" (*folia*).[51] As the biblical account has it, Adam and Eve "sewed fig leaves [*folia*] together and made themselves aprons" (Gen. 3.7). Through wordplay on the double sense of *folia*, botanical and bibliographical, exegetes likened this primal clothing to the "leaves" of the scriptural codex.[52] There can be little doubt that the underlying botanical imagery of the book format preferred by Christians is what prompted patristic authors

---

Scriptorum Ecclesiasticorum Latinorum, vol. 42 (Vienna, 1902), pp. 209–319; trans. Philip Schaff, *On Marriage and Concupiscence*, NPNF, ser. 1, vol. 5 (1887; rpt. Grand Rapids, 1980), pp. 258–308.

48. Matt. 13.23 ("qui audit verbum et intellegit et fructum adfert").

49. An influential late patristic summary of this lore appears in Isidore of Seville, *Etymologiae* 6.13–14 ("De librorum vocabulis," etc.). Cf. *The Oxford English Dictionary* (hereafter *OED*), 1st ed., 13 vols. (Oxford, 1933), s.v. *Book* (from OE *boc*, pl. *bec*, "generally thought to be etymologically connected with the name of the beech-tree"). On tree typology and the Fall, see Robertson, "The Doctrine of Charity," esp. pp. 24–26. See also Yvonne Johannot, *Tourner la page: Livre, rites, et symboles* (Aubenas d'Ardèche, 1988), pp. 39–40; and, for a poststructuralist analysis, Mark C. Taylor, *Erring: A Postmodern A/theology* (Chicago, 1984), pp. 77–78.

50. On book format in late antiquity, see Colin H. Roberts and T. C. Skeat, *The Birth of the Codex* (London, 1987); and articles by the same authors in *CHB* 1:48–66, 2:54–79.

51. *OLD*, s.v. *caudex, codex*.

52. For semantics, see *Thesaurus Linguae Latinae* (hereafter *TLL*; Leipzig, 1900–), s.v. *folium*. In a liminal usage, Virgil refers to the Sybil's writing on "leaves" (*folia*), *Aeneid* 3.444–45; ed. and trans. H. Rushton Fairclough, *Virgil*, 2 vols., rev. ed., LCL (London, 1934). Cf. Horace, *Ars poetica* 60–61 (*folia* = "words"); ed. and trans. H. Rushton Fairclough, *Horace: Satires, Epistles, and Ars Poetica*, rev. ed., LCL (London, 1929); and Dante, *Paradiso* 33.65–66.

to gloss the fig leaves of Genesis 3 as an allegorical reference to the book of Scripture, specifically in its material (or "literal") aspect (fig. 3). Since the leaves of the codex were usually sewn together (in quires) with string or thread, this particular book format offered a special figurative parallel with the fig leaf coverings, manufactured by a similar process—"and they sewed [*consuerunt*] fig leaves together."[53]

On the basis of such etymologies and associations, exegetes incorporated the fruit and leaves of Genesis 2–3 into a single symbolic Tree of Scripture. Under this figure, exegetes linked scriptural "fruit" and "leaves" variously with the Tree of Knowledge, the Tree of Life, and the trees of Paradise at large. An ancient tradition holding that the first humans had taken *both* the forbidden fruit and the leaf coverings from the same tree (i.e., a fig tree) may have favored the Tree of Knowledge as a scriptural emblem, although the medieval identification of the forbidden fruit as an apple tended to divide the source of the fruit and the leaves.[54] Another, later tradition combined the Tree of Knowledge and the Tree of Life into a single tree that bore two kinds of fruit, one life-giving and the other deadly.[55] But the dominant tradition distinguished between the two trees and tended to favor the Tree of Life, with its life-giving fruit, as a scriptural emblem. Some medieval exegetes even contrasted the Tree of Life, as an emblem for Scripture, with the Tree of Knowledge as an emblem for worldly wisdom, or the "Book" of Nature.[56] Whatever specific form it took, however, the notion of Scripture as a tree bearing "fruit" among its "leaves" became a crucial element in the patristic and medieval hermeneutics of the Fall.[57]

53. Vulg. *consuerunt*, OL *suerunt* or *assuerunt* (as in Ambrose, *Par* 13.64). For semantics, see *OLD*, s.v. *consuo*. On sewn leaves and quires in the early Christian codex book, see *CHB* 2:73.

54. E.g., *Apocalypse of Moses* 20.5, *OTP* 2:281 ("I took [fig] leaves and made for myself skirts; they were from the same plants of which I ate"); *Vita Adae et Evae* lacks the parallel passage.

55. E.g., Cyprian of Gaul, *Heptateuchos* 1.68–69, *Corpus Scriptorum Ecclesiasticorum Latinorum*, vol. 23 (Vienna, 1881), as cited and discussed in Evans, *Paradise Lost and the Genesis Tradition*, p. 139, with medieval examples, p. 188, n. 2.

56. E.g., Pierre Bersuire (d. 1362): "the Tree of Life is sacred Scripture, while the Tree of Knowledge is worldly knowledge and teaching" (*Reductorium morale super totam Bibliam*, Gen. 3, in *Opera omnia*, 3 vols. [Antwerp, 1609], 2:3, col. 1, my trans.).

57. For related medieval allegories of the "good" and "bad" trees, see Adolf Katzenellenbogen, *Allegories of the Virtues and Vices in Medieval Art from Early Christian Times to the Thirteenth Century*, trans. Alan J. P. Crick (1939; rpt. Toronto, 1989), pp. 63–68.

3. God with scriptural book, Adam and Eve with fig leaves. The inscription reads, "Behold, Adam [is become] like one of us" (Gen. 3.22). Carved capital, 13th c.: Clermont-Ferrand, Église Notre-Dame du Port, choir. Giraudon / Art Resource, New York.

Later in this chapter we shall see how Augustine analyzed the "fruit" in Genesis 3 as an emblem for textual pleasure, among other things. As for the fig leaves, they acquired a variety of negative textual values in patristic and medieval tradition. The fig leaf garments, being human rather than purely natural products, suggested the status of writing as an instrument of culture, as artifice, as technique. In their concealing properties or opacity they represented the secrecy of writing, its tendency to "cover" or conceal the truth. As coverings for the genitals, they hinted at the link between writing and illicit desire or pleasure. And their dry, dead state, after having been severed from the living branch, suggested not just human mortality, the withering of the human leaves of grass (Ps. 90.5–6), but also death as embodied in the law or letter of Scripture. According to a medieval collection of glosses, the fig leaves signify, among other things, "lies, the asperity of the law, and the itch of marriage."[58] As we shall see, the patristic hermeneutics of the Fall drew heavily on such associations among the leaves, the letter, lust, and death.

Patristic culture overdetermined the Fall as the origin of writing, and of Scripture in particular, by also allegorizing the other clothing image of the Fall—Adam's and Eve's skin garments—as an emblem for the scriptural parchment. This development, introduced into Latin exegesis by Augustine, again involved clever wordplay, as with the "fruit" and "leaves" of Genesis 3. According to the biblical account, "the Lord God made for Adam and for his wife garments of skins [*tunicas pellicias*], and clothed them" (Gen. 3.21).[59] Invoking a common term for the dried and treated animal skins used in the making of manuscript books, that is, *pellis* ("skin, parchment"), Augustine turned this second clothing image in Genesis 3 into yet another evocative image for textuality.[60]

In his earliest Genesis commentary, Augustine indicates that both the fig leaves and the skin garments, as parallel images of postlapsarian "covering," represent various dire consequences of the

58. Melitus, *Clavis cum variorum commentariis* 7.22, s.v. *Ficus*; ed. Jean Baptiste Pitra, *Spicilegium solesmense, complectens sanctorum patrum scriptorumque ecclesiasticorum anecdota hactenus opera*, vol. 2 (Paris, 1855), p. 372 ("*Folia ficus* [id est] mendacia, asperitas legis, vel prurigo nuptiarum. In Genesi: 'Et sumserunt folia ficus, et fecerunt sibi campestria' ").

59. Both Vulg. and OL have *tunicas pellicias* in Gen. 3.21, and this is Augustine's usual phrasing; see *Vetus latina: Die Reste der altlateinischen Bibel*, vol. 2 (Genesis), pp. 75–76, with quotations s.v. "AU" (= Augustine).

60. See *OLD*, s.v. *pellis* 3b.

Fall, including verbal deception, illicit pleasure, and death: "Death was prefigured by the garments of skin. For they made for themselves aprons from the leaves of the fig tree, but God made for them garments of skin. That is, having abandoned the face of truth, they sought the pleasure of lying, and God changed their bodies into this mortal flesh in which deceitful hearts are hidden" (*GenM* 2.21.32). This passage is programmatic for Augustine's later elaborations on textuality and the Fall. As noted earlier, Augustine held that the "mortal flesh" of the postlapsarian human body had turned opaque, thus depriving the human soul of direct, unmediated knowledge of God and relegating humans to external signs and words. By extension, the concealing of the truth by the "flesh" encompasses Scripture, too, in which the divine Word (*Verbum*) is covered or clothed in human words (*verba*).

In the *Confessions*, Augustine uses typology and wordplay on the term *pellis* to liken the skin garments that cover Adam and Eve to the scriptural parchment book that "covers" their fallen descendants: "You clothed men with skins [*pellibus*] when by their sin they became mortal. And so you have like a skin [*sicut pellem*] stretched out the firmament of your book, that is, your words which so well agree together" (13.15). As critics have noted, Augustine here combines several images—the heavenly firmament (Gen. 1.7), the sky as a skin (Ps. 103.2), and Adam's and Eve's skin garments—thereby "relat[ing] the Fall to mankind's need for Scripture, mediating God to man."[61] Yet this matrix of imagery represents for Augustine more than simply the "sublime authority" of Scripture.

In another, longer, and later gloss on Psalm 103.2 ("[He has] stretched out the heaven like a skin [*sicut pellem*]"), Augustine stresses the bodily qualities that Scripture, as a book written on dead animal hides, shares with the primeval skin garments:

> Those two first parents of ours, the authors of the sin of the human race, Adam and Eve, when in Paradise, they disdained God's precept and transgressed God's command by yielding to the serpent's suggestion, were made mortal and exiled from Paradise. And to signify their mortality they were clothed with garments of hide [*tunicis pelliceis*]. . . . What then, if divine Scripture is here signified under the name of a hide, how did God make heaven from a hide, and

61. Robert McMahon, *Augustine's Prayerful Ascent: An Essay on the Literary Form of the Confessions* (Athens, Ga., 1989), pp. 48–49. Cf. the sky as a "scroll," Is. 34.4, Rev. 6.14. In quoting these various passages, Augustine interchanges the terms *pellis*, *liber*, and *codex*.

"spread out the heaven like a hide"? Because they by whom Scripture was preached to us, were mortal.... [But] by what instrument did He bestow upon us what we read? By what was mortal, by mouth, by tongue, teeth, hands. All those means by which the Apostle achieved the whole work which we read of, are bodily functions [*corporis officia*].... With respect to holy Scripture, the discourse of the dead is spread; for this reason then it is spread out as a hide; and much more spread out, since they are dead.[62]

Although Scripture comprises various dualities (divine/human, spirit/flesh, life/death, speech/writing), here Augustine stresses the temporal, bodily, and "mortal" qualities that Scripture shares with its human "authors" or progenitors (*auctores*), from Adam and Eve onward. Moreover, as "the discourse of the dead" (*sermo mortuorum*), Scripture itself will suffer a kind of death at the end of time, when "the heavens shall be rolled together as a scroll."

In likening the scriptural parchment book to the skin garments in which God clothed the bodies of the newly fallen humans, Augustine stresses that the material words (*verba*) of Scripture function similarly as a "covering" or "clothing" for the divine Word (*Verbum Dei*), particularly in its often allegorical, enigmatic images: "The scroll [*pellis*] shall be folded up ... , but Thy word remaineth forever, which now appears to us not as it is but under the dark image [*in aenigmate*] of the clouds and through the glass [*per speculum*] of heaven" (*Conf* 13.15). Alluding here to Paul's figure of seeing God through a glass darkly (*per speculum in enigmate*, 1 Cor. 13.12), and building on the established imagery of "skins" (*pelles*), Augustine traces scriptural enigma and allegory back to the "clothing" necessitated by the Fall.

Augustine's analogy between the primal skin garments and the "clothing" of scriptural allegory is essentially another version of Paul's own textile or clothing trope for the allegorical text—namely, the "veil." In regarding the Law as the "letter" whose "spirit" inheres in the Gospel, Paul treated persons and events in the Jewish scriptures as "allegories" for events of the Christian era.[63] Within this general framework, Paul figured the Law or Old Testament as a "veil," an image deriving from the Mosaic pentecost at Sinai; as Paul explains, Moses "put a veil [*velamen*] over his face so that the

62. *Enar* 103.1.8, trans. LOF, vol. 37, pp. 73–74 (modified); Ps. 103.2 cited from *Conf* 13.15.

63. Gal. 4.24. On biblical typology, see Auerbach, "Figura," in *Scenes from the Drama of European Literature*, pp. 11–76.

Israelites might not see the end of the fading splendor..., [and] to this day, when they read the old covenant, that same veil remains unlifted, because only through Christ is it taken away."[64] Paul's epistles predated the written gospels, but later exegetes reformulated the Law-Gospel relation in terms of the two written testaments, Old and New, and they widely adopted Paul's image of the scriptural "veil," which is the underlying metaphor of "revelation" (re-vela-tio).[65] As Augustine put it, "The Old Testament [is] revealed in the New, the New veiled in the Old."[66]

As suggested earlier, the patristic notion of Scripture as a veil of allegory that has fallen or descended over God's eternal Word applied primarily to the Law, for which the Gospel offered an interpretive gloss. Much as the written law had been a supplement to the inner "writing" erased from Adam's heart by the first sin, so the Gospel in turn formed a supplement to the Law, as exegetes set forth in a vast array of typological correspondences between the Old and New Testaments. Following Paul, patristic exegetes deprecated devotion to the Jewish law alone as adherence to the "dead letter." Yet parts of the New Testament were also obscure and allegorical (e.g., the Gospel parables, the Book of Revelation).[67] Moreover, Scripture as a material whole, in its nature as a book of parchment (pellis), signified the subjection of humans to a fallen, fleshly order that was consubstantial with not only language in general but writing in particular. Patristic authors thus maintained a Neoplatonic ambivalence about the "skin" or "veil" of Scripture as a liminal zone: both earthly and heavenly, obscure and revealing, mimesis and logos.

I have already noted that medieval art of the Fall often shows God holding a book as he addresses the humans in the Garden.[68] This symbolic book represents both divine teaching and the divine word in its specifically scriptural form, the book of parchment leaves that was generated at the foot of the Tree by the Fall, and that

64. 2 Cor. 3.13–14; cf. Rom. 16.25–26; Heb. 10.19–20.

65. On the "veil" as a hermeneutical trope in patristic and medieval tradition, see Robertson, *Preface to Chaucer*, pp. 291–92, 294–95. For a scholastic gloss (veil = letter), see Hugh of St. Victor, *De sacramentis* 2.9.7.

66. *Enar* 105.36, trans. LOF, vol. 37, p. 185 ("Vetus Testamentum in Nouo reuelatum, in Vetere Nouum uelatum uides"). Cf. *Conf* 6.4 ("velamentum"), *Doc* 3.7.11 ("velamen").

67. Paul implies that the Gospel (in the nontextual sense) could be "veiled" to nonbelievers (2 Cor. 4.3). And Augustine cites both "the writings of the prophets and apostles" as containing obscure allegories (*GenM* 2.4.5).

68. See above, Chapter 1.1.

embodies a host of hermeneutical problems founded by the same event.

For patristic and medieval culture, the Fall served as the origin of not only texts as objects but also the scribal task of reproducing texts, above all Scripture. This task, of course, was crucial to the definition and the continuity of the church as a tradition and cult of the Book. Scripture had one divine Author, but many human ones; inspired by God, it had been written by men. And in order to be disseminated it had to be multiplied by human copyists, or scribes. Patristic authors accordingly invested the scribe's work with great moral and theological significance. For example, Cassiodorus (ca. 490–583) said that "every word of the Lord written by the scribe is a wound inflicted on Satan."[69] Furthermore, patristic and medieval culture saw the scribe as a son of Adam laboring in the textual "field." Monks adopted the classical analogy between writing and plowing; parchment was likened to a field, the pen to a plow, and ink to seed.[70] By scholastic times, Adam the scribe was a familiar figure, as eventually immortalized (and secularized) in Chaucer's own "Adam Scriveyn."

Although at least one ancient tradition associates the institution of writing with Eve,[71] patristic and medieval culture viewed inscription as essentially a masculine task. The judgments passed on Adam and Eve after their sin imply that Adam will "sow" his seed in both womb and field, and exegetes developed this analogy. Writerly dissemination was a "natural" extension of this masculine labor in the domains of husbandry and sexual reproduction; from Adam on, men were sowers of seed in field, womb, and text alike. By a series of subtle transformations, the imagery of dissemination associated with the Fall eventually produced one of the key medieval images of textuality—that of Christ (the "Word") as the ultimate Book.

Crucial to this transformation were the typological correspondences between Eve and Mary which hinged on the so-called protevangelium in Genesis 3.15 ("I will put enmity between you and the woman, and between your seed and her seed"). On the basis of this verse, exegetes saw the birth of Christ (who is both Eve's "seed" and the "fruit" of Mary's womb) as fulfilling a prophecy or promise

69. Cassiodorus, *Institutiones* 1.30.
70. On agricultural tropes for writing, see Curtius, *European Literature*, pp. 313–14; and, on organic metaphors generally, Gellrich, *The Idea of the Book*, pp. 210–14.
71. *Vita Adae et Evae* 50.1.

delivered in the Garden.[72] Doubtless prompted by the gospel parables of the field, exegetes also allegorized the "seed" in Genesis 3.15 as a "word" of one kind or another. For example, as early as Tertullian (ca. 200 A.D.) the Serpent's seed was glossed as a diabolical "word" impregnating Eve, by contrast with the divine Word that caused Mary to conceive.[73] Augustine furthered this tradition by glossing the womb, both Eve's and Mary's, as a fertile field for dissemination of various kinds. Thus Adam is said to "sow" (serere) the human race in Eve's womb; Eve's womb represents the soul receiving either a divine or diabolical "word" or "seed," and accordingly "conceiving" virtue or vice; and Mary's womb is like the ground of Paradise as it was when "there was no man who worked on the earth [Gen. 2.5], because no man has worked on the Virgin, from whom Christ was born."[74] In sum, these various allegories linked the Fall with the Redemption through a triple motif of dissemination—verbal, sexual, and agricultural.

For Augustine, the fruit of Mary's womb was not only the divine Word but specifically a divine Book, the ultimate "written" Text. Augustine's most vivid use of this metaphor, in the *Confessions*, appears alongside the image of Scripture as a book of parchment (*pellis*) engendered by the Fall and fated to be rolled up at the end of time. The divine Book, which far and away transcends Scripture, will be "read" by resurrected humans, just as the angels already "read" that Text in the heavenly Paradise: "Their book is never closed, nor is their scroll folded up, for you yourself are their book and you are forever" (*Conf* 13.15).

The divine or celestial book, of course, became a common medieval topos, appearing in the *Dies Irae*, Dante's *Paradiso*, and elsewhere.[75] But medieval exegetes carried this imagery into the realm of the Incarnation also, and in treating Mary's womb as the origin of the ultimate Text, they continued to follow Augustine in marking the Fall as the origin of writing. Thus, for example, Bernard of Clair-

---

72. For doctrinal background, see Pelikan, *The Christian Tradition* 1:149–50 and 3:71. The angel Gabriel blesses the "fruit" (*fructus*) of Mary's womb (Luke 1.42), an image popularized by the liturgy (e.g., "Salve Regina").

73. Tertullian, *De carne Christi* 17; PL 2:751–92, see quotation on cols. 781–82 ("Unto Eve, as yet a virgin, had crept the devil's word, the framer of death. Equally, unto a virgin was introduced God's word, the builder of life" [trans. Phillips, *Eve*, p. 134, with other examples]).

74. Eve's womb as a field: GenL 9.9.15, 9.3.5 (my thanks to Pat Moloney for these references). Word/seed: GenM 2.18.28, 2.21.31. Mary's womb: GenM 2.24.37.

75. On the cosmic or celestial book, see Curtius, *European Literature*, pp. 310–11, 322, 331–32; and Gellrich, *The Idea of the Book*, pp. 157–66.

vaux depicted Mary as praising God for having "written" in her womb with the "pen" of the Holy Spirit in order to engender Christ— "Not [a word] scratched by dumb signs on dead skins, but one in human form truly graven, lively, within my chaste womb, not by the tracings of a dead pen, but by the workings of the Holy Spirit."[76] Bernard's image of Christ as Text alludes to Augustine's image of the divine Book as well as to Augustine's typology of writing as an embodiment of *both* Fall and Redemption. The divine "writing" in Mary's womb fulfills God's (spoken) promise concerning Eve's seed, as Bernard suggests by citing the "dead skins" (*mortuis pellibus*) or parchment of Scripture, an image that in turn points back to the skins covering Adam and Eve.[77] Bernard's Augustinian matrix of images acknowledges that, for the Middle Ages too, the Fall was the ultimate origin of all texts, including that Text which was its own Author.

3. Reading Like Adam and Eve

As we saw earlier, patristic glosses on the Serpent attached doctrinal and hermeneutical significance to the Fall; besides a false teacher, the Serpent was also a deceptive exegete who interfered with Adam's and Eve's proper understanding of the "text" of God's command.[78] In treating the Fall as a hermeneutical episode, however, exegetes tended to dwell most heavily on the errors of the humans themselves, suggesting that to interpret Scripture erroneously was to "read" like Adam and Eve.

The first sin had been, among other things, a symbolic abuse of the constituent parts of Scripture—its "leaves" and "fruit," or letter and spirit. A passage cited earlier in this chapter suggests how patristic authors turned the tree/text analogue to exegetical use; there Ambrose uses Adam and Eve as types for the literalist reader who plucks "leaves" out of Scripture, while ignoring the "fruit," in order to find pretexts ("coverings") for sin. In further developing the ex-

76. Bernard, *Sermones in laudibus Virginis Matris* 4.11, in *Sancti Bernardi Opera*, ed. Jean Leclercq, C. H. Talbot, and H. M. Rochais, 8 vols. (Rome, 1957–77), 4:57; trans. Marie-Bernard Saïd and Grace Perigo, *In Praise of the Virgin Mother*, in *Magnificat: Homilies in Praise of the Blessed Virgin Mary* (Kalamazoo, Mich., 1979), p. 57 (original brackets). I am indebted to Betsy Beckmann for bringing this passage to my attention.

77. Bernard cites the Fall throughout *Sermones in laudibus Virginis Matris*, esp. in *Sermo* 4.8, right before the passage quoted above.

78. See above, Chapter 1.3.

egetical import of the first sin, Ambrose assumes that although Adam and Eve were not to eat of the forbidden fruit, they were allowed to touch it (which Eve falsely denied, Gen. 3.3), and that this "touching" signifies a proper examination of Scripture: "Life exists by touching the life-giving qualities of holy Scripture" (*Par* 12.58).

On the basis of this assumption, Ambrose first likens Adam and Eve as mistaken "readers" or interpreters to the Gentile who fails to "handle" Scripture properly by going beyond the letter of the text. For example, "if he takes up the Scriptures, [he] reads: 'Eye for eye, tooth for tooth. . . .' He does not understand the sense of this. He is not aware of the secret meaning of the divine words [*divini arcana sermonis*]. . . . A careful, not a superficial, examination of the context of the passage should be made" (*Par* 12.58). Comparing the Tree to God's word (as embodied both in Scripture and in Christ), Ambrose goes on to warn readers not to repeat the error of their first parents: "The Word would not perhaps have caused injury to Adam and Eve if they had first touched and handled it, as it were, with the hands of the mind."

Whereas Ambrose suggests that the occasional Gentile may fall into interpretive error, he cites the Jews as a collective example of the sin of literalism inaugurated by Adam and Eve: "Do not the Jews seem to you to be patchers of leaves when they interpret in a material manner the words of the spiritual Law? Their interpretation, condemned to eternal aridity, loses all the characteristic greenness of the fruit" (*Par* 13.66). To read or interpret Scripture in a "material" or bodily manner (*corporaliter*), to choose the letter at the expense of the spirit, is to follow Adam and Eve in choosing "leaves" instead of (spiritual) "fruit." Ambrose here relies on Paul's linkage between the Jewish law and the body, sin, and death.[79] Although Ambrose borrowed his allegorical method from Philo of Alexandria, a Jew, he nonetheless evokes here a stereotype about "Jewish" literalism that became an unfortunate (and inaccurate) commonplace among Christian exegetes during the Middle Ages.

Like Ambrose, Augustine held that Adam and Eve had fallen into sin through an act of misinterpretation. First, Augustine's theory of scriptural exegesis figures in his historical commentary on the Fall. In a famous passage in *De doctrina Christiana*, Augustine adopts Paul's letter/spirit distinction as one of the fundamental prin-

---

79. "Whoever plants this [fruitful and spiritual fig] tree in the souls of every man will eat the fruit thereof, as Paul says: 'I have planted, Apollos watered'" (1 Cor. 3.6).

ciples of scriptural exegesis: "You must be very careful lest you take figurative expressions literally. What the Apostle says pertains to this problem: 'For the letter killeth, but the spirit quickeneth'" (*Doc* 3.5.9). Augustine also warns against the converse error of "tak[ing] literal expressions as though they were figurative" (*Doc* 3.10.14). To the rule against literalism Augustine adds a series of strictures: taking signs for things, and taking figurative expressions literally, is equivalent to a descent into "carnal" understanding, to "the death of the soul," to the life of "beasts," to "a miserable servitude of the spirit," and, finally, to a failure "to raise the eye of the mind above things that are corporeal and created to drink in eternal light."

In their imagery (water, light, labor, death), these strictures hark back to the hermeneutical glosses on the Fall in Augustine's first commentary on Genesis.[80] Equally important, however, echoes of the exegetical rules themselves reappear in Augustine's later historical analysis of the Fall, *De Genesi ad litteram*. Citing Paul (1 Tim. 2.13–14), Augustine there maintains that only Eve was really "deceived" by the Serpent's words, yet he holds that both humans, in different ways, misinterpreted God's command. In Eve's case, Augustine surmises that she erred in thinking God to have spoken figuratively rather than literally: "Since she did not believe that eating [the fruit] could bring about her death, I think she assumed that God was using figurative language [*alicujus significationis*] when He said, 'If you eat of it, you shall die'" (*GenL* 11.30.39). Eve thus violated the converse of Augustine's cardinal rule, namely, "[not] to take literal expressions as though they were figurative." Furthermore, her error signifies precisely the "carnal" (or "fleshly") mode of life that Augustine describes (*Doc* 3.5.9) as the moral and ontological ground of sign abuse: "Perhaps...she was living according to the spirit of the flesh [*sensum carnis*] and not according to the spirit of the mind" (*GenL* 11.42.58). Possibly Eve's error also reflects her "fleshly" nature as woman, which derives from the key role of the "flesh" in her creation.[81] But in this passage Augustine goes on to link Eve's error specifically to her lack of divine knowledge, or even of God's image, which she was to have acquired "gradually" under Adam's "direction and tutelage."

Augustine worries a good deal about whether Adam himself

80. Esp. "to drink in eternal light" (*ad hauriendum aeternum lumen*). Cf. the light and water imagery in *GenM* as cited above, section 1.

81. See Gen. 2.21–23. Nichols, "An Intellectual Anthropology of Marriage," observes that "in the case of Adam's creation, the word *caro* (flesh) does not occur, whereas it figures prominently in Eve's" (p. 74).

misinterpreted God's command, despite Paul's claim that the man was "not deceived." Augustine finds it problematic that Adam, as "a spiritual man, in mind though not in body," allowed himself to fall into an abuse of God's command at all (*GenL* 11.42.58), and he rejects the idea that the Serpent (or Eve) could have succeeded in getting Adam to question the motive or intention behind God's command: "I do not think that Adam, if he was endowed with a spiritual mind, could have possibly believed that God had forbidden them to eat the fruit of the tree out of envy" (*GenL* 11.42.60). Returning to this problem in the *City of God*, Augustine suggests that Adam still may have misunderstood God's command in some way— not by distrusting God's motives, or by doubting the command's content, but by failing to understand the full force of the threat of death: "Since [Adam] was not yet acquainted with the strict justice of God, he might have been mistaken in believing that his offence was pardonable. Hence, though he did not suffer the same deception as the woman, yet he was mistaken [*fefellit*] about the verdict that would inevitably be pronounced" (*Civ* 14.11). This solution, however, does not quite fit with the verbal epistemology that Augustine elsewhere applies to the Fall. That is, how can Adam be said to have understood the meaning of "evil" (*malum*) or "death" (*mors*) by the principle of contraries (*GenL* 8.16.34–35) if, as Augustine asserts here, he was "mistaken" about the verdict eventually to be passed upon him? More than once Augustine suggests that Adam doubted God's threat of "death" when he saw that Eve was still alive after eating of the fruit.[82] So the possibility remains that Adam, even without doubting God, may have thought, as Augustine says of Eve, "that God was using figurative language."

As we have seen, Augustine viewed the Fall as the origin of labor in general, including the labor of interpretation. While exegetes might compare Scripture to a pleasant and fruitful Garden, they also likened it to the hard and thorny field where the fallen Adam had to earn his bread from the ground by sweaty labor. The sons of Adam were thus "plowmen" not only as scribes but also as interpreters. Exegetes developed Adam's field as a symbolic site of scriptural interpretation by using various agricultural tropes, most of which had their roots in the biblical imagery of field and vineyard, harvest and "fruit."

In *De doctrina Christiana* Augustine indicates that readers must

82. *GenL* 11.30.39, 11.42.60.

often work hard for spiritual nourishment among the obscure allegories of Scripture, and he suggests that this readerly and interpretive labor is a direct result of Adam's curse:

> Many and varied obscurities and ambiguities deceive those who read casually, understanding one thing instead of another; indeed, in certain places they do not find anything to interpret erroneously, so obscurely are certain sayings covered with a most dense mist. I do not doubt that this situation was provided by God to conquer pride [*superbia*] by work [*labore*] and to combat disdain in our minds, to which those things which are easily discovered seem frequently worthless. (*Doc* 2.6.7)

By implication, the labor of interpreting obscure scriptural allegories was inflicted on Adam's descendants to curb the same sin of pride that led to their first father's fall. Augustine often mentions labor and pride in connection with the Fall, and here these terms reinforce the link between original sin and the work of textual interpretation.[83]

In the same passage Augustine likens readers and interpreters to Adam as they toil over scriptural allegories to gain spiritual nourishment:

> Those who do not find what they seek directly stated labor in hunger; those who do not seek because they have what they wish at once frequently become indolent in disdain. In either of these situations indifference is an evil. Thus the Holy Spirit has magnificently and wholesomely modulated the Holy Scriptures so that the more open places present themselves to hunger and the more obscure places may deter a disdainful attitude. (*Doc* 2.6.8)

Here Augustine evokes what Peter Brown, in another connection, calls "Adam's primal hunger for the Wisdom of God"; in likening Scripture to a wholesome (*salubris*) and delicious food, Augustine alludes to "the rich feast of spiritual delight from which Adam had turned away in Paradise."[84] Unlike the forbidden fruit, however, the

---

83. On pride (*superbia*) and the Fall, see *Doc* 1.14.13 ("man fell through pride"), *GenL* 11.5.7, and *Civ* 14.13–14. *Labor* ("work, toil") appears at Gen. 3.17 (OL and Vulg.) and is Augustine's most common term for Adam's work after the Fall (e.g., *GenM* 2.20.30, and citations in *Vetus latina* 2:73–74, quots. s.v. "AU" [= Augustine]).

84. Brown, *The Body and Society*, p. 406.

spiritual food to be found in Scripture is often hidden to prevent disdain or distaste (*fastidium*).[85]

Adam's field is also an underlying metaphor in Augustine's many other harvest and threshing images for the work of interpretation. For example, scriptural "secrets are to be removed [*enucleanda*] as kernels from the husk as nourishment for charity" (*Doc* 3.12.18). The trope suggests that to get at the "nutritious" scriptural truth is to crack open the textual shell, or to thresh out its meaning. As yet another version of the letter/spirit distinction, this trope anticipates the common medieval exegetical image of "fruit" and "chaff," and other such agricultural tropes for exegesis.[86] These allegories of garden, field, harvest, and food relate in turn to a larger set of alimentary images that patristic and medieval exegetes developed from scriptural sources.[87] Exegetes often used these images to link the alimentary motif in Genesis 3—namely, the eating of the forbidden fruit and Adam's resulting toil for bread—with other related biblical imagery, such as the food, water, and harvest metaphors for God's word in the New Testament parables (as cited earlier); the eating of the bread at the Last Supper, with its Eucharistic implications; and the eating of the book (Ezek. 3.1, Rev. 10.9–10), with its suggestion that Scripture is "food" for the soul.[88] Augustine's crucial contribution was to theorize more fully, and to place within a formal hermeneutics, the notion that Scripture was the "field" where Adam's descendants labored in order to gather this spiritual food.

85. See also Augustine's image of the hermeneutical harvest in *Enar* 32.2 (Sermo 2.1), as cited in Vance, *Mervelous Signals*, p. 15.

86. Cf. *Doc* 3.7.11. For further medieval examples, see D. W. Robertson, Jr., "Some Medieval Literary Terminology, with Special Reference to Chrétien de Troyes," *Studies in Philology* 48 (1951): 669–92; rpt. in Robertson, *Essays in Medieval Culture*, pp. 51–72. Also Robertson, *Preface to Chaucer*, pp. 316–17; and Gellrich, *The Idea of the Book*, pp. 209–14.

87. See Curtius, *European Literature*, pp. 134–36; and Leo C. Ferrari, "The 'Food of Truth' in Augustine's *Confessions*," *AS* 9 (1978): 1–14.

88. E.g., Ambrose, *Par* 9.42, links the forbidden fruit to the bread of the Eucharist. Augustine, *GenL* 11.31.41, contrasts Adam's and Eve's eye-opening eating of the fruit in the Garden with the supper at Emmaus. The alimentary theme also appears in Augustine's medical glosses on the Fall, where God is a "doctor" (*medicus*) whose dietary prescriptions Adam and Eve ignore, thus losing their spiritual health (e.g., *Ver* 45.83, *Doc* 1.14.13). On medieval food symbolism and the Fall, including typological contrast between the forbidden fruit and the "food" of God's word, see Caroline Walker Bynum, *Holy Feast and Holy Fast: The Religious Significance of Food to Medieval Women* (Berkeley, 1987), chap. 2. For medieval allegories of "eating the book," see Gellrich, *The Idea of the Book*, p. 22.

In his biblical poem, Avitus dramatizes Augustine's notion of the Fall as an abuse of God's word that led to the often fruitless labor of both field and womb. According to Avitus, the Temptation disastrously inverts the order of teaching in Paradise, as shown earlier, and directly attacks God's word *as a sign*. Thus when Eve ill-advisedly asks the Serpent to teach her the meaning of God's command—"What He meant by 'death,' / Do thou willingly explain to me"—she is expressly seeking an explication or interpretation of God's word (*pandere* "explain, comment upon, unfold").[89] When the Serpent, readily assuming the office of exegete, deceitfully answers, "You fear, O woman, a word empty of threats [*uacuum nomen*]" (2.185), he abuses the verbal sign not so much by distorting its significance as by denying that it has any significance at all. The Serpent thus reduces God to both a liar and a source of "empty" or "meaningless" signs—the exact opposite of God's Augustinian role as the ultimate source of signifying plenitude. Avitus shows his debt to Augustine and at the same time adds great poetic irony by having Eve single out for discussion the very word, "death," that signifies the main punishment inflicted by God on the humans for their interpretive error. For mistaking the meaning of "death" in God's precept, Eve flirts with "the death of the soul" that Augustine identifies with sign abuse, and as a result she must suffer physical death itself. Poetic justice indeed!

With Adam, Avitus has less to go on in both Scripture and commentary, and he simply portrays Adam, without discussion, taking the fruit of Eve's interpretation directly from her mouth (*ex coniugis ore* [2.258]). Avitus implicitly follows Augustine's account of Paul's dictum that Adam was "not deceived," never suggesting that Adam really believed Eve's radically revised understanding of God's word, only that he finally gave in to her persuasions. Adam thus abuses God's word, as a sign, mainly in that he disregards it. Like Eve, however, Adam is punished in his distinct sphere of labor for having "emptied" God's word of its significance.

In Avitus's version of God's curse upon Eve, she will suffer "empty" sorrows in childbirth for mistakenly believing God's command to have been an "empty" threat: "When as a woman, exhausted by heavy labor, / You shall have brought forth the hoped-

89. *Poematum* 2.181–82, as quoted more fully above, Chapter 1.3, with Latin text. Citations are from Nodes, ed., *Avitus, The Fall of Man*; translation adapted from Kirkconnell, *The Celestial Cycle*, pp. 3–18. See *Mediae Latinitatis Lexicon Minus*, s.v. *pandere*.

for offspring, / You shall sometimes bewail its death with worthless sorrows."⁹⁰ Eve's worthless or "empty" sorrows (*uacuos dolores*) over the doomed fruit of her womb (i.e., Abel in particular and children in general) clearly recall her earlier abuse of God's word as an "empty term" (*uacuum nomen*). Having emptied the divine word of meaning, she now learns that her own labors will be emptied of significance by the death of her offspring.

As for Adam, he will suffer an "empty" harvest in the field of his particular labors. Despite "heavy tillage" he will be tricked by "lying [*mentito*] seed" and as a result will reap "empty [*uacuus*] husks" and "deceptive [*fictas*] crops."⁹¹ Like Augustine, Avitus here uses the word/seed metaphorics of the gospel parables to turn Adam's field into a figure for language and textuality, and Adam's curse into a figure for the hermeneutical toil of humans in general. Besides dramatizing Augustine's hermeneutical allegories on Adam's field, Avitus anticipates the agrarian metaphorics of the sign that was to flourish during the feudal age, as in the twelfth-century *Jeu d'Adam*, where the fallen Adam prophesies to Eve that her sin will be recorded not only in Scripture but also in the "signs of confusion" springing from the ground.⁹²

4. The Fruit of Interpretation

In transforming the Fall into the genesis of hermeneutics, Augustine did more than just allegorize the historical Adam and Eve as types for readers or interpreters. Probing more deeply into the readerly implications of the Fall than any of his predecessors, Augustine used the first humans as emblems for the faculties involved in the psychology of reading. In particular, he analyzed what Genesis 3 suggested about the pleasure of the text and its problematic role in readerly experience.

As with signs and writing, Augustine's earliest analysis of pleasure and the Fall appears in his first commentary on Genesis. Using wordplay on *fructus* ("fruit") and *frui* ("to enjoy"), Augustine there glosses the Tree of Knowledge as the first object and hence the

90. 3.150–52 ("Nam cum praeduro mulier confecta labore / optatam sobolem tali produxeris ortu, / lugebis uacuos nonnumquam orbata dolores").

91. 3.164–66 ("pinguia decipient mentito germine culta. / Nam pro triticeo lolium consurgere fructu / et fictas segetes uacuasque dolebis hauenas").

92. *Le Jeu d'Adam*, ed. Willem Noomen (Paris, 1971), pp. 51–52, lines 542–45 ("le signes de grant confusion").

ultimate symbol for illicit pleasure. The passage is worth quoting at length, since it sheds light on how Augustine adapts the Fall to the problem of textual pleasure:

> It is called the tree of discernment of good and evil, because the soul ought to stretch itself out toward those things which are before, that is, to God and to forget those things which are behind [Phil. 3.13], that is, corporeal pleasures. But if the soul should abandon God and turn to itself and will to enjoy [*frui*] its own power as if without God, it swells up with pride, which is the beginning of every sin. When punishment has followed upon this sin, it will learn by experience the difference between the good which it abandoned and the evil into which it has fallen. This is what it will be for it to have tasted of the fruit [*fructu*] of the tree of the discernment of good and evil. Hence, it received the commandment to eat from every tree that is in paradise, but not to eat from the tree in which there is the discernment of good and evil. That is, it was not to enjoy [*fruatur*] it, because by eating from it it would violate and corrupt the ordered integrity of its nature. (*GenM* 2.9.12; trans. modified)

Though eating the forbidden fruit signifies illicit pleasure, Augustine stresses that Adam and Eve could, and humans in general can, "enjoy the fruit" in a spiritual sense: "And would that we were enjoying [*frueremur*], as we were commanded, every tree of paradise, which signifies spiritual delights. 'But the fruit of the Spirit is charity, joy, peace.'"[93]

The pleasure principle based on the "fruit" in Genesis 3 is further refined in the psychological allegory (or "tropology") of the Fall that Augustine uses first in the same commentary and repeatedly in later works. In this allegory, the Serpent typically stands for the senses, Eve for appetite, and Adam for reason; hence the Serpent is associated with pleasure, Eve with delight (*delectatio*), and Adam with consent.[94] Together Adam and Eve represent the "marriage" of rea-

---

93. *GenM* 2.25.38, quoting Gal. 5.22–23. Augustine also links *frui* and the forbidden fruit in *Ver* 12.23.

94. *GenM* 2.14.21, *Trin* 12.12.17, and *Dom* 1.12.34; cf. *Conf* 10.30. See also *GenM* 2.11.15 on Adam and Eve as, respectively, soul and body, or "virile reason" (*virilis ratio*) and its "animal part" (*animalis pars*), that is, appetite. For analysis, see Robertson, *Preface to Chaucer*, pp. 65–75. A. Kent Hieatt, "Eve as Reason in a Tradition of Allegorical Interpretation of the Fall," *Journal of the Warburg and Courtauld Institutes* 43 (1980): 221–26, stresses that Augustine's gloss on Eve as "appetite," an aspect of reason, is a crucial departure from Philo and Ambrose, who had equated Eve exclusively with the senses, or the "flesh" (see esp. p. 221).

son and appetite in the soul, a metaphor whose sexual connotations are important to Augustine's hermeneutics, as we shall see. Reason, which "has appetite very near to it," judges "concerning the bodily things which are perceived by the bodily sense; if well, in order that it may refer that knowledge to the end of the chief good; but if ill, in order that it may enjoy [fruatur] them for their own sake."[95] And to consent to the allurement to enjoy oneself (fruendi se) "is to eat of the forbidden tree. But if that consent is satisfied by the pleasure [delectatione] of thought alone," then reason (Adam) has not fallen, and it is "as if the woman alone should have eaten the forbidden food." Augustine's tropology has been aptly summed up by Jesse Gellrich: "The result of Eve's temptation and Adam's capitulation was the inversion of the proper order of masculine control over feminine desire, an 'adultery' of the perfect marriage in the Eden of the soul."[96]

In picturing an interior marriage of gendered faculties, and the tempted soul as poised between "fidelity" and "adultery," Augustine's tropology supplies the moral and psychological framework for his hermeneutics, which essentially translates the narrative and imagery of the Garden into a set of principles about enjoying or taking pleasure in texts. As Adam must govern Eve, and reason control appetite, so the "masculine" reader must resist the temptation embodied by the "feminine" text. Or, in a variation of the same idea, the rational ("masculine") part of the reader must control or govern the appetitive ("feminine") part.

The delight (delectatio) represented in Augustine's tropology by Eve (or woman) is neither good nor evil in itself; it is morally ambiguous; it can go either way. In De doctrina Christiana, referring to signs and texts, Augustine articulates this ambiguity in terms of his fundamental distinction between enjoyment (fructus) and use (usus).[97] Only spiritual things are to be enjoyed (i.e., loved for their own sake) whereas all other things are to be "used" (i.e., employed for obtaining spiritual things). "However," Augustine adds, "enjoyment is very like use with delight [delectatione]. When that which is loved is near, it necessarily brings delight with it also" (Doc 1.33.37). But in the case of lesser things, one must be careful not to "cling to that delight and remain in it, making it the end of

95. Trin 12.12.17.
96. Gellrich, The Idea of the Book, p. 152.
97. Or frui ("to enjoy") and uti ("to use"), Doc 1.3.3, 1.4.4, 1.33.37; and, for commentary, Robertson, Preface to Chaucer, pp. 65–67.

your rejoicing," for only God ("the Trinity") is a worthy object of this kind of enjoyment.

The way in which Augustine's gendered tropology of the Fall informs his scriptural exegesis may be seen from a well-known passage on allegory in *De doctrina Christiana*. Significantly, this passage occurs in the midst of the passages, quoted earlier in this chapter, about the labor and hunger that attend the search for truth in scriptural allegories. Choosing as his example a passage from the Canticle of Canticles (4.2), whose garden inevitably recalls Eden, Augustine asks why scriptural allegory yields pleasure as well as doctrine or truth: "Why is it, I ask, that if anyone [speaks plain doctrine] he delights [*delectat*] his hearers less than if he had said the same thing in expounding that place in the Canticle of Canticles where it is said of the Church, as she is being praised as a beautiful woman [*pulchra quaedam femina*], 'Thy teeth are as flocks of sheep, that are shorn, which come up from the washing, all with twins, and there is none barren among them'?" (2.6.7). Augustine answers that the similitude of the "beautiful woman" provides him as a reader with a certain pleasure: "In a strange way [*nescio quomodo*], I contemplate the saints more pleasantly when I envisage them as the teeth of the Church cutting off men from their errors and transferring them to her body." But precisely why this pleasure arises, Augustine repeats, is "difficult to say."

The reason for Augustine's readerly pleasure is perhaps not so strange or difficult to say as he suggests. The textual image of the woman (*femina*) is able to delight (*delectare*) him as a reader because "she," like Eve, and Woman in general, arouses his sense of pleasure or delight (*delectatio*).[98] The woman of the Canticle, whose body is described more erotically in verses not quoted here by Augustine, clearly represents for him an object of both sensuous attraction and moral anxiety. Apart from textual images per se, texts themselves have a bodily aspect; the idea of the written text as a *corpus* ("body"), and hence as offering erotic potential, a "pleasure of the text," runs from Ovid and Macrobius through patristic and medieval tradition, the text usually being equated with the female body in particular.[99]

---

98. Augustine's usual term for Eve is *mulier* ("woman"), but he designates her as *femina* in contexts both historical (e.g., *Lib* 3.10.31; ed. W.M. Green, *CCSL* 29:205–321; trans. John H.S. Burleigh, *On Free Will*, in *Augustine: Earlier Writings*, pp. 102–217); and tropological (e.g., *Trin* 12.12.17).

99. See *OLD*, s.v. *corpus* 16; Cassiodorus, *Institutiones* 1.15.12; Curtius, *European Literature*, pp. 316–17; and, for other examples, Dinshaw, *Chaucer's Sexual*

The ultimate Text, the divine Book, is a "masculine" and spiritual entity, but earthly texts, including Scripture, belong to a bodily order, and as such they have a specifically "feminine" aspect. Although Augustine can view the text's "feminine" qualities in a favorable light, as when likening Scripture to a "mother" who trains and nourishes her "little ones," or readers (GenL 5.3.6), it is fair to say that, like his contemporary Jerome, he finds the attractively "feminine" body of the text to be profoundly disturbing.[100]

Although the patristic tendency to transfigure the literal woman of the Canticle into a spiritual emblem has precedents going back to rabbinic exegesis, in adopting this tradition Augustine and other patristic exegetes, as ascetic Christian males, betray their wariness of the tempting body of the text—not just of the Canticle but of the often sensuous imagery of the Hebrew Scriptures at large. But Augustine deliberately appropriates sexual language for spiritual experience. For example, in a passage from his Soliloquies that precariously balances sensual image against spiritual intent, Augustine describes divine wisdom as a woman unclothed and sexually embraced—"a most clean embrace; to see and to cling to Her naked, with no veil of bodily sensation in between."[101] Here, from Augustine's male point of view, to pierce the "veil" is not only to strip naked the truth but also to penetrate her feminine being, at once a hermeneutical and a hymeneal act.

The moral ambiguity of pleasure or enjoyment in Augustine's hermeneutics reflects the problematic role of sexuality in the Fall itself. Although Augustine never equates the Tree of Knowledge with "carnal knowledge" per se (unlike more severe authorities such as Jerome), he often describes the Fall in terms of illicit sexual pleasure (and vice versa).[102] For example, he uses his tropology of the Fall to explicate Christ's dictum about adultery (Matt. 5.28), and the same dictum (elsewhere) to explicate the Fall.[103] Augustine views autonomous sexual desire, in its rebellion against the will, as not

---

Poetics, pp. 19–25. Cf. Roland Barthes, "Le texte a une forme humaine..., de notre corps érotique" (Le Plaisir du texte [Paris: Seuil, 1973], p. 30).

100. Cf. Jerome's famous comparison of the pagan text to the beautiful captive woman (Deut. 21.10–13), Epistola 70 (to Magnus); ed. I. Hilberg, CSEL 54–56; trans. Charles C. Mierow, Letters, ACW, no. 33 (Westminster, Md., 1963); as cited and discussed by Dinshaw, Chaucer's Sexual Poetics, pp. 22–25.

101. Sol 1.13.22; PL 32:869–904; as cited in Brown, The Body and Society, p. 394.

102. See Jerome, Epistola 22.18–19 (to Eustochium), on the sexual significance of the forbidden fruit in "the Paradise of virginity."

103. Dom 1.12.33–34, Civ 14.10.

only a major catastrophic result of the Fall but also—as scholars have noted—as an analogue for hermeneutical error.[104] For example, he commonly censures the abuse of signs, words, or texts as "fornication."[105] Sexual connotations flavor his warning not to read "carnally" (*carnaliter*) by subjecting the mind "to the flesh in the pursuit of the letter" (*Doc* 3.5.9). This exegetical principle itself rests on a notion of signs and reference that parallels the sexual politics of Augustine's Garden tropology: to read literally is to fail to "refer" (*referre*) signs to their significance (*Doc* 3.5.9), and the "adultery" of the soul occurs when the "masculine" reason fails to "refer" (*referre*) to higher, spiritual ends the bodily things that attract the "feminine" appetite (*Trin* 12.12.17). Finally, Augustine must have counted on the erotic connotations of *frui* ("to enjoy sexually") in adopting it as a key term for his hermeneutics.[106]

Sexual connotations such as these also shape Augustine's applied hermeneutics. In the case of scriptural allegories, for example, the "masculine" reader may enjoy the "feminine" text insofar as pleasure accompanies the discovery of the truth, for in this case, according to Augustine, "enjoyment is very like use with delight." But one must not read simply for pleasure, or become entrapped by the allure of the text, or enjoy it "for [its] own sake." For to read this way would be, in Augustine's phrase, to "cling" to delight, an echo of the idea that man is to "cleave" to his wife (Gen. 2.24) but without letting her exert undue influence over him, as Eve did over Adam, as appetite may over reason, and as pleasurable texts can over unwary readers.[107] In terms of the example from the Canticle, illicit pleasure occurs if the reader takes delight in the *femina* as simply a pleasurable image rather than as an allegorical sign of spiritual truth (in this case, about the church). To enjoy the text in itself, to take pleasure in the sensuous imagery of its fleshly body, is tanta-

---

104. Augustine's main commentary on sex and the Fall appears in *Civ* 14.15–24; on sexual urges as a direct result of the Fall, see also *GenL* 11.32.42. On Augustine's sexual tropes for signs, language, and texts, see examples and discussion in Robertson, *Preface to Chaucer*, pp. 72–75; Burke, *The Rhetoric of Religion*, pp. 138–41; Vance, *Mervelous Signals*, pp. 6–11, 15–19; and Gellrich, *The Idea of the Book*, pp. 152–54.

105. E.g., *Doc* 3.8.12; *Conf* 1.13, 2.6, 4.2.

106. *OLD*, s.v. *fruor* 4b; cf. Curtius, *European Literature*, p. 316n. *Fructus* has related connotations, "gratification, pleasure, satisfaction" (*OLD*, s.v., 6).

107. *Doc* 1.33.37, to "cling" (*inhaerere*) to delight (as cited earlier). *GenM* 2.24.37, to "cleave" or "cling" (*adhaerere*) to one's wife (citing Gen. 2.24). See quotations in *Vetus latina* 2:54, col. 2, s.v. "AU" (= Augustine); and Burke, *The Rhetoric of Religion*, pp. 129–33.

mount to eating the forbidden fruit and hence to a readerly reenactment of the figurative "adultery" or "fornication" inherent in the Fall. In the same passage, Augustine glosses the woman of the Canticle as Mother Church fructified by "holy men" who "come to the holy laver of baptism and, ascending thence, conceive through the Holy Spirit and produce the fruit [fructum] of a twofold love." Thus Augustine transforms the sexual imagery of the Garden of Eden and its fruit, as echoed in the garden and fruit of the Canticle, into the terms of a spiritual union to be "used" *and* "enjoyed" by the reader.

If Augustine tends to feminize the text, he also recreates the reader in his own—masculine—image. The first-person voice noticeably intrudes during his dealings with the *femina* of the Canticle—for example, "I contemplate [intueor] the saints more pleasantly"—and this voice echoes that of the *Confessions*, a narrative of personal fall and redemption that juxtaposes and even likens to each other the role of texts and women in seducing or saving men. Textual ambivalence and feminine ambivalence mirror each other in the story of Augustine's life: by his own testimony, poetic fictions and heretical tracts appeal to the youthful Augustine's carnal inclinations, and even the sensuous letter of Scripture confounds him, until he is enlightened through Neoplatonic books, Ambrosian exegesis, saints' lives, and the revelation from Paul's epistle; likewise, his concubine and "mistresses" tug on his "flesh" until he is "enticed" into the arms of motherly Continence, faithful Monica, and Mother Church herself. The "feminine" text, then, can be a trap where the "masculine" reader loses his reason, his soul, and his proper Paradise—or a guide enabling him to regain these.

5. The End of the Book

The *Confessions* as a whole contains an autobiographical version of the hermeneutics of the Fall that Augustine bequeathed to the Middle Ages. Laying out a spiritual itinerary whose landmarks include two typological gardens and two symbolic trees, Augustine narrates his life in terms that involve signs and texts, reading and interpretation, at every crucial turn.[108] Hermeneutics not only is a major

108. On Augustine's readerly itinerary, see O'Connell, *Art and the Christian Intelligence*, pp. 97–98.

theme of the *Confessions* but also defines its structure, for the whole work concludes with three books of commentary on Genesis, thus signaling that the proper end of both life and letters is to know and to enjoy the divine Word. Confession turns into exposition, or, as Eugene Vance aptly puts it, *narratio* into *enarratio*.[109] But Augustine's concluding exegesis includes a vision of the heavenly Book that spells out the ultimate limits on all finite, fallen, and material texts, including Scripture itself.

We have already seen how Augustine, in his scriptural commentary and treatises, used the narrative and imagery of the Fall to account for the labors of language that afflict fallen humans. In the *Confessions*, Augustine dramatically suggests how Adam's curse affects humans, as linguistic beings, from birth onward. As an infant feeling the desire for food and other necessities, Augustine is incommunicado, trapped within himself, until he muddles his way from gestures to noises to intelligible speech: "My desires were inside me and those to whom I wished to express them were outside and could not by any sense perception of their own enter into my spirit. And so I used to jerk my limbs about and make various noises, ...and by the end of my infancy I was already trying to find signs [*signa*] by which I could make my feelings intelligible to others" (*Conf* 1.6). This passage hints at Adam's and Eve's "clumsy artifice of language and gestures," as evoked by Peter Brown in a passage cited earlier. Making feelings intelligible requires making them "sensible" in the form of signs, and the signs crossing the gap between inside (*intus*) and outside (*foris*) reflect the various kinds of alienation—of soul from body, of will from desire, of knowledge from intellect—that are among the most divisive legacies of the Fall.

In his continuing account of language, the self, and the Fall, Augustine marks off his growing pains in verbal stages, from being "an infant, incapable of speech" (*in-fans*, "without speech"), and then "a speaking boy [*puer loquens*]" (1.8), and eventually a student struggling with the "boring and troublesome" rudiments of grammar (1.13). The work involved in all these stages, but particularly in studying the formal arts of language, leads Augustine back to the ultimate source of all such noisome labor: "I could have learned [those arts] just as well in studies that were not useless; and that is the safe path along which boys should go. But how one must condemn the river [*flumen*] of human custom! Who can stand firm against it? When will it ever dry up? How long will it continue to

---

109. Vance, *Mervelous Signals*, p. 3.

sweep the sons of Eve into that huge and fearful ocean?" (*Conf* 1.15–16). This passage, recalling the river (*flumen*) that "flowed out of Eden" (Gen. 2.10), returns Augustine by an almost Joycean flux of imagery ("riverrun, past Eve and Adam's") to the sorry scene where the labors of language began.[110]

At a more advanced level, too, no longer just "trying to find signs" but now using them to try to make sense of the world, Augustine suffers under the same Adamic curse. For example, "imagining that everything in existence could be placed under [Aristotle's] ten categories, I attempted by this method to understand you, my God" (*Conf* 4.16). The "falsehood" and "fictions" produced by this philosophical labor are said to result directly from Adam's curse: "You gave the order, and so it was done in me, that the 'earth should bring forth briars and thorns to me' and that 'in the sweat of my brows I should eat my bread.'" As one of the "sons of Adam" (*Conf* 8.9), Augustine finds that even to reconstruct the grounds of sign theory, to work out a verbal epistemology—in the functions of memory, intellect, and will—"is hard labor, hard labor inside myself, and I have become to myself a piece of difficult ground, not to be worked over without much sweat" (*Conf* 10.16).

Besides treating the labors of language and knowledge as results of the Fall, Augustine suggests that signs themselves, including things that are signs, can embody a fatal temptation for humans. A major gloss on this idea is the famous story of his youthful theft of pears, long recognized as a recapitulated Fall:

> Near our vineyard there was a pear tree, loaded with fruit, though the fruit was not particularly attractive either in color or taste. I and some other wretched youths conceived the idea of shaking the pears off this tree and carrying them away. We...stole all the fruit that we could carry. And this was not to feed ourselves; we may have tasted a few, but then we threw the rest to the pigs. Our real pleasure was simply in doing something that was not allowed. (*Conf* 2.4)

It is not the inherent qualities of the forbidden fruit that tempt Augustine but, as with Eve and Adam, what the fruit represents as

---

110. At Gen. 2.10, Augustine's OL Bible has *flumen* (e.g., *GenM* 2.1.1, 2.10.13; *GenL* 8.7.13). James Joyce, *Finnegans Wake* (1939; rpt. Harmondsworth, 1976), p. 3. Cf. *Conf* 13.20 ("from [Adam's] loins [flowed] the brackishness of that sea which is the human race").

a sign: for him, forbidden behavior; for them, forbidden knowledge.[111]

In another hermeneutical reprise on the Fall, Augustine specifies that signs are dangerous, for himself and other fallen humans, precisely as media for knowledge. Having been collectively exiled from the Garden, humans now find themselves in a vast and bewildering forest (*silva*) where the tempter lurks with false signs of the divine truth that was lost or obscured with the Fall: "In this enormous forest, so full of snares and dangers, many are the temptations which I have cut off and thrust away from my heart, as you, God of my salvation, have granted me the power.... Yet, my Lord God, to whom I owe my humble and pure service, there are all kinds of artifices of suggestion by which the enemy urges me to seek for some sign [*signum*] from you" (*Conf* 10.35). Signs are suspect in a fallen world, and simply to seek signs for their own sake can lead to worse results than having no signs at all.

Augustine's hermeneutics of the Fall climaxes in the *Confessions* with its most famous episode, the conversion in the garden at Milan, which symbolically reverses the first sin of sign abuse in the Garden of Eden. Augustine's conversion story, with its fig tree, tempting voices, and other typologies of Genesis 3, has long been recognized as an allegory of both the Fall and the Redemption. In particular, however, the central role of signs, texts, and interpretation in this episode thematizes the hermeneutics of the Fall—and of Redemption. In Augustine's garden, the spoken word and the written word, in the form of the *tolle lege* and the *sortes biblicae*, not only redeem the individual but also betoken a redemption of language itself, including written texts. Augustine's conversion story had an immense literary legacy, not least of all in medieval hermeneutical glosses on the Fall.[112] And it also set a pattern for medieval modes of typological expression, which often depend on a "dual referentiality whereby the language of the Passion also evokes the language of the Fall."[113]

111. As with Adam and Eve, however, "all I tasted in [the fruit] was my own iniquity"; and, like the sign abuse in the first Garden, the theft of pears was "fornication" (*Conf* 2.6).

112. On Fall typology in *Conf* 8, see Forsyth, *The Old Enemy*, chap. 24. On the role of language in particular, see Colish, *The Mirror of Language*, pp. 31–32; Freccero, "The Fig Tree and the Laurel," pp. 36–37; and Vance, *Mervelous Signals*, pp. 24–26. For medieval hermeneutical glosses, see references in Mazzotta, *Dante, Poet of the Desert*, p. 166.

113. Stephen G. Nichols, Jr., *Romanesque Signs: Early Medieval Narrative and Iconography* (New Haven, 1983), p. 111, referring to an 11th-century Passion poem.

As Augustine tells it, he is lying "under a fig tree" when he hears a voice singing or chanting, "Take it and read it [*tolle lege*]," a voice that prompts the sequence of readerly and exegetical actions involved in the climax of his conversion (*Conf* 8.12). On the precedent of St. Anthony, he decides that he must interpret these words as a divine command concerning the book of Paul's letters that lies nearby:

> I snatched up the book, opened it, and read in silence the passage upon which my eyes first fell: "Not in rioting and drunkenness, not in chambering and wantonness, not in strife and envying: but put ye on the Lord Jesus Christ, and make not provision for the flesh in concupiscence" [Romans 13.13–14]. I had no wish to read further; there was no need to. For immediately I had reached the end of this sentence it was as though my heart was filled with a light of confidence and all the shadows of my doubt were swept away.

Besides depicting the climax of his conversion as an act of reading, Augustine employs a matrix of images—food, light, shadow, flesh, clothing—that incorporate into this moment his hermeneutical allegories of Genesis. As embodied in this imagery of the Fall, Augustine's conversion expresses the true end of the hermeneutics that embraces the *Confessions* itself as a rhetorical production, which is to lead the fallen soul—by reading—back to God.

The forbidden fruit of the first Garden is here converted, figuratively and redemptively, into scriptural fruit. Led to the book by a voice, intent upon it through his eyes, Augustine "snatches" it up with a gusto and an appetite that is, however, spiritual rather than fleshly in nature. Spiritual, scriptural food is set off against forbidden food by the passage opportunely picked from Paul, which mentions "rioting and drunkenness," the first term of which (*comisatio*) also suggests "feasting."[114]

As for the visual imagery of the scene, the interior light (*lux*) sweeping away the shadows (*tenebrae*) of doubt reverses the loss of inner light that Augustine cites in his Genesis commentaries as

---

See also p. 133, on Redemption as reversing and transforming the Fall's "rhetoric of negativity."

114. Augustine stresses this sense of the term in *Epistola* 22.1.2; in *PL* 33:61–1162; trans. Wilfrid Parsons, *St. Augustine, Letters*, 5 vols., FOC, nos. 12, 18, 20, 30, 32 (New York, 1951–56); as cited by Brown, *Augustine of Hippo*, p. 207; and, in Paul's letter, the subsequent context of the passage is a discussion of questionable food.

being an immediate result of the Fall. Like many other motifs that Augustine incorporates into his hermeneutics of the Fall, the flash of illumination is ultimately Platonic.[115] Up to this moment of illumination, Augustine has been lying in the shadow of a tree, both in body and soul, an echo of Adam and Eve's hiding among the trees after their sin. (He also has been suffering the "darkest [*tenebrosissimae*] agonies of the sons of Adam" [8.9].) These shadows recall those that encroached on Adam and Eve "toward evening, that is, when the sun was already setting for them, that is, when the interior light [*lux*] of the truth was being taken from them" (*GenM* 2.16.24, as cited earlier). An act of reading is what restores to Augustine the paradisal inner light.

The clothing imagery in this famous passage also suggests how Augustine's conversion reverses the Fall in hermeneutical terms. To "put on" (*induere*) Christ is also to put off the garments of skin in which God clothed Adam and Eve.[116] The fleshly coverings resulting from the Fall represent not only human error, carnality, and mortality but also the "veiling" of the truth by the corporeal words and allegories of the scriptural parchment book. To put on Christ the Word, therefore, is to put on again the paradisal "cloak of grace" as well as to draw back the "veil" of the scriptural words covering the truth. Though converse images, these acts of covering and uncovering are spiritually analogous. In reading and understanding, Augustine finds revealed for him the truth that lies behind the fleshly garment of scriptural words.

Apart from its significance for Augustine's life, the sexual imagery of the Pauline text, "chambering and wantonness" and fleshly "concupiscence," serves to recuperate desire as a hermeneutical impetus that had been corrupted with the Fall. Augustine's act of reading Scripture, unlike his youthful "fornication" through reading Virgil's poetry (*Conf* 1.13), appears to have an *an*aphrodisiac function at its crucial point in the episode as a whole. The tempting voices of the "mistresses" fade away; Continence hovers into view as an apotheosized mother figure; a neutered voice ("the voice of a boy or

115. Plato, *Letter* 7 (341c). See Albin Lesky, *A History of Greek Literature*, trans. James Willis and Cornelis de Heer (New York, 1966), p. 878.

116. Both Vulg. and OL use *induere* in Gen. 3.21, as does Augustine in quoting this verse; see *Vetus latina* 2:75–76, with quotations s.v. "AU" (= Augustine). Augustine, *Civ* 14.17, refers to a "cloak of grace" (*indumentum gratiae*) worn by humans before the Fall; cf. *GenL* 11.32.42. In the more immediate context, to "put on" Christ is also to recover from being "stripped naked" by his conscience (*Conf* 8.7) and from being tempted in "the garment of my flesh" by his "mistresses" (8.11).

a girl, I don't know which") chants *tolle lege*; Augustine reads that he should "make not provision for the flesh"; and before the chapter closes he is avowing that God has converted him "in such a way that [he] no longer sought a wife." Whereas the biblical narrative of the Fall ends with Adam "[knowing] Eve his wife" (Gen. 4.1), Augustine's conversion narrative, with its reversal of the Fall, resoundingly ends with his swearing off the idea of having a wife at all (and hence of Monica's having any "grandchildren of my flesh"). That nothing further be sought from his flesh (*caro mea*) is the thought that closes the chapter and the book.

Augustine's rapid and overflowing harvest of spiritual fruit from just one brief passage of Scripture suggests that in the garden he is seeking not only for himself but also for his hermeneutics a renewed paradisal innocence and abundance. Human knowledge of God must still be mediated by signs and words, but readers and exegetes are to be purified of any carnal desires, any illicit urges toward pleasure "for its own sake," that may subvert their spiritual understanding of God's word or world. This notion, at least, is what is symbolically suggested by the episode of redemptive reading and exegesis in the garden—an attempt to return to Paradise, undo the Fall, and regain a knowledge of God that is "pure" in every sense. Augustine will return, for a time at least, to the realities of teaching rhetoric to unworthy souls for secular ends. But while still in the garden he sketches a tableau of his hermeneutical ideal. Alypius at his side, the new convert examines the text again, discussing it with his friend. As an emphatically asexual couple, they together form a symbolic community of chaste readers seeking spiritual fruit in God's word, unlike their carnally minded first parents who, after enjoying the wrong fruit, went on to beget the race.[117]

Various details in the climactic scene (Augustine's reading "in silence," his reading "[no] further," his "shutting the book") have been seen as symbols for transcending the letter of the text, or corporeal language, or language altogether.[118] Certainly the rapid inward movement from an audible voice (the *tolle lege*) to silent reading

117. Augustine, *GenL* 9.5.9, states that Adam's female companion was a concession to reproductive necessity and that a male companion would have better suited his intellectual needs.

118. "For St. Augustine all dialectic, true rhetoric, and thought itself were but attempts to reascend to that silence from which the world fell into the perpetual clamor of life as fallen men know it" (Mazzeo, "St. Augustine's Rhetoric of Silence," p. 192). Colish finds a more affirmative view of language in Augustine, especially in his conversion narrative; see "St. Augustine's Rhetoric of Silence Revisited," *AS* 9 (1978): 15–24.

and to a nonverbal illumination in the "heart" (*cor*) suggests something of this sort.

On the one hand, Augustine's conversion stresses the moment or instant of reading and hence the temporality of language. By the time he reaches the end (*finis*) of the sentence, Augustine is a changed man. Through his readerly conversion Augustine represents himself as finally making sense of his life by making sense, at the same time, of a scriptural text. Reading Scripture gains him a point of view from which to read and to articulate his own life—a narrative pattern of Fall and Redemption that retrospectively explains the whole, even as his life continues to unfold and move forward in time.[119]

But all has happened as though "in no time." The flash of readerly understanding, which changes Augustine's life in the twinkling of an eye, points not only backward and forward in time but also beyond time into eternity.[120] Augustine has no wish or need to read further because in coming to the end of the sentence, he also has come to the end—the *telos*—of all words and texts, the God in whom his heart can rest. Having searched many books for the truth, and having now found in a book what he has sought, Augustine closes a chapter of his life by "shutting the book" (*codicem clausi*), and in so doing he also suggests a kind of closure for language itself. The gesture has a practical purpose—he wants to tell others what has happened, an affirmative return from self and silence to language and society—but it is more than just that.

In the same chapter of the *Confessions* where he likens the parchment book of Scripture to the garments of skin (*pellis*) worn by Adam and Eve after the Fall, Augustine, nearing the end of his own book, invokes the temporal limits of God's written word: "Your Scripture is stretched out over the peoples until the end of time" (13.15). The end of Scripture envisioned here is part of a totalizing scheme of language, history, and cosmos. As noted earlier, Augustine envisions Scripture itself, at the end of time, being transcended by the "book" of God's face. Even now the angels "read" this divine "book," which is eternally open to them: "For they al-

---

119. See Kermode, *The Genesis of Secrecy*, p. 16, on Wilhelm Dilthey's citing the "moment" of Augustine's readerly conversion as a synoptic "impression-point" of self-understanding (though as applied to aesthetics). Freccero, "The Fig Tree and the Laurel," remarks that Augustine "reads the passage that interprets him and is thereby converted" (p. 36).

120. There is no verb, no linguistic marker of temporal process, in the phrase that describes the act of reading itself ("statim quippe cum fine huiusce sententiae").

ways see your face, and there they read without syllables that are spoken in time what is willed by your eternal will.... Their book is never closed [non clauditur codex eorum], nor is their scroll folded up, for you yourself are their book and you are forever." The image of the unclosed book verbally echoes and typologically fulfills Augustine's earlier gesture, in the garden at Milan, of closing the temporal book of Scripture, and it helps bring to a close Augustine's own book, which like all other earthly words and texts, including Scripture, will pass away at the end of time. The restored vision of God's face (faciem) in the heavenly Paradise also answers to Augustine's glosses on Adam's exile from God's "face" in the earthly Paradise.[121] For resurrected humans to "read" the "book" of God's face is to return to a "natural" language, a language "without syllables," identical with the interior discourse enjoyed by Adam before the Fall.

If the Fall in the Garden of Eden represents for Augustine the beginning of hermeneutics, and his conversion in the garden in Milan a middle phase based on an earthly hermeneutical ideal made possible by Christ's redemptive agony in another garden, then the vision of the Book in the heavenly Paradise signifies an end of hermeneutics altogether. The end of hermeneutics, as embodied by the heavenly book, is at once a purpose, a conclusion, and an apotheosis. The end of time is the end of the book because it is the end of earthly language itself, which subsists on the slowly passing yet ephemeral world of time and of moribund bodily life—the once fallen, now redeemed, but yet unresurrected Creation. After their heavenly reincarnation, humans, like the angels themselves, will again enjoy, as formerly in Paradise, a vision of God no longer mediated by ambiguous signs or embodied in transient words or misted over by the breath of earthly desire.

6. Conclusion

A patristic scriptural hermeneutics, as developed largely by Augustine, seized on the Fall as an originary scene for signs, writing, and interpretation. This hermeneutics posited the Fall as an exile from direct, unmediated knowledge of God to indirect knowledge by signs; and from God's original, vocal presence into a realm of supplementary, written revelation. By allegorizing the characters,

121. See GenM 2.21.32 ("the face of truth"), as cited above, section 1.

events, and images of Genesis 3, exegetes also turned the Fall into the paradigm of sign abuse and textual error, warning readers and interpreters not to abuse Scripture as Adam and Eve had abused God's word and the other signs given them in the Garden. Finally, patristic authors prophesied the eventual end of signs, texts, and hermeneutics altogether by envisioning a divine Book to be "read" by resurrected humans in the heavenly Paradise.

Clearly, this hermeneutics of the Fall involves several problematic circles. That is, Scripture is said to recount a Fall, which in turn is held to explain the need for Scripture; furthermore, allegorical methods are used to explicate the hidden meaning of the Fall, which again is used to explain the need for allegory. The Fall thus represents both a genesis of hermeneutics and a genesis of secrecy—to use Frank Kermode's phrase for interpretive approaches that cultivate an aura of hidden meaning available only to a privileged elect.[122] Virtually equating holy writ with recondite truth, Augustine repeatedly invokes the "secrets" (*secreta*) enclosed in Scripture (*scriptura*), two terms that actually have the same archaic origin.[123] As Kermode points out, however, the genesis of secrecy, as practiced by ancient, medieval, and modern exegetes alike, not only finds the text full of hidden meaning but also tends to inscribe there—or to find already inscribed—a self-reflexive hermeneutical scene. Such a scene is exactly what patristic exegetes found, or founded, in the biblical story of the Fall, whose hermeneutical yield came to rival even that of the gospel parables of the Word. Furthermore, by virtue of the story's capacity to posit and define an anterior event, the historical Fall came to be nothing less than the *felix culpa* of hermeneutics, having made possible the totality of God's scriptural dispensation in the first place.

Augustine's hermeneutics of the Fall set the basic pattern for a medieval scriptural hermeneutics that later exegetes, including the great scholastic authors, extended and elaborated along essentially Augustinian lines. But the vernacular literature that arose in the Middle Ages posed new difficulties for this hermeneutics and did not just borrow but also challenged and sometimes even subverted

---

122. On patristic and medieval forms of this hermeneutical method, see Kermode, *The Genesis of Secrecy*, pp. 35–39.

123. E.g., *Doc* 2.16.23, 3.12.18; also *Conf* 11.2 ("paginarum opaca secreta"). On the shared etymology of *scriptura* and *secretum*, see Calvert Watkins, comp., "Indo-European Roots," in *The American Heritage Dictionary of the English Language* (Boston, 1969), s.v. *skeri-* ("to cut, separate, sift"), p. 1540.

its basic terms and assumptions. Religious vernacular literature, whether practical or mystical, presented anew the problem of using "fallen" language, inextricable from the corporeal world, to convey spiritual truths. The confrontation between an oral pagan culture and a literate Christian one, as in Anglo-Saxon England, enhanced the Fall's significance as a representational ground for the difference between speech and writing. A rise in readership (and eventually authorship) among both religious women and laywomen created new problems for the Augustinian dialectic of reading and interpretation, with its "masculine" and "feminine," or rational and appetitive, aspects. Furthermore, many of the new vernacular genres (romance, lyric, fabliau, etc.) frankly celebrated "carnal" or material values such as sexual love, earthly wealth, and worldly fame. This secular scripture, which developed its own poetics of literary fiction, and eventually its own poetics of the book as well, co-opted theological sign theory and hermeneutics for its own secular ends. The fact that this secular literature often proceeds from Augustinian premises about language and the Fall, only to arrive at very non-Augustinian conclusions, further complicated the immense legacy of patristic hermeneutics to medieval culture.

Chapter 3

The Garden of Eloquence

[Whoever] violates the command of God has become naked
and...wants to cover himself with fig leaves, sewing
together, as it were, insubstantial and shady words which
he interweaves word after word with patched-together
lies in order to make a veil.
—*Ambrose*

FOR PATRISTIC AUTHORS the Fall was the archetypal seduction
through language, especially as embodied in its two episodes of
temptation. The Serpent had verbally persuaded Eve to eat of the
forbidden tree, and the text hinted that Eve had mimicked her own
tempter in similarly persuading Adam. Moreover, after their sin the
humans had covered themselves not only with fig leaves but also,
when questioned by God, with evasive excuses, a further sign that
something had gone wrong with eloquence in the Garden. Finally,
all the rhetorical abuses implicated in the Fall could be instructively
set against the "divine eloquence" used by God himself, before the
Fall, in urging the humans to obey his command and not eat of the
forbidden Tree.

Genesis 3 lent itself easily to rhetorical issues, just as it did to
doctrinal and hermeneutical ones. Exegetes and poets brought to
this text a number of crucial assumptions that vastly enriched the
Fall as a scene for matters of eloquence. First, they widely assumed
that the Serpent spoke for Satan, Augustine even maintaining that
Satan had used the Serpent as his mouthpiece, manipulating its body
to make the sounds of speech and to offer a convincing performance
to Eve. This notion, accepted by the rest of patristic and medieval
tradition, greatly enhanced the Fall as a scenario for rhetorical artifice. Second, patristic authors inferred that Eve felt a desire for the

forbidden fruit largely as a result of verbal rather than visual—or other sensory—stimulation. The text suggests that Eve responds to the fruit's allure *because* she has heard it described attractively: "So when the woman saw that the tree was good for food . . . , she took of its fruit and ate" (v. 6). The idea that a tempting speech was the mainspring of Eve's desire for the fruit put the psychology of language at the center of the Fall.[1] Third, patristic authors generally assumed that Eve accompanied the proffered fruit with persuasive words. Although Eve's temptation of Adam is only briefly mentioned in the biblical account, which initially refers to no exchange of words at all ("she also gave some to her husband, and he ate" [v. 6]), God's later remarks to Adam include a direct hint that Eve persuaded Adam verbally ("you have listened to the voice of your wife" [v. 17]). This hint, or a logical assumption from the first temptation, or an idea about what suited Eve's "nature" as a woman, became the basis for this third assumption. Eve's verbal persuasion of Adam suggested that the "fall" of eloquence inaugurated by the Serpent quickly spread along the chain of discourse in the Garden.

Dwelling on matters such as these, exegetes elaborated the psychology, politics, and sexuality of rhetoric involved in the historical Fall. Furthermore, they allegorized key images in Genesis 3—for example, the sensory allure of the fruit; the concealing fig leaves; the erotically charged bodies of Adam, Eve, and the Serpent—as emblems for the verbal temptation and rhetorical artifice originating with the Fall. They also drew heavily on Paul's seduction typology, which had likened the Serpent's "cunning" to that of false preachers or apostles who might "seduce" the church ("Eve") away from Christ ("Adam").[2] On this model, Augustine used the Fall to define the

1. In the Vulgate text the crucial transition ("So when") is a conjunction of consequence—*igitur* ("therefore"). Robertson, *Preface to Chaucer*, pp. 65–75, largely ignores the key role of verbal persuasion in both the text and exegesis, emphasizing instead the fruit's inherent visual attractions: "The fact that Eve saw that the forbidden tree was 'fair to the eyes and delightful to behold' is obviously a matter of profound significance" (p. 72). A corrective comes from an unexpected source: Geoffrey H. Hartman, *Saving the Text: Literature/Derrida/Philosophy* (Baltimore, 1981), cites Augustine's attention to "aural experience" in temptation scenarios (p. 125, with n.), noting, "There exists a lust of the ears as strong and auspicious as the lust of the eyes about which so much has been written since Saint Augustine" (p. 123). Augustine cites the "lust of the eyes" (1 John 2.16) in *Conf* 10.30 (also 10.35); significantly, he deals with "the delights of the sense of hearing" (10.33) *before* "the pleasure of these eyes of my flesh" (10.34).

2. 2 Cor. 11.3 ("as the serpent deceived Eve by his cunning [Vulg., *astutia*], your thoughts [may] be led astray"). V. 4 mentions false preaching; vv. 13–14, false apostles (*pseudoapostoli*), with reference to Satan disguised "as an angel of light."

crucial role of eloquence, both seductive and redemptive, in the lives of individuals and the church. Meanwhile, poets such as Avitus dramatized Genesis 3 in metrical versions full of speeches and narrative detail that emphasized the art of rhetoric and the psychology of persuasion involved in the Fall.

1. A Theology of Eloquence

Augustine's long training as a rhetoric teacher prior to his conversion, and his experience as a preacher and bishop afterward, allowed him to see the Fall's manifold rhetorical implications in the practical sphere. Furthermore, his depth as a theologian enabled him to theorize about these implications on the grandest scale. In the course of his career, Augustine developed what could be called a "theology of eloquence," a framework of rhetorical theory that treats eloquence as either a direct manifestation, or a subversion, of the divine Word. This framework addresses the main problems of rhetoric and the Fall as recognized and defined by patristic culture.

In his early treatise *On Free Will* (388–95 A.D.), Augustine used biblical typology to project the crucial role of verbal persuasion in the Fall onto all of sacred history by assigning an equivalent role to eloquence in the dynamics of salvation. According to Augustine, humankind (*homo*) ignored God's word in the form of the command about the Tree, was persuaded to evil by Satan in the guise of the Serpent, and consequently had to be persuaded to the good by the divine Word as incarnated in Christ:

> The Word of God, God's only Son, assuming human nature, brought the devil . . . under subjection to man. . . . For the devil, having deceived the woman, and by her having caused her husband to fall, claimed the entire offspring of the first man . . . so that he might keep possession of all born of them, as fruits of his own tree. . . . Those whom the devil has persuaded [*persuasisset*] to persist in unbelief, he is justly allowed to keep as his companions in eternal damnation. So man was not snatched from the devil by force, seeing that the devil had taken him captive not by force but by persuasion [*persuasione*]. And man, who was justly brought low so as to serve him to whose evil persuasion he had consented, was justly set free by him to whose good persuasion he had consented.[3]

3. *Lib* 3.10.31.

Augustine adds that "man sinned less in consenting than the devil sinned by persuading [*suadendo*] him to sin."

This passage points to at least five major rhetorical themes connected with the Fall. First, the Fall was a matter not of force but of persuasion—specifically *verbal* persuasion. Second, the Fall involved rhetorical deception, primarily Satan's deception of Eve. Third, the Fall, with its two separate temptations, involved a kind of rhetorical imitation whereby Eve mimicked her own tempter in persuading Adam. Fourth, one of the "fruits" of the Fall is the continuing abuse of eloquence itself. And, finally, as already suggested, the Fall as the archetypal abuse of eloquence had required an answer and reversal in the divine eloquence of the Redeemer.

Augustine's rhetorical typology of the Fall provides a useful thematic itinerary for this chapter, but it addresses only the overall features of his rhetorical theory. A more detailed, psychological account of eloquence and the Fall appears in Augustine's familiar tropology of Genesis 3, one of his earliest glosses on the Fall and later a commonplace among medieval exegetes and moralists. Augustine's tropology—which renders the psychology of sin as a series of transactions among the senses (Serpent), appetite (Eve), and reason (Adam)—is in fact an internalized rhetorical scenario.[4] That is, Augustine not only "introjects" the spoken exchanges involved in the Fall but also uses expressly rhetorical terms to describe how the various faculties "address" one another within the soul. For example, when the senses tempt the appetite, "a certain measure of suasion [*suasio*] is put forth, as it were, by the serpent." And, if the appetite is moved, it is "as though the woman were already persuaded [*persuasum*]." But if reason does not consent to appetite, the bodily members are "restrained by the authority of higher counsel [*consilii*]."[5]

Although an internal scenario, Augustine's tropology implies certain rhetorical roles for the historical Serpent, Eve, and Adam. The Serpent, as "suggestion," embodies the danger of autonomous eloquence or persuasion (*suasio*), of rhetorical art when divorced from truth or wisdom and used instead in the service of falsehood. Eve's role in representing appetite suggests that in the historical Fall she, as woman, was especially vulnerable to the delights of eloquence, to verbal appearances rather than substance, to emotional

---

4. On Augustine's tropology, see references and analysis above, Chapter 2.4.

5. *Dom* 1.12.34 (*suasio*); ed. Almut Mutzenbecher, *CCSL* 35; trans. William Findlay, NPNF, ser. 1, vol. 6 (1887; rpt. Grand Rapids, 1980), pp. 1–63. *Trin* 12.12.17 (*consilii*). *GenM* 2.14.21 (*persuasum*).

appeals instead of rational ones. Finally, Adam's role in representing reason, with its arbitrating power of judgment or consent, suggests that in the Garden he should have shunned the superficial delights or emotional appeals of tempting eloquence, holding to the truth as known to him through rational conviction. It is especially significant for the historical Fall that in Augustine's tropology, appetitive delight (Eve) performs a dual, mediating role, being both an "audience" to the senses (Serpent) and a "persuader" of reason (Adam).

The danger of illicit rhetorical delight is precisely what Augustine stresses in his historical account of the Fall. For example, in *The City of God* he states that "delight" in the Serpent's words was the stimulus for the Fall of generic humankind (*homo*): "The devil would not have trapped man by the overt and manifest sin of doing what God had forbidden to be done if man had not already begun to be pleased with himself. This is why he was also delighted [*delectavit*] with the words: 'You will be as gods.' "[6] With respect to the psychology of persuasion, this passage suggests the important role of words in stimulating delight or pleasure. Despite the reference to generic humankind, it also implies a link between illicit delight and Eve, for the quoted words were pronounced specifically to her by the Serpent.

As with his hermeneutics, Augustine's tropological and historical accounts of the Fall as a rhetorical scenario share a wariness of the "lower" psychological functions. Augustine characteristically places under suspicion the crucial mediating role of appetitive delight (*delectatio*), which he typically associates with Eve and with the feminine in general.[7] Just as a psychological "fall" occurs when appetite usurps authority over reason within the soul of the individual, so a rhetorical "fall" occurs when the speaker's or listener's pleasure in verbal delight takes precedence over rational functions such as teaching (or being taught) doctrine or the truth.

The problematic role of delight or pleasure in the dynamics of persuasion, and in Augustine's theology of eloquence at large, is most fully analyzed in *On Christian Doctrine*, book 4, written late in Augustine's career (427). From classical tradition Augustine inherited the threefold distinction among the aims or offices of eloquence: "[The orator] should speak in such a way that he teaches,

---

6. *Civ* 14.13.

7. E.g., *GenM* 2.18.28: "We cannot be tempted by the devil except through that animal part, which reveals, so to speak, the image or exemplification of the woman in the one whole man."

delights, and moves."[8] In adapting classical eloquence to Christian use, however, Augustine arranged the traditional offices into a hierarchy that clearly subordinates delighting (and moving) the audience to teaching them: "To teach is more important than to move. . . . To move is not a necessity because it need not always be applied if the listener consents through teaching and even through delight also. . . . But to delight [delectare] is not a necessity either" (Doc 4.12.28, trans. modified). As Augustine goes on to explain, the very teaching of the truth can itself delight the audience and gain their consent. Although "delight has no small place in the art of eloquence" (4.13.29), it is often superfluous to the teaching of the truth. Most important, when separated from the truth, the delight aroused by eloquence is very dangerous, as when things are urged "only for the sake of pleasure [delectatio]" (4.14.30). This theme is pervasive in Augustine's rhetorical theory, which typically links delight with deception.[9]

Further rhetorical glosses on the Fall appear in the Confessions, where Augustine describes in more personal terms the potential dangers of verbal pleasure. Not only do humans use language to express desires (whether good or evil), but also, by a reciprocal pleasure principle, words themselves can evoke desire in humans.[10] Augustine describes at length, and censures as "fornication," his youthful delight in the passions aroused by reading the pagan poets (1.13), as well as his delight in rhetoric for its own sake: "Not that I blame the words themselves; they are like choice and valuable vessels. What I blame is the wine of error which is put into them. . . . [Yet] I myself (poor wretch) took easily to these studies and indeed was delighted [delectabar] with them" (1.16). This alimentary imagery, anticipating the typological episode of the pear-tree early in the next book, places Augustine's youthful sins of rhetorical pleasure squarely in the shadow of the Fall, for the abuse of eloquence belongs to the "river of human custom" that sweeps away "the sons of Eve" (1.16).

For Augustine, the rhetorical crux of the Fall is precisely the

---

8. Doc 4.12.27 ("ut doceat, ut delectet, ut flectat"). Augustine is paraphrasing Cicero, Orator 21.69 (ed. and trans. H.M. Hubbell, Cicero: Brutus, Orator, rev. ed., LCL [London, 1962]), with docere ("to teach") substituted for probare ("to prove"). For the third office ("to move"), Augustine freely alternates movere with flectere (e.g., Doc 4.12.28).

9. E.g., Doc 2.37.55, Conf 6.6 (contrasting docere with placere). Yet see Ord 2.13.38 on the need sometimes to move (commoveri) an audience.

10. See Conf 1.13–17, as discussed by Vance, Mervelous Signals, pp. 11–19.

abuse of the "vessels" of eloquence to delight Adam and Eve, and their descendants, in order to serve them the fatal "wine of error." Patristic authors relate the alimentary motif in Genesis 3 to similar imagery in both Christian rite (the Eucharist) and rhetorical tradition, which is rich in oral imagery of various kinds. A key term in Augustine's rhetorical glosses on the Fall is *suavitas*. *Suavitas*, traditionally coupled with rhetorical "delight," means primarily "the quality of pleasing the senses," especially taste and smell, associations that it carries over into its figurative application in rhetorical art.[11] *Suavitas* and related words (e.g., *suavis, suaviter*) overlap in form and meaning with another family of terms that includes *suasio* ("persuasion") and *suadere* ("to persuade"). All these terms spring from the same Indo-European etymon meaning "sweet."[12] Augustine acknowledges *suavitas* as a desirable rhetorical quality, but he warns that it must be used only to flavor the "wholesome" or "nutritious" substance of truth or wisdom; if used to add appeal to evil or falsehood, it offers merely a "pernicious" sweetness.[13] Exegetes had a convenient figure for rhetorical *suavitas* in Genesis 3 itself. The Old Latin version of the Bible cited by Augustine refers to Paradise as a "garden of delight" (*paradisum suavitatis*), and the Vulgate Bible describes the trees of the Garden as "sweet" (*suave*) to the taste; in Augustine's version, the latter verse instead reads "good" (*bonum*), but he himself associates the forbidden fruit with *suavitas* when he glosses Eve's proffering of "the unlawful food" to Adam as the soul contemplating sin "with pleasure" (*suaviter*).[14]

Another important term in Augustine's rhetorical glosses on the Fall is *decorum*, which similarly denotes verbal appeals to "taste," though not so literally as with *suavitas*. A traditional rhetorical ideal, *decorum* signifies mainly what is fitting or appropriate to the

11. Cicero, *Orator* 21.69 ("delectare [est] suavitatis"). *OLD*, s.v. *suauitas* 1 (literal sense), with taste, smell, sound, and sight listed in that order. Cf. *suauis*, which reflects the same sensory hierarchy.

12. See Watkins, "Indo-European Roots," s.v. *swad-* (p. 1544). Cf. Chaucer, *Clerk's Tale* IV.32, "rethorike sweete" (in *The Riverside Chaucer*, ed. Larry D. Benson, 3d ed. [Boston, 1987]).

13. *Doc* 4.5.8: "A pernicious sweetness is always to be avoided. But what is better than a wholesome [*salubris*] sweetness or a sweet wholesomeness?" On beneficial *suavitas*, see also *Doc* 3.16.24, 4.12.27; and, harmful *suavitas*, *Doc* 4.14.31, *Lib* 3.25.74 (*dulcedo*), and loci from *Conf* cited later in this chapter.

14. OL: Gen. 3.23 ("paradisum suavitatis"), quoted in *GenM* 2.1.2, 2.22.34. Vulg.: Gen. 2.9 ("omne lignum . . . ad vescendum suave"). *Trin* 12.12.17 ("suauiter"). Some OL versions of Gen. 3.6 have "vidit mulier quia *suave* esset lignum ad esca" (*Vetus latina* 2:60, and quots., 61). Cf. Avitus, *Poematum* 2.211, as discussed later in this chapter.

speaker and the occasion.[15] As Augustine himself puts it, "that should not be called eloquence which is not appropriate to the person speaking."[16] *Decorum*, too, has a figurative basis in the rhetorical dynamics of the Temptation: according to the Old Latin text used by Augustine and other exegetes, Eve listens to the Serpent's words and thus finds the fruit "delightful" or "pleasing" (*decorum*) to look upon (v. 6).[17]

The intersection of rhetorical tradition and the biblical story of the Fall in terms like *suavitas* and *decorum* provided exegetes and poets alike with powerful and vivid imagery for their glosses on eloquence and the Fall. In associating eloquence with food in the oral dynamics of Genesis 3, patristic authors implicitly contrast the tempter's "sweet" and "pernicious" words with the equally "sweet" but "wholesome" word of God. Furthermore, Augustine's theology of eloquence asserts that the human disdain for God's word in the Garden is what set the stage for the divine eloquence that eventually was incarnated in the nutritious Word of Christ and Scripture.

2. Persuasion in the Garden

Patristic exegetes held that Adam and Eve, in allowing themselves to be persuaded by the Serpent, had at the same time turned away from a divine eloquence embodied in the command they had received from God. Medieval preaching manuals extended this patristic line of thought: God's speech about the trees of Paradise in general and the forbidden Tree in particular (Gen. 2.16–17) became the original precedent for the art of preaching (*ars praedicandi*), with God "preaching" to Adam in order to "persuade" him to virtuous conduct.[18]

In his treatise *On Free Will*, Augustine pointedly contrasts God's persuasive speech with the diabolical urgings by which Adam and Eve allowed themselves to be swayed instead: "In the Garden of Eden the commandment of God came to man's attention from above.

15. See Cicero, *Orator* 21.71.

16. *Doc* 4.6.9, in a passage using *decere* ("to befit, suit").

17. Vulg., *delectabile*. Augustine, *GenL* 11.1.1 ("decorum ad cognoscere"), 11.30.39 ("decorum ad aspectum"). Cf. *GenM* 2.1.2 ("bonum"). For patristic vrr., see *Vetus latina* 2:60–61, quotations.

18. E.g., Robert of Basevorn, *Forma praedicandi* 6; trans. Leopold Krul, *The Form of Preaching*, in *Three Medieval Rhetorical Arts*, ed. James J. Murphy (Berkeley, 1971), p. 126.

From beneath came the suggestion of the serpent. Neither the commandment of God nor the suggestion of the serpent was in man's power. But if he has reached the healthy state of wisdom he is freed from all the shackles of moral difficulty, and has freedom not to yield to the enticing suggestions of inferior things" (*Lib* 3.25.74). While yet in the Garden, the humans had this freedom. But presented with the conflicting voices, the divine voice "from above" and the diabolical voice "from beneath," they chose to be persuaded by the wrong one.

To explain this choice, exegetes waxed metaphorical about God's speech, ascribing to it *spiritual* attractions that the humans, in turning toward bodily pleasures, had ignored or spurned. For example, Ambrose compared God's command to delicious and nutritious food which Adam and Eve had passed by, although "we surely ought to fill the belly of our souls with the Word of God rather than with the corruptible things of this world."[19] And, as noted earlier, Augustine equated God's command, as directly received by Adam (if not Eve), with the actual presence of God, notwithstanding which Adam "despised" God "as present in His command" (*GenL* 11.30.38). The identity of God's presence with his word also underlies Augustine's notion that in order to compensate for the Fall, God later incarnated his eloquence (and wisdom) in Christ and Scripture.

As we have seen, patristic authors held that God's speech to Adam in the Garden embodied an act of divine teaching, which was subverted by the false teaching of the tempter. God's pronouncing of the command coincides with the first—and, for Augustine, the most important—office of eloquence, which is to teach (*docere*) the truth.[20] But Augustine implies that Adam and Eve lost the belief or conviction that God had originally instilled in them through persuasion: "They could not be persuaded [*persuaderi*] to sin unless they were first persuaded that they would not die as a result" (*GenL* 8.16.35). As we shall see, Augustine wrestles at length with the problem of why Adam and Eve so readily gave up the truth as taught them by God in exchange for a falsehood purveyed through an inferior form of persuasion.

Patristic authors saw the crisis of eloquence in the Garden embodied primarily in the Serpent who tempted Eve into sin by means of

19. *Par* 15.74.

20. Scholastic authors elaborate on God's command as a form of teaching, dividing it into parts whose significance they then analyze; e.g., Hugh of St. Victor, *De sacramentis* 1.6.7.

persuasive words. Scripture said that Satan was the "father of lies" (John 8.44), and patristic authors tended to identify the arch-persuader at work behind the scenes in the Garden. But prior to Augustine they were likely to take the Serpent as only a *sign* of Satan; even Augustine, in his first commentary on Genesis, stopped short of a literal, corporeal identification of Satan with the Serpent.[21] But in his later, historical exegesis, Augustine went beyond his predecessors in identifying the Serpent as also Satan's bodily *instrument* of persuasion—a physical agent employed in order to speak the words that persuaded Eve to sin.

Augustine suggests that Satan used the Serpent's body much as a ventriloquist uses a puppet, although in this case acting *from within* the proxy. The ventriloquistic motif appears earlier in the pseudepigraphal *Apocalypse of Moses* (1st c. A.D.), though other early sources, including the Jewish scholar Josephus, claimed that the Serpent (like the other animals) had shared a common tongue with the humans before the first sin.[22] But for theological reasons requiring an ever-closer identity between Satan and the Serpent, Augustine chose the ventriloquistic motif instead, incorporating this idea into literary tradition as a detailed explanation for the mechanics of the Temptation.

Ventriloquism was usually associated with possession by a divine or demonic spirit, and thus Augustine himself mentions it in connection with the possessed slave girl exorcised by Paul (Acts 16).[23] Essentially the same notion of demonic possession informs Augustine's account of how the Devil was able to speak with Eve.[24] As a demonic spirit, Satan required a bodily means for speaking to Eve, and so he assumed the body of the Serpent, causing it to produce audible words: "In the serpent it was the Devil who spoke, using that creature as an instrument [*velut organo*], moving it as he was able to move it and as it was capable of being moved, to produce the sounds of words and the bodily signs by which the woman would

---

21. E.g., Ambrose, *Par* 2.9; Augustine, *GenM* 2.14.20. Forsyth, *The Old Enemy*, notes Augustine's "reluctance" in *GenM* "to treat the story entirely as a literal, physical event" (p. 424). For patristic views specifically on Satan, see Russell, *Satan*, esp. chap. 7 (Augustine).

22. *Apocalypse of Moses* 16.5, *OTP* 2:277; see Forsyth, *The Old Enemy*, p. 233. Common language: *Jubilees* 3.28, *OTP* 2:60; and Josephus, *Jewish Antiquities* 1.41, who adds (1.50) that God punished the Serpent afterward by exchanging its power of speech for poison.

23. *Doc* 2.33.35 ("ventriloqua femina").

24. Augustine, *GenL* 11.28.35, cites examples of demonic possession to explain the passage quoted below.

understand the will of the tempter" (*GenL* 11.27.34). By this account, the Temptation was the worst sort of rhetorical trick, the Serpent being merely a mask or mouthpiece for Satan's machinations. Furthermore, whereas some earlier authorities had endowed the Serpent itself with speech, holding that God deprived it of this power only after the first sin, Augustine innovatively placed the key verbal rupture, in the form of a dislocated voice, at the *beginning* of the Temptation. For patristic tradition from Augustine onward, this notion greatly enhanced the Fall as the original scenario of rhetorical artifice.

Augustine further maintains that in persuading (*suadens*) Eve by means of a proxy, Satan resorts to an abuse of signs (*signa*), the sounds and gestures that not only convey a false message but also constitute a convincing persona in themselves. Apart from the signs emitted by the Serpent, the tempter's body itself signifies deceptively, being a disguise that hides, or dissimulates, the underlying presence of Satan even as it speaks—or is made to speak. False speech is an extension of falsified being, as later, scholastic exegetes emphasize.[25] Regarding ventriloquism, fictive speech, illusion, and the like, the Fall was very much a paradigm for theater—in the pejorative sense of the term favored by patristic authors and persistent throughout the Middle Ages.[26]

Significantly, Augustine's account of rhetorical ventriloquism in the Fall relies on a musical analogy. Satan used the Serpent "as an instrument" (*velut organo*), phrasing that echoes Quintilian's account of articulatory mechanics, which compares the orator's windpipe to the pneumatic pipe organs of antiquity.[27] Augustine also employs a rhetorical, though not strictly musical, analogy in discussing the same topic in *The City of God*: "[Satan] chose as his mouthpiece a serpent in the corporeal paradise.... This slippery animal, of course, which moves in twisting coils, was a suitable tool for his work. By his stature as an angel and his superior being he made it subject to him in spiritual wickedness, and misusing it as his instrument [*instrumento*] he conversed deceitfully with the

25. E.g., Hugh of St. Victor holds that God allowed Satan to take the Serpent's shape (*forma*) because this form, though "fraudulent," did not "entirely" conceal him (*De sacramentis* 1.7.2).

26. For patristic and medieval links between the Fall, demonic possession, and theatrical fictions, see Camille, *The Gothic Idol*, pp. 59–61.

27. Quintilian, *Institutio oratoria* 11.3.16 ("velut organa"), in *The Institutio Oratoria of Quintilian*, ed. and trans. H.E. Butler, 4 vols., LCL (London, 1920–22). See also *OLD*, s.v. *organum* 2; and *Mediae Latinitatis Lexicon Minus*, s.v. *organum* 3, 5 ("mouthpiece," "power to move"). The voice/organ analogy appears in Job 30.31.

woman" (*Civ* 14.11). The term *instrumentum* was commonly applied by rhetoricians to the orator's physical or mental "equipment"; thus, here it stresses Satan's rhetorical ruse.[28] The notion of the Serpent as the Devil's "instrument" has a long literary and artistic legacy. At least one medieval Temptation scene shows the Serpent projecting from the Devil's mouth as he offers the fruit to Eve; and Milton's Satan speaks "with Serpent Tongue / *Organic*, or impulse of vocal Air."[29]

When he discusses the Serpent's rhetorical performance, Augustine dwells on the tempter's body, not only as a disguise for Satan, and as a vehicle for the art of dramatic gesture practiced by orators, but also as a "suitable" (*congruus*) physical form.[30] In describing the Serpent's bodily form as "twisting" (*anfractus*) and "tortuous" (*tortuosus*), Augustine uses terms commonly applied to an involved or roundabout style.[31] Circumlocution of course marks the Serpent's opening gambit with Eve—"Did God say . . . ?" In the Serpent's flexible body, patristic authors found a usefully androgynous form that could be either phallic or enveloping, thrusting or alluring, masculine or feminine. *Serpens*, the biblical term for the Serpent and the most common term in Latin exegesis, can be of either gender, a fact that probably helps explain the Serpent's androgynous variability in patristic and medieval tradition.[32]

Augustine puts chiefly masculine terms on the Serpent. His literal commentary on Genesis brings out the Serpent's masculine features by likening that creature to the two physical agents (and emblems) of spoken and written eloquence, tongue and pen: in his cleverness (*astutia*), Satan employed the Serpent, who is called "astute" just as "we speak of a subtle or astute tongue [*lingua*] which a subtle or acute person moves to persuade subtly or acutely"; sim-

28. See *OLD*, s.v. *instrumentum* 3b. In *Civ* 14.11 the substantive terms for the Serpent are *coluber*, *animal*, and *instrumentum*; "mouthpiece" and "tool" are the translator's expansions.

29. *The St. Albans Psalter* (12th c.), ed. Otto Pächt et al. (London, 1960), pl. 14. *Paradise Lost* 9.529–30, emphasis added.

30. On gestures, see Pseudo-Cicero, *Rhetorica ad Herennium* 3.15.26 ("motus corporis"); ed. and trans. Harry Caplan, LCL (London, 1954).

31. See *OLD*, s.v. *anfractus* 5a ("tortuosity of style, circumlocution"); and *tortuosus* 2 ("complicated, tortuous").

32. Exegetes also designate the Serpent as *coluber* (fem. = *colubra*), a term associated with monsters (Hydra, Furies) in antiquity. The usual adjectives in Gen. 3.1 are of ambivalent gender: Vulg. *callidior* ("wiser, subtler"); OL *sapientior*, *prudentior*, *astutior*, and so on. But some exegetes, including Augustine (e.g., *GenL* 11.2.4), use masculine forms such as *prudentissimus* and *sapientissimus*. For patristic quotations, see *Vetus latina* 2:56–58.

ilarly, "a pen [*stilus*] is said to be lying when a liar tells his lies with it; and this would be the case if the serpent were called a liar because the Devil used it like a pen for his deceitful purpose" (*GenL* 11.29.36). Here "tongue" and "pen" suggest not only spoken and written rhetoric per se but also the whole phallocentric culture of rhetoric in the late classical and patristic environment.[33] Elsewhere, invoking the expressly phallic Serpent cited by Paul and other early exegetes, Augustine states that "Eve" must guard against the tempter's "seed" (*semen*): "She watches his head so that she may exclude him in the very beginning of his evil persuasion [*mala suasio*]."[34]

Although Augustine may have thought of the original tempter's voice as primarily masculine, his influential notion that Satan (a traditionally male figure) entered and possessed the Serpent's body suggests not only a demonic violation but also a sexual one, thus reinforcing the Serpent's potentially "feminine" qualities. Moreover, during the Middle Ages a specifically feminine form of the Serpent—a reptile with a woman's face—emerged in a wide range of literature as well as in an abundance of visual art. The twelfth-century scholastic author Peter Comestor, the first to mention explicitly a Serpent with a woman's face, attributed this idea to his eighth-century predecessor Bede; the attribution is false, but it rightly points in the direction of earlier influences.[35]

In dealing with Eve's temptation, Augustine infers from Scripture that the Serpent's persuasive words directly prompted a desire for the forbidden fruit. Of course, the Serpent could not have persuaded Eve "if there was not already in her heart a love of her own independence and a proud presumption on self." But Augustine implies that Eve desired the fruit for its appearance or taste only *after* the Serpent's words had aroused her appetite: "*Not content with the words of the serpent*, she also gazed on the tree and saw that it 'was good for food and a delight to behold' " (*GenL* 11.30.39; emphasis

33. On "phallic" eloquence in Augustine, see Vance, *Marvelous Signals*, pp. 6–8, 18–19. Augustine, *Civ* 14.15, glossing Adam's and Eve's punishments, illustrates the "lust" (*libido*) of anger by citing the man who "in his rage smashes his style or breaks his reed pen when it writes badly."

34. *GenM* 2.18.28 ("temptation" altered to "persuasion"); see also *GenM* 2.17.25 on the historical Eve's responsibility to keep (*custodire*) God's command and not to let in (*admittere*) the Serpent's words. On the phallic Serpent, see 2 Cor. 11.2–3; and Tertullian, *De carne Christi* 17, as cited above, Chapter 2.2.

35. Peter Comestor, *Historia scholastica* 1.21, PL 198:1053–1722 (col. 1072). See Hans A. Kelly, "The Metamorphoses of the Eden Serpent during the Middle Ages and Renaissance," *Viator* 2 (1971): 301–28 (with plates).

added). Augustine here stresses that verbal prompting preceded desirous looking and the "satisfaction" of eating. That is, Eve was not "satisfied" (*contenta*) with the pleasure or the mere promise of the Serpent's words themselves, and her verbally elicited desires urged a fulfillment in deed. The term *consideravit* ("gazed on") can refer to not only looking at or examining something but also noticing it (as for the first time), contemplating it mentally, or even considering it from a certain point of view (as from that of the Serpent's "eye-opening" account).[36] Although Eve may have already looked at the Tree, Augustine implies that she was prompted by the Serpent's words to look at it now in a new way. Later on, scholastic authors took Augustine's point even further.[37]

Drawing on technical terms from the art of rhetoric, and emphasizing the critical role of delight (*delectatio*) in the psychology of persuasion, Augustine specifies that the Serpent's words ("Your eyes will be open," etc.) persuaded Eve by "pleasing" and "moving" her: "When curiosity was stirred up [*mota*] and made bold to transgress a commandment, it was eager to experience the unknown, to see what would follow from touching what was forbidden, being delighted [*delectata*] in taking a dangerous sort of liberty by bursting the bonds of the prohibition" (*GenL* 11.31.41; trans. modified). Besides underscoring the key role of verbal stimulus in Eve's temptation, this passage implies that the Fall was tantamount to a subversion of the art of rhetoric, especially the proper relation among the three offices—to teach, to move, and to delight. Eve was merely "moved" and "delighted" by what the Serpent said; "teaching," in the proper sense, had no part in the act of persuasion.

Augustine's account of Adam's temptation by Eve similarly stipulates the importance of verbal persuasion, implying that Eve turned around and used on her husband the same rhetorical art just used by the Serpent/Satan to seduce her. As noted earlier, Scripture furnished a hint for this second rhetorical episode, namely, in God's censuring words upon Adam after the sin ("you have listened to the voice [*vox*] of your wife" [v. 17]). Almost as a matter of course, Augustine assumes that persuasive words were involved in Adam's fall and, moreover, that Eve spoke as Satan's rhetorical proxy: "In the woman, who was a rational creature and able by her own powers to speak, it was not the Devil who spoke, but it was the woman

36. See *OLD*, s.v. *considero*.
37. E.g., Peter Lombard, *Sententiae* 2.22.2, *PL* 192:519–962 (col. 697), as cited below in Chapter 5.1.

herself who uttered words and persuaded the man, although the Devil in a hidden way interiorly prompted within her what he had exteriorly accomplished when he used the serpent as an instrument" (*GenL* 11.27.34). The idea that Eve, though no ventriloquist's puppet, may have been "interiorly prompted" to speak reflects the patristic notion that Satan could speak *through* humans acting under their own will, using the speaker's "breast" or "tongue" to convey false-hood or sinful persuasion.[38] Apart from interior "prompting," Eve in tempting Adam also imitates the rhetorical example set by her own tempter; her *imitatio diaboli* is also important to the Fall as a rhetorical paradigm, as will be shown later in this chapter.

Augustine further specifies that Eve used "persuasive" words in tempting Adam to eat of the fruit: "She took some of the fruit and ate and gave some also to her husband, who was with her, using perhaps some persuasive words [*verbo suasorio*] which Scripture does not record but leaves to our intelligence to supply" (*GenL* 11.30.39). The descriptive term applied to Eve's words, *suasorius* ("persuasive, seductive"), points specifically toward the domain of rhetorical art. Augustine here qualifies his supposition about Eve's persuasive words ("perhaps"), going on to add that "perhaps [Adam] did not need to be persuaded [*suaderi*], since he saw that she was not dead from eating the fruit," though usually he assumes that Eve did use such persuasion.[39]

Regarding *what* Eve may have said in persuading Adam, Augustine leaves this open to the "intelligence" (or the imagination) of readers, exegetes—and poets. His later remark, "The sin was urged [*persuasum*] in accordance with the way in which such things are urged [*persuaderi*]," merely begs the question and leaves this crux open to the same speculation.[40] As one of the major narrative gaps in the story of the Fall, the encounter between Adam and Eve itself became a kind of temptation—a place in the text that, ironically, inspired a good deal of eloquence itself. Augustine's vague reference to "some persuasive words" only gave more license to poets already eager to "supplement" Scripture on this intriguing point.

Although inclined to think that Eve used verbal persuasion in tempting Adam, Augustine does not hold that Adam *believed* what Eve said. Citing Paul's influential dictum, "Adam was not deceived,

38. E.g., *Conf* 8.4, the Devil uses an orator's breast (*pectus*) as his "stronghold" and his tongue (*lingua*) as a "weapon." Cf. *Conf* 6.12; and 5.3, Faustus as the Devil's "snare."

39. Trans. modified. See *Ver* 45.85, *Civ* 14.11.

40. *GenL* 11.42.60, trans. modified.

but the woman was" (1 Tim. 2.14), Augustine maintains that Adam, unlike Eve, did not capitulate *intellectually*: "A seduction in the proper sense occurs when one is persuaded [*suadebatur*] to accept as true what in reality is false; for instance, that God forbade Adam and Eve to touch the tree because He knew that if they touched it they would be like gods.... I do not think that Adam, if he was endowed with a spiritual mind, could have possibly believed that God had forbidden them to eat the fruit of the tree out of envy" (*GenL* 11.42.60). Implicit here is the same assumption about male intellectual superiority that shapes Augustine's paradisal hierarchy of instruction. If Adam taught the command to Eve in the first place, she could not have truly persuaded him to disbelieve it.[41]

But then *why* did Adam give in to Eve's persuasion? Augustine, setting a precedent followed through the Middle Ages down to Milton, holds Adam to have been swayed not by what was said but by *who* said it: "After the woman had been seduced and had eaten of the forbidden fruit and had given Adam some to eat with her, he did not wish to make her unhappy, fearing she would waste away without his support, alienated from his affections, and that this dissension would be her death" (*GenL* 11.42.59). In *The City of God* Augustine repeats essentially the same explanation: Adam was persuaded by "his woman" (*sua femina*) because of "the close bond of their alliance"; "[he] refused to be separated from his sole companion even in a partnership of sin" (14.11). In terms of Aristotle's rhetorical theory, Adam was persuaded by an emotional appeal (*pathos*) or by the character of the speaker (*ethos*), rather than by reason (*logos*).[42] More simply put, Eve herself embodied his main temptation.

More than once Augustine compares the tempted Adam to Solomon, who, without in the least believing in idol worship, was unable to resist "the love of women" or feminine "blandishments" and so fell into sin.[43] Despite the sexual overtones of this comparison, however, Augustine stresses that sexual seduction was *not* involved in Adam's fall, since in his yet-unfallen state he did not feel sexual desire rebelling against his will: "He was not overcome by the concupiscence of the flesh, which he had not yet experienced in the law of the members at war with the law of his mind, but by the sort of attachment and affection [*benevolentia*] by which it often

41. Augustine, *Lib* 3.24.72, says of collective mankind (*homo*) that "it is not surprising that he could be seduced [*seduci*]," but he always defends Adam, as an individual man (*vir*), from the charge of having been deceived.

42. Augustine discusses speaker-audience relations in *Cat* 15.23.

43. *GenL* 11.42.59 ("mulierum amori"); *Civ* 14.11 ("blanditiis femineis").

happens that we offend God while we try to keep the friendship of
men" (*GenL* 11.42.59). As Peter Brown summarizes matters, "Augustine was adamant that Eve had used no sexual attraction to lure
Adam to eat the fatal fruit."[44] But Augustine says only that Adam
was not "overcome" (*victus*) by carnality. He does not say whether
Eve—who had already eaten of the fruit and presumably felt already
"the law of the members"—*attempted* a sexual seduction of Adam.
Could her feminine "blandishments" (charm, flattery, coaxing,
promises) have included sexual overtures?

Literary tradition by and large accepted Paul's and Augustine's
dictum that Adam was not persuaded by Eve's arguments ("was not
deceived"), whatever form these arguments took. Still, Augustine's
verdict that Adam did not succumb to feminine sexual allure, but
only to the tie of "friendship," never sat well with poets (or painters),
and for centuries since Augustine they have liberally interpreted
Adam's fall, and Eve's too, in terms of a sexual rhetoric. This interpretation is rampant in medieval literature and art, where Eve and
the Serpent often seem to be engaged in a sexual dance, and where
the Adam-and-Eve episode commonly suggests a comparison between the forbidden fruit and the erogenous zones of the body, especially between the fruit and Eve's breasts.[45]

3. "Some Persuasive Words"

As one of the earliest Latin poets to dramatize the Temptation in
detail, Avitus stresses the abuse of rhetorical art and the psychology
of persuasion involved there, giving imaginative form to a number
of key Augustinian ideas about rhetoric and the Fall. Besides depicting Eve and the Serpent as rhetorical proxies for Satan, and emphasizing the crucial role of verbal persuasion in both temptations,
Avitus stresses the "fall" of eloquence from its proper offices in the
Garden. And in a departure from the letter of Augustine's exegesis,
Avitus brings out the sexual aspect of both temptations, mainly
through a suggestive use of the story's inherent imagery.[46]

44. Brown, *The Body and Society*, p. 402 (citing *GenL* 11.42.59).

45. See illustrations in Phillips, *Eve*, esp. p. 65 (Jacopo della Quercia), p. 86 (Hans
Baldung Grien); and discussion of "fig" motif (Michelangelo), pp. 67–69. Sources for
the apple/breast motif include Cant. 7.7–8; and Isidore of Seville, *Etymologiae*
11.1.74.

46. In the prologue to his poem Avitus worries over the traditional problem of
combining Christian truth with the poetic "license to lie" (*licentia mentiendi*), that

Avitus offers a reference point for the rhetorical abuses involved
in the Fall by establishing God, the divine *rhetor*, as the ultimate
model of eloquence. This requires no fewer than three speeches in
the poem's first book, which dramatizes the prelude to the Fall. The
third of these, which concerns the forbidden Tree, exemplifies an
ideal eloquence not only by favoring the first office of rhetoric—
teaching—but also by presenting a model of orderly and restrained
persuasion.

God begins his speech with the orator's standard appeal to the
goodwill of his audience (*captatio benevolentiae*) and then amplifies
the biblical injunction to eat the fruit of the trees of Paradise:

> O highest work of the Creator, alone made by our hand,
> While the other creatures I called into being by voice,
> Do you see with what abundance this most beautiful grove
> Is furnished with good things? All of these
> Shall be given you to eat without limit.[47]

God continues a little longer in this positive vein, promising that
the humans will enjoy (*frui*) a long earthly life, and then He turns
to the prohibition, expressing it in didactic terms, as detailed in
Chapter 1.[48] Cast in the high style, as befits the Father, the speech
has some grandiose touches, like the promise of food without limit
(*sine fine*), which echoes Jupiter's prophecy in the *Aeneid*, and transforms Paradise into the ultimate imperium.[49] But as a whole, the
speech employs measured terms that offer an excellent gauge for the
tempter's forthcoming effusions of flattery.

In dealing with the Temptation, Avitus accepts Augustine's

---

is, to use certain rhetorical figures and pagan mythology (ed. Nodes, p. 16, l. 25).
Roberts, "The Prologue to Avitus' *De spiritalis historiae gestis*," explains Avitus's
"unusually rigid" stand on poetic license (p. 406) in terms of his episcopal role as an
opponent of heresy. But Avitus hints that his caution may also be due to his subject,
the Fall, particularly its theme of rhetorical art and artifice: he seeks divine rather
than human approval in shunning poetic license and thus taking on a task "more
difficult than fruitful"—*plus arduum quam fructuosum* (ed. Nodes, ll. 34–35; trans.
altered from Roberts, p. 400).

47. Avitus, *Poematum*, 1.302–6 ("O summum Factoris opus, quos sola creauit
/ nostra manus, nasci cum cetera uoce iuberem, / aspicitis quanto pulcherrimus
ubere lucus / per multas famuletur opes? Haec cuncta dabuntur / ad uestros sine fine
cibos").

48. 1.309 ("fruens longaeuo in tempore uita").

49. *Aeneid* 1.279 ("imperium sine fine dedi").

statement that "in the serpent it was the Devil who spoke." Avitus illustrates this notion in terms of an uncanny metamorphosis:

> It happened that the serpent, wise in heart, surpassed
> In subtlety all living things. His form the wicked one
> Above all others decided to assume. His aery body
> He changed suddenly to a serpent's and covered
> With viperous flesh, a snake with outstretched neck.[50]

As a disguise for Satan, the Serpent's body is not only a dissimulating sign but also a "covering" (*tegmen*) that suggests the concealing function of rhetorical art in the temptations and their aftermath.[51] Later, as the Serpent creeps toward Adam and Eve, Avitus stresses that Satan, the arch-persuader, has "put on" (*induit*) the Serpent's form because he is bent on rhetorical fraud (2.137).

Avitus's Serpent is expressly masculine, and the phallic significance of its "outstretched neck" soon becomes manifest in relation to Eve's eroticized ear.[52] Furthermore, the Serpent's body (*forma*) has a certain "terrible" or "fearful" beauty (*decorem*), an external allure that it shares with Eve's body, the forbidden fruit, and language itself in the episodes of temptation.[53] Avitus details the Serpent's verbal equipment by likening his voice to the sound of song: "Simulating mildness, in its throat it whispers the hisses / Of incessant song, and from its mouth extends a triple tongue."[54] Possibly Avitus is glancing at Augustine's musical trope, that Satan used the Serpent "as an instrument" (*velut organo*). Avitus has described earlier the human tongue producing the sounds of speech against the palate as a plectrum does in striking a lyre.[55] As a counterpoint

50. 2.118–23 ("Forte fuit cunctis animantibus altior astu, / aemulus arguto callet qui pectore, serpens. / Huius transgressor de cunctis sumere formam / eligit, aerium circumdans tegmine corpus / inque repentinum mutatus tenditur anguem: / fit longa ceruice draco").

51. The Serpent's body as a *tegmen* (repeated, l. 129) recalls Augustine's notion that the Fall inaugurates verbal "covering" in both the hermeneutical and rhetorical senses. Cf. Ambrose and Augustine on verbal coverings (*integumenta*), as cited later in this chapter.

52. E.g., "aemulus . . . serpens," in quoted passage; also, "coluber" (2.130).

53. 2.131 ("terribilis metuendum forma decorem").

54. 2.134–35 ("nunc simulat blandum, crebro ceu carmine fauces / ludunt, et trifidam dispergunt guttura linguam").

55. "The supple tongue is matched to the hollow palate / That modulated language may resound upon the smitten air, / When it is forced in the sound-chamber as by plectrum-stroke [*ut in cameram pulsantis uerbere plectri*]" (1.87–89).

to this musical analogy, the Serpent's "song" or "poem" (*carmen*) suggests the imminent abuse of eloquence in the Temptation.

Even before the Serpent speaks, much is suggested about the role of rhetoric in Eve's temptation. Bent on his "evil persuasion," the tempter "proceeds / With climbing coils to mount an upright tree."[56] As the source of both tempting words and tempting fruit, the Tree of Knowledge now becomes the Tree of Eloquence, too. Supported by the Tree, the Serpent manages to reach "Eve's ear in subtle wise," and "With gentle voice he seizes hold of her."[57] Eve's eroticized ear, the target of the phallic Serpent's "sly injected poison [*ueneno*]" (2.141), keeps the emphasis on verbal rather than visual stimulation. In Avitus's account, the fruit looks good to Eve and arouses her appetite only after it starts to "sound good."

The Serpent's first speech to Eve has little to do with the fruit at all. Most of it is a long flattering prelude mainly about Eve's own beauty and fertility. Whereas God's speech had made only a modest opening appeal to the audience (*captatio benevolentiae*), the tempter's praise knows no such bounds:

> O ornament of the world, most beautiful woman,
> Whom a resplendent form adorns more than a rosy virtue,
> Thou art the destined mother of the race,
> And the whole world awaits thy motherhood.
> Thou art the first and certain joy of man....[58]

The speech has a total of sixteen lines, of which fully twelve are given to such flattery—a swelling exordium out of all proportion to the whole and as such, a sure sign of rhetorical abuse. This overture, though it eventually leads to the fatal question about the Tree, clearly is meant to signal that Eve was seduced not so much by the fruit itself as by a new vision of herself glimpsed in the flattering mirror of the Serpent's words.

The bodily beauty stressed in the Serpent's speech complements the seductive "body" of the speech itself and, in the absence of spiritual concerns, is another warning sign. In expressing admiration

---

56. 2.136, 142–43 ("malesuada fraude," "arboris erectae spiris reptantibus alto / porrigitur tractum"), perhaps echoing Augustine, *GenM* 2.18.27 ("mala suasio"), or *Civ* 14.11 ("malesuada versutia").

57. 2.143–44 ("sublimibus aequans, / auditum facilem leni sic uoce momordit").

58. 2.145–49 ("O felix mundique decus, pulcherrima uirgo, / ornat quam roseo praefulgens forma pudore, / tu generi uentura parens, te maximus orbis / expectat matrem; tu prima et certa uoluptas / solamenque uiri").

for Eve's body or physique (*forma*), the Serpent draws attention to what, after his own recently mentioned body (*forma*, 2.131) has served its rhetorical purpose, will become Satan's next instrument of persuasion.[59] Also, in describing Eve as the "most beautiful woman" (*pulcherrima uirgo*), the tempter subtly transfers to her body an epithet earlier applied by God, in Eve's hearing, to the grove containing the forbidden Tree.[60] This association with the fruit itself further embellishes Eve's body as a tempting medium.

Drinking it all in—"seductile Eve into her ears / Received the deadly poison and accepted / Praise without warrant"—Eve betrays in her very first words of reply how attractive and persuasive she finds the Serpent's overture:

> O viper, with sweet words most charmingly endowed,
> Thou art mistaken to think that God urges us to fast,
> Forbids us food....[61]

Eve's pleasure in the Serpent's "sweet words" (*suauibus dictis*) ominously foreshadows her delight in the forbidden fruit itself, soon afterward described as "sweet" (*suauis*, 2.211). By investing the Serpent's language with the qualities of the forbidden fruit, Avitus emphasizes that persuasive language itself is mainly what stimulates Eve's desire. Eve's adjacent mention of God as "urging" (*suadens*) the humans further elevates the Serpent's *suavitas* to legitimacy by putting it in company with divine eloquence.

The Serpent's next speech "explains" to Eve the meaning of God's word, particularly the word "death," while promising her great rewards for eating the fruit.[62] The narrative sequel stresses that Eve's attention is rapt on her tempter's words—the medium of temptation—rather than on the object of temptation itself:

> The credulous woman, with a yielding look, marvels
> Upon him as he promises such gifts with

59. In the art of rhetoric, *forma* denotes a figure of speech; see *OLD*, s.v., 6c.

60. 1.304 ("pulcherrimus lucus"). The Serpent's many terms in *prae-* (implying preeminence) and various positive forms of the superlative (*maximus, prima*, etc.) are further marks of his flattering style.

61. 2.166–67, 169–70 ("mortiferum seductilis Euua uenenum / auribus accipiens laudi consensit iniquae"; "Suauibus O pollens coluber dulcissime dictis, / non ut rere Deus nobis ieiunia suasit").

62. See above, Chapter 2.4.

> Whisper false. Now more and more she wavers
> And turns her mind aside. . . . [63]

Here using a technical term from the art of rhetoric, Avitus specifies that the Serpent's words have now begun to sway, move, or "turn" (*flectere*) Eve's mind, clearly suggesting an abuse of the offices of eloquence.

Only after this substantial verbal prelude consisting of two long speeches from the Serpent, and Eve's intervening reply, does the fruit itself, as a sensory object, begin to take on a significant role in the temptation:

> When he perceived that she was vanquished now
> By an impending judgment, mentioning once more
> The name and station of the gods, he pulled
> One apple down from all of those upon the fatal tree,
> Enveloped it in sweet odor, recommended it
> For pleasing sight, and offered it to her. . . . [64]

The "sweet" (*suauis*) odor that now envelops the fruit makes good on the Serpent's "sweet" words, but sensory qualities are a secondary temptation that now merely reifies the "sweetness" already embodied in the Serpent's utterance. Avitus does not explain how the Serpent continues speaking with the fruit in his mouth—the tempter is thus pictured by other early poets and artists, as well as by medieval tradition—but certainly this gesture symbolically transfers the fruit's qualities to the tempter's words.[65]

The delayed attention to the fruit as a tempting object suggests that Eve's impression of its alluring sweetness even *results* from its attractive verbal presentation by the tempter's "sweet" words—that the tempter's words shape Eve's perception. By this point, the fruit is no longer an object in itself to Eve but the sum total of the qualities she has heard the Serpent ascribe to it. Avitus stresses the crucial

63. 2.204–7 ("Talia fallaci spondentem dona susurro / credula submisso miratur femina uultu. / Et iam iamque magis cunctari ac flectere sensum / incipit").

64. 2.208–12 ("Ille ut uicino uictam discrimine sensit, / adque iterum nomen memorans arcemque deorum, / unum de cunctis letali ex arbore malum / detrahit et suaui pulchrum perfundit odore. / Conciliat speciem nutantique insuper offert").

65. E.g., Dracontius (5th c.), *Carmen de Deo* 1.472, where the Serpent approaches Eve "bringing food full of cruel death in his mouth [*ore cibos crudeli funere plenos*]" (ed. F. Vollmer, *Auctores Antiquissimi*, MGH, vol. 14 [Berlin, 1905], pp. 23–113; as quoted and trans. in Evans, *Paradise Lost and the Genesis Tradition*, p. 132). Early art of the Fall with this motif is cited below, section 5.

role of verbal stimulus by picturing Eve's first bite of the apple—
"greedily she bit [*momordit*]" (2.231)—in terms that recall the Serpent's persuasive overture: he "seized hold of [*momordit*] her."[66] By
implication, Eve swallows the forbidden fruit because she has already swallowed the Serpent's lies.

In dealing with Adam's temptation, Avitus reflects the patristic
consensus that Satan used Eve as his rhetorical proxy because of her
intimacy with Adam, as well as Augustine's specific idea that Adam's consent to Eve had less to do with what was said to him than
who said it or even how it was said. An understudy to her own
tempter, Eve copies the Serpent's techniques of persuasion, beginning with her opening appeal to Adam:

> Take food, sweet husband, from the seed of life,
> Whose potency, perhaps will make thee like
> The Thunderer and equal to the gods.[67]

In urging that Adam "take food" (*sume cibum*), Eve echoes the
Serpent's urging that she take his advice (*consilium sumere*) instead
of God's.[68] When eventually Adam "takes" both Eve's advice and
the fatal fruit, the poem reifies her words themselves as something
to be tasted, swallowed, and digested.[69]

Eve also copies her own tempter in not just speaking but *whispering* to Adam: "The unfortunate man receives her whispered
words / Of evil suasion and is quite dislodged from his firm re-
solve."[70] This description implies the same ear-to-mouth intimacy
of her own temptation. Furthermore, the sibilance of the Latin phrasing (*malesuade uerba susurri*) lends a serpentine quality to Eve's
speech, and the term *malesuade* ("evilly suasive"), applied earlier
to the Serpent's words (2.136), suggests that Eve's rhetorical persuasion of Adam both imitates her own seduction and perpetuates
the new, falsified art of eloquence that has come into being.

66. 2.144, as cited earlier; Nodes, ed., p. 36n, notes the wordplay.

67. 2.242–44 ("Sume cibum dulcis uitali ex germine coniux, / quod similem
summo faciet te forte Tonanti / numinibusque parem").

68. "Take rather my counsel [*Consilium mage sume meum*]" (2.194); she also
echoes God's injunction, "take the given fruits [*sumite concessas fruges*]" (1.307),
applying it to the wrong object.

69. Eve's offering Adam "the dish of death" (*fercula mortis*, 2.252) suggests the
"vessels" of eloquence, as in Augustine, *Conf* 1.16 (*vasa*); 5.6 (*pocula*). On the transferred use of *ferculum*, see Curtius, *European Literature*, p. 135.

70. 2.254–55 ("Accipit infelix malesuade uerba susurri, / inflexosque retro deiecit
ad ultima sensus").

Although Avitus indicates no overtly sexual seduction of Adam by Eve, he suffuses the scene with sexuality. The most suggestive detail in the episode, and the one that most directly links eloquence with illicit desire, is the striking oral image that renders the climax of Adam's fall:

> From the mouth of her, his wretched wife,
> The unfirm man seizes with firmness on a poisonous gift,
> And fills his open throat with deadly food.[71]

Just as Eve's biting into the apple recalls how the Serpent has previously "seized hold" of her through his eloquence, so Adam's fatal bite is conjunct with the persuasive words he "swallows" at the same time. Adam's fall comes doubly "from the mouth" of his wife (*ex coniugis ore*), which offers him both fatal advice and fatal fruit. As in Eve's encounter with the Serpent, who likewise offered the apple from his mouth, Avitus focuses here on the sexualized orifices of mouth and ear. For Avitus, the dynamics of the Fall circulate within the ambit of hearing and speech, the primary domain of rhetoric.

As already noted, Eve, in tempting Adam, not only uses "some persuasive words" but also falls into a fatal mimicry of her own tempter, a rhetorical *imitatio*. *Imitatio*, the student's emulation of set pieces from illustrious orators, was a staple of rhetorical education, and in Avitus's poem Eve's rhetorical mimesis suggests an abuse of traditional eloquence—indeed, even a warning about the dangers of that art's powerful appeal to the imitative urge.[72] Some medieval poems and plays of the Fall take the trick of Eve's diabolical *imitatio* even farther by having her repeat not just words or ideas, as in Avitus, but phrases and whole lines from her tempter's performance. Such overt cases of mimicry can suggest either a kind of ventriloquism or the incantatory power of eloquence to take hold of the mind.

At the same time, Eve's seductive mimicry hints at a disturbance

---

71. 2.258–60 ("ex coniugis ore / constanter rapit inconstans dotale uenenum, / faucibus et patulis inimicas porrigit escas").

72. On imitation, see *Rhetorica ad Herennium* 1.2.3; and Donald L. Clark, *Rhetoric in Greco-Roman Education* (New York, 1957), chap 5. Augustine, *Lib* 3.25.76, states that Adam and Eve were persuaded not only by words but also by the "pattern of pride" that the Devil presented for their imitation (*imitatio*); and, in *Conf* 1.19, he censures his own eagerness, while a student of rhetoric, to imitate (*imitare*) "worthless shows." Stephen G. Nichols, "An Intellectual Anthropology of Marriage," discusses *imitatio* in the biblical account (see esp. pp. 75–77).

of the sexual order in the Garden—Eve's insemination with the Devil's seedlike word by means of the phallic Serpent. In the biblical narrative, Eve's apparent receptivity to bad examples (as the Serpent tempts her, so she tempts Adam; as Adam blames her, so she blames the Serpent) may be a symbolic displacing of Eve's fecundity onto language, a verbalizing of the female flux (and fluctuation) feared by men. Eve's womb, after all, bears the brunt of God's judgment upon her: "I will greatly multiply your pain in childbearing" (v. 16). In any case, patristic versions of the Temptation clearly express concern about what fruit the seeds of evil eloquence might bring forth.

4. Fig Leaves and Other Fabrications

In glossing the Fall as a rhetorical scenario, patristic exegetes equated the abuse of eloquence not only with the tempting forbidden fruit but also with certain images of artifice or fabrication. Citing especially Adam's and Eve's attempts to cover themselves after their sin with fig leaves and excuses, exegetes figured fallen rhetoric in terms of various textile tropes—"weaving," "cloth," "veils," "nets," etc.— that signified the capacity of words to hide, entrammel, or deceptively embellish the truth.[73] Most of these tropes derived from ancient rhetorical commonplaces that still have analogues in modern terms for discourse, whether generic ("text"), fictive ("spin a yarn"), or mendacious ("whole cloth," "tissue of lies").[74] But as incorporated into patristic glosses on Genesis 3, these commonplaces came to stand for rhetorical artifice as a function and product of the Fall.

One of the most influential authors to treat the Fall in such terms was Ambrose of Milan. Ambrose produced important glosses on the fig leaves, but he saw the postlapsarian cover-up as belonging to a pattern of artifice and concealment that had begun already with the Serpent's overture to Eve. Using a hunting or catching image

73. For "sewing," Vulg. has *consuerunt*; OL has *suerunt, consuerunt, adsuerunt*, and so forth. For the fig leaf "aprons," Vulg. has *perizomata*; OL has *tegimenta, succinctoria*, and the like. Terms used by Ambrose and Augustine are cited later in this chapter. For the full range of OL and patristic terms, see *Vetus latina* 2:61–62, quotations.

74. See *OLD*, s.v. *texo* 3b, *intexo* 4b, *textum* 1b, *textus* 3, *consuo* 1b. Rhetorical commonplaces include Horace, *Ars poetica* (*Epistola* 3.2) 15–16 (the "purple patch"); and Quintilian, *Institutio oratoria* 8.pref.20 ("things are dressed [*verborum habitu vestiantur*] by words"). Augustine, *Conf* 12.26, uses *texere* nonpejoratively of his own writing.

that likens deceptive language to a "trap," Ambrose writes (*Par* 12.56) that the Serpent's opening words to Eve show the Devil as he "sets his snares" or "weaves his nets" (*intexit dolos*). Ambrose later specifies that the Serpent's whole speech was a patchwork of lies "composed" with the express intention of deceiving Eve:

> Of the things that he promised, scarcely one of them seems to be true. He contrived [*composuit*] falsehoods..., [saying] "You shall not die." Here we have one falsehood, for man, who followed the promises of the serpent, is subject to death. Hence he added [*addidit*], "For God knows that when you eat of it, your eyes will be opened." This alone is true.... But his composition [*agglutinatum*] is still a falsehood, for the serpent quickly attached [*adjunxit*] this: "And you will be like gods, knowing good and evil." (*Par* 13.61; trans. modified)

In rhetorical tradition, the orator is said to "compose" (*componere*) set speeches; sometimes, as here, the term implies not just persuasion but outright verbal deception.[75] In this passage, the series of words having the prefix *ad-* ("to, with") emphasizes the contrived or artificial nature of the Serpent's discourse. When he describes the speech as an "agglutination" of lies, in particular, Ambrose calls up various associations with glue and papyrus to imply the speech's "patched-together" quality, its holding power or "stickiness," or possibly even its association with food (through wordplay on *gluttio*, "to swallow, gulp down").[76]

Developing his main allegory for rhetorical artifice, Ambrose morally and figuratively aligns Adam's and Eve's making and wearing of fig leaf coverings (Gen. 3.7) with the narrative sequel, their evasive excuses to God (vv. 9–13), a case of verbal fabrication and cover-up.[77] The process by which Ambrose turns the fig leaves and excuses into emblems for rhetorical artifice is somewhat involved but worth following in its details, for it shows the genesis of a very important trope for language and the Fall.

Ambrose begins by allegorizing the first part of the key verse (Gen. 3.7):

> "And their eyes were opened," we are told, "and they realized that they were naked." They were naked, it is true, before this time,

75. See *OLD*, s.v. *compono* 5d, 8a–d, 10a.

76. *OLD*, s.v. *gluten* ("glue"), *glutino* ("to glue"), etc., and *gluttio* (v. 1).

77. Exegetes sometimes invoke also the intervening episode, the hiding "among the trees of the garden" (v. 8).

but they were not devoid of the garments of virtue. They were naked because of the purity of their character and because nature knows nothing of the cincture of deceit. Now, on the other hand, the mind of man is veiled in many folds of deception. (*Par* 13.63)

Here humankind's original state of virtue is represented by nakedness, whereas the deceit that enters the world with the Fall is symbolized by coverings of various kinds: "garments," "cincture" (or toga), "veil," and "folds" (or wrappings).[78] Although "naked truth" and verbal "clothing" are ancient tropes, Ambrose here invests these images with patristic values.[79]

Continuing, Ambrose invokes the second part of his text—"they sewed fig leaves together and made themselves aprons"—to turn Adam's and Eve's makeshift clothing into an emblem, first of all, for self-deception and sensuality:

When, therefore, they saw that they had been despoiled of the purity and simplicity of their untainted nature, they began to look for objects made by the hand of man wherewith to cover the nakedness of their minds. They added delight to delight so as to increase the shady pleasures of this world, sewing, as it were, leaf upon leaf [*folia foliis assuentes*] in order to conceal and cover the organ of generation. (*Par* 13.63; trans. modified)

The primal coverings here represent human artifice in general, "objects made by the hand of man" (*manufacta*), as well as sensuality ("shady pleasures").

Ambrose goes on to associate "nakedness" and "clothing," as embodied in the episode of the fig leaves, with the hermeneutics of the Fall discussed in Chapter 2 of this book (e.g., the literalist "patching" together scriptural "leaves"). Ambrose thus underscores the Fall's significance as the moment when language in general, like the fallen human body, turned opaque and began to "cover" (rather than display) the truth, whether in a hermeneutical or rhetorical sense.

78. I.e., *integumentum, amictus, vela, involucrum.*

79. Besides the cloth and clothing tropes for language already mentioned, classical Latin authors used the term *nudus* ("naked") for the absence of deceit in general as well as for unadorned language in particular; see *OLD*, s.v. *nudus* 8b, 14a–b, esp. Horace, *Carmina* 1.24.7, "naked truth" (*nuda veritas*). Note also the later, scholastic distinction between "innocent" and "guilty" nakedness, cited in Erwin Panofsky, *Studies in Iconology: Humanistic Themes in the Art of the Renaissance* (1939; rpt. New York, 1972), p. 156.

In the context of this hermeneutical gloss, Ambrose also associates the fig leaves with Adam's and Eve's self-excusing speeches to God, making the leaves into emblems for specifically rhetorical "covering":

> Whoever . . . violates the command of God has become naked and despoiled, a reproach to himself. He wants to cover himself with fig leaves, sewing together, as it were, insubstantial and shady words which he interweaves word after word with patched-together lies in order to make a veil for his genitals and to cover his own awareness of his deed. Desiring to conceal his fault, he throws leaves over himself, at the same time indicating that the Devil is responsible for his crime. He offers allurements of the flesh or the counsels of another individual as excuses for his wrongdoing. (*Par* 13.65; trans. modified)

This gloss completes a richly woven texture of images and ideas that requires some unraveling itself.

First, Ambrose stresses in this series of passages that Adam and Eve, imitating the Serpent's verbal artifice, make or fabricate language into a covering for themselves. As the tempter "weaves" his verbal "nets," so they weave together (*intexit*) words; as he pieces together or composes lies, so they use patched-together (*compositis*) excuses. Second, Ambrose suggests that fallen humans in general, following the example of Adam and Eve, use verbal artifice to cover (*operire*), conceal (*contegere*), or veil (*velare*) the truth. In combination with these verbs of "covering," Ambrose employs a series of textile nouns to figure fallen language as deceptive "clothing": *integumentum* ("covering, cloak"), *amictus* ("mantle, cloak"), *involucrum* ("wrapping"), *tunica* ("garment"), and *velamen* ("veil"). Just as the fig leaves are denatured into bodily coverings, thus becoming signs of cultural artifice, so language degenerates after the Fall into a medium that humans can artfully manipulate to "veil" themselves from God, from one another, and from self-knowledge (fig. 4). Paul Ricoeur's modern gloss on the fig leaf episode is apposite here: "The nakedness of the innocent pair and the shame that follows fault express the human mutation of all communication, marked henceforth by dissimulation."[80]

In likening the fig leaves to words that hide or cover the truth,

---

80. Ricoeur, *The Symbolism of Evil*, p. 247. See also Burke, *The Rhetoric of Religion*, p. 220, on the primal clothing as signs of "social estrangement or differentiation by status."

4. Adam and Eve hiding from God among the trees of the Garden. Carved capital, 13th c.: Cluny, Abbey Church, choir; in Cluny Museum. Foto Marburg / Art Resource, New York.

Ambrose emphasizes that verbal signs, in either their hermeneutical or rhetorical capacity, often function more as an opaque *material* than as a transparent *medium*. Fallen language can be not only an instrument of temptation, a means for articulating "lies," "allurements," and "excuses" (all mentioned here by Ambrose), but also a temptation in itself. The veils, garments, and other clothing metaphors that Ambrose uses suggest how language, by covering and concealing the naked truth, implicates its users in its own sensuous and alluring texture.

We have seen how exegetes such as Ambrose used the sexual connotations of the fig leaves to censure the illicit pleasures of the text as a hermeneutical object. In the passages quoted here, Ambrose stresses the sexual motif in the fig leaf episode in order to censure also the specifically rhetorical abuses of language. First, using an important term from patristic moral psychology and the traditional art of rhetoric, Ambrose says that Adam and Eve, in covering themselves with fig leaves, "added delight to delight" (*delectationes delectationibus*). Then he links specifically erotic delight or pleasure to the abuse of rhetoric by saying that just as Adam and Eve sewed leaves together to increase their "shady pleasures" (*umbratiles voluptates*) and "to conceal and cover the organ of generation [*genitale*]," so the sinner weaves "shady words" (*umbratiles sermones*) to "make a veil for his genitals [*pudenda*]." Significantly, Adam and Eve and their sinful descendants use "shady words" to cover or conceal their sin not only as a moral fault (*culpa*) and as a mental awareness (*conscientia*) but also as a bodily event that is situated, actually or symbolically, in the sexual organs. As coverings specifically for the genitals, the fig leaves thus come to represent the inextricable relation between language and desire after the Fall.

Augustine follows his teacher Ambrose in using the fig leaves as emblems of verbal artifice, but the converted rhetorician extends their application much further in the realm of verbal culture.[81] First of all, in his earliest commentary on Genesis, Augustine similarly employs the primal clothing of Adam and Eve as a sign of lost innocence and of the urge to deceive that begins with the Fall. Originally Adam was "naked [*nudus*] of dissimulation" and instead was "clothed [*vestiebatur*] with the divine light" (*GenM* 2.16.24), but with sin the humans fell into the arts of dissimulation, as symbolized by the fig leaves: "The leaves of the fig tree signify a certain itching... which the mind suffers in wondrous ways from the desire and pleasure of lying" (*GenM* 2.15.23). Thus the leaves represent carnality and dissimulation as well as a certain desire (*cupiditas*) or pleasure (*delectatio*) with respect to lying. Like Ambrose, Augustine uses the sexual connotations of the fig leaves to stress the bodily aspect of fallen eloquence and its tendency to elevate the least important rhetorical office, "delight."

Linking up the episode of the fig leaves with its immediate narrative sequel, the hiding among the trees of Paradise (v. 8), Augustine suggests that Adam and Eve got their first clothing from the Tree of Knowledge itself: "Clothed in lying coverings [*cooperimenta*

---

81. Augustine's gloss on the fig leaves and its medieval legacy are noted by Robertson, "The Doctrine of Charity," pp. 24–28.

mendacii] . . . , they hid near the tree that was in the middle of paradise" (*GenM* 2.16.24; trans. modified). For Augustine, the fatal tree represents not only knowledge and hermeneutics but also eloquence, its leaves being emblems for fallen language as used to "clothe" or "cover" sin. Elsewhere Augustine compares the fig leaves to words unaccompanied by the "fruit" of good deeds: "Like the leaves of sweet fruits, but without the fruits themselves, [Adam and Eve] so weave together good words [*bona uerba contexunt*] without the fruit of good works, as while living wickedly to cover over their disgrace as it were by speaking well" (*Trin* 12.8.13). "To speak well" (*bene loqui*), a byword for rhetoric, here suggests the whole art of eloquence as abused in the aftermath of the Fall.[82]

In his first commentary on Genesis, written against the Manicheans, Augustine also compares the "lying coverings" made and worn by Adam and Eve to falsehood in the form of heretical "myths" or "fables" that threaten the truth as taught by the church. The Christian who abandons the doctrines of the church is said to gather "carnal coverings of lies [*carnalia tegumenta mendaciorum*] like the leaves of the fig tree, from which [Adam] made himself an apron. [The Manichean heretics] do this when they lie about Christ and preach that he has lied. They, so to speak, hide themselves from the face of God after they have turned to their lies from his truth, as the Apostle says, 'They will turn their hearing from the truth and will turn to fables'" (*GenM* 2.26.39). Citing here the heretical "myths" or "fables" (*fabulas*) censured by Paul (2 Tim. 4.4), Augustine extends the significance of the fig leaf emblems to verbal artifice at large, including false doctrine.

Elsewhere Augustine uses the same terms, "covering" and "fabular" speech, for pagan beliefs as embodied in the rhetoric and poetry of the schools.[83] Moreover, evoking the commonplace that rhetorical art is a "weaving" of words (*texere* "to weave"; hence *textus*, "text"), Augustine glosses the fig leaves as emblems for not only spoken but also *written* heresy, a more permanent form of rhetorical abuse that threatens church doctrine. For example, in another polemical context, he likens the writings of Pelagius, one of his main theological opponents, to the verbal artifice of Adam and Eve: "Do not the words in question appear to you to be the fig-

---

82. Cf. Augustine, *Doc* 4.3.4 ("dicere bene"). O'Connell, *Art and the Christian Intelligence*, p. 30, defines the *ars bene loquendi* as "the [art] of speech."

83. E.g., *Conf* 1.13, "curtains [*vela*] are hung at the doors of Schools of Literature . . . as a covering [*tegimentum*] for error"; and *Conf* 1.14, Homer used to compose or "weave" (*texere*) "stories and fables" (*fabulosas narrationes*).

leaves [*folia*], under cover of which is hidden nothing else but that which he feels ashamed of? For just as they of old sewed [*consuerunt*] the leaves together as a girdle of concealment, so has this man woven a web of circumlocution to hide his meaning. Let him weave out [*contexat*] his statement."[84] As we noted earlier, "to sew together leaves" (*consuere folia*) alludes to books and bookmaking.[85] Although Augustine (like Ambrose) can use such wordplay to evoke the Tree/Text of Scripture, here he suggests instead the "book" of heresy and deceitful eloquence that was also founded with the Fall. There is a special irony in Augustine's applying the fig leaf trope to Pelagius, who disputed the doctrine of original sin, holding that sin was an individual fault rather than a collective, inherited deficiency. In saying that Pelagius "weaves" together deceptive words as Adam and Eve did, Augustine, through typology, neatly implicates his opponent in the sins of his "first parents," including the abuses of eloquence stemming from the Fall.

In developing the fig leaf trope into an emblem for the various abuses of eloquence arising from the Fall, exegetes such as Ambrose and Augustine set important patterns for the Middle Ages, where this trope shows up in a wide variety of contexts. In penitential literature, for example, medieval authorities censure self-excusing or euphemistic speech as so many "fig leaves" that compromise the ideal of "naked confession." In sermons and moral treatises, "leaves" continue to represent (among other things) the shady words and deeds of fallen humans. And even in the poetry of Petrarch and Chaucer, among others, tree leaves of various kinds continue to signify eloquent "coverings," though not always in a negative sense.

5. The Tree of Eloquence

As we have seen, patristic exegetes tend to associate fallen eloquence with either the seductively sweet fruit or the enveloping leaves of the forbidden Tree. This tendency is consistent with early Christian art of the Fall, which often shows the Serpent entwined around the Tree or even proffering the fruit in its mouth, thus juxtaposing the Tree's attributes with rhetorical abuses. Medieval art of the Fall commonly reproduces both motifs.[86] Moreover, medieval authors

---

84. *Nup* 2.17.
85. See above, Chapter 2.2.
86. The Serpent curls around the Tree in the earliest-known depiction of the

commonly allegorize the seven liberal arts, including rhetoric, as trees.[87]

Augustine treats the Tree of Knowledge as a symbol especially for the morally ambiguous state of eloquence after the Fall. In book 4 of *On Christian Doctrine*, he introduces the moral dilemma posed by rhetoric in the fallen world by locating this art in a moral middle ground whose features recall the allegorized landscape of the Garden:

> Since by means of the art of rhetoric both truth and falsehood are urged, who would dare to say that truth should stand in the person of its defenders unarmed against lying? ... Who is so foolish as to think this to be wisdom [*quis ita desipiat, ut hoc sapiat*]? While the faculty of eloquence ... is in itself indifferent [*in medio posita*], why should it not be obtained for the uses of the good in the service of truth if the evil usurp it for the winning of perverse and vain causes in defense of iniquity and error? (*Doc* 4.2.3)

As a faculty placed or planted "in the middle" (*in medio posita*), eloquence resembles the Tree planted "in the middle of paradise" (*in medio paradisi*) as well as the place where Adam and Eve hide after their sin—"among the trees" (*in medio ligni*)."[88] For Augustine, the Tree's medial position signifies not only the soul's "middle state" (*medietas*) but also Adam's and Eve's fall into rhetorical abuses, as "clothed with a lie" they hide "near to the tree that was in the middle of paradise [*in medio paradisi*], that is, near themselves."[89]

Besides planting eloquence "in the middle," between good (*bonum*) and evil (*malum*), Augustine here suggests the scene of the Fall through a pun on *sapere*, meaning both "to taste" and "to know."[90] Tasting/knowing is the central metaphor of Genesis 3, and the tempter/"taster" is figured in the Serpent's usual Old Latin ep-

---

Fall, the *Sarcophagus of Junius Bassus* (4th c.), Rome, Vatican Museum; reprod. in Phillips, *Eve*, p. 100. The fruit in the Serpent's mouth is a very common motif.

87. See Katzenellenbogen, *Allegories of the Virtues and Vices in Medieval Art*, p. 64, n. 3; and Bloch, *Etymologies and Genealogies*, p. 89.

88. Gen. 2.9, 3.3 ("in medio paradisi"); Gen. 3.8 ("in medio ligni paradisi"). See *OLD*, s.v. *pono* 4, "to plant (trees, etc.)."

89. *GenM* 2.9.12 ("middle state," my trans.); *GenM* 2.16.24 ("clothed with a lie," etc.), as cited earlier in an alternate trans. Cf. *GenM* 2.16.24 (Adam and Eve "in the middle rank of things [*in medio rerum*]").

90. See *OLD*, s.v. *sapio*.

ithet, *sapientior* ("wiser").[91] Augustine thus implies that the Fall has left humans with a mixed rhetorical legacy—namely, an art of persuasion that can be turned to either good or evil use.

Long before he codified his rhetorical theory in *On Christian Doctrine*, Augustine put down in his *Confessions* a vivid account of actual rhetorical abuses harking back to the Fall. As we have already seen, Augustine's portrait of himself as a young rhetorician relies heavily on Fall typologies. Besides scattered allusions to illicit verbal delight, and censures on particular rhetoricians, these typologies include the two famous garden scenes, both of which involve a symbolic tree of eloquence. Furthermore, his conversion story contains both a temptation scenario based on Genesis 3 and an affirmative vision of the redeemed and redemptive eloquence that Augustine seeks to put into the service of the church.

The first major rhetorical typology of the Fall in the *Confessions* is the famous story of the stolen pears (2.4). Augustine mentions no prelude of verbal temptation in this escapade, though his committing the theft with "some other wretched youths" implies its genesis in social, and hence ultimately verbal, contracts.[92] Furthermore, as noted earlier, Augustine describes the whole episode as a violation of "a law written in men's hearts which not iniquity itself can erase." Noting the insipidity of the fruit itself ("not particularly attractive either in color or taste"), Augustine points to Paul's notion of the Law itself as a stimulus to sin: "Our real pleasure was simply in doing something that was not allowed." The episode of the pear tree thus suggests that the Fall afflicts even divine eloquence with the capacity to undo—to unravel, or to negate—itself, whether as embodied in an "inner law," Scripture, exegesis, preaching, or yet some other form.

In his analysis of Augustine's pear tree story, Kenneth Burke notes the various motives, including his membership in a "band of sinners" (*consortium peccantium*), that incite Augustine to sin. But in his complementary analysis of Genesis 3, and of Adam's and Eve's original theft of forbidden fruit, Burke cites the dialectical problem

91. *Sapientior*, the usual OL reading in Gen. 3.1 (*Vetus latina* 2:56), is used by Augustine, *GenM* 2.1.2, 2.14.20; and noted, *GenL* 11.2.4 (as *sapientissimus*; vr. with *prudentissimus*, used in *GenL* in 11.1.1). Augustine, *Civ* 12.16, plays on the gustatory sense of *sapere*, citing Rom. 12.3 ("non plus sapere quam oportet sapere"). Cf. Bernard of Clairvaux, *De gradibus humilitatis et superbiae* 10.30, citing this verse in reference to Eve's temptation and fall.

92. Vance, *Mervelous Signals*, p. 19, refers to "an unworthy social bond that incites Augustine's 'fall.' "

of "language and the negative" that informs the Fall and its recapitulations. In brief, the discourse of authority or the law contains the seeds of its own subversion: "The thou-shalt-not is itself implicitly a condition of temptation, since the negative contains the principle of its own annihilation." As a result, in the original Garden, and elsewhere, "the 'No trespassing' signs of empire . . . both stimulate desires and demand their repression."[93] Like Adam and Eve themselves, the youthful Augustine can resist everything except temptation.

In turning Fall typology upon rhetoricians and their abuses of eloquence, Augustine censures not only himself, his fellow students, and his schoolteachers but also heretical preachers such as Faustus, the Manichean bishop whom he encountered in Carthage during his twenty-ninth year. Like his story of the pear tree, Augustine's picture of Faustus as a seductive master of eloquence offers yet another gloss on the Tree of Eloquence. Comparing Faustus to the archetypal Tempter, he depicts him as using "snares," as offering dangerous food or drink disguised with *suavitas*, as deceptively using *decorum*, and so forth.

Augustine introduces Faustus (*Conf* 5.3) as "a great snare [*laqueus*] of the Devil," an image for rhetorical entrapment that he elsewhere links directly to the Serpent's speech.[94] The typological gloss on the Manichean as a tool of the Devil harks back to Augustine's first commentary on Genesis, which compares Manichean preachers in general to the Serpent.[95] According to Augustine, the bishop's appeal lay mainly in his *suavitas*: "What charmed people was the smoothness [or "sweetness"] of his language [*suaviloquentia*]." Enriching the alimentary imagery to suggest the forbidden food of the Fall, Augustine goes on to say that Faustus used "the dish and adornment of a fine style" to attract his audience to the knowledge (*scientia*) that he would set before them to be "consumed" (*comedendum*). Knowledge is of course what the Tree represents

93. Burke, *The Rhetoric of Religion*, pp. 93–101 ("band," etc.), 187 ("language and the negative"), 218–19 ("thou-shalt-not," "signs"). Augustine, *GenL* 8.13.29, notes that evil did not inhere in the forbidden Tree and that God's decree alone defined the offense.

94. *Conf* 6.12: "It was by means of me that the serpent began to speak to Alypius himself. My tongue was used to weave sweet snares [*dulces laqueos*] and scatter them in his path to trap his free and unsuspecting feet"; the verb *inplicare* ("to catch, trap") appears in both passages. The Devil's "snare" (*laqueus*) originates in 1 Tim. 3.7, with reference to bishops; cf. 2 Tim. 2.26.

95. *GenM* 2.25.38 ("[the serpent] signifies the poisons of the heretics and especially of these Manichees").

and what the Serpent offers to Eve in the form of the forbidden fruit.[96]

A few chapters later, Augustine reinforces the Fall typology by citing again the Manichean's *suavitas* and now also his verbal *decorum* as a "waiter" (*ministrator*) tempting his audience with delicious but deadly "drink": "He came out with exactly the same things as the others are always saying, but he did it much more elegantly [*multo suavius*]. However, my thirst could not be relieved by expensive drinking vessels and a well-dressed waiter.... Nor could I consider the soul wise because the face was attractive and the words well chosen [*decorum*]" (*Conf* 5.6). The tempter's "attractive" (*congruus*) face recalls the Serpent's qualities as a "fitting" instrument for Satan's rhetorical purposes.[97] There follow further allusions to the original tempter and the meretricious verbal "delight" involved in the Fall: "And as to those who promised me so much of him, they were not good judges of things. Their reason for thinking him wise and intelligent [*prudens et sapiens*] was simply that his way of speaking gave them pleasure [*delectabat*]."

To sum up, Augustine's satirical portrait of Faustus as a suave waiter promotes the Fall as the archetypal pattern of rhetorical abuse. At the same time, it adapts the typology of the Fall to Roman eloquence in particular and to the life of the leisured and lettered class whose secular rhetorical education Augustine condemns as a marketplace where souls are bought and sold.[98] Furthermore, while the Faustus episode highlights the youthful Augustine's own susceptibility to fallen rhetoric, in the larger cultural sphere it exemplifies the patristic notion that the tempter's voice was still to be heard in heretical preachers and other enemies of the church.

As with Augustine's hermeneutics, his main gloss on rhetoric and the Fall in the *Confessions* appears in the conversion narrative, with its typological garden, tempting voices, and fig tree—yet another symbolic Tree of Eloquence. The conversion, as a recapitulation of the Fall, embodies not only Augustine's return to "redeemed speech" after years of abusing eloquence in the service of unworthy ends but also a symbolic redemption of eloquence

96. The Vulg. uses the verb *comedere* ("to eat") throughout Genesis 2–3, though the OL cited by Augustine uses the related term *edere*, in alternation (some versions) with *manducare*.

97. *Civ* 14.11 ("operi suo congruum," as cited earlier). As a "well-dressed [*decentissimus*] waiter," Faustus further embodies *decorum*.

98. "I would gently withdraw from [teaching rhetoric].... I had been bought by you and was not going to return again to put myself up for sale" (*Conf* 9.2).

itself from pagan and secular uses.[99] Before his conversion, as a secular teacher of rhetoric, Augustine was "weaving words" and "wearing lies" in the fashion of Adam and Eve. Afterward, quitting his post as a self-described "vendor of words" and "professor of lies" (4.2, 8.6, 9.2), he turns instead to professing God's word and to preaching in emulation of the divine eloquence embodied in Scripture. Augustine's conversion sets a pattern for the rest of his life and work as a rhetorician and for the rhetorical mission of patristic culture at large.

In describing his rhetorical conversion, Augustine uses the garden at Milan not only typologically to represent the original Garden of temptation but also tropologically to symbolize the "paradise of the soul." Thus Augustine specifies that his inner crisis takes place in a "little garden" (*hortulus*): "To this garden the tumult in my heart [*tumultus pectoris*] had driven me, as to a place where no one could intervene in this passionate suit which I had brought against myself until it could be settled."[100]

A lengthy temptation scenario precedes Augustine's readerly epiphany, and consistent with his other glosses on the rhetoric of the Fall he highlights here the psychology of persuasion. Having already identified himself as a "son of Adam" (8.9, 10), Augustine plays Adam to an Eve embodied by tempting female "voices," which represent seductive stimuli that address the soul from either the senses, or the memory, or the imagination. Describing these tempting "voices" at length, Augustine emphasizes the carnal nature of their urgings:

> Toys and trifles, utter vanities had been my mistresses, and now they were holding me back, pulling me by the garment of my flesh and softly murmuring in my ear: "Are you getting rid of us?" and "From this moment shall we never be with you again for all eternity?" and "From this moment will you never for all eternity be allowed to do this or to do that?" My God, what was it, what was it that they suggested in those words "this" or "that" which I have just written? I pray you in your mercy to keep such things from the soul of your servant. How filthy, how shameful were these things they were suggesting! And now their voices were not half

---

99. On "redeemed speech," see Colish, *The Mirror of Language*, pp. 30–33; and, on Augustine's rhetorical conversion, Vance, *Mervelous Signals*, pp. 24–27.

100. *Conf* 8.8; the "suit" (*litem*) against himself, like the later forensic trope, "the controversy [*controversia*] in my heart" (8.11), points to the rhetorical nature of his crisis.

> so loud in my ears; now they no longer came out boldly to con-
> tradict me face to face; it was more as though they were muttering
> behind my back, stealthily pulling at my sleeve as I was going away
> so that I should turn and look at them. (8.11)

Although some tangible and visual stimuli are suggested here,
the temptation is cast mainly in verbal (and specifically vocal) terms:
"murmuring in my ear," "words," "voices," "muttering."[101] Furthermore, like the original tempter, Augustine's temptresses are
fond of questions, particularly rhetorical ones. As part of a Fall tropology, the female voices represent the "feminine" appetite ("Eve")
"persuading" the "masculine" reason ("Adam") into sin. Though
disembodied, these voices are sensual, suggesting the "feminine"
power of language or eloquence to arouse desire.[102] In their feminine
quality, in their whispering or murmuring, and in their suggested
subject matter ("How filthy, how shameful!"), they embody the
pleasure principle of language stressed by Augustine's rhetorical theory and practice.

In calling "shameful" (*dedecora*) the sins to which he here alludes, Augustine heightens the incongruity between decorous word
and sensual deed, between eloquence itself and the sinful motives
it serves. That Augustine's own temptation scenario might be dangerous to the reader only underscores the power of eloquence to
elicit sin. Having veiled the exact nature of his fleshly temptations,
he retreats from the narrated moment to the moment of narration:
"What was it that they suggested in those words 'this' or 'that' which
I have just written?" Putting things down not only selectively but
also in narrative retrospect gives Augustine a kind of moral distance
from his former temptations and keeps the unspeakable "this" or
"that" (however eloquently spoken) below the reader's threshhold
of hearing.

As he struggles with himself in the garden of his soul, Augustine
hears the voices of the mistresses fade away with the approach of
the motherly figure of Continentia (Continence), rather as the seductive muses do at the approach of Lady Philosophy in Boethius's

---

101. Cf. *Conf* 10.33 on "the delights of the sense of hearing," and Hartman on
the "lust of the ears," as cited above, note 1.

102. Although here subordinated to the tropological Eve ("appetite"), the Serpent
("suggestion") is also figuratively present—that is, "these things they were suggesting" (*suggerebant*).

later variation of this scene.[103] By contrast with various temptresses modeled on Eve, Continentia is one of several redemptive female figures in the story of Augustine's life. Accordingly she personifies a chaste eloquence: "She was calm and serene, cheerful without wantonness, and it was in truth and honor that she was enticing [*honeste blandiens*] me to come to her" (8.11). Continentia's virtuous "enticement" accords completely with Augustine's rhetorical question why eloquence, so often used in the service of falsehood or evil, should not be used to serve the truth (*Doc* 4.2.3, as cited earlier). Here the verb *blandiri* ("to coax, flatter"), which Augustine elsewhere applies to Eve's temptation of Adam (by way of Solomon's wives), boldly asserts the rightful use of persuasion in a good cause.[104]

Augustine dramatizes this virtuous eloquence by putting words in the mouth of Continentia and making her plead for his soul as she "smiles" at him encouragingly. Through a verbal echo, this "encouraging" (*hortatoria*) gesture renews the association of the garden (*hortulus*) with eloquence, though now the virtuous and redemptive art rather than the tempting, seductive one. Accompanied by figures who represent the sexual virtue that she personifies, Continentia "speaks" to Augustine: "Can you not do what these men and these women have done? Or do you think that their ability is in themselves and not in the Lord their God? It was the Lord God who gave them to me. Why do you try and stand by yourself, and so not stand at all? Let Him support you. Do not be afraid. He will not draw away and let you fall [*cadere*]. Put yourself fearlessly in His hands. He will receive you and will make you well." Like the mistresses, Continentia begins with questions, but these queries soon modulate into encouraging indicatives and imperatives. Moreover, her speech, though brief, displays the tightly controlled rhetorical style so typical of Augustine's prose.[105]

Continuing in this new, contained, rhetorical mood, Continentia concludes by warning Augustine against the "lust of the ears" in particular: "Stop your ears against those unclean members of

103. Boethius (480?–524), *De consolatione philosophiae* 1.1 (prose); ed. and trans. S.J. Tester, *Boethius: The Theological Tractates, The Consolation of Philosophy*, rev. ed., LCL (London, 1973).

104. *Civ* 14.11 ("blanditiis femineis"). Cf. Avitus, *Poematum* 2.134, "nunc simulat blandum" (of the Serpent).

105. Continentia speaks in clauses of similar length (*compar*), repeating terms at the beginnings and ends of clauses (*repetitio, conversio*), with implied contraries or antitheses (*contentio*), zeugma (*conjunctio*), and rhetorical questions (*interrogatio*).

yours, so that they may be mortified. They tell you of delights, but not of such delights as the law of the Lord your God tells" (quoting Ps. 118.85). The contrast between divine law (lex) and seductive delights (*delectationes*) recalls the conflict between the "higher" (divine) and "lower" (diabolical) voices in the first Garden.[106] Here "they" (*illa*) are obviously the tempting voices, but the "delights" that they tell of (*narrant*) can stand for any abuse of eloquence that Augustine has so far placed in the shadow of the Tree: pagan myths, poetic fables, heresies, or lies and falsehood in general. In medieval moral literature, Augustine's temptation scenario, with its quotation from the Psalmist, helped make "stopping the ears" into virtually a physical strategy for warding off verbal temptation.[107]

In the next chapter (8.12), Augustine uses typology to emphasize that a crisis and conversion of rhetoric are under way. In his emotional tumult he throws himself down and weeps under a fig tree (*sub quadam fici arbore*). Pointing back to the fig tree of Genesis 3, among other biblical antecedents, this tree is not only a hermeneutical emblem but also a specifically rhetorical one. As a rhetorician, Augustine has for many years been hiding among the "leaves" of false eloquence, "weaving" false coverings for himself and improperly enjoying the sweet "fruit" of secular eloquence. But now a divine eloquence, both sweet and nutritious, offers itself to him instead of the "pernicious sweetness" of the false and fatal art.

Marcia Colish notes that the climax of Augustine's conversion is expressly rhetorical in its dynamics: it takes place "through speech —literally, the words of Scripture, and figuratively, the eloquence of moral example."[108] Augustine's response to both the spoken *tolle lege* and the silent, readerly *sortes biblicae* presumes that God is addressing him, even "speaking" to him, through other agents. Thus Augustine hears the chanting voice "as a divine command to me [*mihi*]"; and he reads the text, on the model of St. Anthony, "as though the words read were spoken directly to himself [*tamquam sibi*]." The divine "oracle" addresses Augustine in the imperative voice ("Take it and read it"; "Put ye on the Lord Jesus Christ"), reinforcing the dialogical, I-Thou, relation between the divine "speaker" and the human audience. Of course, both of these redemptive "speech" acts involve mediating agents—the child's voice, the apostolic book—but Augustine treats them as though they em-

106. *Lib* 3.25.74, as cited earlier.
107. E.g., *Ancrene Wisse*, as discussed below, Chapter 5.2.
108. Colish, *The Mirror of Language*, p. 32.

body and articulate the *vox Dei* itself.[109] In its typological setting, this divine "ventriloquism" provides a counterpoint to the diabolical ventriloquism that runs like a leitmotif through Augustine's glosses on the Fall.

Occupying the role of audience rather than rhetor, Augustine registers the rhetorical dynamics of his conversion in terms of outward and inward responses to both voice and written text. The singing or chanting voice literally *moves* him excitedly toward God: "I went eagerly back [*concitus redii*] to the place where...I had left the book." As for the climactic act of reading, its rhetorical power is measured by its aftereffects: "I had no wish to read further [*nec ultra volui legere*]; there was no need to. For immediately I had reached the end of this sentence it was as though my heart was filled with a light of confidence." Motion, excitement, fulfillment—Augustine's affective responses bespeak the legitimate power of divine eloquence not only to teach but also to move and to delight the audience.

Ambrose had said that in Scripture "we seem to be listening to the very voice of the Lord," and Augustine defined Scripture as a divine eloquence (*eloquentia*) "perfectly adjusted to stir the hearts of all learners."[110] Not only did God speak the highest wisdom and truth through Scripture, but also in literary terms the Bible was the equal of classical literature—in Peter Brown's words, "a classic as inexhaustible and as all-absorbing as Vergil or Homer had been to the pagans."[111] As a trained rhetorician, Augustine is at no loss to demonstrate the divine eloquence embodied in Scripture, enumerating a wide array of stylistic devices used there.[112] Yet he does not reduce Scripture to the traditional "precepts of eloquence" or a mere catalog of rhetorical devices, for he holds that Scripture's eloquence depends on the listener's active engagement with the text: "A good listener warms to it not so much by diligently analyzing it as by pronouncing it energetically [*ardenter pronuntietur*]. For these words were not devised by human industry, but were poured forth from the divine

109. One MS. has *diuina domo* (instead of *uicina domo*), implying a divine voice (ed. Skutella, p. 177, apparatus).

110. Ambrose, *Par* 8.39 ("vocem Domini"). Augustine, *Epistola* 55.7.13, as cited in Brown, *Augustine of Hippo*, p. 259.

111. Brown, *Augustine of Hippo*, p. 263.

112. See *Doc* 4.20.39–4.21.45. Later authors emulated this rhetorical analysis of Scripture, also citing Scripture as the ultimate source of poetic genres and figures. On biblical rhetoric, see Curtius, *European Literature*, pp. 46–48; and, on biblical poetics, his chap. 12.

mind both wisely and eloquently" (*Doc* 4.7.21). Such "warmth" was crucial to the art of preaching, whose fifth and final part was oral "delivery" (*pronunciatio*).[113]

For Augustine, divine eloquence must engage the whole being—both body and soul—of speaker, listener, and reader. Precisely this total absorption by God's word is what he puts in the place of classical literary culture, especially pagan poetry, with its distracting ability to seduce the individual away from the truth. Besides weeping for Dido while reading Virgil and thus "wandering" in the "tracks" of poetic fictions, Augustine during his school days had competed in rhetorical declamations on pagan themes for which the prize went to whoever performed "the best imitation of the passions of anger and grief and found the most appropriate words to express his meaning" (*Conf* 1.17). By contrast with this passionate fallen rhetoric, Augustine's ideal for the redemptive art of preaching is the "ardently" uttered divine word. This word is the basis for the church's whole rhetorical continuum of "interpreting, expounding, teaching, discussing, praising, and praying" (*Conf* 13.23; trans. modified). Though Augustine may read "in silence" the text that converts him back to God, as a result he spends much of his remaining life proclaiming that word aloud.[114] Furthermore, in preaching God's word, Augustine does not rely ultimately on his own invention or style but takes inspiration directly from the *vox Dei*, submerging his own voice in scriptural paraphrase or quotation, as in the powerful cadences that close the *Confessions*: "This must be asked of you, sought in you, knocked for at you. So, so shall it be received, so shall it be found, so shall it be opened."[115] In such fashion, the divine eloquence that converts Augustine away from fallen rhetoric embodies also his broader vision for a culture of redeemed and redemptive eloquence.

6. Conclusion

Patristic culture defined the Fall as the archetypal crisis of eloquence and hence as a source for both the theory and practice of rhetorical

113. On preaching and "warmth," see also *Doc* 4.18.37.

114. Right after his conversion Augustine engages in a discussion of Scripture with Alypius.

115. *Conf* 13.38 ("A te petatur, in te quaeratur, ad te pulsetur; sic, sic, accipietur, sic invenietur, sic aperietur"; cf. Matt. 7.7–8). See Curtius, *European Literature*, p. 74 ("Here rhetoric becomes poetry").

art, as framed by an overarching theology of eloquence. On the historical level, patristic glosses on the Fall as a rhetorical scene stressed the abuse of persuasive technique by the tempter and his understudy Eve as these contributed to Adam's fall and hence to the collective Fall of humankind. Allegorically, the fruit and leaves of the forbidden Tree stood for the "sweet" and "covering" tendencies of fallen rhetoric in general, as abused by Adam and Eve and their descendants. The fall of rhetoric in turn had made necessary the divine acts of redemptive eloquence embodied in Christ and Scripture and imitated in the eloquence of the church. Patristic culture thus found in the Garden, or founded there, a comprehensive vision for the corporate and personal practice of rhetoric in the service of the divine Word.

Patristic culture left to the Middle Ages not only a substantial body of lore about eloquence and the Fall but also some persistent problems, problems complicated by the dispersal of this lore through vernacular literature. In their prose treatises, exegetes could isolate and disarm the rhetoric of temptation through moral commentary and critique. But as poets increasingly dramatized the Fall, and as moralists sketched social and domestic scenarios based on Genesis 3, it became necessary to compose more speeches for the characters, thus activating the fictive and seductive resources of language that the Fall, as a moral exemplum, was supposed to warn against and check. There was little danger that the audience would mistake Satan, the villain of the piece, for a hero; or Eve, the femme fatale, for a clever wench or witty noblewoman deserving emulation. But as they adapted the Fall in increasingly detailed terms to the lives, needs, attitudes, and circumstances of medieval people, authors had to confront the problem of language and the Fall in terms of audience response to these supposedly edifying works.

This problem can be seen quite early in the Anglo-Saxon poetry on the Fall that is modeled largely on Avitus and that emerges about the time of Charlemagne. As composed in (or translated into) the language and culture of Anglo-Saxon England, the story of the Fall continued to reflect concern with heresy and seductive eloquence (as embodied in Augustine's satire of Faustus the Manichean) as well as more local themes. The Fall was used to address the sexual politics of persuasion, but even more so the crisis of eloquence embodied by the conflict between the old tradition of oral poetry and a new scriptural poetry written in the monasteries. Claiming the moral high ground in the garden of eloquence, monks used the Fall to warn against the rhetorical arts of the old Serpent still lurking in the native vegetation.

Another problem of rhetoric and the Fall emerged later in the context of moral treatises and handbooks written for an increasingly literate laity. Medieval moralists liked to evoke seduction scenarios based on the Fall for the benefit of their readers, especially women. But moralists could go only so far in detailing what such seductions might involve, verbally and otherwise, as anticipated by Augustine in his temptation/conversion story, which mutes the sensual suggestions of his "mistresses." Medieval moralists were similarly aware that a too-detailed account of sin could itself lead into temptation, thus defeating their own purpose. Medieval penitential literature confronts the related problem that confession brings men and women not only into close quarters but also onto dangerous topics. Evoking a patristic emblem for fallen rhetoric, moralists urged their readers to "strip off" the "fig leaves" of self-excusing words and to confess themselves "nakedly"—but not *too* nakedly, lest the confession arouse either themselves or the priest.

Finally, secular poets writing in the vernacular also inherited certain problems of rhetoric and the Fall. Some poets were obviously concerned that the laity, in reading books of their own, might abuse texts in specifically rhetorical ways. In perhaps the most famous medieval example, Dante links Paolo and Francesca to Adam and Eve, offering a palinode to readers and authors alike about the seductive power of literary rhetoric. Furthermore, the very rise of a vernacular secular literature raised anew the old question of whether such rhetorical art was of a piece with the "weaving" of words inaugurated in the Garden. Even as a typological emblem, the tree in Augustine's garden points toward the autotelic potential of language, a rhetoric and poetics of the self.[116] Increasingly worldly, sensual, and self-preoccupied, the secular literature of the later Middle Ages often seems to play and revel in the very shade of the Tree of Eloquence that patristic culture regarded with such suspicion.

116. See Freccero, "The Fig Tree and the Laurel."

Part Two

The Medieval Garden

Chapter 4

The Old English Epic of the Fall

[The monks] should not put their trust in spoken words,
but in the reading of the truth. These are perilous times, as
the apostles foretold, for many false teachers now rise up
and, introducing new sects, strive to darken the
purity of the catholic faith.
—*Alcuin of York*

DURING WHAT USED to be called the Dark Ages, when the schools
of the Roman Empire had died out and the medieval universities
had not yet been born, the garden of letters was to be found mainly
in the monasteries, which kept patristic learning alive and also nourished an early vernacular poetry on religious subjects, including the
Fall. English is the vernacular with the oldest extant poetic tradition,
including one of the best early poems on the Fall—*Genesis B*, an
anonymous ninth-century work that recounts the Fall in some 600
lines of native alliterative meter. One of several biblical poems collected in the Junius manuscript (ca. 1000), *Genesis B* once was
thought to be the work of Caedmon but now is recognized as the
product of later and more learned clerics using native oral-heroic
poetry as a vessel for Christianity. It was translated (or transliterated)
from a slightly earlier Old Saxon poem on the Fall and reflects the
close literary ties prevailing between England and the continent
while Alcuin was Charlemagne's chief scholar (780–804), and renewed during the reign of Alfred the Great (871–99), the English
king at whose court the poem may have been translated. As a learned
religious poem in the native Germanic poetic style, *Genesis B* thus
locates the Fall at various linguistic and cultural junctures. The
hybrid nature of the poem makes it especially fruitful for early medieval ideas about language and the Fall. In particular, *Genesis B*

recounts the Fall from the viewpoint of a clerical Christian culture based on written tradition and superseding a pagan heroic culture based on oral tradition.[1]

For much the same reason that Luther set church hymns to tavern songs ("Why should the Devil have all the good tunes?"), English clerics appropriated the powerful vehicle of native oral poetry to promulgate sacred history and doctrine.[2] During the eighth and ninth centuries, tribal poetry, if it still existed, "tended to disappear," giving way to religious poems in the heroic style as "biblical epics came to be written in the monasteries."[3] Although the fortunes of English monasticism fluctuated during this period, biblical epics were written and read by English monks from as early as the time of Caedmon (fl. 670) until the Conquest, when Norman influences in the English church shifted patronage away from the Anglo-Saxon poetic tradition.[4]

As a poem converting heroic motifs to Christian uses, *Genesis B* characterizes Satan as a disloyal thane of God who is exiled to Hell, where he plots out his revenge against the Lord, planning to persuade Adam and Eve to a similar disloyalty in Paradise and, hence, to an exile like his own. After God gives his command to the humans and departs from the Garden, the Tempter (a thane of Satan who answers his fettered lord's call for a volunteer) "arms" himself with crafty words, travels from hell to earth, and there represents himself—first to Adam and then to Eve—as a messenger

1. *Genesis B* (or *The Later Genesis*) is so-called to distinguish it from the older (8th c.) *Genesis A* into which it is interpolated in Oxford Bodleian MS. Junius 11. All citations are from *The Junius Manuscript*, in *ASPR*, ed. George Philip Krapp and Elliott Van Kirk Dobbie, 6 vols. (New York, 1931–53), 1:9–28 (ll. 235–851). Unless otherwise noted, translations (incl. *Genesis A*) are from Charles W. Kennedy, *Early English Christian Poetry Translated into Alliterative Verse* (New York, 1952), pp. 35–37, 48–71. Other editions include Benno J. Timmer, *The Later Genesis*, rev. ed. (Oxford, 1954); John F. Vickrey, "*Genesis B*: A New Analysis and Edition" (University of Indiana diss., 1960); and, most recently, Alger N. Doane, ed. and comm., *The Saxon Genesis: An Edition of the West Saxon Genesis B and the Old Saxon Vatican Genesis* (Madison, Wis., 1991). Major criticism is reviewed in Stanley B. Greenfield, Daniel G. Calder, and Michael Lapidge, *A New Critical History of OE Literature* (New York, 1986), pp. 209–12. On the poem's provenance, see *ASPR* 1:xxv–xxvi; Michael J. Capek, "The Nationality of a Translator: Some Notes on the Syntax of *Genesis B*," *Neophilologus* 55 (1971): 89–96; and now Doane, *Saxon Genesis*, pp. 51–54.

2. See Greenfield et al., *New Critical History*, chaps. 7 and 8; and Jeff Opland, *Anglo-Saxon Oral Poetry: A Study of the Traditions* (New Haven, 1980), chap. 5.

3. Opland, *Anglo-Saxon Oral Poetry*, p. 160.

4. On the monastic background to OE literature, see references in Greenfield et al., *New Critical History*, chaps. 1–3.

from God, eventually tricking the humans into breaking God's command. On one level, then, *Genesis B* is a traditional Germanic war story in which a defeated lord seeks revenge against the victorious overlord by promising rewards to a thane who is successful in a quasi-military raid against the other lord's thanes.[5] In thus pouring the new wine of sacred history into the old skins of Germanic heroic poetry, *Genesis B* furthered the biblical poetics that held Scripture to be the true and original epic.[6]

While the biblical poetics broadly implicit in *Genesis B* imitates the example of Avitus and other Christian Latin poets who converted pagan poetry to religious use, the poem also follows specific patristic themes, particularly in treating the Fall as a paradigm for language. Patristic ideas about language and the Fall were widely available in Saxon and English monasteries during the eighth and ninth centuries, when scholars such as the Venerable Bede (d. 735), Alcuin (d. 804), Hrabanus Maurus (d. 856), and John Scotus Erigena (d. 877?) perpetuated and amplified Augustinian glosses on the Fall in their own treatises and biblical commentaries.[7]

Augustine and other seminal exegetes had treated the Fall as a crisis of instruction in which Satan taught falsehood or "heresy" to Adam and Eve and subverted the lines of authority in Paradise. A central theme of *Genesis B* is that the Tempter, as a self-claimed messenger from God, persuades the humans to exchange God's teaching for his own, false doctrine (*lar*). Following patristic hermeneutical themes, the poem also depicts the Fall as a crisis of signs and interpretation, with the Tempter offering Eve a false vision which she in turn uses as a sign (*tacen*) to persuade Adam that the Tempter indeed speaks for God. Finally, *Genesis B* shows its continuity with patristic tradition by casting the Fall as a crisis of rhetoric. The many persuasive speeches in the poem, like those in

5. See John M. Evans, "*Genesis B* and Its Background," *RES*, n.s. 14 (1963): 1–16, (and esp.) 113–23; and Michael D. Cherniss, "Heroic Ideals and the Moral Climate of *Genesis B*," *MLQ* 30 (1969): 479–97. The mixture of patristic and native Germanic elements in OE poems on the Fall, including *Genesis B*, is also examined in the early study by Charles Abbetmeyer, *Old English Poetical Motives Derived from the Doctrine of Sin* (Minneapolis, 1903). For texts, see Friedrich Klaeber, ed., *The Later Genesis and Other Old English and Old Saxon Texts Relating to the Fall of Man* (Heidelberg, 1913).

6. See Curtius, *European Literature*, chap. 12 (especially pp. 219–20).

7. On sources and influences, see Evans, "*Genesis B* and Its Background," pp. 1–16; Susan Burchmore, "Traditional Exegesis and the Question of Guilt in the Old English *Genesis B*," *Traditio* 41 (1985): 117–44; and Doane, *Saxon Genesis*, chap. 7, and pp. 148–50 (Ambrose, Augustine). On Avitus in particular, see Evans, pp. 12–15.

Avitus, dramatize the major role of seductive eloquence in the Fall and suggest that the Fall involves a corruption of this art; moreover, the Tempter instructs Eve in the art of successfully persuading Adam, as Eve shows by repeating many of her teacher's words.

Genesis B reflects not only patristic ideas about language and the Fall but also the more local concerns and attitudes of the churchmen who composed, translated, and preserved the poem. During the eighth and ninth centuries in England and Saxony, the church was assailed by heathens from without and riven by heresy within. Boniface was martyred by pagan Frisians in 754, and from the late eighth century and throughout the ninth, hordes of heathen Vikings repeatedly fell upon England and Saxony, sacking and burning, extorting and killing. The terrifying Norsemen clearly represented to Christians a militant diabolism that may well be personified in the helmeted Tempter of Genesis B—"God's enemy ready in his wargear"—whose raid on Paradise involves lies, threats, and ultimately death.[8] The Norse, eventually settling in England and holding large territories there even after the English resurgence under Alfred, embodied not only a material threat but also a spiritual one to the English church, as may be seen from a papal letter (ca. 891–96) castigating the English bishops for their laxity toward the "unspeakable rites of the pagans" in their midst.[9]

Besides a rampant paganism, serious questions were raised in the ninth century about the prevailing "Augustinian synthesis" of doctrine within the church itself.[10] Authorities such as John Scotus Erigena and Ratramnus claimed that although the fathers had laid to rest many heresies in their own day, the Devil was now again attacking "the fortified walls of the faith" and spreading "new poisons of unbelief."[11] During the ninth century, the most notable heresy to touch Saxony, where Genesis B originated, was that of Gottschalk, a Saxon monk who taught so severe a doctrine of predestination that his teachings were condemned as heretical (in 847

8. 442–43 ("godes andsaca / fus on frætwum"), trans. modified. The Battle of Maldon (based on events in 991 A.D.) emphasizes that lies were crucial to the Viking strategy (l. 86) and that the raiders were heathens ("hæþene," 55); ASPR 6:8–9.

9. ("nefandos ritus paganorum") Cartularium Saxonicum: A Collection of Charters Relating to Anglo-Saxon History, ed. Walter de Gray Birch, 3 vols. (1885–93; rpt. New York, 1964), 2:215 (no. 573). On the letter's authenticity, see Frank M. Stenton, Anglo-Saxon England, 3d ed. (Oxford, 1971), p. 435.

10. See Pelikan, The Christian Tradition, vol. 3, chap. 2.

11. John Scotus Erigena, De praedestinatione (On Predestination) 1.4; PL 122: 347–440; Ratramnus, Liber de nativitate Christi (On the Parturition of Saint Mary) 1.1; PL 121:81–102; as cited and trans. in Pelikan, The Christian Tradition 3:51.

and again in 849). Scholars differ over whether *Genesis B* reflects this particular crisis—and, if so, exactly how.[12] But certainly the general problem of heresy is indicated by the poem's thematic treatment of the Fall as a paradigm of false teaching or doctrine (*lar*).[13] Regarding continental affairs, *Genesis B* (as originally an Old Saxon poem) may also allude to court intrigues involving Charlemagne's son, Louis the Pious (d. 840), and his influential second wife, Judith.[14]

Apart from pagan threats, heresy, and political turmoil, *Genesis B* mirrors the attitudes of the continental and English clerics involved in writing biblical poems in the native oral style while striving to transcend the traditional ethos of the latter.[15] Even more or less secular heroic poems such as *Beowulf* are clerical productions that embody an antagonism toward the older, oral culture they depict, dramatizing that the volatile, violent, and ultimately doomed nature of tribal culture is linked to its exclusive reliance on oral tradition and memory for its sense of identity and social cohesion. *Genesis B* similarly depicts the Fall as a tragedy of oral culture by showing how easily oral tradition is corrupted when Adam and Eve abandon their direct memory of God's word and accept instead the Tempter's "report" of God's speech. The poem dramatizes how oral

12. Evans, *Paradise Lost and the Genesis Tradition*, p. 166, suggests that *Genesis B* reacts against Gottschalk by showing Adam and Eve with a relatively free will and intellect, thus "accepting the letter while excluding the spirit of Augustinianism." For the theological points at dispute, see Pelikan, *The Christian Tradition* 3:80–98; and Doane, *Saxon Genesis*, pp. 102–7.

13. For semantics, see Joseph Bosworth and T. Northcote Toller, eds., *An Anglo-Saxon Dictionary* (Oxford, 1898) and *Supplement*, ed. T. Northcote Toller (1921), with *Enlarged Addenda and Corrigenda to the Supplement*, ed. Alistair Campbell (1972), s.v. *lar*. (This work is hereafter cited as B-T, *Dictionary* or *Supplement*.) On the poem's instructional terms and themes, see Margaret J. Ehrhart, "Tempter as Teacher: Some Observations on the Vocabulary of the Old English *Genesis B*," *Neophilologus* 59 (1975): 435–46. Burchmore, "Traditional Exegesis," p. 137n, links this vocabulary to heresy as "an important theme" in the poem. The Fall as a crisis of teaching is thematic in Aelfric's homilies, roughly contemporaneous with the Junius MS. (ca. 1000); for example, "death came to us through Adam from the teaching [*lare*] of the Serpent who mistaught [*forlærde*] him" (*Homilies of Aelfric: A Supplementary Collection*, ed. John C. Pope, 2 vols., EETS OS 259–60 [London, 1967–68], 2:656).

14. See the fascinating study by Carol A. Bradof, "*Genesis B*, Carolingian History, and the Germanic Heroic Tradition" (Columbia University diss., 1990).

15. Scholars have recently stressed the ways in which manuscript culture defined itself over and against oral tradition. See Michael T. Clanchy, *From Memory to Written Record, England, 1066–1307* (Cambridge, Mass., 1979); Jesse Gellrich, "Orality, Literacy, and Crisis in the Later Middle Ages," *PQ* 67 (1988): 461–73; and, on the Anglo-Saxon scene in particular, Seth Lerer, *Literacy and Power in Anglo-Saxon Literature* (Lincoln, Nebr., 1991).

tradition keeps a society unstable, threatening its political order, kinship ties, and inherited knowledge. Before we examine the poem itself, it will be useful to look briefly at the monastic culture of the written word that produced and preserved *Genesis B*.

1. The Word Made Script

As repositories of learning, both classical and Christian, monasteries exalted manuscript books as virtually their sole link with the past. Rather than authoring new books, monks busied themselves mainly with collecting, copying, glossing, illuminating—and of course reading—old ones. Learned men had traditionally held script to be superior to fallible memory, an attitude that had ample precedent in passages like the one in Augustine's *Soliloquies* that calls into question the power of unaided memory to hold on to the truth:

> *Reason:* Can your memory properly preserve all your thoughts?
> *Augustine:* That would be difficult, nay impossible.
> *Reason:* Then you must write [them] down.[16]

Writing, Augustine says, is a way of preserving what is "worth remembering."[17] But it was medieval monastic culture that enshrined writing—in the form of often elaborately illuminated manuscript books—as a vastly superior medium for knowledge and discourse, by comparison with memory and oral tradition.

In monastic culture the sacral aspect of writing received an impetus, particularly in northern lands, from the Germanic cult of runic letters as magical talismans, a cult that partly transferred itself to the Latin alphabet brought by the church.[18] As noted in Chapter 2, Cassiodorus, one of the founders of monastic book culture, had declared that scribes fought against the Devil with pen and ink and that every sacred word written by a scribe was "a wound inflicted on Satan."[19] An Old English metrical gloss on the Lord's Prayer, dating from as late as the tenth century, concretizes this notion by describing the Latin letters (and corresponding runes) that make up

---

16. *Sol* 1.1 ("Ergo scribendum est"); *PL* 32:869–904; trans. John H. S. Burleigh, *The Soliloquies*, in *Augustine: Earlier Writings*, pp. 17–63.

17. *Ord* 2.12.37.

18. See Ralph W. V. Elliott, *Runes: An Introduction*, 2d ed. (Manchester, 1989), chap. 6, esp. p. 81 (citing Bede, etc.).

19. Cassiodorus, *Institutiones* 1.30

the *Pater noster* as weapons for attacking and wounding the Devil: "*P*, for example, has a long rod to scourge the devil," and "T stabs at the devil's tongue."[20]

The monastic notion that knowledge was best embodied and conveyed in books, and that in this form it not only preserved the truth but also could ward off evil, is particularly well attested in the writings of Alcuin, the English scholar and head of the episcopal school at York, who was recruited by Charlemagne (in 780) to direct the emperor's monastic and educational reforms. Alcuin himself wrote a commentary on Genesis that recapitulates many patristic glosses on the Fall and that was later translated into Old English; the Latin original has been cited as a possible source for *Genesis B*.[21] But it is especially Alcuin's ideas about books as cultural repositories—articulated in his treatises, letters and poems—that offer a useful vantage point on *Genesis B*, particularly that poem's virtual equation of the Fall with corruptible oral tradition.[22]

Alcuin regards books as a divine gift helping to compensate for the loss of knowledge incurred with the Fall. Thus one of his poems celebrating Scripture begins by invoking Adam's exile from the "beautiful garden" and various divine compensations for this exile, chief among which is "the great gift of books"; if one hopes for eternal life, "let him read and remember books."[23] Books can restore humans to Paradise, Alcuin suggests elsewhere: "We must bring the flowers of England to France in order that the school of York be no longer merely [a] garden enclosed: the fruits of Paradise will also be able to be plucked in the school of Tours."[24]

20. *Solomon and Saturn I* 84–169, *ASPR* 6:35–37, as paraphrased by Greenfield et al., *New Critical History*, p. 274. On dating, see Neil R. Ker, *Catalogue of Manuscripts Containing Anglo-Saxon* (Oxford, 1957), no. 70A (p. 119).

21. Alcuin, *Interrogationes et responsiones in Genesin*, PL 100:517–66. For analysis, see Evans, "*Genesis B* and Its Background," pp. 1–4. Aelfric, trans., OE version (ca. 1000), ed. George E. MacLean, "Aelfric's Version of *Alcuini Interrogationes Sigeuulfi in Genesin*," *Anglia* 7 (1884): 1–59.

22. Whitney F. Bolton, *Alcuin and Beowulf: An Eighth-Century View* (New Brunswick, N.J., 1978), uses Alcuin's literary theory and practice as a framework for understanding the reception of heroic poetry in the eighth century, a methodology that also makes sense for a ninth-century religious "epic" such as *Genesis B*. For many of Alcuin's remarks cited in this chapter, I am indebted to Bolton's valuable discussion of Alcuin's ideas about writing, books, etc., pp. 13–27. Some of these themes are also noted briefly in Johannot, *Tourner la page*, pp. 79–81.

23. *Carmina* 69.1, 13, 19 ("pulchro fuerat homo pulsus ab horto"; "maxima dona librorum"; "hos legat et teneat"); ed. Ernest Dümmler, *Poetae latini aevi Carolini*, vol. 1, MGH (Berlin, 1881), 288; my trans.

24. *Epistola* 121; ed. Ernst Dümmler, *Epistolae Karolini Aevi*, vol. 2, MGH

While Alcuin values books for preserving past words and deeds and for making these widely available in time and space, he often honors them at the expense of the spoken word. For example, he sees script as a crucial aide-mémoire for speech.[25] Thus he sends one of his own works to a student so that in reading it the latter may refresh (*recreare*) his memory of their discussions, for memory "often loses what it should preserve unless it retains it laid up in the treasurehouse of writing."[26] Alcuin says that Paul's epistles similarly helped readers recall oral instruction in Paul's absence: "The daily reading of letters [fixed] a lasting memory of the father's precepts in the minds of his sons."[27]

For Alcuin, written tradition is a means not only for preserving the truth but also for avoiding error; God's word is too important to be entrusted to mere oral tradition.[28] Thus in the poem praising Scripture he states that "without these [books of the Bible], false knowledge will wickedly seduce the mind that does not wish to learn the holy words of God."[29] Alcuin distrusts oral tradition because it is susceptible to corruption in the form of false teaching or heresy. A letter advising an abbot to have his monks read Scripture warns of the doctrinal contamination associated with oral tradition: "Encourage the brethren to read the Holy Scripture most diligently. They should not put their trust in spoken words [*linguae notitia*], but in the reading of the truth. These are perilous times, as the apostles foretold, for many false teachers now rise up and, introducing new sects, strive to darken the purity of the catholic faith with impious assertions."[30] Calling for soldiers "to defend the city of God," Alcuin echoes Augustine as well as Benedict, whose Rule likens monks to warriors. Alcuin thus anticipates several important motifs in *Genesis B*, particularly the threat posed by false teachers

---

(Berlin, 1895), 177, lines 8–10; as cited in Jean Leclercq, *The Love of Learning and the Desire for God: A Study of Monastic Culture*, trans. Catharine Misrahi, 2d ed. (New York, 1977), p. 52.

25. Bolton, *Alcuin and Beowulf*, p. 14.

26. *Epistola* 80, p. 122, lines 22–23; trans. Bolton, *Alcuin and Beowulf*, p. 14.

27. *Epistola* 83, pp. 126–27, lines 36–01; trans. Bolton, *Alcuin and Beowulf*, p. 14.

28. The clergy's Latin, too, suffered from unchecked oral tradition: "[Alcuin] understood that incorrect speech was caused by the lack of books and of schools" (Leclercq, *The Love of Learning*, p. 52).

29. *Carmina* 69.179–80, ed. Dümmler, p. 292; my trans.

30. *Epistola* 74, p. 117, lines 10–16; trans. Bolton, *Alcuin and Beowulf*, pp. 14–15 (modified and augmented).

(*pseudodoctores*) to true doctrine, the enemy's attack on God's war-rior-thanes, and of course the corruptibility of oral tradition.

Alcuin is well aware, of course, that written tradition, too, is fallible. He himself prepared a corrected text of the Bible at the emperor's behest, and he described heresy as "a defect in literary tradition" and equally as a mistake requiring erasure from the "tables of the heart."[31] But Alcuin sees God's word as mainly a *written* text that provides the basis for a renewed oral proclamation. For Alcuin, the fugitive spoken word as contemplated by Augustine achieves at least partial permanence in writing: "Words have sound-ed from the fleshly mouth and have gone forth in flying sounds ...; but the things themselves, of which the sounds are signs, drawn to some extent into the recollection of those who heard the sounds, have come down to us by means of letters, which are visible signs."[32] As shown earlier in this book, patristic culture regarded writing as not only a sign of the Fall but also a potentially redemptive medium. Stressing the positive aspects of the letter as a sign, monastic culture sought divinity in script itself.[33]

As is well known, medieval readers, especially monks, tended to read aloud "with the lips, pronouncing what they saw, and with the ears, listening to the words pronounced, hearing what is called the 'voices of the pages.' "[34] Thus the daily monastic round of read-ing, liturgy, and divine office converted script back into sounds, but these spoken (or sung or chanted) words still were grounded in writ-ing, even when memory intervened. In the poem on Scripture quoted above, Alcuin details this vocalizing of the text: "Whoever shall read in the sacred body of this book, declaiming in church the sub-lime words of God, let him in speaking distinguish between sen-tences, rubrics, phrases, and breathing pauses, so that he may know how to sound the intonations with his mouth. Let his flowing voice sound at length in the ears of the church, so that every listener may praise God with his mouth."[35] Whereas Augustine had tended to equate spirituality with *silent* reading, a nonbodily discipline of the

---

31. Bolton, *Alcuin and Beowulf*, pp. 22 ("defect"), 20. In the latter passage, Al-cuin urges a heterodox churchman to "erase" heresy from "the pages of your breast [*tabulis tui cordis*]" (*Adversus Elipandum Toletanum* 2.14, *PL* 101:270).

32. *Commentaria in S. Johannis evangelium* 5.31 (John 12.50), *PL* 100:924; trans. Bolton, *Alcuin and Beowulf*, p. 14.

33. Johannot, *Tourner la page*, p. 79 ("c'est maintenant dans le texte qu'on va trouver la divinité").

34. Leclercq, *The Love of Learning*, p. 19.

35. *Carmina* 69.183–88 (p. 292); my trans.

word, Alcuin—and medieval monastic culture generally—equated spirituality with reading *aloud*.[36]

In vocalizing (and memorizing) Scripture, monks were said to "ruminate" on God's word, an alimentary trope that suggests a continual recourse to script to nourish the soul. Augustine had valued a silent "rumination" on God's word with "the mouth of the heart," but monastic culture, following Benedict, reified this metaphor in the active pronunciation of the written word, especially in the *lectio divina*, the scriptural reading that accompanied monastic meals in the refectory.[37] As Jean Leclercq defines it, *ruminatio* meant "assimilating the content of a text by means of a kind of mastication which releases its full flavor."[38] Alcuin alludes to this practice in a famous letter written in 797 to Hygbald, bishop of Lindisfarne: "Let the words of God be read when priests are eating. There let the reader be heard, not the harp; the words of the fathers, not the songs of the people. What has Ingeld to do with Christ?"[39] Another letter likens the *lectio divina* to a repast: "While the body is fed at the meal, let the mind be nurtured by the divine reading."[40] Whereas patristic authors commonly speak of God's word as nourishing the soul, Alcuin tends to stress that this nourishment comes from Scripture as such—a *written* text. The scriptural word is food, and reading is eating. This characteristically monastic notion is an important reference point for *Genesis B*, where Adam and Eve receive but fail to feed on God's *spoken* word, instead swallowing a false oral tradition.

Alcuin's famous rhetorical question—"What has Ingeld to do with Christ?"—often has been taken to suggest that secular heroic songs and poems were common fare in English monasteries and that they competed there with scriptural and other religious material.[41]

36. Augustine, *Conf* 6.3, 8.12; see Gellrich, *The Idea of the Book*, pp. 117–18.

37. Augustine, *Conf* 6.3. *Sancti Benedicti regula* 38: "At the meals of the brethren there should not fail to be reading" (trans. Justin McCann, *The Rule of Saint Benedict in Latin and English* [London, 1941], p. 93).

38. Leclercq, *The Love of Learning*, p. 90; see also pp. 18–22. Augustine, *Conf* 10.14, uses *ruminatio* for the recollection of words and images from memory, "the stomach of the mind" (*venter animi*); but in *Conf* 11.2 he describes readers of Scripture as stags "chewing the cud" (*ruminantes*).

39. *Epistola* 124, p. 183, lines 21–22 ("Verba Dei legantur in sacerdotali convivio. Ibi decet lectorem audiri, non citharistam; sermones patrum, non carmina gentilium. Quid Hinieldus cum Christo?").

40. *Epistola* 173, p. 287, lines 24–25, my trans. Cf. *Carmina ad varios* 260, lines 28–29, *PL* 101:797.

41. However, Opland, *Anglo-Saxon Oral Poetry*, pp. 144–47, contests the view that Alcuin is referring to "the performance of ballads or Heldenlieder concerning

Although it is not clear exactly what Alcuin means by invoking Ingeld, the Germanic hero who figures in *Beowulf*, his puzzling remark seems to disparage oral tradition, in the form of popular songs (*carmina gentilium*), by comparison with the vocalized *lectio* of Scripture that here and elsewhere he so fervently recommends.

Clearer evidence for how monastic culture circumscribed oral poetic tradition appears in the main source for early English church history, the *Ecclesiastical History* written by the Venerable Bede earlier in the eighth century (731). Bede's account of the beginning of English religious poetry, embodied in the Caedmon legend, reflects clerical suspicions of popular oral tradition. In his famous story, Bede tells of how the illiterate cowherd, hearing Scripture read aloud to him, could turn it into poetry overnight: "He by thinking again with himself upon all that he could hear and learn, and chewing [*ruminando*] thereon as a clean beast cheweth the cud, would turn it into a very sweet song; and by melodiously singing the same again would make his teachers to become in their turn his hearers."[42] Here Bede adapts to Caedmon's unusual situation the ideas of "ruminating" on God's word and of memory as the "stomach" of the soul.

Bede's image of the cowherd turned cow-poet, an organ for turning Scripture into poetry, reflects clerical anxiety about the dangers of an oral poetry that is ungrounded in learned, literary tradition. After Caedmon's gift has been revealed, he immediately begins to be "instructed in the regular course of holy history." (Bede notes also that the clerics ask Caedmon to recite his first poem so that they may examine it; that they test new material on him; that after he is approved the abbess urges vows and instruction on him; and that Caedmon never made secular but only religious poems.) Writing more than a century and a half later, the Alfredian translator adds to Bede's account that the clerics who listened to Caedmon's productions also *wrote* them down (*æfter his muðe writon and leornedon*).[43] One may interpret this added detail variously; it suggests not only the fleeting nature of oral poems but also a clerical distrust

---

legendary or heroic figures like Ingeld in the eighth-century Anglo-Saxon monasteries" (p. 147).

42. Bede, *Ecclesiastical History* 4.24; *Baedae opera historica*, trans. J. E. King, 2 vols., LCL (London, 1930), 2:140–51. See Lerer, *Literacy and Power*, pp. 33–34, 42–48, for a detailed analysis of how Bede's story of Caedmon "takes Germanic oral forms and grounds them in texts" (p. 42).

43. *König Alfreds Übersetzung von Bedas Kirchengeschichte*, ed. Jacob Schipper, Bibliothek der angelsächsischen Prosa, vol. 4 (Leipzig, 1899), 486 (col. 2). For discussion, see Opland, *Anglo-Saxon Oral Poetry*, p. 114.

of memory, and perhaps a sense that fire, water, and worms threaten human repositories of the word even more than they do parchment.[44] After Caedmon's "stomach" makes the poetry, it is transferred to a safer place for permanent storage.

Bede provides a list of Caedmon's poetic subjects that includes "the creation of the world, and beginnings of mankind, and all the story of Genesis." *Genesis B* was for a long time ascribed to Caedmon, as part of a "Caedmonian Genesis," partly on the basis of this list. This view of the poem's composition is no longer seriously maintained, but it still suggests an important characteristic of *Genesis B*. The poem is very much in line with the clerical program for religious poetry reflected in Bede's account, particularly the idea that poetry should be grounded on script and Scripture rather than being entrusted to vulnerable oral tradition.

2. The Fall of Oral Tradition

Genesis B equates the Fall with fallible oral-mnemonic tradition by dramatizing that such a tradition is vulnerable to error and misrepresentation.[45] When God addresses Adam and Eve and confides to them his command, he creates an oral tradition based on the *vox Dei*. Adam's initial rebuff to the Tempter preserves this tradition. But when Eve accepts the Tempter's word for God's, this tradition is falsified; and when Adam in turn accepts Eve's word, the new and false oral tradition is extended by yet another link. As long as the humans hold to what they themselves have heard God say, the *vox Dei*, they keep hold of the truth; but when they accept the mediated account of God's word from the Tempter, they open themselves to error.

The first scene in the extant poem is a fragmentary one containing the last two lines of God's command about the forbidden Tree.[46] Significantly, this scene shows God pronouncing the command to *both* Adam and Eve:

"Enjoy every other,   from this one tree refrain;
Beware of its fruit!   Nor shall ye know want,

44. On the mortality of manuscripts, see *Riddle 47, ASPR* 3:205.

45. Parts of this section are drawn from my article "Invoking/Revoking God's Word: The *Vox Dei* in *Genesis B*," *ES* 71 (1990): 307–21.

46. *Genesis B* features a contrasting Tree of Life and Tree of Death (460–90). On this motif, see Katzenellenbogen, *Allegories of the Virtues and Vices in Medieval Art*, pp. 63–68, with reference to poem by Boniface (p. 63, n. 1).

Or dearth of good things." Then they bowed them down
Before heaven's Lord and with grateful hearts
Gave thanks for His counsels.[47]

By including Eve in God's audience—a detail following Avitus rather
than Ambrose and Augustine—the poem unites God and the humans
into an oral community.[48] Each human thus carries a direct oral
memory of God's teaching (*lar*) into his or her encounter with the
Tempter, who appeals to remembered, reported speeches to disrupt
this unmediated oral community.

Before the scene changes, the narrative indicates that after his
speech God returns (*hwærf*, 240) to heaven, thus creating the sense
of divine distance and absence on which the Tempter's ploys will
turn.[49] The narrative also states that Adam and Eve "were God's
beloved / As long as they heeded His holy word"—or as long as they
would "hold" (*healdan*) that word, in the poem's metaphor.[50] The
poem returns to this metaphor repeatedly, though the Temptation
and Fall that follow illustrate the difficulty of "holding" God's word
on the basis of a purely oral, mnemonic tradition, especially when
that word is challenged by a rival oral tradition based on a similar
appeal to memory.[51]

The long scene in Hell that follows (246–441), in which the
fettered Satan procures a volunteer (the Tempter) to go to earth and
deceive the humans, not only sets up a counterplot to the promul-
gation of God's word but also, in terms of narrative structure, sugges-
tively interrupts the course of events in the still unfallen part of
Creation. In terms that stress the imminent assault on the oral
tradition established between God and the humans, Satan, offering
rewards, urges his thanes to make the humans "relinquish God's
word," "abandon his teaching," "break his bidding."[52] A missing

47. 235–39 (" 'ac niotað inc þæs oðres ealles, forlætað þone ænne beam, / wariað
inc wið þone wæstm. Ne wyrð inc wilna gæd.' / Hnigon þa mid heafdum heofon-
cyninge / georne togenes and sædon ealles þanc, / lista and þara lara").

48. Avitus, however, does not emphasize the fallibility of oral tradition.

49. Cf. Karen Cherewatuk, "Standing, Turning, Twisting, Falling: Posture and
Moral Stance in *Genesis B*," *NM* 87 (1986): 537–44.

50. 244–45 ("Heo wæron leof gode / ðenden heo his halige word healdan wol-
don").

51. E.g., 526, 537. Alfred/Augustine, *Soliloquies* (as cited earlier), uses
ge)healdan ("to hold") of words retained by memory; see *King Alfred's Version of
St. Augustine's Soliloquies*, ed. Thomas A. Carnicelli (Cambridge, Mass., 1969), p. 49.

52. 405, 428–30 ("onwendon þæt he mid his worde bebead," "hie word godes /
lare forlæten," "brecað his gebodscipe"), my trans.

passage (after line 441) obscures what comes directly after these exhortations, but the devil who evidently volunteers to go to earth and tempt Adam and Eve is said to have "craft of speech and cunning of word."[53] The Tempter's marks of verbal craft, which keep language at the center of the conflict, recall those of Unferth, the royal spokesman (*thule*) in *Beowulf*, who is said to "unbind words of contention" in beginning an account of Beowulf's past that challenges the hero's own oral résumé.[54]

When the Tempter arrives on earth, he approaches Adam first. (This rare motif also occurs in a few other medieval versions of the Fall.)[55] Now begins a series of three separate temptation episodes (Tempter/Adam, Tempter/Eve, Eve/Adam) that repeatedly test the humans' ability to keep the oral tradition of God's word. The separate tempting of Adam and Eve structurally underscores that the Tempter's challenge to their shared oral memory of God's word divides them from each other as well as from God.[56]

The Tempter begins his temptation of Adam by claiming that he comes at God's bidding with a message (*ærend*):

> Have you any longing,   Adam, that looks to God?
> I come at His bidding,   faring from afar;
> Nor has the time been long   since I sat at His side.[57]

By saying that he has only recently (*ne...fyrn*) left God's presence, the Tempter suggests that he carries a fresh memory of God's words. Continuing, the Tempter pretends to paraphrase God's command, invoking a direct, aural experience of God's voice by sprinkling his "report" with locutive verbs referring to God's supposed speech:

53. 445–46 ("wiste him spræca fela, / wora worda"); literally, "he knew many speeches, wicked words."

54. *Beowulf* 499–501 ("Unferð maþelode..., / onband beadurune"); cited from *Beowulf and the Fight at Finnsburg*, ed. Friedrich Klaeber, 3d ed. (Boston, 1950); trans. E. Talbot Donaldson, *Beowulf: A New Prose Translation* (New York, 1966).

55. On this and other unconventional details in the poem, see Rosemary Woolf, "The Fall of Man in *Genesis B* and The *Mystère d'Adam*," in *Studies in Old English Literature in Honor of Arthur G. Brodeur*, ed. Stanley B. Greenfield (Eugene, Ore., 1963), pp. 187–99.

56. The poem makes clear that the Tempter seduces Adam and Eve separately; after conversing with Adam, the Tempter is said to move (*wende hine*), apparently some distance, to the location where (*þær*) he tempts Eve (547–48).

57. 496–99 ("Langað þe awuht, / Adam, up to gode? Ic eom on his ærende hider / feorran gefered, ne þæt nu fyrn ne wæs / þæt ic wið hine sylfne sæt"), trans. modified.

On this errand He *bade* me go,   *bade* you eat of this fruit
Said your power and might   and mind will be greater,
Your body brighter,   your form more fair,
Said you will lack naught   of the world's wealth.[58]

The locutive verbs (*hatan*, "to command"; *cweðan*, "to say, speak")
surround the false command with the suggestion that God himself
pronounced it, while the juxtaposed pronouns in "he bade me" (*het
he me*) reinforce the impression that the Tempter has directly heard
God's speech.

Having offered this fictitious report of God's spoken word, the
Tempter tries to persuade Adam to obey God's new "command" by
appealing to traditional lord-thane obligations and the cult of fame
celebrated in heroic poetry:

Because you have done His will   and won His favor,
And served Him with gladness,   you are dear unto God.
In His heavenly light   I have heard Him speak
Of your way of life,   praising your words and works.[59]

The Tempter, exhorting by way of praise, here urges Adam to serve
(*þegnian*) his Lord as any good thane would, to earn his Lord's favor
(*hyldo*), and to seek an orally perpetuated fame (*lof*).[60] Old English
religious verse that evokes the heroic ethos typically transcends
secular fame with appeals to heavenly glory. Abusing this spiritual
ideal, the Tempter promises a fictitious fame for deeds that would
actually offend God and earn notoriety and punishment for Adam.
The fictional nature of the divine praise reported here, and of the
future fame promised, dramatizes that oral tradition is easily falsified.

Describing himself as God's messenger, *boda* (510), the Tempter
accounts for his role in the new oral dispensation by explaining that
God himself could not be troubled to come and speak to Adam:

58. 499–504 ("Þa *het* he me on þysne sið faran, / het þæt þu þisses ofætes æte,
cwæð þæt þin abal and cræft / and þin modsefa mara wurde, / and þin lichoma leohtra
micle, / þin gesceapu scenran, cwæð þæt þe æniges sceattes ðearf / ne wurde on
worulde"), trans. modified, emphasis added.

59. 504–8 ("Nu þu willan hæfst, / hyldo geworhte heofoncyninges, / to þance
geþenod þinum hearran, / hæfst þe wið drihten dyrne geworhtne. Ic gehyrde hine
þine dæd and word / lofian on his leohte and ymb þin lif sprecan").

60. By contrast with the Tree of Death, the Tree of Life and its fruit are "praise-
worthy" (*lofsum*, 468). On semantics, see B-T, *Dictionary*, s.v. *lof*; and Vickrey,
Genesis B, Glossary, s.v. *lof* and its compounds.

He does not wish   to have the hardship
Of making this journey   but sends His servants
To tell His commandments,   bidding us teach
Wisdom by precept.   Now do His will,
Take this fruit in your hand,   taste it and eat.[61]

As a self-claimed messenger and "servant" (*gingra*) of God, the
Tempter here borrows terms commonly used of the disciples and
apostles, ironically pretending to have a role in the proclamation of
God's word.[62] At the same time, the Tempter tries to disguise his
intervention in oral tradition by talking as if God were directly
commanding Adam (*he þe . . . het*), craftily eliding the first-person
pronoun (*ic, me*) that would stress his own self-insertion into that
tradition.

Faced with this first temptation, Adam refuses to fall for the
new oral tradition. Moreover, he refutes the Tempter's claims by
expressly appealing to what he himself has heard directly from God.
Although Adam also cites the Tempter's unfamiliar appearance and
his failure to present a sign (discussed later in this chapter), his first
criterion of authority, and the one to which he returns again later
in his speech, is his own auditory memory of God's command:

Then Adam answered   where he stood on earth,
The first of men: "When I heard the Almighty,
The Victor Lord *speaking   with stronger voice*,
And He *bade* me dwell here   and do His will,
Gave me the woman,   this glowing bride,
And *bade* me guard   that I be not beguiled
Or ever tempted   to the tree of death,
He *said* that blackest hell   shall hold him fast
Who harbours in his heart   aught of evil."[63]

Significantly, Adam first mentions God's word in terms of an enun-
ciating voice (*stemn*) and only then in terms of the message or com-

61. 513–19 ("Nele þa earfeðu / sylfa habban þæt he on þysne sið fare, / gumena
drihten, ac he his gingran sent / to þinre spræce. Nu he þe mid spellum het / listas
læran. Læste þu georne / his ambyhto, nim þe þis ofæt on hand, / bit his and byrige").

62. See B-T, *Dictionary* and *Supplement*, s.v. *boda, gingra.*

63. 522–31 ("Adam maðelode þær he on eorðan stod, / selfsceafte guma: 'Þonne
ic sigedrihten, / mihtigne god, mæðlan gehyrde / strange stemne, and me her stondan
het, / his bebodu healdan, and me þas bryd forgeaf, / wlitesciene wif, and me warnian
het / þæt ic on þone deaðes beam bedroren ne wurde, / beswicen to swiðe, he cwæð
þæt þa sweartan helle / healdan sceolde se ðe bi his heortan wuht / laðes gelæde' "),
trans. modified, emphasis added.

mand (*bebod*) itself; God's voice, heard and remembered, remains the index of authority, especially in that it is louder or stronger (*strangre*) than the Tempter's.[64] The phrase *mæðlan gehyrde* ("heard say") also bespeaks Adam's vocal immediacy to God's original command, though this formula can also evoke the multiple links of extended oral tradition.[65] Adam's repeated use of the first-person pronoun (*ic, me*) reinforces his role as a direct audience to God's words and actions.

The Tempter's failure to persuade Adam to abandon God's command shows that oral tradition, in its simplest form, at one remove from the original utterance, can be truthful despite its exclusive reliance on memory. But the poem goes on to suggest that when oral tradition is extended through a mnemonic chain, it is only as strong as its weakest link. Approaching Eve, the Tempter begins *not* by announcing the false command (as with Adam) but by threatening that when he returns to heaven and reports the humans' "disobedience," God will be very angry and (ironically) will have to come down himself and speak to the humans:

> I know well that God
> Will be angry at you both   after my errand,
> When I come from my weary journey   over this long way
> To tell Him you two will not heed   the new behest
> He sends hither from the east.   He alone, it seems,
> Must come to instruct you;   His messengers may not
> Tell you His bidding!   Truly I know
> The Almighty's wrath   will be roused against you both.[66]

Pretending that it is normal for him to carry messages himself (*selfa*) to God, but that only in unusual circumstances would God himself (*sylf*) come to speak directly to the humans, the Tempter turns the very basis of authority, the *vox Dei*, into a threat. Twice here the

64. For the vocal, enunciative connotations of *stefn* (acc. *stemn*), see B-T, *Dictionary*, s.v. *stefn* I.

65. E.g., *secgan hyrdan* (*Beowulf* 273, 582, 875, 1346); *nemnan hyrdan* (2023).

66. 551–59 ("Ic wat, inc waldend god / abolgen wyrð, swa ic him þisne bodscipe / selfa secge, þonne ic of þys siðe cume / ofer langne weg, þæt git ne læstan wel / hwilc ærende swa he easten hider / on þysne sið sendeð. Nu sceal he sylf faran / to incre andsware; ne mæg his ærende / his boda beodan; þy ic wat þæt inc abolgen wyrð, / mihtig on mode"), trans. modified.

Tempter conjures up the image of an angry or wrathful (*abolgen*) God confronting the guilty humans, and he skillfully uses dual pronouns (*git, incre, inc*, "you two, you both") to emphasize that Eve's fate is joined with Adam's.[67]

To gain Eve's compliance with the "new" command—"Eat of this fruit!" (564)—the Tempter promises her an even rosier garden: she will gain knowledge ("your mind will be freer, your wit more firm"), a new vision of things ("your eyes shall have light to look afar / Over all the world"), and influence over Adam ("Over [him] thereafter you shall have sway"); he also flatters her ("O fairest of women)."[68] But fundamentally he appeals to Eve's fear of God's wrath, as threatened in the speech above. The narrative suggests that the Tempter *begins* with an appeal to fears based on maternal feeling: "He said that thereafter her offspring would suffer / The worst of all evils."[69] This remark sets the tone for the scene.

Critics continue to dispute whether the Tempter's appeals, and Eve's ready compliance, reflect a traditional patristic model of the feminine—weak, gullible, and easily swayed by emotional appeals— or a substantial departure from that tradition.[70] Clearly Eve as wife and (future) mother responds in part to powerful emotional appeals, but the poem does not fault her for this reaction. Rather, it implicitly censures her, in her intellectual capacity, for *believing* the Tempter's claims in the first place, given their suspect source, content, and function as speech acts.

67. Dual pronouns occur here in lines 551, 554, 557, 558. On their use in the poem generally, see J. R. Hall, "Duality and the Dual Pronoun in *Genesis B*," PLL 17 (1981): 139–45.

68. 561, 564–66, 568, 578 ("þu meaht his þonne rume ræd geþencan"; "Æt þisses ofetes! Þonne wurðað þin eagan swa leoht / þæt þu meaht swa wide ofer woruld ealle / geseon siððan"; "Meaht þu Adame eft gestyran"; "idesa seo betste").

69. 549–551 ("cwæð þæt sceaðena mæst / eallum heora eaforum æfter siððan / wurde on worulde"). Ironically, vengeance on Adam's offspring (*eafrum*, 399) is precisely what Satan had plotted in hell.

70. A major crux is the reference to Eve's weak (*wac*) or weaker (*wacran*) mind (649, 590), possibly relative to the Tempter rather than Adam (as critics often have assumed). On Eve's representation in the poem, see Jane Chance, *Woman as Hero in Old English Literature* (Syracuse, N.Y., 1986), chap. 5; Pat Belanoff, "The Fall(?) of the Old English Female Poetic Image," *PMLA* 104 (1989): 822–31; Alain Renoir, "Eve's I.Q. Rating: Two Sexist Views of *Genesis B*," in *New Readings on Women in Old English Literature*, ed. Helen Damico and Alexandra Hennessey Olsen (Bloomington, Ind., 1990), pp. 262–72; and Gillian R. Overing, "On Reading Eve: *Genesis B* and the Readers' Desire," in *Speaking Two Languages: Traditional Disciplines and Contemporary Theory in Medieval Studies*, ed. Allen J. Frantzen (Albany, N.Y., 1991), pp. 35–63.

As the poem goes on to show, Eve believes the Tempter's misrepresentations of not only God's speech but also Adam's, whose reported words (unlike God's) she could double-check. In his first speech to Eve, the Tempter refers in passing to the "deadly strife" caused by Adam's "evil answers."[71] And he winds up this speech with a highly distorted summary of the same:

> If you can accomplish this,   O fairest of women,
> I will hide from your Lord   Adam's harmful speech,
> His churlish words.   He charges me with falsehood,
> Says I am eager in evil,   no angel of God
> But a servant of fiends![72]

In his second speech to Eve, the Tempter returns to this theme, referring to Adam's "slanderous words" and "the ill will he uttered against me."[73] Taken as a whole, the Tempter's account of Adam's speech ominously extends his mediating role from the God/human relation to the Adam/Eve one as well. That Eve believes the Tempter's distorted accounts of Adam's speech, and that they have a key role in persuading her, may be seen from the fact that she herself later appeals to these accounts in persuading Adam to change his mind.[74] Although Eve could question Adam about the Tempter's representations, she does not, perhaps fearing the visitor's further wrath. The Fall thus involves a corruption of discourse not only between God and the humans but also between the humans themselves.

Before turning to Eve's persuasion of Adam, the narrative stresses that she accepts and believes the Tempter as God's bonafide messenger: "She believed that his counsel came from God / As he cunningly said."[75] Though the "vision" granted to Eve helps "corroborate" the Tempter's words (see discussion later in this chapter), emphasis is placed on the fictive power of those words themselves, which are spoken "cunningly" (*wærlice*)—or "truly," "like the

71. 572–73 ("þone laðan strið, / yfel andwyrde"), trans. modified.

72. 578–82 ("Gif þu þæt angin fremest, idesa seo betste, / forhele ic incrum herran þæt me hearmes swa fela / Adam gespræc, eargra worda. / Tyhð me untryowða, cwyð þæt ic seo teonum georn, / gramum ambyhtsecg, nales godes engel"), trans. modified.

73. 621–22 ("þa womcwidas"; "þæs fela he me laðes spraec"), trans. modified.

74. 661–64, quoted and discussed below, section 3, as an example of Eve's rhetorical mimicry of the Tempter.

75. 650–52 ("[heo] geleafan nom / þæt he þa bysene from gode brungen hæfde / þe he hire swa wærlice wordum sægde").

truth," in that Eve takes them as such.[76] Once Eve gives up her memory of God's voice as an index of authority, she can be duped by a fiction of suffcient verisimilitude. At more than one remove from its source, oral tradition is only as true as it sounds.

When Eve has eaten of the forbidden fruit, and at the Tempter's bidding tries to persuade Adam to do the same, she constructs her appeal strictly on the basis of a *mediated* version of "divine" authority. Abandoning the *vox Dei* itself as a reference point, she now appeals instead to the Tempter's voice:

> Here in my hands
> I bring this fruit   and give of it freely.
> O good my lord,   I do believe
> It is come from God   and brought by His bidding,
> As in truthful words   this herald has told me.
> It is like naught else   in all the earth
> Except, as he says,   it is sent by God.[77]

Eve's appeal to "truthful words" (*wærum wordum*) continues the theme of her trust in words spoken "truly" (*wærlice*). Constituted as an appeal to words whose actual truth is unverifiable, her persuasion of Adam is symptomatic of oral tradition as represented in the poem.

Adam, in turn, mistakenly relies on Eve's claims—"he trusted the promise / Which the woman spoke to him in words"—thereby adding a final link to the false oral tradition and completing the Fall.[78] Adam's fall thus encapsulates the power of oral tradition to perpetuate truthlike fictions through a chain of speakers progressively removed from the supposed source. More than a half-dozen times in the Temptation scenes, the poem uses another, plainer term for the fictions passed on by oral tradition from the Tempter to Eve and from Eve to Adam—"lies" (*ligen*).[79]

In sum, the Tempter insinuates himself into oral tradition and

---

76. For this sense of the term, see B-T, *Dictionary*, s.v. *wær*; and Vickrey, *Genesis B*, p. 242 (line note).

77. 678–83 ("Nu hæbbe ic his her on handa, herra se goda; / gife ic hit þe georne. Ic gelyfe þæt hit from gode come, / broht from his bysene, þæs me þes boda sægde / wærum wordum. Hit nis wuhte gelic / elles on eorðan, buton swa þes ar sægeð, / þæt hit gegnunga from gode come").

78. 706–7 ("he þam gehate getruwode / þe him þæt wif wordum sægde"), my trans.

79. *Ligen* (or *lygen*), occurring at 496, 531, 588, 601, 630, 647, 699 (*ligenword*).

distorts speech and memory in two different lines of communication, from God to the humans and from Adam to Eve. Thus the Tempter ends up mediating all formerly direct verbal relations, completely subverting the original structure of oral tradition in the Garden. This result is emphasized near the end of the extant poem, where Adam and Eve, discursively uncoupled, sit apart in silence while awaiting God's return.[80]

3. Oral Formulas and the Fall

Oral tradition is a fallen medium, *Genesis B* suggests, not only because it is vulnerable to tampering but also because it creates its own compelling versions of reality that cast a spell over the minds of its recipients. In Old English heroic poetry the orally constructed past, as embodied in songs and lays as well as less formal utterance, can provoke powerful—even violent—emotional responses. In *Beowulf*, for example, the hero himself testifies to how an old warrior's tales may stir a young warrior to revive a suppressed but scarcely forgotten feud, thus breaking a fragile peace with renewed violence and bloodshed.[81] *Genesis B* suggests the incantatory fictive power of oral tradition, and its destructive potential, mainly through Eve's rhetorical imitation of the Tempter, her credulous repetition of significant words and phrases from his speeches in her own speeches to Adam.[82]

Strife and conflict in *Genesis B* have their impetus in an oral recitation similar to those that provoke violence in secular epics and lays—namely, Satan's long speech to his *comitatus* of devils, in which he recounts his unresolved feud with God in order to spur his thanes to vengeance. Offering a very distorted account of matters, Satan calls Adam a usurper of his former domain, urges revenge, and promises reward to any thane who successfully avenges him against God:

80. 842–43 ("sæton onsundran, bidan selfes gesceapu / heofoncyninges").

81. *Beowulf* 2032–69. Here I am indebted to my colleague R. W. Hanning, who elucidated this passage in "Recollection and Its Discontents," a paper presented to the Columbia Medieval Guild in 1989.

82. Parts of this section are drawn from my article "Tempter as Rhetoric Teacher: The Fall of Language in the Old English *Genesis B*," *Neophilologus* 72 (1988): 434–48.

> He has wrought us wrong,
> In hurling us down   to the fiery depths of hell,
> Deprived of heaven.   He has marked those heights
> For man to settle.
>
>   . . . . .
>
>   We must earnestly ponder
> How we on Adam   and on his offspring,
> If ever we can,   may avenge this wrong
> And pervert His will   by any device.
>
>   . . . . .
>
> I will let him sit next myself   who returns to tell,
> In this hot hell,   that the will of the King of heaven
> Unworthily they forswore   by their words and works.[83]

In the main action of the poem, the Tempter's success in arousing Eve to disobedience through false promises and threats similarly illustrates the emotive power of oral tradition and its inherent threat to social stability.

The poem dramatizes the power of the Tempter's fictions over the humans, particularly over Eve, by having her repeat, in her speech to Adam, many key elements from his own speeches to her. The frightened and credulous Eve simply mimics a good deal of what she hears from him. Again, Eve's credulity is due not to an inferior intelligence (after all, Adam is said to believe her) but rather, it would seem, to the power of oral tradition to create a compelling fiction. The Tempter exploits this power by explicitly urging Eve to convey his message to Adam and by offering a kind of metapersuasion in which he sketches out how she, in turn, should persuade Adam.

In his first speech, the Tempter urges Eve to "hear [his] words" (the crucial first stage of an oral tradition) and then to speak to Adam in such a way "as [he] shall show [her]" (the second stage of Eve's role in that tradition).[84] Alluding to the power of speech, the Tempter states that Eve will be able to rule Adam "if [she has] his will and

---

83. 360–64; 397–400; 438–41 ("Næfð he þeah riht gedon / þæt he us hæfð befælled fyre to botme, / helle þære hatan, heofonrice benumen; / hafað hit gemearcod mid moncynne / to gesettanne"; "We þæs sculon hycgan georne, / þæt we on Adame, gif we æfre mægen, / and on his eafrum swa some, andan gebetan, / onwendan him þær willan sines, gif we hit mægen wihte aþencan"; "Sittan læte ic hine wið me sylfne, swa hwa swa þæt secgan cymeð / on þas hatan helle, þæt hie heofoncyninges / unwurðlice wordum and dædum / lare").

84. 559–60, 563 ("minum . . . wordum hyran"; "swa ic þe wisie").

he trusts in [her] words."[85] This remark makes explicit that the Tempter, having been rebuffed by Adam, plans not only to employ Eve's persuasive power as Adam's wife but also to create a more elaborate oral tradition to overcome Adam's doubts. With his subtle shift from "my words" (*minum wordum*) to "your words" (*þinum wordum*), the Tempter seems to say that Eve will persuade Adam on her own terms, but the terms that she actually uses turn out to be mainly *his*. The covert meaning of the pronoun shift from *minum* ("my") to *þinum* ("your"), with its suggestive acoustical echo, is that the new oral tradition being invented here will rely heavily on borrowed formulas and mimicry.

The Tempter next invokes the instructional and hortatory functions of oral tradition when he says to Eve, "Persuade him [Adam] earnestly to follow your teaching."[86] The implied purposes of Eve's speech—to pass along information and to urge certain kinds of behavior—resemble the gnomic and ethical uses of oral tradition in secular poetry. The terms *span* ("persuade") and *lar* ("teaching") also coincide with the themes of persuasion and instruction central to the patristic view of the Fall as a paradigm of verbal abuses.

The Tempter's second, shorter speech to Eve (611–22), which takes place *after* she has eaten of the forbidden fruit, elaborates the new oral tradition by specifying what Eve is to say to Adam. Beginning with a summary of what Eve has seen in the "vision" he has offered her, the Tempter goes on to prompt her to report this experience to Adam:

> O worthy Eve! You may see for yourself
> How you now have altered, nor need I tell
> How bright your beauty or your form how fair,
> Since you have trusted my words and followed my teaching.
> All round about you shines radiant light
> Which I brought from God, blazing from heaven.
> Lo! You may touch it! *Tell Adam in truth*
> *What vision you have,* what virtue, through my coming.[87]

Here the Tempter essentially rehearses what Eve is to say to Adam, prompting and cueing her reportage in great detail. Again, "your words" turn out to be mainly "my words."

85. 569 ("gif þu his willan hæfst and he þinum wordum getrywð"), trans. modified to reflect *his willan* ("his will").
86. 575–76 ("Span þu hine georne / þæt he þine lare læste"), trans. modified.
87. 611–18 ("Þu meaht nu þe self geseon, swa ic hit þe secgan ne þearf, / Eue

Eve's credulous adoption of a new, erroneous oral tradition is evident from the texture of her speech to Adam (655–83), which relies heavily on motifs, phrases, individual words, and even syntax occurring in the Tempter's speeches to her. For example, in terms of themes and phrasing, the Tempter tells Eve that he is God's messenger, *boda* (558), a term which she uses twice in speaking to Adam, embellishing it with formulaic epithets—"this beautiful messenger" and "your lord's messenger."[88] Also mimicking the Tempter's repeated mention of his mission or errand, *ærend* (555, 557), Eve repeats this key term in a reference to the messenger (*ærendsecg*) and in her remark to Adam that the Tempter can represent (*ærendian*) the humans to God (658, 665). The Tempter had used the term *ærend* in speaking to Adam (497), but Adam did not use it in return, so that Eve's use of it stands out. Moreover, whereas *ærend* and *ærendian* are common terms in the Old English corpus, the compound used by Eve, *ærendsecg*, is unique to *Genesis B*.[89] As a rarity likely to be noticed by the audience, and as an echo of the Tempter's diction, the term betrays that Eve studiously repeats the Tempter's words.

Another important motif that Eve borrows from the Tempter's repertoire is that of the human chest or breast (*breost*) as the locus of thought, appetite, and verbal activity. (The poem's "breost" motif is discussed later in this chapter.) Again, Adam's speech furnishes a contrast here. Although the Tempter promises Adam that the fruit will enlarge his thoughts in his "breost" (519), Adam does not mention the term in his reply. With Eve, the Tempter mentions the "breost" fully three times (562, 571, 574). Eve's very first words to Adam, declaring that the apple is delightful *on breostum* (656), register the shaping influence of this motif on her sensibility. In a related example, the Tempter urges Eve to consider matters fully or amply, *rume* (561), and Eve, in the only other use of this adverb in the poem, tells Adam that after her "vision" she can see and hear *rume* (673) throughout the world. The related adjective *gerum* ("wide") is used only by the Tempter (519, 759), confining the stem *rum-* to the Tempter's fallen discourse as mimicked by Eve.

---

seo gode, þæt þe is ungelic / wlite and wæstmas, siððan þu minum wordum getruwodest, / læstes mine lare. Nu scineð þe leoht fore / glædlic ongean þæt ic from gode brohte / hwit of heofonum; nu þu his hrinan meaht. / *Sæge Adame hwilce þu gesihðe hæfst* / þurh minne cime cræfta"), emphasis added.

88. 656, 664 ("þes boda sciene," "þines hearran bodan"), my trans.

89. *A Microfiche Concordance to Old English*, comp. Antonette diPaolo Healey and Richard L. Venezky (Toronto, 1980), s.v. *ærendsecg*.

Concerning Eve's "vision," the Tempter tells her to report that she can see (*geseon*, 611) for herself the things she describes to Adam; Eve accordingly says to Adam that she sees (*geseo*) the Tempter's veracity from his appearance, that she can see (*geseon*) God, and that she can see (*geseon*) widely through the universe (657, 666, 674). The Tempter also mentions several times the light (*leoht*) that Eve sees as a result of her "vision" (564, 614, 619); Eve duly mentions to Adam the light shining within her and around her (676–77).

One of Eve's most striking evocations of the Tempter's speech involves the adverb *georne* ("eagerly, earnestly"). Although the Tempter urges Adam to obey him *georne* (517), Adam neither complies with this urging nor uses the term himself. But after the Tempter urges Eve to persuade Adam *georne* (575), repeating this sonorous term in subsequent lines,[90] Eve not only follows the Tempter's rhetorical coaching but in so doing even adopts the term herself: "Here in my hands / I bring this fruit and give it to you eagerly [*georne*]."[91]

Besides motifs and individual words, Eve repeats or closely mimics some of the Tempter's phrases when she invokes Adam's dispute with the stranger:

If today you answered him   with harmful words
He will still forgive   if we do his service.
What do you want   with deadly strife
Between us   and the angel of God?[92]

In repeating nearly verbatim the Tempter's claim that Adam spoke "harmful words" (*hearmes gespræc*) that have caused "deadly strife" (*laðan strið*), Eve reveals not only her misguided trust in his false report but also the tendency of unchecked oral tradition to create its own reality.[93] In addition, Eve closely echoes the Tempter's description of the light or "vision" as something "brought from God."[94]

Syntactical patterns provide a final example of how the Tempter's language shapes Eve's. First, Eve mimics the Tempter's ma-

90. 581 (*georn*), 585 (*geornlice*).

91. 678–79 ("Nu hæbbe ic his her on handa...; gife ic hit þe georne"), trans. modified.

92. 661–64 ("Gif þu him heodæg wuht hearmes gespræce, / he forgifð hit þeah, gif wit him geongordom / læstan willað. Hwæt scal þe swa laðlic strið / wið þines hearran bodan?"), trans. modified.

93. Tempter: "laðan strið" (572), "hearmes...gespræc" (579–80). Eve: "laðlic strið" (663), "hearmes gespræce" (661).

94. Tempter: "þæt ic from gode brohte" (615). Eve: "hit from gode come, / broht from his bysene" (679–80).

nipulation of the dual pronoun, as when advising Adam that the Tempter's favor "is better *for us two* / To win than his ill will."[95] Second, Eve picks up and repeats the Tempter's use of the conditional term *gif* ("if"). Clauses with *gif* appear obsessively already in Satan's speeches as he twists and turns in his world of straitened possibilities; and, as Satan's thane, the Tempter echoes his master, using this term extensively in his speeches to Eve.[96] Eve in turn uses *gif* no fewer than three times in addressing Adam. In the passage quoted above she doubles the term, first to soften the accusations against Adam and then to tempt him with the possibility of "forgiveness": "*If* today you answered him with harmful words / He will still forgive *if* we do his service." Later Eve uses *gif* again to shore up her argument for the Tempter's authority as God's messenger: "Who could bestow such virtue and vision / *If* it came not from the heavenly King?"[97] After capitulating, Adam too falls into this verbal tic (806, 828, 834). Since the Tempter does not use *gif* in speaking to Adam, nor Adam in replying, Adam appears to have contracted it from Eve and hence (indirectly) from the Tempter and ultimately from Satan himself. By the end of the poem, even Adam, who at first had refused both the forbidden fruit and the Tempter's false word, is echoing Satan.

On one level, these various repeated formulas amount to a dramatic realization of Augustine's gloss on dissemination and the Fall: "The command came from the Lord through the man to the woman, but sin came from the Devil through the woman to the man."[98] The errors and rhetorical tics passed on from the Tempter to Eve and from Eve to Adam are discursive signs of an original sin that passes like a stomach flu through the inhabitants of the Garden and, by extension, the whole human race. But the transmission of verbal patterns from the Tempter to Eve—and, in at least one case, all the way from Satan, via the others, to Adam—suggests the power of oral-mnemonic tradition to enthrall individuals bound by the social chain of speech. Augustine had perceived a mimetic aspect in the rhetoric of the Fall, surmising that just as the Serpent used words

95. 659–60 ("His hyldo is *unc* betere / to gewinnanne þonne his wiðermedo"), trans. modified, emphasis added. Hall, "Duality and the Dual Pronoun," p. 143, cites this example, among others.

96. Satan: 398, 400, 409, 413, 427, 430, 434. Tempter (to Eve): 559, 569, 570, 578, 618.

97. 671–73 ("Hwa meahte me swelc gewit gifan, / *gif* hit gegnunga god ne onsende, / heofones waldend?"), trans. modified, emphasis added.

98. *GenL* 11.34.45. See above, Chapter 1.1.

to persuade Eve, so Eve must have used "persuasive words" with Adam. Avitus dramatized this idea, with Eve's flattery and pseudo-learning imitating the Serpent's. In *Genesis B* mimetic patterns pervade the very diction, phrasing, and syntax of the tempting speeches, suggesting how oral tradition can only repeat itself. Even the poem's narrative uses verbal repetition to suggest that Eve, in persuading Adam, imitates the speeches of her own Tempter:

> He *mistaught* with lies   the lovely woman,
> Told her untruths,   until she,
> The fairest of women,   spoke as he willed,
> Helped him to *misteach*   the work of God's hand.[99]

Besides reiterating the poem's major theme of false doctrine (*lar*), the repetition of *forlæran* ("to misteach") suggests that Eve misteaches Adam as she herself has been mistaught by the Tempter.[100] The comment that Eve spoke according to the Tempter's will (*on his willan spræc*) indicates that *his* oral tradition becomes *hers*, too.

The poem suggests the contagious power of oral tradition in one of the Tempter's remarks to Eve: "Different to you / Are shapes and forms, since you have trusted my word, / Followed my teaching."[101] Although this passage alludes to Eve's "vision," it also points to the important role of language in Eve's perception of reality. To Eve the Tempter's words (*wordum*) and teaching (*lar*) have made everything different, new, or alien (*ungelic*). Having exiled herself to the "region of unlikeness" where the fallen Augustine found himself, Eve experiences not only strange "shapes and forms" but also the strange power of language itself to shape and form reality.[102] If Eve no longer "holds" God's word or teaching but instead the Tempter's, it is equally true that the Tempter's discourse now holds *her*, just as she herself will soon hold Adam in the thrall of her own language.

4. The False Sign

Besides altering Eve's language and sense of reality, the "vision" she receives upon eating of the fruit is a sign or proof used by the Tempter

---

99. 699–703 ("he *forlærde* mid ligenwordum / to þam unræde idese sciene, / wifa wlitegost, þæt heo on his willan spræc, / wæs him on helpe handweorc godes / to *forlæranne*"), my trans., emphasis added.

100. On the significant repetition of *forlæran*, see Ehrhart, "Tempter as Teacher," p. 442.

101. 612–14, trans. altered from version quoted earlier.

102. Augustine, *Conf* 7.10 ("regio dissimilitudinis"); see above, Chapter 2.1.

to corroborate his word. As a sign, Eve's vision suggests the patristic notion of the Fall as a crisis of interpretation. At the same time, her vision reflects the important role of visual proofs in oral culture, furthering the poem's equation of the Fall with fallible oral tradition. Like the Tempter's word and the apple, Eve's vision is used to suggest that oral tradition tends to abuse signs by turning them into seductively corporeal *things*.

In his initial rebuff to the Tempter, Adam states that God warned him not to be tricked or deceived about the Tree—"[He] bade me guard that I be not beguiled / Or ever tempted to the tree of death"— a remark foreshadowing the semiotic theme soon to become explicit in the poem.[103] After rehearsing his direct knowledge of God's command (535), Adam adds that the Tempter has offered him no sign or token of his report's veracity:

> You are not like
> Any of His angels   that ever I saw,
> Nor do I find in you   any token of faith
> That God has sent me   as sign of His favor.[104]

The term *tacen* ("token, sign") occurs three more times in the poem, always in connection with Eve's vision.[105] It next appears when Eve is said to trust in the *tacen* shown her by the Tempter (653). The term occurs again to indicate that Adam, too, interprets Eve's vision, secondhand, as a validating sign: "She showed the token and swore the truth / Until Adam within his breast / Changed his mind."[106] Ironically, having first rejected the Tempter's message for lack of a *tacen*, Adam now accepts that message on the basis of a *tacen* merely reported to him by Eve, thus compounding his abuse of signs, both visual and verbal.

103. 527–29, as cited above.

104. 538–42 ("Þu gelic ne bist / ænegum his engla þe ic ær geseah, / ne þu me oðiewdest ænig tacen / þe he me þurh treowe to onsende, / min hearra þurh hyldo"), emphasis added.

105. Evans, "*Genesis B* and Its Background," p. 114, mentions *tacen* as one of three important leitmotifs in the poem. *Genesis A* "continues" the *tacen* motif with the fig leaves when Adam says, "Now I bear the mark [*tacen*] plainly on my self" (885–86), trans. modified.

106. 713–16 ("heo þam were swelce / tacen oðiewde and treowe gehet, / oðþæt Adame innan breostum / his hyge hwyrfde"), trans. modified. See John F. Vickrey, "The Vision of Eve in *Genesis B*," *Speculum* 44 (1969): 86–102: "The poem offers no evidence that Adam sees the vision himself. Eve describes it to him without suggesting that he see for himself, and the very fact that she describes it implies that he could not see it" (99).

Critics have argued that the content of Eve's vision reflects a false view of God characterized by diabolical fears of judgment; as a false sign, it should arouse the suspicion of both humans.[107] This idea is also supported by the poem's final mention of Eve's vision as a false sign (*untreowa / tacen*, 773–74) that fades away after both humans have eaten of the fruit. By implication, both humans make a serious interpretive error in failing to see that Eve's vision is a *false* sign. Consistent with patristic tradition, the poem's *tacen*-motif puts hermeneutics at the center of the Fall.

As a term commonly used to render Latin *signum*, *tacen* is closely associated with traditional sign theory. In the Alfredian literature, *tacen* denotes miracles and wonders, the typological events of sacred history, symbols such as the Cross, and so forth.[108] (The term is related to *tæcing*, "teaching.")[109] As discussed in Chapter 2, Augustine's later exegesis equates the Temptation with a semiotic crisis that challenges Adam and Eve to interpret God's command correctly. Clearly *Genesis B* follows this precedent: while yet innocent, Adam is warned by God not to be beguiled or deceived (*bedroren ne ... beswicen*) about the Tree, and the ensuing Temptation is a series of hermeneutical tests involving verbal and visual signs. Perhaps the poem means to show Adam erring even in *asking* for a sign (a mediation, and hence a diminishment of God). But it is more likely that *Genesis B* (following the later Augustine) equates the Fall not with mediation and signs themselves but with their abuse. On this reading, Adam's request is reasonable (though it evidently prompts the Tempter to a semiotic ruse), and Adam's fault lies in *accepting* the false sign that he is eventually offered.[110] That Adam accepts a false vision of God as a sign of divine authority is even more ironic given the fact that, as he himself tells the Tempter, he has already seen God: "well I know / What our Saviour said when last I saw [*geseah*] Him."[111] By comparison with the false sign proffered by the Tempter, Adam's own vision of God is a genuine proof, or *tacen*.

The Tempter as a bringer of false signs recalls Augustine's ac-

---

107. See Vickrey, "The Vision of Eve," and Robert E. Finnegan, "Eve and 'Vincible Ignorance' in *Genesis B*," *Texas Studies in Literature and Language* 18 (1976–77): 329–39.

108. B-T, *Dictionary* and *Supplement*, s.v. tacn, tacen.

109. Cf. *tæcan* ("to show, present"), *tæcnian* ("to prove"), and other cognates.

110. See Vickrey, "The Vision of Eve," p. 98.

111. 535–36 ("Ic wat hwæt he me self bebead, / nergend user, þa ic hine nehst geseah").

count of how, in the vast "forest" of temptations that is the world, "there are all kinds of artifices of suggestion by which the enemy urges me to seek for some sign [*signum*] from you."[112] In a nearby passage, Augustine describes how the Devil comes offering delusory visions: "Many people in their attempts to return to you and not being able to do so by their own strength have, so I hear, tried this way [the help of angels] and have fallen into a desire for strange visions [*visionum*] and have become, rightly, the victims of delusions.... They were seeking a mediator through whom to become clean, but this was not he. It was the devil, transforming himself into an angel of light."[113] In *Genesis B*, Adam's reference to the Tempter as an unlikely angel (*engel*), and the vision offered by the Tempter to Eve, reflect Augustine's account of the Devil as a false mediator deceiving humans with "signs" from God and the notion of the Fall as a crisis of signs in general.

But *Genesis B* also uses Eve's vision in its capacity as a sign to address more local concerns, particularly to deprecate oral tradition. As is well known, oral societies often supplement the spoken word with visual proofs and signs of authority that are also "a means of impressing the occasion upon the memory of participants and by-standers alike," a practice "particularly useful in a society where few people knew how to read."[114] The special use of *tacen* in *Beowulf* shows how in secular heroic poetry this term was used for visual proofs of a hero's exploits. In one instance, Beowulf sets up Grendel's arm and shoulder in the hall as a sign (*tacen*) that he has fulfilled his boasts; and, later, Beowulf presents Grendel's head as "a sign [*tacen*] of glory" when recounting his recent exploit at Grendel's mere.[115] In these—the only—instances of the term in *Beowulf*, *tacen* has to do with the process of making things into signs (at two levels, event and narrative). Beowulf says that he and his men have "brought" the trophy to Hrothgar; to function as a sign, Grendel's head must be carried, bodily, into a social, signifying context.[116] In an oral culture, the objects brought back from exploits are actually part of the process of reporting (*re-port*, "carry back"); "bringing"

112. *Conf* 10.35, as cited above, Chapter 2.5.

113. *Conf* 10.42, citing 2 Cor. 11.14. Cf. *GenL* 12.14.30 ("the Devil [may] cozen the soul with a spiritual vision"). Woolf, "Fall of Man in *Genesis B*," pp. 191–93, cites 2 Cor. 11.14 as source for Tempter/angel motif. Augustine, *Civ* 8.18, associates demonic messengers with paganism.

114. Dorothy L. Sayers, trans., *The Song of Roland* (Harmondsworth, 1937), p. 32.

115. *Beowulf* 833, 1654, my trans. See also Ann W. Astell, "Holofernes's Head: *Tacen* and Teaching in the Old English *Judith*," *ASE* 18 (1989): 117–33.

116. 1653–54 ("brohton / tires to tacne").

word usually involves bringing visual signs as well. Although visual signs can be used truthfully, as presumably by Beowulf, *Genesis B* depicts how a false *tacen* can just as well be used to substantiate false reporting.

But not only does oral culture supplement the spoken word with signifying things; it also tends to treat the vocable itself *as a thing.*[117] In Old English secular poetry, for example, the spoken word is reified variously as a constituent of a "word-hoard," as a weapon, and as a bodily entity issuing from the speaker's chest.[118] *Genesis B* points up how this tendency to reify speech makes oral culture vulnerable to certain errors or deceptions. The Tempter's claim to have "brought" word from God likens the false command to a bodily thing comparable to the other media of temptation, the apple and the vision. The verb *bringan* ("to bring"), as applied to these various signs abused by the Tempter, runs like a leitmotif through the Temptation: the Tempter claims that he brings (*bringað*) God's word to Adam (510) and that he brought (*brohte*) the vision (or light) to Eve (615); Eve believes that the Tempter has brought (*brungen*) God's word (651). Moreover, in tempting Adam she virtually equates the apple with the word "brought" by the Tempter:

> My heart is illumined   from without and within
> Since I ate of the apple.   Here in my hands
> I have this fruit   and give of it freely.
> O good my lord,   I do believe
> It is come from God   and *brought* by His bidding,
> As in truthful words   this herald has told me.[119]

Following the Tempter's lead, Eve here reifies words as things that are "brought" from elsewhere, rather than treating them as transient vocables that emerge anew from each speaker in the chain of oral tradition.[120]

Although only Eve's vision is called a sign (*tacen*), the spoken word and the apple are also signs that are falsified and abused by

117. For more on this point, see my article "Speech and the Chest in Old English Poetry: Orality or Pectorality?" *Speculum* 65 (1990): 845–59.

118. *Beowulf* 259, 2791–92, 2550–51.

119. 676–681 ("Wearð me on hige leohte / utan and innan, siðþan ic þæs ofætes onbat," and as quoted earlier, with *broht* at line 680).

120. *Genesis B* offers one of the earliest examples of this sense of the verb "bring"; see *Dictionary of Old English* (hereafter *DOE*), ed. Angus Cameron et al. (Toronto, 1986—), s.v. *bringan* 4a ("to convey information, instructions"), citing *Genesis B* 509.

the Tempter and in turn by the humans. Likened to one another as
things allegedly "brought" from God, the word, vision, and apple
revert from signs to things, objects that distract the humans from
their signifying function and the abuse thereof. Adam and Eve's
deception by these various abused signs puts patristic semiotics at
the center of the Fall. At the same time, their willingness to swallow
false signs suggests how oral tradition seductively reifies signs—
spoken words, in particular—as bodily things.

5. Swallowing the Lie

In *Genesis B* the bodily and spiritual center of the Fall clearly is the
human chest or breast (*breost*), which is the exclusive site of various
crucial interior functions—verbal, psychological, and alimentary.[121]
Enjoined to "keep" or "hold" God's word by not eating of the forbidden fruit, Adam and Eve instead "take in" or "consume" both
that fruit and the Tempter's false message. In the poem, the "*breost*"
serves not only in an alimentary metaphorics derived from patristic
sources but also as the source or sanctum of oral tradition as construed in Old English poetic tradition. In this respect, the "*breost*"
motif in the poem stresses that vulnerable oral tradition subsists
solely on a mnemonic word kept "within."

The chest or breast is important in patristic commentary on the
Fall because it appears in God's curse on the Serpent, "Upon your
[breast] you shall go" (Gen. 3.14), where the Latin Bible has *pectus*
("chest, breast") in the Vulgate, along with *venter* ("stomach, belly")
in the Old Latin version.[122] Like Old English *breost*, *pectus* is a
polyvalent term having verbal, psychological, alimentary, and mammary senses, among others.[123] In rhetorical tradition, the breast was
both the source of speech and the site of its emotional effects. Thus
Augustine describes a certain rhetorician's breast as the Devil's "im-
pregnable stronghold," hinting at the role of the Serpent's "breast"
in Satan's ventriloquism.[124] The curse on the Serpent valorized *pec-*

---

121. Parts of this section are drawn from my article "The Word in the 'Breost':
Interiority and the Fall in *Genesis B*," *Neophilologus* 75 (1991): 279–90.

122. For patristic vrr., see *Vetus latina* 2:66–67.

123. See B-T, *Dictionary* and *Supplement*, s.v. *breost* (with compounds in -*cofa*,
-*hord*, etc.), and now *DOE*, s.v. *breost*; and *OLD*, s.v. *pectus*, especially 3c ("considered
as a source or organ of speech, prophecy, etc.").

124. *Conf* 8.4 ("inexpugnabile receptaculum"), citing also the rhetor's tongue
(*lingua*) as the Devil's "weapon." On the chest (*pectus*) as the "house" of eloquence
and center of rhetorical dynamics, see *Doc* 4.6.10, 4.18.37, 4.20.42.

tus for patristic poetry on the Fall; for example, Avitus hints at the curse by locating the Serpent's guile in his heart or chest.[125] Patristic poetry also uses the pectoral motif in connection with the inner dynamics of persuasion. In another early Latin poem on the Fall, for example, the Serpent's words move Eve within her breast, soon conquering that region; subsequently, God condemns the Serpent to crawl on his breast, and the humans too suffer there.[126] The pectoral motif in these earlier Latin poems on the Fall may have provided a model for the "breost" motif in *Genesis B*.

As documented extensively in the first part of this book, patristic authors liked to figure God's command to Adam and Eve as healthful and delicious "food" which they rejected in exchange for the fatal fruit and the tempter's false word. In reference to Genesis 3.14, Ambrose develops this alimentary metaphorics in terms of the human obligation to carry God's word uncorrupted within oneself. The breast (*pectus*) "is frequently referred to as the seat of wisdom"; therefore humans should not "crawl" like the Serpent, "minding the things of earth," but "surely ought to fill the belly of [their] souls [*ventrem animae*] with the Word of God rather than with the corruptible things of this world."[127] This and similar patristic glosses underlie the pectoral motif in *Genesis B*. But whereas patristic authors used various bodily terms to designate the interior dynamics of the Fall—verbal, mental, and alimentary—*Genesis B* places all interior functions under a single polyvalent term: *breost*.

Besides patristic tradition, the pectoral motif in *Genesis B* evokes the secular heroic idea of the "breost" as the center of verbal functions, particularly as the repository of oral-mnemonic tradition. Old English secular heroic poetry typically describes the chest (*breost*) as an organ of speech and the seat of speech faculties. In *Beowulf*, for example, spoken words issue forth from the "breost."[128] *The Wanderer* similarly situates speech in the *breostcofa* ("breast-chamber"), which "holds" thoughts or feelings before they are released as utterance.[129] In *Genesis B* the ease with which the Temp-

---

125. Avitus, *Poematum* 2.119 (*pectore*), 3.122 (*pectora*). Avitus does not use *pectus* systematically of the humans, describing their interior states variously in terms of the *mens, sensus, cor,* or *uiscera* (e.g., 2.190–95, 206, 224, 239, 245); but his example may have contributed to the thematic use of "breost" in *Genesis B*.

126. Cyprian of Gaul, *Heptateuchos* 1.76 (*sub pectore*), 82 (*pectora*), 109, 122 (*pectore*). *Pectus* is similarly prominent in Claudius Marius Victor, *Alethia*, bk. 1 (the Fall).

127. *Par* 15.74 (using also *uterus*).

128. *Beowulf* 2550, 2792.

129. *Wanderer* 17–18, *ASPR* 3:134 ("Forðon domgeorne dreorigne oft / in hyra

ter's word dislodges God's word from the human "breost" suggests its vulnerability as a repository for oral tradition.

The "breost" is first mentioned in the Tempter's speech to Adam, where the promise that knowledge will ensue from eating the fruit is cast in terms of the "breost" instead of the eyes (as in Scripture): "Take this fruit in your hand, taste it and eat. / You will grow greater within [on þinum breostum]."[130] The promise of a wide or roomy "breost" seems to refer primarily to mental or cognitive powers, though the knowing/eating imagery also draws on the term's alimentary sense ("stomach"). In making the organ of knowledge the "breost" instead of the eyes, the poem begins to centralize crucial functions in the pectoral region.[131]

When the Tempter, unsuccessful with Adam, turns to Eve, he continues his attack on the "breost" as the inner sanctum of the divine word that both humans still "hold" within themselves. Mentioning the "breost" no fewer than three times, mainly as the center of thought and speech, the Tempter suggests that everything now depends on Eve's receiving God's "new" command in her "breost" and properly conveying it to Adam's:

> Plan in your *breast*
> That you both may avert   the vengeance to come,
> As I shall show you.   Eat of this fruit!
>
> . . . . .
>
> If you tell him truly   the command kept
> In your *breast*,   God's bidding that you obey
> The true teaching,   he will cease this strife,
> Will abandon   the evil answer
> In his own *breast-chamber*,   as we both bid him.[132]

The "evil answer" in Adam's "breast-chamber" is presumably his rebuff to the Tempter—a synecdoche for God's word itself, which

---

breostcofan bindað fæste"). Cf. the words stifled in the chest, *ferðlocan* and *hordcofan* (13–14).

130. 518–19 ("nim þe þis ofæt on hand, / bit his and byrige. Þe weorð on þinum breostum rum"), trans. modified.

131. The visual motif is still present in the poem, of course. On Eve's vision as a reflex of Gen. 3.5 in particular, see Vickery, "The Vision of Eve," p. 90.

132. 562–64; 570–75 ("Gehyge *on þinum breostum* þæt þu inc bam twam meaht / wite bewarigan, swa ic þe wisie. / Æt þisses ofetes! / . . . Gif þu him to soðe sægst hwylce þu selfa hæfst / bisne *on breostum*, þæs þu gebod godes / lare læstes, he þone laðan strið, / yfel andwyrde an forlæteð / *on breostcofan*, swa wit him bu tu / an sped sprecað"), trans. modified, emphasis added.

Adam had expressly invoked in the Tempter's presence by recalling the sound of God's voice, rehearsing the substance of God's command, and repeating that God had ordered him faithfully to "hold" his word. As an enclosure, Adam's "breast-chamber" signifies the bodily and spiritual interior that "holds" the remembered word of oral tradition, whether good or ill.

In addressing Eve, as quoted above, the Tempter invokes the "breost" not only as a receptacle for words, as held by the mind or memory, but also as an organ for producing and reproducing speech. The chest's function as the source of speech is consistent with rhetorical tradition, with the pectoral psychology passed on by patristic culture, and with the native poetic notion that words issue from the "breost." Having invoked a great chain of communication extending from God to himself (551–56), from himself to Eve (559–60), and now from Eve to her husband, the Tempter suggests that everything depends on Eve's properly conveying the "new" command from her "breost" to Adam's.

The Tempter's plan to use Eve's "breost" as his rhetorical instrument suggests not only the "ventriloquism" traditionally associated with the Fall but also persuasion in its sexual or seductive aspect.[133] The female breast was traditionally associated with fruit, especially in the metaphorics and iconography of the Fall, and in this episode Eve's "breost," in its mammary sense, adds erotic significance to the specifically verbal role of Eve's "breost" in persuading Adam.[134] In yet another of its senses, as a womb, the "breost" is associated with conception and gestation.[135] As noted earlier in this book, exegetes held that Eve (by contrast with Mary) had "conceived" the Devil's "word" and "brought forth" its evil "fruit."[136] The Tempter's clear intention to reproduce his false teaching from Eve's "breost" seems to draw on this traditional notion of Eve as a fertile womb for the Devil's word.

In carrying out the Tempter's advice to convey his word or teaching from her "breost" to Adam's, Eve begins her persuasive speech with an appeal to the pleasurable effect of the fruit in the "breost":

133. On ventriloquism, see above, Chapter 3.2.

134. For the mammary sense of the term, see B-T, *Dictionary*, s.v. *breost* II; *Supplement*, s.v. *breost* IV. The apple/breast motif appears in Cant. 7.7–8; and Isidore of Seville, *Etymologiae* 11.1.74.

135. B-T, *Supplement*, s.v. *breost* III.

136. E.g., Tertullian, *De carne Christi* 17. An Old English metrical expansion of the creed (10–11th c.) has Christ conceived in Mary's *breostcofan* (*The Creed* 16, ASPR 6:79).

"Adam, my lord, / This fruit is so sweet and blithe in the breast [*on breostum*]."[137] Here "breost," again, means mainly the stomach.[138] But since the term is by now fraught with verbal and psychological significance, its use suggests that the humans "consume" the Tempter's word just as they consume the apple itself. Furthermore, as the "belly of the soul" (in Ambrose's terms), the "breost" will experience the bitter results of the Tempter's word once it is taken in or ingested. Like the apple itself, which Eve calls "sweet" but which the narrative consistently describes as "bitter," the Tempter's false word, as conveyed by Eve, is a bitter food flavored with a merely rhetorical *suavitas*.[139]

The "breost" motif comes full circle as the Temptation culminates in Adam's "breost," the symbolic site to which the Tempter had originally pitched his appeal. There Eve's persuasive words now take effect as Adam yields to her urging that he eat of the fruit:

> Over and over   the most winsome of women
> Pled with him
>
> . . . . .
>
> Until Adam   *within his breast*
> Changed his mind   and his heart began
> To follow her will.[140]

This passage locates both mind (*hyge*) and heart (*heorte*) in the "breost," stressing that the pectoral dynamics of the Fall include not only verbal and alimentary but also psychological aspects.[141] "Heart" and "mind" may here represent appetite and reason, respectively, with their traditional functions in the tropology of the Fall—sinful "suggestion" appealing to the "delight of appetite,"

137. 655–56 ("Adam, frea min, þis ofet is swa swete, / bliðe on breostum").

138. B-T, *Dictionary*, s.v. *breost* I, and *Supplement*, s.v. *breost* III, cites this line for the sense "stomach" and compares Gen. 3.6 ("bonum ad vescendum").

139. The tree of death (645), its fruit (479), the Tempter's appearance (725), and the fallen Adam's hunger pangs (803) are all "bitter" (*bitre*). The Tempter himself is "most bitter" (*bitresta*, 763).

140. 704–5, 715–17 ("Heo spræc ða to Adame idesa sceonost / ful þiclice... / oðþæt Adame innan breostum / his hyge hwyrfde and his heorte ongann / wendan to hire willan"), trans. modified, emphasis added.

141. On this "early medieval conception of the physiological basis of human emotion and cognition," see Thomas D. Hill, "Notes on the Old English 'Maxims' I and II," *N&Q* 215, n.s. 17 (1970): 445–47 (p. 445).

which in turn gains the "consent of reason."[142] In any case, this passage highlights the psychology of persuasion in the Fall, stressing the capacity of Eve's words to "turn" (*hwerfan*) Adam's will and to make him "follow" (*wendan*) after her bidding, terms consistent with the traditional notion that eloquence is able to "move" the soul, whether for good or ill.[143]

Further centralizing the dynamics of persuasion in the "breost," the poem stresses the analogous *interior* effects of the two main tempting media, the forbidden fruit and the Tempter's false word. When Eve approached Adam with the fruit, "Some she bore in her hands, some lay at her heart [*æt heortan*]," suggesting its active presence *within* her.[144] In addition, Eve's mind "took in" (*genam*, 710) the Tempter's command or teaching. Finally, after Adam capitulates and eats, "the apple within him touches at his heart [*æt heortan*]."[145] Like the fatal apple itself, the Tempter's word is not only an illicit object of consumption but also a dangerous physic or drug.

An earlier Old English poem, *Guthlac* (8th c.), offers a summary of the Fall in which the Devil pours a "bitter cup" for Eve, who in turn pours one for Adam, thus suggesting the "flow" of evil discourse in the dynamics of the Fall.[146] *Genesis B* makes much the same point even more directly. At the climax of the Fall, when he eats of the fruit (fig. 5), Adam is said to consume various evils, including evil persuasion itself:

> From the woman's hand   he took death and hell,
> Though it bore not these names   but the name of fruit.
> Yet the sleep of death   *and the devil's persuasion*,
> Death and damnation,   perdition of men,
> Were the fatal fruit   whereon they feasted.[147]

142. The affective sense of *heorte* is attested in B-T, *Supplement*, s.v. *heorte* VI ("intent, will, desire, inclination"), where *Genesis B* 716 is cited as an example (see also senses VIII, IX).

143. On the offices of eloquence, esp. to "move" (*movere*) or "turn" (*flectere*) the will of the audience, see above, Chapter 3.1.

144. 636–37 ("Sum heo hire on handum bær, sum hire æt heortan læg, / æppel unsælga"), trans. modified. Kennedy, translating 636b as "some on her breast," suggests the fruit's collocation with Eve's breasts (the sexual motif).

145. 723–24 ("hit him on innan com, / hran æt heortan").

146. *Guthlac* 982–85, ASPR 3:77 ("The enemy first gave the woman to drink, and she afterwards poured forth the bitter cup [*bittor bædeweg*] for her own dear Adam"); see also line 868, "bitter drink" (*bitran drync*).

147. 717–23 ("He æt þam wife onfeng / helle and hinnsið, þeah hit nære hatan

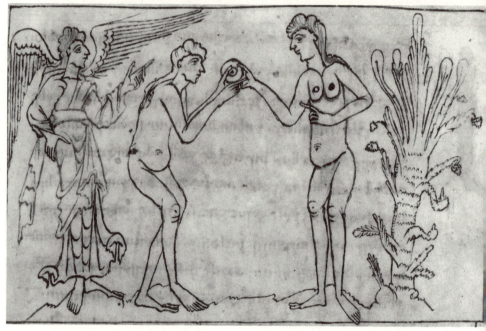

5. Eve proffering the forbidden fruit to Adam while the Tempter urges her on. Manuscript drawing, ca. 1000 A.D.: Oxford, Bodleian Library, MS. Junius 11, p. 31. Bodleian Library, Oxford.

Here the noun *gespon* ("persuasion") reifies the action of the verb *spanan* ("to urge, persuade"), which hitherto the poem has used repeatedly for the rhetorical aspects of the Temptation.[148]

The poem's gloss on the fruit as a "vessel" for evil anticipates later medieval wordplay on Latin *malus* ("apple"/ "evil"), the apple here signifying evil in its multiple forms.[149] But the apple is more than a polyvalent sign. By foregrounding the distinction between word and thing, name (*nama*) and referent, this passage evokes the

---

swa, / ac his ofetes noman agan sceolde; / hit wæs þeah deaðes swefn *and deofles gespon*, / hell and hinnsið and hæleða forlor, / menniscra morð, þæt hie to mete dædon, / ofet unfæle"), trans. modified, emphasis added.

148. E.g., the Tempter's urging Eve that she persuade Adam strongly, "*Span* þu hine georne" (575), as cited earlier; cf. lines 274, 588, 684, and 687.

149. E.g., Peter Riga (12th c.), *Aurora* 1.343–44, ed. Paul E. Beichner, *Aurora, Petri Rigae Biblia versificata: A Verse Commentary on the Bible*, 2 vols. (Notre Dame, Ind., 1965), 1:40. *Genesis B* makes evil consubstantial with "the tree of death, which bore many bitter things [deaðes beam, / se bær bitres fela]" (478–79), my trans.

ambiguity or slippage of signs themselves in the course—and the aftermath—of the Fall. As a sign for language, the apple suggests in particular the confusion of terms involved in the Fall, perhaps most obvious in Eve's calling "sweet" what is "bitter." Of course, the polyvalent apple can be *both* bitter (in its effects) and sweet (in its allure). But Eve's error of naming suggests a confusion about the oppositions or antitheses that construct the Garden, with its two Trees, and indeed all of Creation, which originates in a series of primal divisions: heaven/earth, light/darkness, male/female, and so on. Eve's confusion dramatizes a scriptural passage about naming that Augustine cites in connection with the Fall: "Woe to those who call evil good and good evil, who put darkness for light and light for darkness, who put bitter for sweet and sweet for bitter."[150]

In eating the sign, the humans swallow the legacy of fallen language, though without yet feeling its full effects. Soon they begin to, however. The final pectoral reference in the extant poem, voiced by Adam, links the humans' transgression of God's word (*waldendes word*) to a hunger and thirst that he now feels "bitterly" in his "breast"—an inner bitterness that clearly stems from having consumed not only the "bitter" fruit but also the word or teaching brought by the "bitter" messenger.[151] The poem thus equates the forbidden fruit with fallen language itself and oral tradition in particular—ever so sweet to the taste but fraught with bitter qualities and often having deadly effects.

6. Ruminating on the Fall

The ultimate failure of the "breost" in *Genesis B* to hold God's word and to resist the persuasions of a false oral tradition reflects the clerical idea that written tradition is more reliable than an oral one. And the Alfredian literature roughly contemporary with *Genesis B*

---

150. Is. 5.20, with *dicere* and *ponere* as the operant verbs. Cited in Augustine, *Ench* 13, 19, with discussion of sin in chaps. 12–28, tree imagery in 15, and analysis of the Fall in 24–28; CCSL 46:21–114; trans. J. F. Shaw, *The Enchiridion*, NPNF, ser. 1, vol. 3 (1887; rpt. Grand Rapids, 1980), pp. 237–76.

151. 798, 802–3 ("wit waldendes word forbræcon.../ Nu slit me hunger and þurst / bitre on breostum"). Two intervening passages (spoken by the Tempter) refer to Satan's "breost" (734, 751), perhaps alluding to Gen. 3.14; another refers to the sorrow "burning" there in the fallen humans (777). Line 13 in the OS *Genesis*, equivalent to *Genesis B* 803, omits "breost" (text in *ASPR* 1:171; and now Doane, *Saxon Genesis*, p. 234). Possibly the OE translator/redactor added the pectoral theme to the poem.

suggests that English clerics were quick to convert the "breost" from an oral repository to one for written tradition instead. For example, the Old English version of Gregory's *Pastoral Care*, a key work in Alfred's program for English church reform, has a metrical preface and epilogue that cite the important role of the "breost" in the transmission of book-learning. First, in the preface, the heroic-epic motif of messages borne over the seas is adapted to script culture:

> This written message   from the mainland
> Augustine brought   over the ocean,
> As the Lord's prince,   the Pope in Rome,
> Had dictated it before.[152]

The message that travels over the sea is not a song or tale in the oral tradition, an oral-mnemonic message like the Tempter's *ærend*, but an expressly written one—an *ærendgewrit*. The far-flung network of discursive and political authority created specifically by the technology of writing is personified here by a "speaking" text: "Thereafter King Alfred turned me into English, every word, and sent me through his scribes south and north, commanding them to make many more copies of this message, that he might send them to his bishops."[153] Talking letters (or runes), a common device in Old English verse, here embody the monastic ideal of script-based oral proclamation.[154] All the functions of authority (to command, send, bring, etc.) here take the forms peculiar to manuscript culture (books, dictation, copies, etc.). Significantly, in the metrical epilogue that closes Alfred's version of the *Pastoral Care*, these ideals are recapitulated in terms of the "breost" as a sanctum for expressly *written* tradition: the "stream" of sacred knowledge flows from heaven into the "breost" of holy men for further proclamation, but the only permanent and reliable earthly source of this knowledge is to be found in "sacred books."[155]

As part of a book of scriptural poetry, *Genesis B* itself may have

152. ("Þis ærendgewrit Agustinus / ofer sealtne sæ suðan brohte / iegbuendum, swa hit ær fore / adihtode dryhtnes cempa, / Rome papa") *The Metrical Preface to the Pastoral Care* 1–5; ASPR 6:110; my trans.

153. *The Metrical Preface* 11–15 ("Siððan min on englisc Ælfred kyning / awende worda gehwelc, and me his writerum / sende suð and norð, heht him swelcra ma / brengan bi ðære bisene, ðæt he his biscepum / sendan meahte"); my trans.

154. E.g., prosopopoeia appears in *The Dream of the Rood* and *The Husband's Message*.

155. *The Metrical Epilogue to the Pastoral Care* 7, 11, 16; ASPR 6:111–12 ("wæterscipes welsprynge," "halga bec," "on weres breostum").

nourished the "breost" of monks and others with food for ruminative thought or with edifying drink. *Genesis B* is a fairly short interpolation into an older and longer poem, *Genesis A* (8th c.), which frequently cites manuscript books as sources. To validate its own authority, *Genesis A* repeatedly uses the formulas "books tell us" (*us secgað bec*), and "writ tells us" (*us gewritu secgað*), phrases that also occur in the works of Cynewulf, a literate poet who probably wrote in the ninth century.[156] In the Junius manuscript, these formulas occur right before and soon after the interpolated text of *Genesis B*. If we keep in mind that the manuscript presents Genesis as one continuous scriptural paraphrase, with a series of linking illustrations, and without any formal divisions to indicate where *Genesis B* (a unit defined by modern scholars) takes up or leaves off, it is reasonable to suppose that the poem's original readers or audience experienced the Genesis poem as a single unified narrative.[157] Indeed, it has been recently argued that the manuscript as a whole, with its carefully chosen biblical excerpts and its liturgical echoes, represents a single literary "epic of redemption."[158] Accordingly, the appeals to "holy books" that bracket *Genesis B* would have heightened the poem's thematic links between oral tradition and the Fall, as would the many drawings in the manuscript that depict God holding a book, especially the scenes where he addresses Adam and Eve.[159]

As discussed earlier, monks typically read aloud, "ruminating" on God's word as part of their spiritual regimen. Significantly, the first lines of the first work in the Junius manuscript (i.e., *Genesis A*) enjoin vocal, communal praise of God, "It is proper and right that

---

156. *Bec*: 227, 969, 1239, 1723, 2613. *Gewritu*: 1121, 1630, 2565, 2612. On Cynewulf, see Opland, *Anglo-Saxon Oral Poetry*, pp. 157–60. Lerer, *Literacy and Power*, chap. 4, analyzes references to written authority in other poems of the Junius manuscript and cites (p. 155) the appeal to "what books tell us" (*us secgað bec*) in Aelfric's homilies, which—like the Junius poems—were performative texts.

157. Although a lost leaf in the MS. at the beginning of *Genesis B* (before line 235) makes it impossible to determine the degree of continuity between the two poems at that point, it is significant that *Genesis B* ends (851) with a complete clause, with no break in the text or change of leaf, and with a smooth narrative segue to *Genesis A*.

158. See J. R. Hall, "The Old English Epic of Redemption: The Theological Unity of MS. Junius 11," *Traditio* 32 (1976): 185–208. The last poem in the MS., *Christ and Satan*, "replies" to *Genesis B* by recounting the Fall (408–19) and recapitulating it in Christ's Temptation. On liturgical links, see James W. Bright, "The Relation of the Caedmonian *Exodus* to the Liturgy," *MLN* 27 (1912): 97–103.

159. See the MS. facsimile by Israel Gollancz, ed., *The Caedmon Manuscript of Anglo-Saxon Biblical Poetry* (Oxford, 1927), pp. 7, 10–11, 16–17, 41, 44–45.

we praise [Him] aloud," a note that is echoed a few lines later as the heavenly host is shown praising God.[160] Moreover, the manuscript contains physical evidence—punctuation and accent marks—suggesting that its poems, particularly *Genesis B*, may have been read aloud, chanted, or declaimed.[161] The main punctuation in the Junius manuscript is a point or dot used between the poem's half-lines, or hemistichs. Scarce and costly parchment was saved by transcribing verse in run-on lines right across the leaf, though this practice tended to obscure line divisions and caesuras. Points or dots between hemistichs helped to mark these divisions. According to one editor, George P. Krapp, the medial points in the Junius manuscript are very regular and correct, so that they would have been "of the very greatest assistance to anyone who undertook to read the poems of the manuscript aloud."[162]

The Junius manuscript also contains an abundance of accent marks reflecting established pronunciations of biblical names and other words. These accents, according to G.C. Thornley, "must have been inserted for a purpose related to pronunciation in some form of public utterance," most likely "to assist a lector, probably in a monastery."[163] There are "remarkable parallels" between the rhythms of liturgical recitation (Gregorian chant) and those of Old English poetry, and though an Old English text probably would not have been used in a liturgy, it may have been "intoned to the faithful on various occasions." Canterbury, where the Junius manuscript seems to have originated, was a center of instruction in liturgical chant, whose use was compulsory in England after the middle of the eighth century. Possibly, then, the manuscript represents "the original attempt to set Gregorian chant to the English language." In being read or chanted aloud, especially to a communal audience,

160. *Genesis A* 1–2 ("Us is riht micel ðæt we [him], / ... wordum herigen"); 15–16 ("they honored their Prince, praised Him with gladness [þeoden heredon, / sægdon lustum lof]"), trans. modified.

161. See Krapp, *ASPR* 1:xxii–xxiv; G. C. Thornley, "The Accents and Points of MS. Junius 11," *Transactions of the Philological Society* 1954: 178–205; Vickrey, *Genesis B*, pp. 17–26; and Doane, *Saxon Genesis*, pp. 35–36.

162. Krapp, *ASPR* 1:xxiii, transcribing sample lines, with punctuation. Not all OE verse is punctuated.

163. Thornley, "The Accents and Points," p. 182; further quotations in this paragraph are from pp. 199 ("remarkable parallels"), 190 ("intoned," "original attempt"), 184 ("Canterbury"). On provenance, see Ker, *Catalogue of Manuscripts*, no. 334, pp. 406–8 (Canterbury); and Peter J. Lucas, "Manuscript Junius 11 and Malmesbury," *Scriptorium* 34 (1980): 197–220; 35 (1981): 3–22. Red ink suggests that the corrector added the accents (Ker, p. 407) and hence that the MS. may have been selected and prepared for oral use sometime after it was produced.

Genesis B would have censured oral tradition not only through its content but also as a scripted performance based on literary tradition.

At the same time, oral delivery—in part by dramatizing the poem's many speeches—would have brought out the poem's epic qualities.[164] A major function of epic is to commemorate the history of a people (or a noble elite), who share with their heroes a real or imagined identity through language, tradition, and often kinship. As Eugene Vance notes, even epic in the form of a vocalized script such as the *Song of Roland* appeals to "the genealogical conscious-ness of its audience," as the audience recognizes "distant ancestors" in the poem's warrior-heroes. Whether the kinship bond is real or imagined, oral performance can evoke it through the resonance of the spoken word: "Poet [or performer], hero, and audience re-create each other in a common, phonic space; yet their presence to each other is consummated only in a magnetic alignment, through speech, with some anterior, originary, sacred presence."[165]

Like *Roland*—or, nearer to home, *Beowulf*—*Genesis B* is an epic, complete with heroic ancestors, a military conflict, a tragic (if not ultimate) defeat, and a pervasive appeal to kinship bonds between characters and audience. But *Genesis B* purports to be an epic of not just one people or a social elite thereof. In oral performance the poem would have invoked a lineage far more inclusive than that of Charlemagne's barons in *Roland*. The central characters in the poem, Adam and Eve, would have been recognized as the "distant ancestors" not only of everyone present but of the whole human race. And the poem's numerous references to Adam and Eve's de-scendants, and to the universal inheritance of the Fall, do not just invite but *compel* the audience to recognize their kinship with its characters. For example, like their father Adam, "the sons of men" will thenceforth face the same temptation; in the Fall "so many of [God's] servants" were corporately misled; and the "children" of Adam and Eve must suffer for their parents' sins.[166]

The kinship bond invoked between the poem's audience and characters is of course more than genealogical; it is also theological.

164. Vickrey, "On *Genesis* 623–5," *ES* 70 (1989): 97–106, suggests that the poem's gnomic "quotations" might be evidence that it was "intended for oral pre-sentation" (106n).

165. Vance, *Marvelous Signals*, p. 56.

166. 464–65 ("yldo bearn," "gumena æghwilc"), 597 ("þegn swa monig"), 623 ("hire eaforan"). Note also Satan's avenging designs on Adam's offspring, "eafrum" (399) and "monna bearnum" (403); and the Tempter's threats against Eve's children, "eallum heora eaforum" (550), as cited earlier. The latter threat is false in its context but ironically true in its effect.

A monastic audience, familiar with the doctrine of the transmission of original sin from Adam and Eve to all their posterity, thus would have felt themselves to be doubly the descendants of the first humans. In repeatedly mentioning Adam and Eve's "children," *Genesis B* insists that the audience shares corporately in the momentous fate of their ancestors. And presenting the poem orally would have made its events dramatically "present" by situating characters and audience together in the imaginative space of the Garden of Eden. Poet, performer, and audience thus would join the characters as participants in history, which Augustine, in a passage relating to the Fall, compares to "an exquisite poem enhanced by what might be called antitheses."[167]

7. Conclusion

As a native English poem based on the patristic tradition preserved in the monasteries, *Genesis B* reflects the notion of the Fall as a paradigm for the perennially renewed threats to ecclesiastical verbal culture—to the teaching, hermeneutics, and eloquence that were essential to the church's continuing mission. In this respect, the poem dramatizes the Fall as a crisis of false teaching (*lar*), an abuse of the sign (*tacen*), and a case of evil persuasion (*gespon*)—probably with reference to the church's battles against residual heathenism or new heresies in ninth-century Saxony and England.

In addition, *Genesis B* turns the Fall into a tragedy of oral tradition. Monastic poets using native meters inevitably wrote literate attitudes into their religious poems. As a product of monastic culture, *Genesis B* both adapts the native heroic ethos to its biblical plot and censures the old pagan culture whose exclusive reliance on memory and speech makes it vulnerable to errors and contingencies that a script-based culture could ward off, at least to some extent. According to the poem, the tempter's voice is heard not only in the Devil's allurements, in womanly wiles, and in heresy at large but in the old oral tradition—now on the retreat but still a powerful memory, possibly even in the monasteries. In the poem's typology of fallen and redemptive language, oral tradition is seductive, fallible, "bodily," whereas script is corrective, authoritative, "spiritual." As part of a manuscript book, and perhaps as a vocalized script aiding

---

167. *Civ* 11.18 ("pulcherrimum carmen etiam ex quibusdam quasi antithetis honestaret").

the traditional "rumination" on God's written word, *Genesis B* dramatizes the Fall as a crisis having great cultural resonance for the embattled Anglo-Saxon church.

With the next chapter we move from the precincts of the monastery to a wider sphere. We consider how the Fall was used during the later Middle Ages to interpret and regulate verbal culture as it related to not only religious but also social and domestic matters, particularly in the lives of women. At the same time we follow medieval glosses on the Fall as they turn increasingly inward toward the links between language, psyche, and sexuality. Although *Genesis B* deals with sexual politics and psychological themes, the poem tends to subordinate these issues to larger problems such as the conflict between oral and written tradition. In the Fall literature written by men for women in the later Middle Ages, however, writing and speech themselves become markedly gendered as "male" and "female" discourse, respectively. And even as medieval women gain literacy and access to books, clerical culture tends to perpetuate and enforce other discursive hierarchies that hark back to the Garden. Adam and Eve, soul and body, reason and appetite—these old structures translate now into distinctions like those between Latin and vernacular, writing and reading, authority and experience. Yet, in writing cautionary tales for the newly literate but still vulnerable daughters of Eve, the sons of Adam must face the realization that the tempter's voice may be lurking in the pages of their own books.

Chapter 5

The Seducer and the Daughter of Eve

[Eve] thought that [the Serpent] spoke the truth, believing
him through desire and beautiful words, just as do foolish
women who easily believe the beautiful words of liars who
urge them with flattery and empty promises to commit
folly against their honor and their rank.
—*Geoffrey de la Tour Landry*

AFTER ABOUT THE year 1200, as books increasingly found an audience beyond cloister and school among the laity, there appeared
in Europe certain vernacular writings about the Fall written by men
expressly for women. Part of a growing body of courtesy books and
spiritual guides, these writings recount and explain Genesis 3 in
contemporary terms, adapting it to the everyday life—social, domestic, and religious—of medieval women. Not surprisingly, in using Genesis 3 to instruct women in manners, morals, and devotional
practice, these writings dwell on Eve's actions and experience. In
particular, they turn Eve's encounter with the Serpent into cautionary tales about sexual temptation, especially as embodied by eloquent male seducers. Tending to focus on the dynamics of language,
psyche, and sexuality in Genesis 3, these cautionary tales assert a
large degree of control over women's bodies, mental life, and conversation. Moreover, these tales typically construct their female audience, the vulnerable "daughters of Eve," according to certain ideas
about language, the feminine, and the Fall that were founded by the
church fathers and that descended through an exclusively male literary tradition into the Middle Ages.

The two books for women discussed in this chapter were written
more than a century apart, in different countries, and for quite dis-
similar audiences and purposes: *Ancrene Wisse* is one of the earliest

extant spiritual guides for medieval women, whereas *Le Livre du Chevalier de la Tour Landry* represents the courtesy literature in full bloom by its day. A guide for anchoresses (female religious recluses), *Ancrene Wisse* was written in the early thirteenth century (ca. 1225) by an English cleric for three women who had taken up the life of seclusion, celibacy, and contemplation. On the other hand, the *Livre du Chevalier*, a manual of morals and manners, was written in the later fourteenth century (1371–72) by a French nobleman for his three young daughters, who were destined for courtship, marriage, and life in society. Both books soon achieved popularity beyond their original audience and were widely read, copied, and translated into various other languages.[1]

In playing out the various implications of the Fall for the lives of medieval women, both books draw on the rich tradition of marriage and seduction topoi based on Genesis 3. The first marriage triangle had preoccupied exegetes ever since Paul, likening Adam to Christ and Eve to the church, compared Eve's "seduction" by the Serpent to the threat of heresy.[2] Patristic writers had enhanced the Fall's sexual implications by using the first couple as a paradigm (good and bad) for marriage and by casting the psychology of sin in terms of a hierarchy among the "animal" senses (the Serpent), the "feminine" appetite (Eve), and the "masculine" reason (Adam). In addition, medieval exegetes such as Bernard of Clairvaux (1091–1153) extended Paul's notion of a "marriage" between Christ and

1. *The English Text of the Ancrene Riwle: Ancrene Wisse* (Corpus MS.), ed. J. R. R. Tolkien, EETS OS 249 (London, 1962); trans. Mary B. Salu, *The Ancrene Riwle: The Corpus MS.: Ancrene Wisse* (London, 1955), with occasional minor changes. In parenthetical citations, reference to ME text (by folio) precedes reference to translation (by page). Other MSS. cited as indicated; for editions, see bibliography under *Ancrene Wisse* (= *AW*). For scholarship, see Roger Dahood, "*Ancrene Wisse*, the Katherine Group, and the *Wohunge* Group," in *Middle English Prose: A Critical Guide to Major Authors and Genres*, ed. A. S. G. Edwards (New Brunswick, N.J., 1984), pp. 1–33.

Le Livre du Chevalier de La Tour Landry pour l'enseignement de ses filles, ed. Anatole de Montaiglon (Paris, 1854), hereafter cited parenthetically, with my translations. Scholarship on this work is scant; besides Montaiglon's preface, see *The Book of the Knight of La Tour-Landry, Compiled for the Instruction of His Daughters*, ed. Thomas Wright, rev. ed., EETS OS 33 (London, 1906), Introduction; and Anne-Marie de Gendt, " 'Por ce a cy bon exemple': Morale et récit dans *Le Livre du Chevalier de la Tour Landry*," in *Non Nova, Sed Nove: Mélanges de civilisation médiévale dédiés à Willem Noomen*, ed. Martin Gosman and Jaap van Os (Groningen, 1984), pp. 67–79. For the work's generic context, see Diane Bornstein, *The Lady in the Tower: Medieval Courtesy Literature for Women* (Hamden, Conn., 1983), esp. pp. 49–52.

2. 2 Cor. 11.2–4; see above, Chapter 1.1.

the church to a similar spiritual union between Christ and the soul, as similarly threatened by worldly temptations.[3] Using the garden imagery of Genesis 3 and the Canticle to create contrasting paradigms of seduction and redemption, Bernard describes Christ, the true Spouse, as having to woo the soul, his Beloved, away from the tempting voice of worldly pleasure. *Ancrene Wisse* relies heavily on Bernard's typology, as well as the traditional tropology of the Fall. The *Livre du Chevalier*, on the other hand, uses mainly the domestic paradigm, comparing Adam, Eve, and the Serpent (respectively) to husband, wife, and adulterous rival. Both books take gardens as sexual emblems for the female body: in their feudal idiom, the woman belongs to her lord alone, whether Christ or husband, and, as his property, she is to be "kept" solely by him.

In the two books the marriage triangle is colored by the courtly idiom that was commonly employed, from the twelfth century on, in not only secular literature but also moral and religious writings, including vernacular versions of the Fall. Both *Ancrene Wisse* and the *Livre du Chevalier* put polite flattery into the mouths of their seducers, who are described (respectively) as using *feire* speech and *l'art de bel parler* to deceive women. But both books also use the courtly idiom to reach and persuade their own female audience, employing romance topoi and courteous diction to appeal to women of elevated taste.[4] A certain moral ambiguity thus clings to eloquence (as for Augustine), and although each author's "edifying" language constructs and circumscribes its rival discourse of seduction, this rhetoric of redemption is inevitably implicated in the crisis of language that is the Fall.

Besides feudal and courtly values, the two books reflect new spiritual impulses that emerged during the twelfth century. As romance and love lyric came to focus on the inner emotional life of the individual, moral and religious writings began to dwell introspectively on personal spirituality. Widely influential writings such as Bernard's, for example, carried the spiritual and devotional ideals of the monastic reform movement into lay religious literature. Church reforms also encouraged an introspective turn in lay religious life and literature; for example, the Fourth Lateran Council

3. See Joan M. Ferrante, *Woman as Image in Medieval Literature, From the Twelfth Century to Dante* (New York, 1975), pp. 27–29.

4. On *AW*'s audience, see Eric J. Dobson, *The Origins of "Ancrene Wisse"* (Oxford, 1976), p. 3. While *AW* enjoins courtesy (*curteisie*), it also insists on maintaining a "clear distinction" between "an anchoress and the lady of a house [*huses leafdi*]" (17b; 30–31).

decreed in 1215 that all believers must make formal confession at least once each year. Personal piety and devotion are key themes in *Ancrene Wisse* and the *Livre du Chevalier*, and both books encourage women to make confession regularly, pointing out that the sacrament of penance (like marriage) was instituted in the Garden of Eden.

In stressing personal piety, devotion, and the inner life, these books reflect the growth of private space in medieval households and the developing notion of privacy itself. Upper- and middle-class dwellings increasingly offered more privacy for women, as did the anchorhold (usually a cell attached to a church building); and more privacy allowed women more time alone with friends, with themselves, and also—as the literacy rate rose among laywomen—with books.[5] Deportment books and spiritual guides stepped into this new private space, so to speak, to act as surrogate parents, teachers, spiritual advisers, companions, and chaperones.

As written proxies for the male author, who was also father or priest to his female audience, *Ancrene Wisse* and the *Livre du Chevalier* give voice to many male medieval stereotypes about women.[6] Just as Eve supposedly had sprung from Adam, so most medieval commonplaces about Eve and her "daughters" sprang from the male imagination and were embodied in an antifeminist tradition founded largely on biblical exegesis.[7] In both its institutions and ideology, this tradition tended to associate men with literacy and women with orality; even when male literary culture accommodated women as readers, as with the two books under discussion here, it excluded women from the learned (Latin) and active (writerly) spheres, limiting them to the role of passively receptive readers of male vernacular writings. Although the number of documented female readers, book owners, and literary patrons grew steadily from the twelfth century on,[8] the number of women writers remained relatively very small, and medieval literature about the Fall continued to be an

5. On women and privacy, see Philippe Ariès and Georges Duby, eds., *A History of Private Life*, trans. Arthur Goldhammer, 5 vols. (Cambridge, Mass., 1987–91), 2:3–6 (*privé* and related terms), 77–85 (privacy in the noble household), and 351–53 (the *Livre du Chevalier*). On private reading and medieval women, see Susan Groag Bell, "Medieval Women Book Owners: Arbiters of Lay Piety and Ambassadors of Culture," in *Women and Power in the Middle Ages*, ed. Mary Erler and Maryanne Kowaleski (Athens, Ga., 1988), pp. 149–87 (p. 152).

6. On stereotypes, see Gloria K. Fiero, Wendy Pfeffer, and Mathé Allain, eds., *Three Medieval Views of Women: La Contenance des Fames, Le Bien des Fames, Le Blasme des Fames* (New Haven, 1989); on Eve in particular, see pp. 60–66.

7. See Ferrante, *Woman as Image*, chap. 1.

8. See Bell, "Medieval Women Book Owners," p. 151 (table).

almost exclusively male domain, even—or, perhaps, especially—in the case of books written for women. Not until quite late in the Middle Ages did women authors begin directly to challenge traditional teachings about Eve, the feminine, and the Fall.[9]

The two books discussed here represent women as irrational, appetitive, sensual, gullible, vain, and fickle—in short, as embodiments of the "lower" part of human nature and hence as needing the guidance of fatherly, husbandly, or priestly authority. They also emphasize women's perilous beauty: even as victims of seduction, women are still faulted for *tempting* men into seducing them. *Ancrene Wisse* borrows various strictures on Eve and her "daughters" from a line of authorities with a strong antifeminist streak, including Paul, Augustine, and Bernard. And the *Livre du Chevalier*, in enumerating the "nine follies" of Eve, retails many traditional antifeminist commonplaces, some no doubt contributed by the clerics who helped the author compile his book.[10] Bernice Kliman finds the author of *Ancrene Wisse* to be "genial and humane" and "not a misogynist" yet unquestionably "a sexist and an anti-feminist."[11] And Diane Bornstein remarks that the *Livre du Chevalier*, "written entirely from a man's point of view," aims to "turn women into docile creatures who would cause men the least possible trouble and expense."[12]

One major medieval idea about the feminine and the Fall that was popularized by male clerics (and artists), and that requires a brief word here, is the legend of the woman-faced Serpent.[13] Patristic authors had established the Serpent's essentially androgynous nature by alternately stressing (and allegorizing) its soft feminine curves or its hard masculine thrust, as suited their interpretive needs. The woman-faced Serpent of medieval art and literature gave concrete form to the feminine tempter, though without diminishing its male counterpart, for authors (and artists) continued to depict Eve's tempter not only as her alter ego, or confidante, but also as a masculine seducer who takes advantage of his intimacy with her.[14] And though the female Serpent shows up briefly in both *Ancrene Wisse* (as the

9. E.g., Christine de Pizan, *Le Livre de la cité des dames* (1405); trans. Earl Jeffrey Richards, *The Book of the City of Ladies* (New York, 1982).

10. The chevalier mentions the help of "deux prestres et deux clers" (p. 4).

11. Bernice W. Kliman, "Women in Early English Literature, *Beowulf* to the *Ancrene Wisse*," *Nottingham Mediaeval Studies* 21 (1977): 32–49 (p. 43).

12. Bornstein, *The Lady in the Tower*, p. 49.

13. See above, Chapter 3.2, on this notion—its patristic origins, earliest medieval mention (Peter Comestor, *Historia scholastica* 1.21), and related scholarship.

14. On the tempter as alter ego, see Marina Warner, *Monuments and Maidens: The Allegory of the Female Form* (New York, 1985), p. 296.

related Scorpion of Lechery) and the *Livre du Chevalier* (as the Edenic Serpent itself), these texts subordinate this image to that of its seductive male counterpart.

1. Eve's Ear

Medieval moralists tended to localize the dynamics of Eve's temptation and fall not so much in her eyes as in her mouth and ears, orifices which they endowed with not only verbal significance but also sexual symbolism. In the first place, they typically blamed Eve for conversing with the Serpent and thus providing her tempter with strategic information about his intended victim—a charge going back to ancient biblical libels on the dangerous "feminine" flow of words.[15] But these moralists faulted Eve principally for the other side of her fatal conversation—for credulously *listening* to the Serpent. And during the scholastic period, both Latin and vernacular authors furthered the patristic notion that *verbal* temptation was the mainspring of Eve's fall by focusing on the crucial role of her ear.[16]

Peter Lombard, for example, in his *Sententiae* (ca. 1150), an extremely influential commentary on patristic writings, went even further than Augustine in stressing that the Serpent's words aroused Eve's desire for the forbidden fruit: "Such then was the order of events: the Devil, in tempting her, said, 'If you eat, you shall be as gods, knowing good and evil.' As soon as the woman heard this [*quo audito statim*], pride took hold of her mind and a certain love of her own power, whence she was pleased to do what the Devil had persuaded, and assuredly she did so."[17] At about the same time, authors of vernacular retellings of the Fall were introducing certain narrative devices, like the internal monologue, to make the same point. For example, in an early Middle English version of the Fall (ca. 1250) Eve withdraws into herself for a moment after listening to her tempter's promises: "Then thought Eve in her mind, / 'Then is this fruit awfully good, / Fair to the eye and soft to the touch; / Of this fruit

---

15. E.g., Ecclesiasticus (Sirach) 25.24–25 (= Vulg. 25.33–34): "From a woman sin had its beginning, and because of her we all die. Allow no outlet to water, and no boldness of speech in an evil wife."

16. On scholastic treatments in general, see Evans, *Paradise Lost and the Genesis Tradition*, chap. 6.

17. *Sententiae* 2.22.2, PL 192:697 (my trans.). GenL 11.30.39.

will I have a taste.' "[18] *Ancrene Wisse* and the *Livre du Chevalier* seize on the same moment in Genesis 3 and the same interiorizing device to represent Eve's—and woman's—enchantment by the tempter's voice.

Both books also rely on specifically Augustinian theories about language as a medium of ideas, images, and feelings—theories that were now acquiring great practical importance in medieval rhetoric and poetics. On Augustine's essentially Neoplatonic model, the body was imagined as a kind of container that admitted words and images into the soul by means of the senses. According to the moral psychology also adopted from Augustine, "feminine" appetite was easily moved by mental images (as by all sensory stimulation), and "masculine" reason was supposed to control "feminine" delight in such images, just as Adam should have governed Eve in Paradise. Although Augustine regarded words as crucial in both seduction and redemption, temptation and edification, he tended to stress their role in depositing or stirring up illicit ideas or images within: after the Fall, the truth must enter solely through the ears (and eyes), "and it is difficult to resist the phantasms which enter the soul through these senses." In theory Augustine held that words merely *signify* ideas already present in the mind, but in practice he treated words as media capable of contaminating (or enlightening) the soul.[19]

The notion of words as potentially contaminating media appears in the Latin anchoritic literature that inspired vernacular works such as *Ancrene Wisse*. For example, Aelred of Rievaulx's influential *Rule* (ca. 1160–62), which *Ancrene Wisse* explicitly cites (99b; 162), contains a temptation scenario in which an old woman "feeds" lascivious gossip to the anchoress through the latter's cell window, thus introducing dangerous images into her mind:

> Her mouth widens in laughter and the sweetened poison that she drinks spreads throughout her whole body. When finally they part, ... quiet returns, but the poor wretch turns over and over in her heart the fantasies [*in corde versat imagines*] born of her idle listening; her reflections only fan more fiercely the flame enkindled

---

18. *The Middle English Genesis and Exodus*, ed. Olof Arngart (Lund, 1968), p. 62, lines 333–36 ("Þanne ðogte eue on hire mod, / 'Þanne is tis fruit wel swiðe good, / Fair on sigðhe and softe on hond, / Of ðis fruit wile ic hauen fond' ").

19. Words, images, and memory: *Conf* 10.8, 14, 30. Phantasms, *GenM* 2.20.30. Words as signs, *Mag* 12.39. On memory and images in medieval rhetoric, see Frances A. Yates, *The Art of Memory* (Chicago, 1966), chap. 3. On images and moral psychology, see Robertson, *Preface to Chaucer*, pp. 69–75.

by her chatter. Like a drunkard she staggers through the psalms, gropes through her reading, wavers while at prayer.[20]

Here mouth, window, and ear form a conduit of verbal temptation having psychological and sexual overtones. Aelred's alimentary trope, with its allusion to "forbidden food," relies on the same imagery (mouth, ear, poison, sweetness) used in traditional accounts of the Fall, like that of Avitus.

Adhering more closely than Aelred to the Serpent-Eve episode as a paradigm of male-female seduction, Bernard of Clairvaux focuses explicitly on Eve's ear as a symbol for the verbal and psychosexual dynamics of temptation.[21] For example, in a dramatic apostrophe to Eve at the moment of her fall, where Bernard engages Eve in "dialogue" about her actions, he stresses that although she was tempted by the sight of the apple, it was the Serpent's powerfully persuasive words that prompted her to "drink the poison" (as he puts it a few lines later):

> What about you, Eve? You were in Paradise, charged along with your husband to tend it and care for it. . . . You are forbidden to eat that fruit, why do you look at it? "Oh!" you answer, "I am only looking. . . . " It may not itself be a sin but it is leading you on to sin. . . . While your attention was taken up with this the serpent quietly slipped into your heart and his soft words are being spoken, gentle persuasive words, lies to lull fear to sleep. "No, you will not die," he says. He strengthens your attention, he rouses your appetite, he whets your curiosity, he stirs up your greed.[22]

The list of rhetorical effects ("strengthens," "rouses," "whets," "stirs up") stresses that Eve was seduced *verbally*. At the same time, the Serpent "slipping in" points to the psychological and sexual dynamics that also interest Bernard.

These various aspects of Eve's seduction converge in another

20. Aelred of Rievaulx, *De institutione inclusarum* 2, *Corpus Christianorum, continuatio medievalis*, vol. 1 (Turnholt, 1971), p. 638; trans. Mary Paul Macpherson, *A Rule of Life for a Recluse*, in *The Works of Aelred of Rievaulx*, vol. 1 (Spencer, Mass., 1971), p. 46 (modified).

21. Bernard's works are cited from *Opera*; unless otherwise indicated, translations are mine.

22. *De gradibus humilitatis et superbiae* 10.30, *Opera* 3:39–40; trans. M. Ambrose Conway, *The Steps of Humility and Pride*, in *The Works of Bernard of Clairvaux* (Spencer, Mass., and Washington, D.C., 1970–) 5:58–59 ("Auget curam, dum incitat gulam; acuit curiositatem, dum suggerit cupiditatem").

Bernardine passage that uses traditional Eve/Mary typology to make Eve's ear the conduit of seduction and sin. Reviving the old patristic topos of Eve's erotic encounter with the Serpent, as contrasted with Mary's pure impregnation by the divine *Logos*, Bernard makes the sexualized feminine ear the receptacle of a masculine word/seed (either divine or diabolical): "The winding serpent was sent by the Devil so that it might pour venom through the ears [*per aures*] of the woman into her mind, and thus pour it thence into the source of all posterity; but the angel Gabriel was sent by God so that he might cast forth the Word of the Father through the ear of the Virgin into her belly and mind, so that the antidote might enter by the same path as the poison."[23] In each case, Bernard sets up the crucial linkage of language, psyche, and sexuality by having the word (*verbum*) pass through the woman's ear into her mind so as to bear fruit in her womb, the fruit of Eve's womb being a sinful race and that of Mary's being the Redeemer.[24] In receiving the phallic Serpent's verbal venom, Eve's ear becomes a vivid image for sexual seduction through language. As a path or entrance (*via*) into the woman's body and soul, the ear (with its sexual implications) evokes not only the (male) medieval notion of the female body as a penetrable container but also the (male) notion of the soul itself as a vulnerable (feminine) interior.[25]

Eve's ear is also central to Bernard's tropological version of Genesis 3. Relying on Augustine's moral psychology to recount the inner life of a tempted monk, Bernard uses Eve's ear to symbolize susceptible "feminine" appetite: "[The Serpent] finds the neglected opening in the wall of circumstance and enters the paradise of my mind unresisted, discovers me sleeping within the very retreat of evil, and creeping up to the little ear of my Eve [*auriculum Evae meae*] and hissing into it the poison of evil persuasion, awakens her by the side of the sleeper and leads her away along the path of curiosity to the tree of the knowledge of good and evil."[26] In evoking "the little ear of my Eve," Bernard combines two key Augustinian

23. *Sermo secundus in die pentecostes* 3, *Opera* 5:167.

24. On the Serpent's "seed" (*semen*, Gen. 3.15), see above, Chapter 2.2. Medieval and Renaissance paintings of the Annunciation often show the divine *Logos* as a ray of light penetrating Mary's ear.

25. Doubtless this notion was influenced by the feminine gender of Latin *anima* ("soul").

26. *Parabola de octo beatitudinibus*; *Opera* 6/2:299. The monk is lazily lying "in the bosom of my Eve [*in sinu Evae meae*]" (p. 299). Bernard, *Sententiae* 3.107 (*Opera* 6/2:174) explicitly glosses the Serpent as sensory suggestion, Eve as "feminine" appetite, and Adam as "masculine" reason.

ideas: the "inner ear" (*auris interior*), and the "feminine" appetite ("Eve") that is easily moved to delight by the images admitted through the senses ("Serpent").[27] Although here the feminized inner "ear" is a trope, and as such is part of an interiorized temptation scenario, it suggests that women are especially responsive to verbal temptation. At the same time, Eve's "ear" again has sexual implications, as reinforced here by such images as the opening (*foramen*) in the wall, the phallic Serpent's "poison," and Eve's arousal from "sleep."

Eve's ear and the aural dynamics of the Fall, along with their sexual symbolism, also figure in the visual art of the scholastic period, as, for example, in the sculpture at Chartres. A carving on the central bay of the North Portal (13th c.) shows the Devil standing behind Eve and speaking into her ear. A typological echo of this scene appears in a carving located in a homologous position on the opposite portal (dating from the same period) and which depicts the Devil, with a phallic serpent dangling from his waist, similarly tempting a woman attired in elegant (noble) dress (fig. 6).[28] The latter carving evokes not only the aural dynamics of temptation but also its sexual overtones. Much like this pair of carvings, *Ancrene Wisse* and the *Livre du Chevalier* use Eve's temptation as a paradigm for the seduction of her medieval "daughters."

2. Falling into Conversation

The first mention of the Fall in *Ancrene Wisse* occurs early in part 2 ("The Custody of the Senses"), which deals with the dangers of the various senses (or sensory organs) as represented by the windows of the anchorhold.[29] Walled up in her cell for life as a living icon or exemplum of spirituality, the anchoress typically was waited on by servants in an adjoining cell and supported by alms from the community at large.[30] Thus she could communicate with the outer world

27. *Conf* 12.11, and 1.5 (*aures cordis*).

28. Eve and Devil: north portal, central bay, right side. Woman and Devil: south portal, central bay, right side. Reproduced in Étienne Houvet, *Cathédral de Chartres*, 5 vols. in 7 pts. (Chelles, 1919–21), vol. 3, pt. 2, pl. 34; and vol. 4, pt. 2, pl. 2.

29. On the logic and organization of part 2, see Alexandra Barratt, "The Five Wits and Their Structural Significance in Part II of *Ancrene Wisse*," MAE 56 (1987): 12–24.

30. On the cell and its furnishings, see Janet Grayson, *Structure and Imagery in "Ancrene Wisse"* (Hanover, N.H., 1974), pp. 6–8. For general background, see Ann K. Warren, *Anchorites and Their Patrons in Medieval England* (Berkeley, 1985).

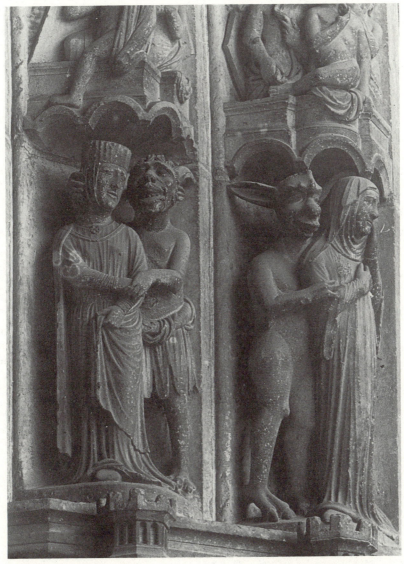

6. Devils tempting women. Stone carving, 13th c.: Chartres Cathedral, south portal, central bay, right side. Foto Marburg / Art Resource, New York.

only through her cell's windows, which *Ancrene Wisse* treats as dangerous avenues of personal contact (visual, verbal, and even tactile) and as sexual and psychological symbols. Just as the walled cell represents a typological garden, so its windows represent Bernard's polysemous "openings" in the "paradise" of the soul that can give entrance to the "Serpent."[31]

At her windows the anchoress was allowed to receive visitors, particularly men, only in carefully prescribed ways. On the one hand, any male visitor—even a cleric—might be a seducer. On the other hand, the anchoress, as seen or heard through her window, might "tempt" men by her feminine beauty. Fearing "harmful friendships," the author lays down strict rules about window protocol.[32] For example, windows (small openings in the masonry) normally are to be covered with a cloth, and when a man is at the window the anchoress should never unveil her face, for she is like a "pit" into which animals fall—an image clearly alluding to female sexual anatomy as transformed by the author into moralized landscape.[33] As E. J. Dobson remarks, "When any question of sex arises, the author reveals a distinct streak of morbid imagination: about the consequences of hands touching through windows, the methods of seducers, secret strainings and gropings."[34]

The author exploits the sexual and psychological symbolism of the windows by setting up "an extended though submerged series of analogies between the anchoress's cell and her body," and between the cell and the soul, using wordplay on *þurl* ("opening") to make the windows represent bodily or sensory apertures.[35] For example, the anchoress is to close "the windows of her eyes"(*eiþurles*) against various tempting sights (Nero 14v; 26–27), and likewise to shut her ears (*eare*) and window (*ehþurh*) against tempting talk (17b;

31. This sexual symbolism was enhanced by the belief that sometimes the cell opening (*foramen*) was enlarged "to allow [the anchoress] to pass through or her paramour to enter" (Aelred, *De institutione inclusarum* 2). Cf. Bernard, *Parabola*, as cited earlier, on "the neglected opening" (*foramen*); also Canticle 5.4.

32. Salu, p. 27, trans. from MS. Vitellius F.7 11b where Corpus MS. has lost a leaf.

33. "The pit [*put*] is her fair face, and her white neck, and her light eye, and her hand if she holds it out before his eyes; and further, her speech is a pit, if it is not controlled, and all things whatsoever that belong to her, through which sinful love may be aroused" (Nero 13v; 25; cf. Prov. 23.27).

34. Dobson, *The Origins of "Ancrene Wisse,"* pp. 155–56.

35. Barratt, "Five Wits," p. 13. *AW* compares the cell to the body by describing both as "houses" (*huses*) for the soul, and Mary as Christ's "anchor-house" (102b; 167); also, *chambre* is used for both the cell (27a; 45) and the soul or "heart" (23b; 40).

31).[36] Clearly regarding lechery rather than pride as the deadliest of the sins, the author spells out his anxiety about the penetrable female body by urging that the cell windows be covered by curtains bearing a cross symbolizing "clean maidenhood" and be "fastened and well locked on every side" (13a; 22). Garden imagery for the female body enhances this sexual symbolism, as when he asks, "Your flesh, what fruit does it bear at all its apertures [*openunges*]?" (75b; 123).[37]

Following a hierarchy of the senses that traditionally puts eyesight first, the author initially evokes the Fall—and Eve's experience in particular—as an example of visual temptation: "Of Eve, our first mother, it is recorded that at the very beginning of her sin its entry was through her eyes. 'And the woman saw that the tree was good to eat....' Observe how Holy Writ speaks of this, telling how sin began in an inward manner; this inward sin went before and made way for evil desire, and the deed followed, the consequences of which are felt by all mankind" (13b; 23). Following Bernard's apostrophe to Eve, as quoted earlier, the author goes on to "question" Eve at the moment of her temptation, and likewise to censure her "reply" that simply looking at the apple is not a sin.

As a whole, this passage sets a pattern for the later seduction scenarios, which are modeled on the Fall, by concretizing the entry (*inʒong*) of sin through the senses and emphasizing that sinful impulses work inwardly (*inwardliche*), first arousing the desire that leads to the external sin itself. The author translates Eve's experience for his female audience by generalizing the forbidden fruit as an object of desire ("This apple . . . symbolizes [*bitacneð*] all those things towards which desire and sinful delight turn"), by attaching a specifically sexual meaning to the fruit ("When you look upon a man, you are in Eve's case; you are looking on the apple"), and by evoking a moral and genealogical link between Eve and the anchoress ("Eve . . . has many daughters who, following their mother, answer in the same way" [13b–14a; 23]). The interpretive principles used here—symbolism, typology, and genealogy—typify how the author turns the Fall into a cautionary tale for the anchoress.

---

36. In the first quotation, Nero is used because Corpus is missing a leaf at this point. See also Corpus 20b (Salu, p. 35): "Close your ears [*tunen ower earen*] . . . , and if need be, lock your windows [*spearren ower þurles*]."

37. Also, as Christ's beloved, the anchoress is to make Christ's "arbour" (*herbearhe*) within herself from the flowers of her virtues (92a; 150); and she is to till or cultivate her heart (*tilie wið þe heorte*, 104a; 170), echoing Adam's duty to keep (*custodire*) the Garden (Gen. 2.15).

In the passage on Eve and the apple, the author not only attaches sexual meaning to the Fall but also assigns the initiative to the woman ("When you look upon a man"). Continuing, he describes her desire as "leaping" like an animal from her soul to its male sexual object: " 'But do you think,' someone will say, 'that I shall leap upon him because I look at him?' God knows, my dear sister, more surprising things have happened. Your mother Eve leaped after her eyes had leapt; from the eye to the apple, from the apple in paradise down to the earth, and from earth to hell." Despite his later warnings about seductive male overtures toward the anchoress, the author continues to worry about this active female desire, fearing that it will collaborate in her seduction.[38]

Moving from the eye to the mouth, the author next evokes the Fall—and, again, specifically Eve—to illustrate the dangers of excessive speech. He stresses that Eve gave herself away by talking too much: "In Paradise Eve talked a great deal to the serpent and told him all that God had taught her and Adam about the apple, and so the devil [feond] soon learned her weakness through her own words, and found out how to destroy her" (16a; 29). Using traditional typology, the author goes on to contrast Eve's "cackling" with Mary's reserve ("Eve had no fear when she spoke with the serpent. Our Lady was full of fear at the words of Gabriel"), and he adds a warning that the anchoress is not to speak too freely to her confessors, though "it would be very surprising if any of them were to allow his eyes to stray toward the woodland glade" (16b; 29).[39] The "woodland glade," alluding to a popular lyric about a woodland tryst, evokes the locus amoenus of medieval garden typology.[40] The motif recurs later in a crucial place.

The notion that Eve gave herself away by talking too much is consistent with the clerical commonplace about feminine loquacity and about women as faulty and leaking vessels of spirituality. Eve is said to give away "all that God had taught her and Adam about the apple," as though having violated her marriage by sharing privileged or intimate knowledge with a prying interloper. With this remark comes a shift in emphasis from visual prompting in the Fall to verbal dynamics, particularly the idea that Eve opened herself to

38. R. E. Kaske, "Eve's 'Leaps' in the Ancrene Riwle," MAE 29 (1960): 22–24, contrasts Eve's sensual "leaping" with the redemptive "leaps" of Christ.

39. I have restored the phrase towart te wude lehe ("toward the woodland glade"), omitted by Salu.

40. E.g., Le Jeu d'Adam (Ordo representacionis Ade), p. 17, s.d. (amenissemus locus). On the lyric, see Eric J. Dobson, ed., The English Text of the Ancrene Riwle (Cleopatra MS.), EETS OS 267 (London, 1972), p. 77n.

further temptation through her words (*þurh hire word*)—or, as a later version adds, through her excessive speech (*mychel speche*).[41] Janet Grayson points out that this passage is *logically* prior to the earlier discussion of sight: "Eve looked upon the apple and fell; but first she gave away her secrets through babbling in conversation with the serpent, so that when he learned her weakness, he knew how to destroy her. In this way, sins of speech lead to sins of sight."[42] As in the passage about the apple, where Eve looked and "leaped," woman here has an active (speaking) role in her own seduction.

Significantly, the exemplum about Eve's talkativeness is framed in terms of a gendered hierarchy of teaching and knowledge that reflects patristic notions about the order of instruction in Paradise.[43] Just before mentioning how Eve told the Serpent all of God's teaching (*al þe lesceun*), the author criticizes the anchoress who would be a *savante*: "A woman who ought to be an anchoress sometimes sets up as a scholar [*meistre*], teaching those who have come to teach her, and wishes to be soon recognized and known among the wise. Known she is, for by those same sayings by which she wants to be considered wise, [the priest] sees that she is foolish, for she is looking for esteem and instead she incurs blame" (16a; 28–29). Citing Paul, the author restricts the anchoress to teaching *only other women*: "Do not preach to any man, nor let any man ask you for advice or give you advice; give your advice only to women. St Paul forbade women to preach: 'I suffer not women to teach' [1 Tim. 2.12]" (17b; 31). Although the author does not quote the verses about Genesis 3 that directly follow, Paul's politics of Paradise clearly are the grounds for this gendered order of instruction. Moreover, the Adam/Eve hierarchy obviously extends to that of author and reader as well, providing a pattern of male authority and female submission that embraces the rhetorical function of *Ancrene Wisse* itself.

Having dealt with the eyes and the mouth, *Ancrene Wisse* turns to the ears, and to the dangers of hearing. This section repeatedly evokes the Fall through a matrix of imagery—serpents, poison, orifices—and through various scriptural texts traditionally used to gloss Genesis 3:

> Against all evil speech, my dear sisters, stop your ears, and hold in abhorrence the mouth which pours out poison.... Evil speech

41. Pepys MS. fol. 381a, p. 25.
42. Grayson, *Structure and Imagery*, p. 46. Dinshaw, *Chaucer's Sexual Poetics*, p. 6, cites this passage (Pepys MS.) to the same effect: "Eve's speech ... is said to be the cause of the Fall."
43. See above, Chapter 1.1.

is threefold, venomous, foul, and idle.... Anyone who spits out
such uncleanness into the ears of an anchoress should have his
mouth stopped.... "The devil is a liar and the father of lies...."
Backbiting and flattery and inciting others to do evil things—these
are not true forms of human speech; they are blasts of the devil's
own voice.... "The Serpent," says Solomon, "strikes soundlessly."
(20b–21a; 35–36)

Essentially, all who use evil speech are "the devil's serpents" (23a;
39). In moral-psychological terms, the serpent imagery furthers the
familiar idea that evil speech can contaminate the soul. In sexual
terms, it conveys the author's (by now well-established) anxiety
about the anchoress's vulnerable lower "window." And the hints of
diabolical ventriloquism, which echo Augustine, anticipate the Fall
typology of the later seduction scenarios, where the seducer is
treated as the Devil's mouthpiece.

The book's main seduction scenario, which dramatizes the Fall in
terms of the various sensory "windows" considered so far,[44] does
not directly mention Genesis 3 but implicitly puts the encounter
between the seducer and the anchoress in terms of the established
Serpent-Eve typology, while alluding to Genesis 3 in other ways as
well. Furthermore, the author enhances the Fall typology by con-
trastively framing the seduction scenario with an account of the
marriage between Christ and the anchoress, which is cast in terms
of another allegorized biblical garden.

Quoting from the Canticle of Canticles as glossed by Bernard,
the author describes Christ as a jealous husband who keeps a close
watch on his spouse: "He is jealous of all your conduct.... His ear
is always inclined towards you and He hears everything; if you make
any show of love towards what is not virtuous, His eye always sees
you" (23b; 39–40). Invoking courtly roles and rhetoric, the author
characterizes Christ and anchoress as lover (leofmon) and beloved
(leof), supplying each with appropriate "speeches" to the other. For
example, Christ says: "Show your face to me and to no other.... I
am not a bold lover. I will embrace my beloved only in a retired
place." And the anchoress, following "the lady in the Canticles,"
responds: "I hear my beloved speaking. He calls me and I must go"
(25b–26a; 42–43). This spiritual marriage patterned on the allego-

44. The author explains his procedure: "Sight, speech, and hearing have been
treated separately and in turn. Let us now go back and speak of all these together"
(23a–b; 39).

rized Canticle contrasts with and implicitly censures the infidelity dramatized in the seduction scenario patterned on Genesis 3.

The seduction scenario proper (25a–b; 42) begins by reminding the anchoress that she never should show herself at her window to male visitors: "If any man asks to see you, ask him what good could come of it, for I see many dangers in it, and no good." The more insistent the man who wishes to see the anchoress, the more she should distrust him, the author continues. If he is so senseless (*awed*) as to reach toward the window curtain, she should shut the window immediately. And a verbal overture should evoke even more decisive measures: "As soon as anyone falls [*feleð*] into any harmful speech that inclines [*falle*] toward unchaste love, spar the window at once and give him no answer at all, but walk away saying this verse loudly enough for him to hear it: 'Depart from me, ye malignant, and I will search the commandments of my God [Ps.118.115]. The wicked have told me fables, but not as thy law [v. 85]'; and go to your altar saying the *Miserere*" (trans. modified). Significantly, the seducer's first verbal foray is couched in terms of the verb "to fall."[45] By falling into conversation, the author suggests, the daughter of Eve might recapitulate the original seduction.

This part of the seduction scenario also evokes the Fall by way of a certain moment in Augustine's temptation-and-conversion in the garden, where Continentia says to Augustine, "Stop your ears against those unclean members of yours," and then quotes the same verse about deceptive fables.[46] The anchorhold with its covered windows helps concretize the imagery of "shutting" out tempting voices and contaminating words. Not only is the scriptural verse about divine truth and seductive lies thematically apt to the situation, but, recited *aloud*, as recommended, it would function rhetorically as a spoken counterpoint to the seducer's voice, its recitation helping to "shut" window and ear alike.

Continuing, the author points out that reciting a litany is safer than offering a spontaneous rebuke to the seducer, for such a rebuke might lead him to renew his attempts, likened to breathing upon a spark: "He might answer the rebuke and breathe [*blawen*] gently as it were on the ashes in a way that might make a spark spring into

45. *Middle English Dictionary* (hereafter *MED*), ed. Hans Kurath, Sherman M. Kuhn, and Robert E. Lewis (Ann Arbor, 1952–), s.v. *fallen* (v.) 2, attests application to Genesis 3 prior to 1250 (quot. *Bestiary*). Note also *fal* (n.) as used in *AW*: "[a] great shame it is to lie for so long after a fall [*val*], and especially under the devil" (88b; 144).

46. *Conf* 8.11. See further above, Chapter 3.5.

life" (trans. modified). Although this passage may allude ironically to the "spark" (*scintilla*) of divine love, a traditional mystical image, *Ancrene Wisse* tends to use the imagery of breath and fire for diabolical or sensual prompting, as when characterizing evil words as "blasts" (*bleas*) of the Devil's voice (as cited earlier).[47]

Besides linking the seducer to the Devil, this imagery of exsufflation stresses the corporeal aspect of language, and of speech in particular, which originates inside the body and issues forth as breath. One of the French versions of *Ancrene Wisse*, amplifying the English original, attaches rhetorical labels to the seducer's carnal breathings: "He may speak so beautifully and sweetly that some spark may quicken to life."[48] "Beautiful" and "sweet," with their physical connotations, emphasize the dangerously pleasurable aspect of speech. Another French version warns directly about the sexual implications of the seducer's overture: "He may reply so deceptively and speak so subtly that some spark may enter your heart and come to life so that he embrace all your body."[49]

The author next dramatizes how the seducer, if allowed to speak, might use deceptive language in the form of complaint or lament (*pleinte*) to arouse illicit desires in the anchoress.[50] The seducer's hypothetical speech is cast in the courtly style, for in trying to win Christ's "bride" for himself, he also usurps and subverts Christ's own courtly idiom: " 'I would rather die than intend any unchastity to you' (swearing great oaths), 'but even if I had sworn not to, I would not be able to prevent myself from loving you. Is anyone in worse case than I? It robs me of many nights' sleep. And now I have told you. Yet even if I go mad, you shall hear no more of how things are with me.' " The author adds that the anchoress "forgives" the seducer these words "because he speaks so fairly [*feire*]" (my trans.). The Serpent's "fair" words to Eve are mentioned in English texts dating as far back as the eighth century.[51] Earlier used in *Ancrene*

---

47. Elsewhere the Devil blows (*blaweð*) with his bellows on the sparks of sin (81a; 132). See Hrabanus Maurus, *De universo* 6.3: "The Devil's breath [*halitus diaboli*] is a hidden inbreathing [*inspiratio occulta*] by which the hearts of sinners are made to burn with carnal love" (*PL* 111:180).

48. Vitellius 19r ("si beel et si doucement parler qe askune estencele porreit avenir").

49. Trinity 135b ("si parler sotilment, ke aucune estincele enz en uostre quer purroit entrer, e tantost se auiuer, ke tot uostre cors si enbraceroit").

50. For semantics, see *MED*, s.v. *pleint* 1a; and, for etymology, *OED*, s.v. *Plaint*. The French MSS. also have *pleinte* (Vitellius 19r, Trinity 135b).

51. *Genesis A* 899, *ASPR* 1:30, Eve confesses to God that the Serpent persuaded her "þurh fægir word."

Wisse to describe how the apple looked to Eve's eye, *feire* is a key epithet for seductive speech throughout the work; as either adjective or adverb, it betokens a decorous or courteous style, usually as employed by the Devil or one of his proxies.[52]

The content of the seducer's speech is the stuff of conventional (male) love lyric and complaint, genuflecting before the female object of desire who traditionally causes the lover's sleeplessness, potential madness, and possible death. As such, it represents what the author apparently imagines women as wanting (or expecting) to hear from men—that is, praise of, or at least sly allusion to, the power of feminine sex appeal. As part of a seduction scenario, however, this rhetoric of desire is circumscribed by moral considerations, and the lyrical appeals to passion, madness, and death are implicitly meant to spell out the dire consequences of carnal sin. Typology assists the author in condemning the seducer's abuse of courtly speech. The seducer's language echoes the sort of flattery that was commonly mouthed by the Serpent in contemporary versions of the feudalized Fall, as in the twelfth-century Anglo-Norman play of the Fall, *Le Jeu d'Adam*, where the Serpent flatters Eve in frankly physical terms as a *belle dame*.[53] Furthermore, prior to the main seduction scenario, *Ancrene Wisse* has already used typological imagery to associate flattery with the Fall, condemning it as "venomous" speech, as "blasts of the devil's own voice," and the like.[54]

The author emphasizes the extent to which desire is not only represented by language but also constructed by it. This view is completely consistent with the account of language and desire bequeathed by Augustine to medieval tradition, particularly in the form of glosses on the Fall.[55] Furthermore, it highlights the pleasure principle of language embodied in the medieval art of love, as codified by Andreas Capellanus in his treatise *De amore* (ca. 1180). Like the amorous dialogues presented in that work, the seducer's speech

52. E.g., "[The Devil] sometimes [makes] one of you believe that it would be flattery to speak courteously [*feire*]" (61a; 100). The Scorpion of Lechery ("a kind of serpent") "makes a show of fairness [*feier semblant*]" (55b–56a; 92). For other verbal applications, see *MED*, s.v. *fair* (adj.) 6, 7. Cf. Rom. 16.18–20, linking deception and the appetites to "fair and flattering words" (*dulces sermones*), and alluding to Genesis 3.

53. The Devil praises Eve's *bel cors* and *figure*, citing her exalted station as *dame del mond* (*Le Jeu d'Adam* 253–55, ed. Noomen, p. 37).

54. Trinity MS. describes this speech as "seductive" (*soudiuant*, 135b), a term already used of the Serpent in the 12th century; e.g., *Le Jeu d'Adam* 466, ed. Noomen, p. 48 ("le serpent suduiant").

55. On desire and language, see above, Chapters 2.4, and 3.2.

suggests that "desire does not necessarily precede language" but that "desire is produced by language and seeks its satisfaction *in* it."[56] Even more than he loves the idea of love (as does the youthful Augustine, *Conf* 3.1), the seducer loves amorous language, and the author fears that this discursive love will infect the anchoress as well.

Going on to describe the aftermath of the seducer's flattering speech, the author now focuses on its lingering *inward* effects—the dangerous dynamics of language, memory, and desire in the "feminine" psyche. He is mainly concerned that, once spoken, the seducer's words will continue to exert a seductive pull on the anchoress, even after her tempter has left:

> "The eyes are ever on the woodland glade," the thoughts are always on what he has already said; and even after he has gone, she will go on thinking about those words, often, when she should be giving all her attention to other things. Then he will look out for an opportunity, at which he breaks the promise he has made, swears that it is too much for him—and so the evil grows, ever longer, ever worse. For no friendship is so evil as friendship that is feigned. An enemy who pretends to be a friend is the worst of traitors. So, my dear sisters, to such men refuse any opening for speech. (25b; 42, modified)

Here again the temptation, now internalized, is framed by various allusions to the Fall. As a deceptive "enemy" (*feond*) who pretends to be a friend, the seducer is likened to the treacherous Devil (*feond*) disguised as the friendly Serpent in the earlier passage on Eve's loquacity.[57] The conversational "opening" (*in3ong*) sought by the seducer continues the window imagery that is central to the book's Fall typology, now adding the ear to the eye and the other openings guarded by the daughter of Eve. And, finally, the "woodland glade" (*wude lehe*), mentioned previously in the passage on Eve's loquacity, evokes the scene of Eve's seduction near the forbidden Tree, a traditional emblem for carnal knowledge. The wood or forest was a conventional trysting spot, and as part of the moralized and sexu-

---

56. Toril Moi, "Desire in Language: Andreas Capellanus and the Controversy of Courtly Love," in *Medieval Literature: Criticism, Ideology, and History*, ed. David Aers (New York, 1986), pp. 11–33 (p. 24, orig. emphasis).

57. As a "traitor" (*sweoke*), the seducer is further likened to the Devil, thus described throughout *AW* (e.g., 63b, 74b). The adjacent mention of *feondschipe* recalls how the Tempter speaks to Eve *þurh feondscipe* in *Genesis B* 610 (*ASPR* 1:22).

alized landscape in *Ancrene Wisse*, the "woodland glade" suggests not only the "shady loves," "shady pleasures," and "shady words" variously evoked by patristic authors in connection with the Fall but also the sylvan aspect of female sexual anatomy as construed by the male imagination.[58] The repeated lyrical tag thus gives a local habitation and a name to the recapitulated Fall. At the same time, it completes a punning motif that works its way through the whole scenario—from the seducer's senseless (*awed*) overture, to his mad (*wod*) passion, and now to its fulfillment in the covert, sensual wood (*wude*).

In its verbal dynamics, this passage relies on Augustine's language theory and moral psychology. Augustine's tropology of the Fall specifies that tempting "suggestion" can come either through the senses or through memory; and in the temptation scenario preceding his conversion Augustine dramatizes the seductive power of remembered sensory stimuli, especially words.[59] The possession of verbal memories is in itself morally neutral—"a voice [leaves] a fixed impression on the ear by which it can be recalled as though it were sounding" (*Conf* 10.9). But habit "fixes" certain images in the memory, and, says Augustine, these images "come into my thoughts, and, though when I am awake they are strengthless, in sleep they not only cause pleasure [*delectationem*] but go so far as to obtain assent and something very like reality" (10.30). Deliberately to recall and enjoy illicit words or images, as the anchoress does, constitutes a sinful delight or pleasure of the mind (*delectatio cogitationis*), which Augustine's tropology of the Fall associates specifically with appetitive "Eve."[60] This state of mind is the same one discussed in Aelred's account of the anchoress taking pleasure, after the fact, in "turn[ing] over and over in her heart the fantasies [*imagines*] born of her idle listening." Likewise, in *Ancrene Wisse* the anchoress obsessively ("always," "often") rehearses the seducer's words after he has left, thus keeping temptation alive through memory. In cultivating a state of mind associated with Eve, the anchoress is doubly the daughter of her first mother.

58. Augustine, *Conf* 2.1 ("umbrosi amores"); Ambrose, *Par* 13.63, 65 ("umbratiles voluptates," "umbratiles sermones"). On woodland trysts, see also Andreas Capellanus, *De amore* 1.6 (dialogue 5).

59. Augustine, *Dom* 1.12.34; *Conf* 8.11.

60. On tropology, see above, Chapters 2.4, 3.1. *AW* makes the site of these fantasies the "heorte" (25b, 74b, as quoted; Latin MSS., *cor*). The "heart" can be the soul or mind in general (*MED*, s.v. *herte* 2) or the emotions or appetites in particular (*MED*, s.v., 3). Note reference to "excessive delight, up towards the heart" (75a; 122), as cited below.

A later passage, in part 4 ("Temptations"), describes this perilous state of mind more explicitly, again in terms patterned on Genesis 3 and Augustine's tropology of the Fall:

> The old deceiver speaks to her heart words which she once heard foully spoken aloud, or he recalls something she has seen, or impurities which she herself has at some time committed. All this he sets forth before the eyes of her heart in order to taint her with the thought of past sins when he cannot with new, and in this way he often brings back into the dazed soul, by letting her savour them, those same sins which had long ago been got rid of in repentant grief. (74b; 121)

This passage puts internal temptation into specifically verbal terms, following the pattern of Augustine's tropology (where the Serpent "speaks" to Eve) and recalling Bernard's evocation of the inner Serpent "hissing . . . the poison of evil persuasion" into "the little ear of my Eve."[61] The tempter, now as a voice "speaking" within, is able to "taint" (*bifulen*) the soul with illicit desires by reviving the memory of sinful pleasures.

As discussed earlier in this book, Augustinian tradition regarded words as signs that were to be "used" to reach eternal truths rather than to be "enjoyed" in earthly and temporal terms "for their own sake."[62] Hence the anchoress who deliberately dwells on seductive words (and illicit fantasies) is dangerously fixated on not just temporal things but temporal language itself, a fixation that constitutes an "idolatry" or "fornication" that began with the Fall and the first sins of language. Furthermore, in recalling, contemplating, and enjoying the words of her would-be seducer as opposed to those of her divine Spouse, the anchoress substitutes an illusory temporal presence for the true eternal presence of God. As she futilely tries to embrace ephemeral verbal phantoms rather than the *Verbum Dei*, the anchoress—"wandering" like the youthful Augustine in the "tracks" of verbal "fictions" (*Conf* 1.17)—becomes entrapped in language instead of transcending it. Although the litany of vows and

---

61. The source for this passage seems to be Gregory, *Moralia in Iob* 1.49 (in *PL* 75:499–76:782), glossing 2 Samuel 4 (see Salu, p. 121n). It is followed by an Augustinian gloss on Gen. 3.15: "If your enemy hurts you in the feet, that is to say, tempts you through the desires of the flesh, do not be too much afraid on account of so low a wound, unless there is too much inflammation, through the consent of the reason, with excessive delight, up towards the heart" (75a; 122).

62. On *frui/uti*, see above, Chapter 2.4.

endearments that she is to speak to her divine Spouse also takes the form of temporal and vocalized words, these words are intended not only to counter the romantic appeal of the seducer's "fables" but ultimately to carry her tempted soul above and beyond language altogether and into the transcendent realm of the Word.

3. Fig Leaves and "Naked Confession"

Although the author of *Ancrene Wisse* would like to maintain a strict moral cleavage between seductive and redemptive language, between tempting and edifying words, he realizes that the latter kind of discourse, no matter how well intended, can have corrupting effects. His awareness of this paradox is especially apparent when he is warning the anchoress about sexual sins or trying to define a "safe" language for confessing such sins after the fact. He knows that even the prohibitions in his own Rule can perversely turn into temptations and that explicit confessions can lure the anchoress back down the garden path of sin. In facing this paradox, he reflects an Augustinian awareness that even "redeemed language" is still enmeshed in the moral ambiguities of the Fall.

Paul had maintained that the written Law itself could "arouse" sinful passions "to bear fruit for death" (Romans 7.5). Augustine similarly held that "this Law *begets* the very carnal desire that it forbids,"[63] as evidenced by his own youthful theft of pears (with its typological overtones of the Fall): "Our real pleasure was simply in doing something that was not allowed" (*Conf* 2.4). Medieval doctors of the soul like Bernard recognized that this legacy of the Fall touched even the monastic rule itself, as when (in a sermon) he ironically paraphrases the Serpent: "Does none of you hear in his heart, 'Why did God say to you that you shall keep this Rule?' "[64] In his comparison of Genesis 1–3 and Augustine's *Confessions*, Kenneth Burke explains that to forbid is inevitably to tempt because all negatives imply their positives and because merely naming the forbidden tends to arouse the imagination: "The negative contains the principle of its own annihilation," and "the 'No trespassing' signs of empire . . . both stimulate desires and demand their repression."[65]

A patristic corollary to the idea that the Law begets sin (or sinful

63. Vance, *Mervelous Signals*, p. 10 (orig. emphasis); see pp. 6–11.

64. *Sermones de diversis* 22.4, *Opera* 6/1:172 ("Cur praecepit vobis Deus ut istam Regulam teneretis?").

65. Burke, *The Rhetoric of Religion*, pp. 218, 219.

desire) was that merely mentioning certain sins, especially sexual
ones, could prompt the sinful imagination. Paul urged that such sins
not even be named (Eph. 5.3), and Augustine held that the Fall had
so compromised language and the human mind that merely naming
the sexual organs, even in an edifying context, inevitably aroused
tainted thoughts in the imagination: "[Adam and Eve] incurred exile
from paradise before they could unite with one another dispassion-
ately and deliberately in the work of propagating their kind. Hence
it is impossible that when [sexual intercourse] is mentioned, it
should now bring before our imagination anything but our own
experience of turbulent lust rather than any speculative notion of a
calm act of will." Attempting to write with equanimity about what
sex was like—or would have been like—in the Garden of Eden,
Augustine confesses that because of the Fall's lingering effects on
language, "a sense of shame [pudor] impedes my speech."[66]

Following Paul and Augustine, the author of *Ancrene Wisse*
realizes, in the first place, that to affix a "No trespassing" sign to
the tree of forbidden sexual knowledge is inevitably to risk arousing
the reader's curiosity about the sexual acts he forbids. His awareness
that to forbid is also to tempt, a theme throughout *Ancrene Wisse*,
is especially well illustrated in part 4 ("Temptations") by a passage
on "the Scorpion of Lechery," an emblem associated with Genesis
3.[67] Alluding to the dangerous power of words to "soil" the mind
by way of the ears, and to his own Augustinian "shame" at sexual
language, the author refuses to name certain sexual sins:

> The Scorpion of Lechery has young which are such that it is not
> fitting for a well-bred mouth even to name some of them, for the
> name alone might hurt well-bred ears, and soil [sulen] hearts that
> are clean.... I dare not name the unnatural offspring of this poison-
> tailed Scorpion of the devil.... I may not speak, out of shame
> [scheome], and dare not, for fear anyone should learn more of evil
> than she already knows, and should be thereby tempted. (55a–
> b; 91)

Going on to condemn whatever lecherous fantasies (*fundles*) the
anchoress may entertain in her mind, the author cautions those

66. *Civ* 14.26. Cf. *GenL* 12.15.31.
67. E.g., "The scorpion is a kind of serpent, with a face, so it is said, rather like
a woman's" (55b–56a; 92).

"who know nothing of such things" that they "need not wonder or try to think what I mean" (55b; 92).[68]

The same anxiety about the corrupting potential of even edifying words pervades the author's attempt to define a confessional idiom that is properly "naked" and yet that does not reveal sexual sins in such detail as to arouse illicit desires in either the anchoress or her confessor. This concern appears mainly in part 5 ("Confession"), which deals at length with the formal requirements (or "conditions") of auricular confession, traditionally sixteen in number, including the stipulation that confession be naked (*nuda*)—that is, stripped of all verbal adornment, excuse, or other "covering."[69]

Patristic authors had treated the rite of confession as a direct result of the Fall, holding that God asked questions of Adam (and Eve) after his sin "because he was forcing him to confess his sin," and medieval penitential literature followed this typology.[70] In introducing the first of the sixteen conditions, *Ancrene Wisse* evokes the same typological parallel with Genesis 3: "Adam and Eve defended themselves, . . . Adam accusing Eve and Eve accusing the serpent" (82b; 135). As explained earlier in this book, patristic authors had linked the fig leaf episode to confession, allegorizing the leaves as Adam's and Eve's excuses to God, and broadly applying this allegory to any verbal "coverings" used by sinners to conceal or embellish their sins.[71] By the early thirteenth century, medieval authorities had linked up this fig leaf allegory with the ideal of naked confession. Scholastic authors distinguished between two kinds of symbolic nakedness, one "a symbol of innocence (preferably acquired through confession)," and the other "a sign of lust, vanity and the absence of all virtues," which Adam and Eve had originally tried to conceal beneath fig leaves.[72] As an established part of pen-

---

68. *MED*, s.v. *findles* 1b ("devices or deeds contrived by the mind"), citing this passage.

69. On the sixteen "conditions," see Thomas N. Tentler, *Sin and Confession on the Eve of the Reformation* (Princeton, 1977), pp. 106–9. On "naked" confession, see also *Moralia super evangelia*, as cited in Eric J. Dobson, *Moralities on the Gospels: A New Source of "Ancrene Wisse"* (Oxford, 1975), p. 155 (no. 48).

70. Augustine, *GenM* 2.16.24. See also *GenL* 11.35.47 (with judicial trope); and, among medieval authorities, Bernard, *Sermo primus in annuntiatione dominica* 8, *Opera* 5:21, lines 24–25 ("Dominus confessionem tentabat elicere"); and Alan of Lille, *Liber poenitentialis*, s.v. "Confessio praefigurata," PL 210:300.

71. See above, Chapter 3.4.

72. I.e., *nuditas virtualis* and *nuditas criminalis*, as cited in Panofsky, *Studies in Iconology*, p. 156, from Bersuire, *Repertorium morale*, s.v. *Nudus, Nuditas*.

itential literature, the amplified fig leaf trope began to show up in vernacular writings such as *Ancrene Wisse*.

Bernard of Clairvaux, a key medieval figure in developing and disseminating the fig leaf trope, is one of the main sources for the penitential ideals embodied in *Ancrene Wisse*.[73] Citing Bernard, the author equates the Fall with the origin of verbal artifice and the fig leaves with the verbal coverings to be shunned in naked confession:

> "O," says St Bernard, "what confusion, what shame there will be [at the Judgment], when the leaves are scattered and dispersed, and all iniquity is laid bare...." He was thinking of how Adam and Eve, when they had sinned in the beginning, gathered leaves and made coverings [*wriheles*] of them for their shameful members. So do many since their time, "inclining their hearts to evil words, to make excuses in sins" [Ps. 140.4]. (87b; 143)

Unlike her first parents, the anchoress should "strip" herself of verbal coverings when confessing her sins to a priest: "Confession must be naked [*naket*], that is, it must be made baldly, not made fair with periphrasis or flavoured with courtly expression, but the words used should be according to the deeds. When we hate a thing greatly, it is a sign of our hatred to strike it violently. If you hate your sin, why do you speak of it in honourable terms? Why do you hide its uncleanness?" (86a; 140, modified). With this passage, courtly speech—the "fair" (*feire*) style earlier associated with seduction—now becomes linked not only with sexual temptation but also with fallen language as used to conceal sexual sin after the fact. Significantly, the Latin versions of this passage use expressly rhetorical terms for *feire* speech, whereas the French texts use class-laden terms, urging that confession be spoken not in a high style (*courtoisement*) but in a lowly fashion befitting commoners (*vileinement*).[74] Just as the *sermo humilis* of early Christianity had

---

73. The fig leaf passage ascribed by *AW* to Bernard (as quoted here) may paraphrase *Sermones de diversis* 5.2, *Opera* 6/1:100: "The parching wind disperses those leaves; you will be left entirely naked [*nuda*] and wretched." Elsewhere Bernard states that confession should be "naked [*nudam*] and stripped of any concealing garment [*velamine*]" (*Sermones de diversis* 40.6, *Opera* 6/1:240). Cf. *Sermones in Psalmum* "Qui Habitat" 11.5, *Opera* 4:451–52; *Sermones in annuntiatione dominica* 1.8, *Opera* 5:21; *De consideratione* 2.9.18, *Opera* 3:425; and *Sermones super Cantica canticorum* 82.3, *Opera* 2:293–94.

74. MS. Merton 144b (*parobolice, pulcre, decenter, ornate*); MS. Vitellius 50a (French). MS. Trinity 56c–d similarly insists that confession be neither *beaus ne nobles*.

challenged classical rhetorical norms, so did its confessional analogue in medieval times transcend the prevailing social boundaries.[75]

As in his main seduction scenario, the author goes on to offer
an example of the sort of speech he is censuring, as well as an
example of the style that he recommends:

> Speak of its shame with obloquy and strike it violently just as you
> would want wholeheartedly to injure the devil. "Sir," a woman
> will say, "I have had a lover," or she will say, "I have been foolish
> about myself." This is not naked confession. Do not wrap [*biclute*]
> it up. Take off the trimmings. Uncover [*Vnwrih*] yourself and say:
> "Sir, God's mercy! I am a foul stud mare, a stinking whore." Give
> your enemy a foul name, and call your sin foul. Strip it, in your
> confession, stark naked, that is, conceal nothing that is connected
> with it. (86a; 140–41, modified)

This passage uses the fig leaf trope in a traditional way to link
language, sex, and the Fall; but, as a script for how women should
(and should not) represent themselves in confession, it also reflects
traditional clerical antifeminism, with its stress on woman's "animal" or "sensual" nature.

In allegorizing the fig leaf episode in Genesis 3, patristic authors
had forged a special link between the verbal and the sexual consequences of the Fall, turning the leaves into emblems for the urge to
dissemble sexual desire, sin, and guilt. For example, Ambrose had
said that the sinner "wants to cover himself with fig leaves, sewing
together, as it were, insubstantial and shady words...in order to
make a veil for his genitals and to cover his own awareness of the
deed."[76] In *Ancrene Wisse* the typology of the Fall pervades the
discussion of coverings in general, bodily and verbal clothing alike
being ultimately products of the Fall.[77] Within this context, the style
of confession censured by the author—"I have had a lover [*leofmon*]"—is meant to illustrate how courtly language can be used to
"cover" sexual sin in particular.[78] In contrast, the recommended

75. See Auerbach, "*Sermo humilis*," in *Literary Language and Its Public*, pp.
25–66.

76. *Par* 13.65. See above, Chapter 3.4, as quoted with modified translation.

77. E.g., the anchoress "shall cover [*wrihen*] her shame, as a sinful daughter of
Eve..., and not use the covering[s] [*wriheles*] as a means of adorning herself" (113b;
186).

78. Where the ME versions have *leofmon*, the French texts have *ami* ("lover"),
also a courtly term.

style, "I am a foul stud mare, a stinking whore" (*a ful stod meare, a stinkende hore*), with its animal imagery and aroma of the brothel, reduces sexual sin to "naked" terms meant to have no appeal whatsoever.

Despite the penitential ideals he is here promoting, the author bespeaks an attitude of revulsion from female sexuality. His bestial terms for the imagined couplings of the "adulterous" anchoress evoke the old patristic libel about Eve's figurative (or not so figurative) coupling with the phallic Serpent.[79] Moreover, the dangerous "pit" of feminine beauty, that part of the female anatomy earlier disguised as moralized landscape, is scarcely covered here by the author's own verbal fig leaves.

At the same time, however, the author worries that naked confession might lead to a dangerous degree of sexual frankness, becoming, as it were, *too* naked: "One can speak in too foul a manner. One need not call the foul deed by its own foul name, nor the shameful members by theirs. It is enough to speak in such a way that the holy confessor clearly [*witerliche*] understands what you mean" (86a–b; 141, trans. modified). Here, as in the preceding passage, the term *ful* ("foul") is the common denominator of the sexual organs, sexual sin, the sexual sinner ("foul stud mare"), and sexual language itself (e.g., "foul name"). Under this recurring epithet, the author virtually coalesces word and thing, or word and deed; and he verges on reifying sexual language itself by suggesting that the "foul" words of an all-too-naked confession might evoke "foul" thoughts, and that these in turn might stimulate "foul" deeds. Ironically, redemptive verbal signs could become corrupting ones.

The author's concern about this matter extends beyond the anchoress to her confessor. Auricular confession, essentially a dialogue consisting of questions and answers, necessarily involves the risk that the priest himself might be aroused and tempted by a woman's excessively "naked" recitation of sexual sins. (The confessional box was not introduced as a safeguard until after the Reformation.)[80] Winding up his treatment of confession, the author returns to this problem, advising the anchoress to be careful about what she confesses to whom. She must have "complete confidence" in a priest to whom she confesses any "temptations of the flesh." To a young priest, she should therefore never go more deeply (*deopluker*) into

---

79. Later the author describes women who fail to yield to Christ's "wooing" as "whores to the Devil [*deofles hore*]" (108a; 177).

80. Tentler, *Sin and Confession*, p. 82. On related matters of medieval confessional protocol, see pp. 82–95.

such matters than as follows: "Sir, a temptation of the flesh which I have, or have had, is gaining power over me through my consenting to it. I am afraid that I may some time push my foolish, and sometimes unclean thoughts too far, as if pursuing pleasure. . . . I am very much afraid that the pleasure of the thought often lasts so long that the consent of my reason is not far off" (93b; 152). "Even so much as this," he adds, "would seem to him monstrous." Here using terms from the standard tropology of the Fall ("pleasure," "consent"), the author seems mainly concerned that the anchoress, now turned unwitting seductress, might play Eve to the young priest's Adam.

Only to her own father-confessor (or "some other man of holy life") should the anchoress confess her fleshly temptations freely. To such a priest, God's probing earthly representative, Eve's daughter may (and must) bare all the details of any sexual fall, though using language that is not so "naked" as gushing: "Let her pour out all that is in the pot, let her vomit out then all that monstrosity; and let her attack that uncleanness [fulðe] mercilessly for what it is, with foul [fule] words, so that she is afraid of hurting the ears of him who is hearing her sins" (93b; 152–53). Reverting to the imagery of filth and foulness, the author here transforms the "pit" of feminine beauty into a "pot," yet another disapproving (and now domestic) image for female sexuality. The alimentary imagery recalls the forbidden fruit, the apple earlier said to symbolize "all those things towards which desire and sinful delight turn"; Eve's sin of eating is thus reversed as her daughter's confessional regurgitation.[81]

The moral ambiguity of fallen language to which *Ancrene Wisse* bears witness in trying to forbid sexual sins while not evoking them, and in attempting to define a rhetoric of confession that is naked yet not too explicit, is grounded in an Augustinian vision of *all* language. As noted earlier, Augustine maintained that from the beginning God had "covered" humans with various kinds of "skin" (*pellis*), including the heavenly firmament, the garments worn by Adam and Eve, and the scriptural parchment itself, all of these being "veils" that will be raised or rolled up to reveal the truth at the end of time.[82] Confession, as a sacrament administered by the church, is situated in history between the first tribunal in Eden, where the fig leaves and skin garments were introduced, and the tribunal of the Last Judgment, where "all the leaves shall be scattered" (in Bernard's words), along with all verbal mediations whatsoever.

81. A little earlier the author evokes the forbidden fruit, stating that God "took revenge on Adam for biting into an apple" (91a; 148).

82. *Conf* 13.15, as discussed above, Chapter 2.5.

Viewing human language through a series of typological events—
Fall, Redemption, Judgment—the author, like Augustine, realizes
that human language is a fallen, temporal anomaly existing within
the limits set by the divine beginning and end of all language. In
the middle, in historical time, within the movement of words and
syllables, naked confession tries to redeem fallen language, as the
church strives to overcome the legacy of Eden, but the anchoress
and the author/confessor remain verbally situated somewhere between the Garden of Eden and the heavenly Paradise.

4. Eve's Nine Follies

Like *Ancrene Wisse*, the *Livre du Chevalier* turns Eve's seduction
into a cautionary tale for medieval women and grafts the moralized
Fall onto a larger program for subjecting women to male authority.
Although it was written for young noblewomen destined for life in
society rather than a life of religious seclusion, the *Livre du Chevalier*'s paternal advice about sleeping, eating, fasting, and piety has
many parallels with the physical and spiritual regimen prescribed
in *Ancrene Wisse*, and the book has been called a "veritable rule of
secular life."[83] On the other hand, whereas in *Ancrene Wisse* the
Fall appears repeatedly as image, allusion, or narrative pattern, suf-
fusing the whole work's treatment of language and sexuality, in the
Livre du Chevalier the Fall provides the basis for a more demarcated
(though extended) discussion of Eve's nine faults or errors (*follies*),
with special emphasis on verbal and sexual matters.

The division of the first sin into a series of separate transgressions, and their allotment among the responsible parties, began with
biblical commentators as early as Bede and continued through the
scholastic period with commentators such as Bernard.[84] By the
twelfth century or so, the enumeration of Eve's faults in particular
had emerged as virtually a literary topos in its own right, perhaps
because it gave respectable scholastic form and "logic" to preexisting
antifeminist sentiment. Passing from Latin into vernacular tradi-

---

83. Ariès and Duby, eds., *History of Private Life* 2:351.

84. Bede, *In Pentateuchum commentarii* (Gen. 3), *PL* 91:212 (five divisions).
Bernard, *Sermones de diversis* 66.3, *Opera* 6/1:301 (six divisions). Cf. Vincent of
Beauvais, *Speculum historiale* 1.42: "The woman sinned more than the man because
she sinned in more things and against more persons," etc. (*Speculum maius*, 4 vols.
[Douai, 1624; rpt. Graz, 1964–65], 4:17, col. 1).

tion, the moral and narrative "analysis" of Eve's share in the Fall became a staple of medieval didactic works directed at women, where antifeminist authors ramified Eve's sin into as many as nine separate offenses. One such work was the *Miroir des bonnes femmes* (ca. 1270–90), from which the *Livre du Chevalier* draws the plan and much of the material for its treatment of Eve's follies, while altering them for its specific audience.[85]

According to the *Livre du Chevalier*, Eve's nine follies were that she (1) spoke with the Serpent, (2) answered the Serpent improperly, (3) incorrectly remembered God's command, (4) looked at the forbidden fruit, (5) touched it, (6) ate of it, (7) did not believe God's warning, (8) persuaded Adam also to eat, and (9) offered excuses afterward. Six of Eve's nine follies are thus explicitly verbal (1–3, 7–9), as the chevalier stresses by using these six to frame Eve's three nonverbal follies (4–6), which focus on the fruit itself. In terms of narrative logic, then, the six verbal follies form a significant verbal prelude and aftermath to the main sin itself, functioning as either "causes" or "effects." Using this framework, the author comments at length on each of Eve's errors in terms of its moral, social, or religious significance in the scheme of values that he wants to teach his daughters.

In dealing with Eve, the *Livre du Chevalier* clearly relies on traditional clerical or popular notions about woman's alleged loquacity (follies 1–2), weaker intellect (folly 3), and sensuality (follies 4–6), as well as about Eve's original challenge to male and divine authority (follies 7–9). But the chevalier's glosses on Eve also incorporate many attitudes and values specific to the feudal aristocracy. Geoffrey de la Tour Landry was an Angevin knight from a distinguished noble line who was intent on marrying off his daughters advantageously.[86] In turning Eve's follies into a series of cautionary tales for the benefit of his daughters, he accordingly treats the Garden of Eden as a representational ground for the social, moral, and economic values of his own class.

Feudal versions of the Fall reflecting the politics of land tenure, vassalage, and the like, survive from about the middle of the twelfth century, one of the earliest and best-known examples being the

85. On the *Miroir* as a source, see extracts and analysis in John L. Grigsby, "A New Source of the *Livre du Chevalier de la Tour Landry*," *Romania* 84 (1963): 171–208.

86. For historical and biographical details, see Wright, ed., *Book of the Knight*, Introduction, pp. vii–xi.

Anglo-Norman play of the Fall, *Le Jeu d'Adam*.[87] Under the usual treatment, Paradise is the original feudal estate (kingdom, fief, manor, etc.), Adam breaks fealty with his divine Seigneur, Eve betrays her own lord and husband, the tempter is a false bailiff or counselor, and so forth.[88] The chevalier's feudal version of the Fall concerns itself less with the estate's administration than with its family politics. In particular, his commentary on Eve's follies plays out the feudal lord's anxiety about the morals of his womenfolk, their purity as vessels of lineage, and their social reputation.

A nobleman had nearly absolute authority over his wife or daughter; she was virtually his legal property, and her *body*, as his property, represented the domain of this authority over her. In particular, the body of the married noblewoman had to be a pure vessel for producing (male) heirs; as primogeniture became the supreme rule of inheritance, "it was of the utmost importance that a wife receive only one seed, that of her husband, lest intruders issued from another man's blood take their place among the claimants to the ancestral inheritance."[89] Furthermore, since the lord's reputation was closely bound to his lady's, he was vulnerable to any taint of scandal attaching to her. In the social semiotics of the feudal nobility, where the lady's "honor" was virtually no more (and no less) than a signifier of her lord's reputation, the catastrophe of the feudalized Fall lay not so much in her fault or "folly" itself as in the damage sustained by her as the lord's *property* and as a *sign* of his good name.[90] Her status was threatened mainly by the destabilizing effects of sexual desire, either her own or the potential seducer's, as the story of Eve was used to dramatize. What Toril Moi observes about the dialogues on love in Andreas Capellanus, *De amore*, is equally true of the chevalier's glosses on Genesis 3: they are "ob-

87. *Le Jeu d'Adam*, ed. Noomen, as cited earlier. The classic treatment of the play's feudal politics is by Auerbach, *Mimesis*, chap. 7.

88. A superb example of this model appears in Bersuire, *Reductorium morale*, Genesis 3; *Opera omnia* 2:3, col. 2.

89. Georges Duby, *Medieval Marriage: Two Models from Twelfth-Century France*, trans. Elborg Forster (Baltimore, 1978), p. 7. The chevalier cites Eve's sin as jeopardizing "her husband and their descendants [*leur lignée*]" (as quoted later in this chapter, under folly seven). See Bloch, *Etymologies and Genealogies*, chap. 3, on how "lineage is disrupted by the deleterious effects of adulterous desire" (p. 110).

90. "Honor" has material connotations, as noted later in this chapter. The semiotics of aristocratic "honor" is staged in the Arthurian romances, where the mere allegation of the queen's adultery jeopardizes Arthur's reputation in the eyes of his court.

sessed with class, and particularly with the threat that desire poses to stable social structures."[91]

Although the section on Eve's follies occurs well into the book (chaps. 39–46; pp. 85–97), the chevalier evokes the typology of the Fall already in his prologue, which describes how the idea for his book came to him in his garden on a certain spring morning in 1371, some twenty years or so after the death of his wife had left his daughters without motherly guidance. Thinking back on his youth, he recalled how certain flatterers (*beaux langagiers*) had often deceived women with false vows for the sake of their own pleasure (p. 2). Suddenly he was struck by the thought that his own daughters, now coming of age, might become victims of such seducers. So he decided to author for them a little book (*livret*) of fatherly advice. Dealing with morals and manners, and offering contrasting examples of women both good and bad, it would teach them honorable behavior and warn them "not to stray like those who had incurred blame, shame, and ill-repute" (p. 3). Besides its twin concerns with piety and certain secular values, "the salvation of the soul and the honor of the earthly body," the book was meant "to teach [them] how to read."[92]

The chevalier's allusions to Genesis 3—the garden typology, the creative and instructional impulse, the knowledge of good and evil— are echoed by an illustration in one of the French manuscripts of his book.[93] The daughters are shown standing in postures of attentive submission before their father, their hands folded across their abdomens, to which he points in instruction or admonition. Three fruit trees appear in the background. The abdominal focus of attention symbolizes the traditional medieval association of women (especially Eve) with the appetites, and the chevalier's manifest concern to control those appetites in his daughters.[94]

In the garden described in the text and shown in this manuscript

91. Toril Moi, "Desire in Language," p. 23, with reference to Andreas, *De amore*.

92. P. 4 ("le sauvement de l'ame et l'onnour du corps terrien"); pp. 3–4 ("pour aprendre à roumancer").

93. Paris, Bibliothèque Nationale, French MS. 1190; reproduced in Ariès and Duby, eds., *History of Private Life* 2:349.

94. The author cautions against the appetites of *le ventre* on pp. 91–92. Proper eating, fasting, and sleeping are all emphasized, as noted in Ariès and Duby, eds., *History of Private Life* 2:351. Bynum, *Holy Feast and Holy Fast*, notes that patristic exegetes "had regularly seen woman (or Eve) as representing the appetites" (p. 262), and that medieval moralists followed a patristic tendency "to associate food and lust" when addressing women (p. 79).

illustration, the chevalier stands *in loco Dei* not only as lord and father but also as an author commanding that his words be put down by scribes, his apostolic foursome of "two priests and two clerics," expressly for the edification of his children.[95] The Middle Ages had inherited from patristic authors a notion of the Garden of Eden as the original place of instruction and as the ultimate source of the scriptures that compensate humans for their fall from divine knowledge. In placing the origin of his own "scripture" in a typological garden, and in stating that his book aims to teach his daughters to read, the Chevalier models himself on the divine Author. He offers a vernacular version of the education—historical, moral, and literary—that medieval culture saw preeminently embodied in Scripture itself, which (as *la Bible*) has first place in the chevalier's own list of sources (p. 4).

The chevalier's concern with his daughters' literacy also points to another, more practical dimension of the problems of language and the Fall addressed in his chapters on Eve's nine follies. As elaborated there, most of Eve's follies are verbal and hence relate to speech, that notoriously unreliable, suspect, "feminine" medium. In using a book as an instructional device, the chevalier, like the author of *Ancrene Wisse*, apparently believes that the stable written word can forestall, or at least forewarn about, the various dangers of volatile speech. Throughout the section on Eve's follies, the authority of the letter sets itself over and against the seductive and destabilizing power of speech, the dangerous orality embodied in Eve's transgression.

Before enumerating and moralizing Eve's various faults, the chevalier introduces her as the prime biblical example of "bad women" (*mauvaises femmes*).[96] He courts his daughters' interest by evoking not just their own genealogical link to Eve but also certain upper-class ideals of womanhood centering on feminine "honor":

> The first example of evil and sin, by whom death entered into this world, is seen in Eve, our first mother, who ill kept God's command and the honor [*honneur*] he had bestowed on her; for he had made her the mistress of all living things under heaven, which obeyed

95. "Deux prestres et deux clers" (p. 4), as cited earlier. In a similar miniature in another manuscript, the author appears to be holding a book or scroll (London, British Library, MS. Royal 19 C.vii, fol. 33a).

96. *Mauvaises femmes* are mentioned at the end of the section on Eve (p. 97), but Eve is cited as *le premier exemple* of evil at the beginning (p. 85).

her and did her will.... Now see and observe carefully how one sin, no more, threw her down from great honor and glory into such low servitude; for she lost all honor and wealth, she gave up all glory and the obedience of others. (p. 85)

By this account, heavy in feudal terminology, Eve's sin cost her the noblewoman's role as ruling mistress (*dame*), the obedience (*obeyssance*) of others, her endowment of wealth (*richesse*), and her renown (*gloire*); without these things, she fell into the servitude (*servage*) fit only for a villein. These social, political, and economic categories clearly reveal how the author filters the story of the Fall through the values and ideals of his own class. His key term, used here no fewer than three times, is *honneur*, indicating that Eve's fall was not only a loss of feminine virtue and good reputation but also a material loss to her lord.[97] With this term as his moral axis, the chevalier begins to transform the law or prohibition (*commandement*) that lies at the center of Genesis 3 into the terms of the upper-class sexual morality and social status that most concern him, and he sets the stage for transforming the forbidden fruit itself into illicit sexual pleasure.

Although the chevalier is concerned mainly with masculine seducers, he initially warns about talkative people in general (*gens qui langaigent*), invoking the woman-faced Serpent as an emblem for them; this embodiment of the Serpent appears only in the section on Eve's first folly.[98] In making an example of Eve's unwise conversation with the Serpent, the chevalier moves back and forth between the Garden and the household (as marked below by bracketed numbers):

[1] The first sin of our mother came through evil acquaintance, in that she held a conversation with the Serpent, who... had a woman's very beautiful and friendly face, which spoke amicably and courteously. Thus she listened willingly and privately, in which she committed a folly. For if at the beginning she had not wanted to listen and had gone to her lord, she would have saved herself from great shame. Foolish listening thus did her great harm. [2] And therefore, lovely daughters, it is not good to listen to people who chatter and who have the art of fine speech, nor to listen to

97. Discussing the feudalized Fall in *Le Jeu d'Adam*, Auerbach notes the "strongly materialistic value" of the term *honneur* as used there (*Mimesis*, p. 147).

98. Surprisingly, he ascribes the female Serpent to Scripture ("ce dit l'escripture"), unless *escripture* here means written authority in general.

sweet and covert words, for sometimes they are deceptive and venomous, and from them one can get a bad reputation. [3] Afterwards the serpent saw its moment, finding her alone and far from her lord, and thus was able to deploy its false speeches at leisure; [4] therefore it is not good to remain alone with a man, except a relative. (p. 86)

The chevalier goes on to warn his daughters against risking their reputation (*honneur*) by replying "more rather than less" to a man, for "one word leads to another," and words might be said that lead to harm or shame. Like the author of *Ancrene Wisse*, he is wary of how conversation between the sexes can take on an unpredictable life of its own.

This passage illustrates how the chevalier likens the two contexts, biblical and feudal, by endowing Genesis 3 with an aristocratic ambiance, while investing the courtly tête-à-tête with typological values from the Fall. Beginning with the biblical story itself (1), he summarizes it in aristocratic terms familiar to his daughters; for example, Eve and the Serpent converse "courteously" and "privately" (terms altered from those in the *Miroir*).[99] Then (2), moving directly to his daughters' world, he points his moral with specific practical advice, now transferring certain qualities from Paradise to polite society, particularly its discourse—conventionally "sweet" but sometimes also dangerously "covert," "deceptive," and "venomous."[100] Next (3), returning to his biblical text, he again puts the Fall into feudal terms, stating that the Serpent approached Eve while she was apart from her lord (*seigneur*). And, finally (4), he points the moral again in terms of his daughters' experience, warning that they should not spend time alone (*seul à seul*) with a man. The increasingly rapid alternation between the Garden and the household aptly serves the author's moral purpose, which is not just to align these two spheres but to offer a very concrete and practical gloss on the text—one that will be readily appreciated by his daughters.

A pervasive term in the above passage, *bel* ("beautiful"), is a particular sign of the author's anxiety about the dangers often concealed by courteous speech. Under the name of beauty, the chevalier successively evokes the Serpent's "attractive female face" (*visaige de femme moult bel*), then his own "lovely daughters" (*belles filles*),

99. I.e., the chevalier alters *atrempeement* ("moderately") to *cointement* ("courteously"), and *ententivement* ("carefully") to *privéement* ("privately"); for the parallel passage, see Grigsby, "New Source," p. 182.

100. I.e., "doulces parolles et couvertes," "decevables et venimeuses."

and finally the "fair speech" (*bel parler*) that so worries him.[101] He thus links language, the feminine, and the Fall by suggesting that the appeal of seductive words is like the allure of female beauty and that both of these in turn resemble the power of the primal tempter. This comparison marks verbal beauty as "feminine" and hence as suspect in much the way that medieval tradition regarded physical beauty as "feminine" (by contrast with "masculine" strength or virtue), the senses or appetites as "feminine" (by contrast with "masculine" reason), and so forth. Furthermore, verbal beauty that has something to hide, like the seductive *bel parler* indicted here, belongs to the seductions begun by the Serpent and Eve, the animal-woman partnership embodied as the feminized Serpent. The chevalier, however, is concerned mainly with *bel parler* as abused by *men* rather than women, and so the female Serpent slips into the shadowy background of the Fall as Lucifer appears on the scene (in the next folly), a figure for the specifically masculine seducer.

In dealing with Eve's second folly, her careless answer to her tempter, the chevalier treats the forbidden fruit as an emblem for the illicit sexual pleasure that male seducers might use to tempt his daughters. Invoking the husband's (and lord's) authority over his wife's conversation, the chevalier first puts Eve and the fruit on the same level as Adam's property:

> The second folly of Eve, our first mother, was that she replied too lightly, without thinking, when the enemy Lucifer asked her why she and her husband ate not of the fruit of the Tree of Life [sic], as of the other trees. That is, she replied without her husband's advice, carrying on a conversation with him, in which she did a foolish thing and wronged her husband besides. For God had given the guardianship of her and of the fruit to her lord [*seigneur*], indicating what fruit they might eat of. (pp. 86–87)

In equating the forbidden tree with the Tree of Life, and thus combining the Garden's two trees into one, the author follows a minor patristic motif that persisted during the Middle Ages.[102] The crucial point here is the introduction of Lucifer, who represents the masculine seducer and his specifically male sexual desire.

Continuing, the chevalier says that Eve should have referred the tempter's question to Adam instead of answering it herself. He

---

101. Here again the chevalier strategically alters his source; none of the phrases with *bel* occurs in the equivalent passage of the *Miroir*.

102. See above, Chapter 2.2, with references.

points up the sexual import of the exchange, and its application to aristocratic life, through a metaphor of "covering" that recalls the allegorized fig leaves:

> Eve could have said that he would have to speak about it to her lord and not to her; thus she could have covered herself [se... couverte] and gotten away. Therefore, lovely daughters, you may learn from this example that if anyone asks folly of you or something that touches upon your honor, you can easily cover yourself [vous... couvrir] and say that you will speak of it to your lord. Thus you will defeat him [i.e., the seducer] and avoid falling into the second folly of Eve, who answered without covering herself [sans ce que elle s'en couvrist] and without seeking her lord's advice. (p. 87)

"Covering" here stands for modesty, chastity, and deference to male authority. Its converse, nakedness, is not the "virtuous nakedness" of proper confession but the "sinful nakedness" that betokens illicit desire, deception, death, and other features of the fallen world, and of which Eve was the first female exemplar.[103] Like their "first mother Eve," the chevalier's daughters expose themselves to sexual vice, shame, and loss of "honor" if they fail to "cover" themselves with their lord's authority when approached by a man.

To illustrate how his daughters can "cover" themselves when propositioned, the chevalier offers a brief anecdote about a lady who silenced her would-be seducer by cleverly invoking her lord's authority:

> I would like you to bear in mind the example of a good lady of Aquila of whom the prince of Aquila begged for foolish love [folles amours]. And, after he had begged it and talked of it at length, she told him that she would ask her lord's opinion. And when the prince saw this, he let her be, never approached her again, and he told many others that she was one of the most perfect ladies in the land, and so this virtuous lady won great reward and renown [honnour]. (p. 87)

The chevalier concludes that all good women should do likewise, rather than "replying for themselves, as Eve did."

This anecdote, whose courtly ambiance helps mediate Eve's his-

103. Panofsky, *Studies in Iconology*, p. 156 (as cited above, section 3).

tory and the author's moral to the audience, again holds up the aristocratic ideal of honor or reputation as the reward for not doing "as Eve did"—that is, not choosing the forbidden fruit of illicit sexual pleasure (*folles amours*).[104] But the anecdote puts a curious construction on Adamic or seigneurial authority, making it into something that a woman can invoke in the absence, the silence, and even the ignorance of her lord. As such, it may reflect the increase of privacy, the division between male and female spheres, as well as the lord's frequent absence from home. In any case, the lady's invoking her lord's opinion (*avis*) is just a ruse to scare off the would-be seducer, and it is not actually necessary to consult it. The author thus departs from the rhetoric of silence (or rote recitation) imposed in *Ancrene Wisse*, instead actually encouraging women to reply to their would-be seducers, though only in a carefully prescribed way. The husband still rules the wife, as in Paul's sexual politics of Paradise, but here Eve's daughter is to internalize the husband's voice of Adamic reason so that when he is absent and she is in need, she can articulate his authority herself.

Eve's third folly—that she incorrectly remembered God's command, adding a "perhaps" to the threat of death—echoes a patristic theme.[105] But the chevalier uses Eve's slip-up to illustrate not doctrinal or textual error but the fact that women sometimes foolishly lead men on by saying maybe when they should say no:

> Eve's third folly was that she did not correctly recall God's command.... When she replied to the Serpent, she failed to speak the truth plainly, saying, "If we eat of it, perhaps [*par adventure*] we will die." Thus she added a condition to her reply, just as many foolish women do when someone speaks to them of folly. God had mentioned no *perhaps*, but simply by saying *perhaps* to the enemy she gave him grounds for speaking further and tempting her more, just as with those women who listen and reply lightly to those seeking foolish love. For, by naive replies and by listening, they give place and time to speak further, as happened with Eve, our first mother, who listened to the false liar. (p. 88)

Like the author of *Ancrene Wisse*, the chevalier alleges that women talk too much, giving themselves away by revealing their weaknesses. But what also worries him is the unpredictable play of lan-

---

104. One French version of *AW* similarly mentions *fol amour* in the main seduction scenario (Vitellius 19a).

105. See above, Chapter 1.2.

guage itself, as embodied in the very phrase *par adventure*, with its echos of sudden love or death in courtly romance.

Turning to how the Serpent took advantage of Eve's faulty reply, the chevalier amplifies the Serpent's biblical speech (as does many a medieval poet) to suggest that Eve fell through flattery: "The enemy tempted her, saying, 'You may well eat of it, nor will you die; rather you shall be as beautiful [*beaulx*] as God, and you will know good and evil. Do you know why he has forbidden that you eat of this fruit? Because, if you eat of it, you will be as beautiful and as bright and as powerful as He.'"[106] Women are still the same, the chevalier goes on to say, true daughters of their first mother in their vanity and gullibility:

> That foolish one thought that he spoke the truth, believing him through desire and beautiful words [*beau parler*], just as do foolish women who easily believe the beautiful words [*belles parolles*] of liars who urge them with flattery and empty promises to commit folly against their honor and their rank, and swear to them many things they do not mean. Many times the foolish women believe them so completely that they go ahead and consent to foolish delight. (p. 89)

Earlier the chevalier linked feminine and verbal beauty to that of the primal tempter (as the female Serpent), but by this point the tempter's dangerous beauty has become completely embodied by language itself, by the masculine thrust of *beau parler* or the feminine allure of *belles parolles*.

In alleging that women give themselves to "foolish delight" (*fol delit*) because they admire their own beauty (real or imagined) as reflected in the mirror of the seducer's flattery, the chevalier suggests that women fall for a mere verbal fiction—a meretricious beauty whose body is language itself. The ultimate trick of the tempter's voice, he implies, is to project, by a kind of ventriloquism, the woman's wishes or fantasies, her desire (*convoitise*), into another person's praise of her. The chevalier is well aware of the pleasure principle of language, and his suggestion that language contains both the beginning and the end (goal) of desire, or at least of such "foolish" desires as those concerned here, is thoroughly Augustinian.

Although Eve's fourth, fifth, and sixth follies (looking at, touch-

106. Pp. 88–89. One of the English versions offers an even more impressive string of flattering qualities: "faire, clere, shyning, bright, puissaunt, and ... mighti" (*Book of the Knight*, ed. Wright, p. 57).

ing, and eating the fruit) do not directly involve words, in these sections the chevalier emphasizes qualities common to both the forbidden fruit and seductive language. For example, in dealing with Eve's "foolish looking" at the forbidden fruit, he says that this object "seemed [*sembla*] to her very beautiful and delightful, wherefore she desired it," and that many women similarly fall into dangerous delight and lechery through their "foolish looking" at seducers' false show (*faulx semblant*) of love (p. 89). Having earlier evoked the beauty and delightfulness that all seductive language borrows from the primal forbidden object, the chevalier here stresses that the fruit only *seemed* attractive, just as the seducer only *seems* to be in love. Implicitly, the seducer's deceptively beautiful speech likewise possesses only the appearance of truth and provides only an apparent delight or satisfaction. With Eve and the Serpent, and with women and seducers, the whole temptation, language included, is grounded on a mere semblance of reality, a *faulx semblant*.[107]

In discussing Eve's other abuses of the fruit, the chevalier cashes out some of the other qualities of seductive language that have been circulating through his discussion. For example, his anxiety about the dangerous orality of conversation between the sexes finds further expression under Eve's fifth folly: "Touching and kissing [*bayser*] move the blood and the flesh such that they obliterate the fear of God and concern about worldly honor. Much evil has come about through foolish kissing and touching, just as happened when Eve touched the fruit" (p. 91). And, under Eve's sixth folly, her actual eating of the fruit, the chevalier warns against taking excessive pleasure in the mere taste (*saveur*) of food (p. 92), thus echoing his earlier censure on seductively "sweet" words.[108]

Finally, in wrapping up his triad of sensory follies, the chevalier restores Eve's various faults to a logical sequence, which he applies to sexual mores in general, as a warning to his daughters. Significantly, the series begins with verbal temptation: "Delight in the apple killed Eve our first mother, who came to sin as do many people; for they proceed from hearing folly [*escouter la folie*] to looking and then to touching, and from touching to kissing, and from kissing to

107. The seducer's *faulx semblant* may allude to the notorious deceiver *Faus Semblant* (False Seeming) in Guillaume de Lorris and Jean de Meun, *Le Roman de la Rose*; ed. Ernest Langlois, 5 vols. (Paris, 1914–24).

108. *Doulces parolles*, p. 86, as cited earlier. He also returns here to the imagery of venom, comparing the fatal fruit consumed by Eve to tasty food laced with poison (*venin*), a detail recalling the seducer's "venomous" (*venimeuses*) words and their fatal effects on reputations (p. 86).

the deed of false delight, as did Eve, who tasted the apple after looking and touching" (p. 92). The chevalier here adapts the traditional analysis of Eve's seduction, which stresses the primacy of the word in her fall, to the temptations of forbidden sexual fruit that he fears may undo his daughters.[109]

Returning now to expressly verbal faults, the chevalier treats Eve's seventh folly, her failure to believe God, as part of the aftermath of her sin, with its various consequences, including death: "Eve's seventh folly was that she did not believe [ne creut pas] what God had said to her, namely that she would die if she ate of the fruit" (p. 93). Touching on a patristic hermeneutical theme, the chevalier points out that God's warning did not specify an immediate death but only (simplement) that Eve would eventually die. But what most interests him are the familial or inherited results of Eve's error: "After her death, Eve descended into the common prison from which none escape, that is, the porch of Hell. Now, she was in prison, she and her husband and their descendants, until the time . . . when God delivered them along with those who had served and obeyed him under the Old Law, while leaving behind the evil ones. He took the grain and left the straw to be burnt." The symbols of prison, lineage, and harvest—here used for original sin, punishment, and divine judgment—have scriptural and patristic precedents but draw on a feudal and manorial vocabulary in particular. Eve, by doubting God's word and eating the fruit, reaped a harvest of death for not only herself and her husband but also their descendants (leur lignée). Likewise, any sexual sins committed by the chevalier's daughters against the seigneurial code threaten the family's lineage, or at least the integrity of the lord's own family unit.[110]

That sexual transgressions are the chevalier's chief concern is evident from the catalog of sins that follows, which begins with murder and theft but ends emphatically with adultery. In concluding, the chevalier warns his daughters that sexual sin means the death of the soul and of one's good name in the world: Death surprises "the sinner coming and going in her foolish pleasures and foolish delight, which is seen and known by all, so that she is defamed and dishonored [diffamée et deshonnourée] before all the

109. This passage may also owe something to the romance (and scholastic) topos of the Five Points of Love (quinque lineae amoris), in which conversation often figures first; see Curtius, European Literature, pp. 512–13.

110. Bloch, Etymologies and Genealogies, pp. 161–64, cites two competing aristocratic models of the family, one linear (genealogical) and the other more nuclear (conjugal).

world and hated by God and his angels" (p. 94). Although he respects spiritual values, the chevalier clearly has pledged his fealty to temporal ones, and he regards the chief sign and attribute of the "fallen woman" as a tarnished reputation in the eyes of the world (*le monde*). Moreover, in the chevalier's feudal perspective on the Fall, original sin tends to be less Augustine's abstract "seed" of sin than the tainted reputation or impaired lineage that might be caused by a noblewoman's fall.[111] The chevalier belongs to a class that places great value on bloodlines and worldly repute, and in this context a fate worse than death is a corrupted family line or a besmirched family name.

Eve's eighth folly, that she persuaded Adam also into sin, reflects the old assumption—beloved by exegetes, poets, and moralists alike—about the crucial role of feminine wiles, including seductive speech, in Adam's fall and in the sins of men generally. At the same time, it indicates the chevalier's special concern with the sexual politics of the feudal estate, particularly the lady's role in influencing her lord's rule over his demesne:

> Eve's eighth folly was that she sought company in her sin; that is, she gave the apple to her husband and urged him [*luy pria*] to eat of it with her. And like a fool he did not wish to disobey her, and therefore both of them became prisoners of sin and of our great calamity. Here is a good example of how, if a wife gives bad counsel to her lord, he should consider whether what she is saying to him is good or evil, and what its likely result will be. For he should not be so inclined to his wife, nor so submissive, that he fails to consider whether she speaks good or evil. For there are many women who are not happy unless their will is carried out. (pp. 94–95)

Breaking with his custom of addressing just his daughters, the chevalier here offers what sounds like advice to the seigneur himself ("he should consider"; "he should not be so inclined to his wife"). This advice could be read as a momentary rhetorical lapse, prompted by his anxiety about the issues at hand, or as a rhetorical device for enlisting his daughters' sympathy with the seigneurial point of view. In either case, however, the author's recommending that the lord not be overly submissive to his lady implies that, up to a point, he ought to solicit and even follow her advice. This position represents

111. With the chevalier's concerns, cf. *Merchant's Tale* IV.2171, 2197–2202.

another departure, however small, from the traditional male silencing of the female voice.[112]

On the negative side, and in keeping with the example of Eve, the chevalier next offers a contemporary anecdote stressing the evil that can come of a husband's undue regard for his wife's advice: "I know a nobleman who so believed his wife that by her foolish counsel [fol conseil] he died, which was a great shame. It would have been better for him had he believed her and concerned himself with her less, as with Adam, who foolishly believed [creut] his wife, to his great sorrow and to ours" (p. 95). The chevalier's assumption that Adam believed Eve, a departure from the consensus that "Adam was not deceived" (1 Tim. 2.14), itself testifies to the power he assigns to a woman's words. On the other hand, he also relies on the old assumption that women persuade men mainly through sex appeal.

Specifying what his daughters should learn from these biblical and contemporary exempla, the chevalier emphasizes that "every good wife should think carefully about the advice she gives her lord so she does not counsel him to do anything shameful or harmful in order to fulfill her own foolish wishes. For, if she is wise, she will consider and assess to what end, either good or evil, the thing will lead; for she will share in it whether it is good or bad" (p. 95). This passage reflects two counterpoised ideas about women. On the one hand, woman is the comparatively weaker sex whose "foolish wishes" (fole voulenté) can threaten her seigneur's interests. On the other hand, she is a rational person capable of being wise (saige), able to think carefully (bien penser), and to weigh and assess (penser et mesurer) her advice. A traditional antifeminist notion of the foolish wife thus coexists here in tension with a more enlightened ideal of woman as her husband's loyal confidante and wise counselor. It must be said, however, that up to now the chevalier has used mainly appetitive terms for feminine psychology and that his resort to cognitive terms in this passage is uncharacteristic.

The chevalier's unusual stress on women's cognitive abilities is, in part, exhortation by way of praise, for clearly his counsel is motivated by seigneurial interests, as signaled in his warning that the wife shall share in (y partira) either the good or evil toward which her advice tends. The important advisory role that he allots to the seigneur's wife reflects conditions of society and class. In the

---

112. The chevalier shows similar respect for women's opinions and advice in the dialogues between himself and his wife, pp. 246–65.

Middle Ages, noblewomen commonly governed the estate in their husbands' absence, a situation that extended their political role from an advisory to a decision-making one.[113] Like the earlier appeals to the family name and line, the mention of the shared fortunes of lord and lady adapts the moralized Fall to the specific concerns of the feudal nobility. As Adam lost Paradise by taking Eve's bad advice, so the seigneur could lose his estate, or even his life, by following bad advice from his wife.

Eve's ninth and last folly, her false confession to God, is said to be her worst. Following medieval penitential theory, the chevalier views confession as having been inaugurated—and subverted—in the immediate aftermath of the Fall, and he stresses that his daughters should never falsify their confessions as Eve did, especially by embellishing their sins in the fine language of their social class:

> [Eve's] ninth and greatest folly was her last, for when God asked her why she had trespassed his command and caused her lord to sin, she excused herself and said that the serpent had made her do it through persuasion.... Giving excuses greatly displeases God, as today when people come for confession to their priest, who is in the place of God, and excuse themselves in confessing before him, and embellish [*pollicent*] their misdeeds, failing to describe their sins as basely as they actually were, and being ashamed to speak of them, while having no shame about having done them. Thus they are like our first mother Eve, who excused herself. But St. Paul said that whoever wants to be washed and cleansed must speak of sin as odiously as it was in fact. (pp. 96–97)

Here, as in *Ancrene Wisse*, polite (or "polished") diction is an impediment to confession; rather than holding up a true mirror to the soul, it flatters the sinner's faults. Accordingly, when confessing their sins to a priest, noblewomen should lower themselves both by kneeling and by speaking basely or humbly (*vilment*) and unbeautify themselves by speaking in an "ugly" fashion (*laidement*) about their misdeeds.

In describing the proper idiom of confession, the chevalier not only uses the imagery of cleansing but also returns briefly to his earlier metaphor of covering and concealment as he compares confession to the public hue and cry (*l'escrie et hue*) that attends crime and punishment:

113. On female regency, see references in Ferrante, *Woman as Image*, pp. 8–10.

> Just as a thief willingly remains where he is hidden along with his theft, not voluntarily going to where it is made public, so with the enemy who steals souls through temptations, who hides himself in bodies and places where there is no hue and cry, and where he is not discovered [descovert] through confession. For whoever confesses herself frequently and rapidly is raising the hue and cry, and this is what [the enemy] hates and fears most. (p. 97)

The image of sin or Satan ("the enemy") hiding in the body (corps) to avoid being discovered (or uncovered) recalls Augustine's notion that after the Fall the human body itself—the opaque flesh—became a repository of lies, illicit desires, and death, as figured by the coverings worn by humans after their fall.

At the same time, the chevalier's image of the thieving "enemy" hiding in the body evokes the seducer (through the Enemy/Satan/Serpent equation) as a threat to his daughters' fertile bodies. The abdomens to which he points in the manuscript illustration cited earlier might become vessels for sexual sin, thus threatening not only his daughters' morals and souls but also their value as marriageable property, and hence the seigneur's name, honor, and legal interests. In strictly material terms, the theft of their virginity would be for him a great misfortune. Yet in such a case the last thing he would want is any actual hue and cry, any public scandal; the only "hue and cry" that he wants is the sort expressed privately in confession to the confidential priest. Of course, sexual sins may confess themselves in their own bodily ways. Possibly the chevalier's mention of a public hue and cry serves as an additional warning to his daughters that they are not to leave themselves—their bodies, their virginity—open to "theft," lest they be forced to undergo this sort of confession as well.

The chevalier's advice about confession adds a third, religious realm to the other spheres of discourse treated under Eve's earlier follies, as well as a third male interlocutor, the priest. The author thereby completes a typological scheme in which each phase of Eve's temptation and fall has a corresponding sphere of practical application in his daughters' lives. That is, Eve's three interlocutors (the Serpent, Adam, and God) have their medieval analogues (seducer, husband, and priest), each of whom occupies a different discursive sphere (social, domestic, and religious). Although the chevalier's glosses on Genesis 3 hardly cover all possible situations, they do turn the story of Eve into a totalizing scheme, a paradigm, for how his daughters are to conduct themselves in key areas of their lives.

By continually moving back and forth between the biblical and feudal realms, the chevalier manages to map the fairly homogenous scriptural material onto the relatively complicated life of the medieval noblewoman, with its multiple discursive spheres.

To be sure, the chevalier performs this practical exegesis strictly from the viewpoint of his own seigneurial interests—from not just "a man's point of view," as Diane Bornstein reminds, but specifically that of a knight, lord, and father. Thus he moralizes and "feudalizes" the Fall differently from the authors of priestly versions like that in *Ancrene Wisse*. As paterfamilias rather than priest, the chevalier uses the story of Eve to instruct his daughters according to his specific interests—that is, his own class-conscious and gender-bound notions of morals and manners, property and piety. Hence the chevalier's reading of Genesis 3 offers at the same time a reading of medieval society itself. Indeed, in turning Paradise into a feudal demesne, the knight's book says much more about medieval culture—as seen from a certain vantage point within that culture—than about any inherent meaning of the text itself.

5. Conclusion

Medieval moralists adapted the Fall as a cautionary tale for women, using the story of Eve in particular to warn her "daughters" about the double danger of being seduced by, or in turn seducing, men; and about the dangers of language itself, not only as a medium of seduction but also as decorative "fig leaves" often used for covering one's sins afterward. As presented in *Ancrene Wisse* and the *Livre du Chevalier*, the story of Eve reflects in differing degrees both learned (patristic) tradition about the Fall—especially its dynamics of language, psyche, and sexuality—as well as the local conditions, ideals, and attitudes that reshaped this story for a specifically female readership in medieval England and France.

Whether adapted to the spiritual ideals of the anchoritic life or to the more material values of the feudal aristocracy, the story of Eve in these texts also attests to the evolving state of language and literacy in medieval Europe. As vernacular literary productions authored by men for women (specifically by "fathers" for "daughters"), both texts reproduce the male/female hierarchy of the Garden not only in their moralizing content but also in their discursive structures. Both *Ancrene Wisse* and the *Livre du Chevalier* use male authority to control rigidly and define narrowly the nature and ex-

tent of female experience. In particular, both try to contain or cir-
cumscribe volatile female speech—the feminine orality regarded by
men with suspicion and fear—by means of a male literary tradition
that stretches back to antiquity in virtual apostolic succession, fixed
and firm. Moreover, even if both books partly break down the medieval gender boundary of literacy, they still respect other male/
female hierarchies ultimately rooted in the sexual politics of Paradise. As readers but not writers, and as an audience to vernacular
but not Latin texts, literate women are kept in a passive, receptive
and relatively unlearned role with respect to literary tradition.

In this connection, it is useful to mention again one of the earliest feudalized versions of Genesis 3, *Le Jeu d'Adam*. The play
includes a scene, after Adam and Eve have eaten of the forbidden
fruit, in which Adam, hurling abuse at Eve as the mother of sin,
adds a specifically clerical threat—"Your sin shall be written in a
book!"[114] This threat of course is a self-fulfilling "prophecy" in several ways, pointing "ahead" not only to Scripture but also to the
sort of antifeminist diatribe contained in the play itself. In the context of medieval literary culture and its scribal means of production,
Adam's curse on Eve signifies the male power of the pen as wielded
threateningly over women. Another twelfth-century antifeminist
diatribe, the popular Latin lyric about "clericus Adam," begins precisely by establishing the Adamic/scribal privilege of cursing Eve in
writing.[115]

Though hardly written by outright misogynists, both *Ancrene
Wisse* and the *Livre du Chevalier* show that the written record of
Eve's faults and follies continued to multiply fruitfully after the
twelfth century. According to a medieval legend invoked in *Ancrene
Wisse*, the Devil writes down everyone's sins and, on Judgment Day,
will read aloud all those sins not "erased" by confession. The author
accordingly warns the anchoress, "Give him as little to write as you
possibly can, for there is no employment he likes better, and whatever he writes, take care to erase it completely" (93a; 152). Although
most medieval antifeminists profess concern for the souls of the
women whom they counsel and admonish as daughters of Eve, often
they seem to be enthusiastically sharing an inkhorn with the Devil
himself. Before the story of Eve, a male narrative, would make room
for Eve's story, a truly female one, women had to take up the pen

114. ("Li toen pecchié iert esscrit en livre!") *Le Jeu d'Adam* 542, ed. Noomen,
p. 51.
115. See references below, Chapter 6.1.

and write books themselves. But the traditional clerical accounts of the Fall were not seriously challenged—in writing, and by women—until about the end of Chaucer's times. And even then a writer such as Christine de Pizan was able to defend Eve only by emphasizing that her sin was a *felix culpa*.[116]

In *The Canterbury Tales*, a fictional female contemporary of the chevalier's daughters affirms vigorously that antifeminist clerics used the story of Eve as their principal brief against women. The unlettered Alisoun of Bath narrates how she was "beten for a book" because Jankyn, her fifth husband and a cleric, used to read aloud to her at the hearth from a misogynist anthology, especially "of Eva first, that for hir wikkednesse / Was al mankynde broght to wrecchednesse."[117] In the skirmish in the battle of the sexes that follows one of Jankyn's reading sessions, Chaucer (like Christine de Pizan) suggests that antifeminist texts were not always passively received but sometimes faced resistance from the female reader—or audience.[118] When Alisoun angrily tears "thre leves" (III.790) out of Jankyn's book—do these loosened *folia* symbolize the first few chapters of Genesis?—there is an exchange of blows, one of which, to Alisoun's head, presumably makes her "somdel deef" (I.446) thereafter to the voice of male authority. It all ends with Jankyn agreeing to burn his book and Alisoun gaining the "governance" of everything, including her husband-cleric's "tonge" and "hond" (III.814–15), which represent speech and writing, among other things.

In looking at Chaucer's (and Alisoun's) challenge to traditional interpretations of the Fall, we leave the thinly documented world of medieval private life and enter the even more uncertain realm of medieval poetic fiction, a realm complicated here, of course, by Chaucer's gendered ventriloquism—a male poet doing women's voices doing men's. But not all of Chaucer's women must, like Alisoun, give up an ear to gain a voice. The richly populated world of *The Canterbury Tales* also contains literate women, both story-

---

116. See Christine de Pizan, *Le Livre de la cité des dames* 1.9.2–3.

117. *The Wife of Bath's Prologue* III.712, 715–16. Further citations are parenthetical, referring to fragment and line numbers.

118. Robert W. Hanning, "From *Eva* and *Ave* to Eglentyne and Alisoun: Chaucer's Insight into the Roles Women Play," *Signs* 2 (1977): 580–99, discusses Alisoun's challenge to clerkly "auctoritee" and to antifeminist tradition derived from Genesis 3, while noting that the Wife of Bath herself has "clerical tendencies" (596n).

tellers and characters, who join Alisoun (or are made to seem to do so) in challenging male assumptions about Eve, the feminine, and the Fall. One of these is May, who takes to writing in order to escape, however briefly, the heavy hand of her old Adam of a husband.

Chapter 6

The Carnal Letter
in Chaucer's Earthly Paradise

> The woman, hearing in the external way the serpent's
> suggestion, failed to read the internal book that was open
> and quite legible.... She kept her mind on the external
> book instead.... [The man], too, turned to the
> external book and to perishable good.
> —*Bonaventura*

DURING THE LATER Middle Ages, lay poets continued the originally monastic project of dramatizing the Fall as a scenario for language, while raising questions that eventually sundered the earlier medieval synthesis of doctrine and poetry—questions about the function of signs, the ambiguities of writing as a fallen medium, and the ultimate end of the book. These and other problems of language and the Fall are richly figured by Geoffrey Chaucer in the *Merchant's Tale*, a fairly late addition to the poet's Canterbury cycle. The tale satirizes Augustine's garden by treating the Fall as a fabliau and by combining the typology of Genesis 3 with an ancient comic narrative, the pear tree story. In this comedy of eros, a squire (Damyan) uses secret signs and letters to seduce the young, newlywed wife (May) of his master, an old and sensual knight (January). Their literary foreplay culminates when the lovers literally fornicate in a pear tree in the old knight's pleasure garden, an act that dramatizes Augustine's glosses on the Fall as an abuse of writing, speech, and signs in general. As recounted by the cynical Merchant, a very unreliable narrator, the tale offers a dark vision of fallen society, marriage, and language alike. But the Merchant does not have the last word, and his tale variously resists his own dire interpretation, as reinforced by its larger context in a redemptive pilgrimage and by Chaucer's own concluding retraction of the carnal letter.

As a learned poet, Chaucer inherited a rich body of lore about language, literature, and the Fall. Patristic culture had maintained an ambivalence toward writing as both a product of the Fall and yet a potentially redemptive medium, and toward the body of the text as both a site of seductive pleasure and a sign enabling spiritual transcendence. The medieval church and its clerics had turned fallen writing to their own advantage, seeking to embody their authority in the written word, while still recognizing that the carnal letter could betray their aims in many devious ways. As stressed in the preceding chapter, the writing/speech hierarchy was a sharply gendered one in medieval culture, with male authors using stable, "masculine" script to control volatile, "feminine" speech and with comparatively few women wielding the pen. Although some women acquired literacy, few gained the privileges of authorship, remaining for the most part in passive, receptive roles with respect to written male authority. This gendered order was supported by the curious duality of the letter, which was regarded both as a feminine entity and yet officially as a male production. Like Eve herself, the letter was born of man and yet could confront, tempt, and even master him. Chaucer complicates this vision of things in the *Merchant's Tale*, where Eve, in the person of the knight's young wife, not only reads but also writes.

In presenting the Fall mainly as a literary seduction, and one that takes place specifically through private letters, Chaucer dramatizes the sexual politics of script as well as the role of writing as representation. From the twelfth to the fourteenth centuries, intellectual life in Europe was dominated by scholastic authors who tended to view the world through books, and human experience through metaphors of the book, a tendency seen in new scholastic glosses on the Fall as a scene for reading and writing.[1] As lay literacy increased, literary versions of the Fall began appearing in more popular literature as well. Dante, for example, produced a scenario of the Fall that features a romance, and Chaucer wrote a Fall scenario featuring love letters.

Chaucer's epistolary version of the Fall both glances at Augus-

---

1. For background, see Curtius, *European Literature*, chap. 16 ("The Book as Symbol"), esp. pp. 315–19, 326–32; and Gellrich, *The Idea of the Book*. On the "lettre" in Chaucer, see Robertson, *Preface to Chaucer*, pp. 315–17; and John A. Alford, "Scriptural Testament in *The Canterbury Tales*: The Letter Takes Its Revenge," in *Chaucer and Scriptural Tradition*, ed. David Lyle Jeffrey (Ottawa, 1984), pp. 197–203.

tine's conversion, which likewise features a letter (an apostolic one), and reflects the growth of reading and writing among the laity in his own time. The later Middle Ages were marked not only by what M. B. Parkes has called "the emergence of the general reader" but also by the general reader's acquisition of writing.[2] Especially among the nobility and bourgeois represented by the characters and narrator of the *Merchant's Tale*, writing was increasingly a part of everyday life, whether in the counting house or the private chamber, at the town hall or on the manorial estate. With the proliferation of writs, charters, account books, and other documents, the private letter also emerged onto the scene, along with manuals for acquiring the specialized art of letter writing (*ars dictaminis*).[3] From this period date the first great collections of English family correspondence, the Stonor letters (1290–1483) and the Paston letters (1422–1509), which provide detailed records of personal and business affairs.

The rise of this art among the laity seems to be reflected in the letters frequently exchanged among characters in Chaucer's works, although literary sources such as Ovid also contribute to this motif.[4] As a rhetorical genre, the medieval letter tended to be heavily stylized, both in fiction and in actuality, even in private or intimate uses.[5] But it is a modern misconception to think that formality precluded the written expression of sincere thoughts or strong emotions. In his early poem *Troilus and Criseyde*, Chaucer dwells at length on the mediation of desire through love letters, a phenomenon familiar to Chaucer's audience as at least a literary convention, if not from personal experience.[6] Many epistolary motifs in the *Troilus*—mediated desire, phallic writing, "writing" on the heart—re-

2. M. B. Parkes, "The Literacy of the Laity," in *The Mediaeval World*, ed. David Daiches and Anthony Thorlby (London, 1973), pp. 555–77 (p. 572). See also Clanchy, *Memory to Written Record*.

3. On types of written records, see Clanchy, *Memory to Written Record*, chap. 3. On the *ars dictaminis*, see James J. Murphy, *Rhetoric in the Middle Ages: A History of Rhetorical Theory from Saint Augustine to the Renaissance* (Berkeley, 1974), chap. 5.

4. Besides *Merchant's Tale*, see *Man of Law's Tale* II.724–899, 953–59; *Summoner's Tale* III.2128; *Clerk's Tale* IV.760–63; *Franklin's Tale* V.837–40; *Troilus and Criseyde* 1.656–721; 2.1002–1337, 1696–1708; 3.190–221, 488, 501–4; 5.470–76, 1292–1435, 1583–1645; and *Legend of Good Women* 1273–76, 1354–67 (Dido); 1564–65 (Hypsipyle); 1670–79 (Medea); 2350–72 (Philomela); 2494–2561 (Phyllis). All quotations and citations of Chaucer's works refer to *The Riverside Chaucer*, gen. ed. Benson.

5. See Norman Davis, "The *Litera Troili* and English Letters," *RES* n.s. 16 (1965): 233–44, which stresses the close ties between Chaucer's literary letters and the medieval *ars dictaminis*.

6. See passages cited above, note 4.

appear in the later *Merchant's Tale*, where letters likewise form the first link between the two lovers, although here the contents of their letters are only summarized, and "love" is treated satirically.

As a central motif in Chaucer's tale, then, the letter embodies and symbolizes not only a fallen writing but also an ascendency of the written word, especially among the laity of Chaucer's time. Before we turn to the carnal letter in the *Merchant's Tale*, it will be useful to glance at some earlier literary versions of the Fall that point to the same development.

1. Misreading, Miswriting, and the Fall

As shown earlier in this book, patristic culture produced a great body of lore about the Fall as an originary myth for reading and writing, among other matters of language.[7] First, the Fall had been a crisis of interpretation in which Adam and Eve had abused the sign of the forbidden fruit and "misread" the "text" of God's word as entrusted to them. At the same time, the Fall had been the origin of writing, since the neglect of God's word, as either spoken aloud or "written" in the heart, had made necessary an external written supplement—first in the tablets of the Law and eventually in Scripture. As a material artifact produced in part by human labor, Scripture was of a piece with the primal human clothing of "leaves" and "skins," emblems for how the Fall had covered God's truth and made necessary a written revelation in the first place.

In this constellation of ideas, Adam was the first namer, the first to wield a hoe or spade, the phallic progenerator of the race, and hence the symbolic inventor of letters or the first scribe. Eve, for her part, bore children and made cloth, progeny and textiles—both traditional symbols for texts. Eve's sewing or weaving begins already (with Adam's) in the fig leaf episode, but Adam's weaving was viewed in writerly terms and Eve's in oral terms. Eve was a type for Mary, mother of Christ, and hence of the ultimate divine Text, but Eve herself was regarded strictly as an oral creature, from her first bite of the apple to her glib excuses afterward. An ancient tradition, known but generally ignored during the Middle Ages, held that Eve, not Adam, had inaugurated writing after the Fall.[8] (In a classical myth popular during the Middle Ages, Philomela's weaving is dis-

---

7. See above, Chapter 2, sections 2, 4, and 5.
8. See the *Vita Adae et Evae*, as cited above, Chapter 2.2.

placed writing, though this art is forced on her by a double violation.)[9] During the later Middle Ages, however, as Eve learns to write,
her potential as an author (and reader) in her own right begins to
bear belated fruit.

One of the traditional accounts of sin and atonement inherited
by the Middle Ages held that Adam and Eve had sold themselves
and their descendants into slavery to the Devil and that Christ's
Passion had been a "ransom" to release them.[10] Corollary to this
ransom theory was the notion that Adam and Eve had executed their
Devil's bargain in "writing." An especially vivid example comes
from Gottschalk, the ninth-century Saxon monk whose ultra-
predestinarian views were finally condemned by the church: "When
our first parents sinned, it was as if they had given a deed [*cartam*]
to the Devil and sold themselves together with us, for the contract
of our damnation is erased by the blood of God's son."[11] The garden
in the *Merchant's Tale* is a scene for similar "chartres."

Another type of textual gloss on the Fall reflects the notion that
Adam and Eve "misread" God's word in the form of a "book" inscribed within them. The trope draws on the ancient metaphor of
inner writing, as used by Paul, as applied to the Fall by patristic
exegetes and as reiterated by numerous scholastic authors.[12] A famous example appears in the writings of St. Bonaventura (1221–74),
the great Franciscan exponent of Augustine.[13] According to Bonaventura, God provided humankind with "two books, one written
within [*scriptus intus*], and that is [inscribed by] God's eternal Art
and Wisdom; the other is written without [*scriptus foris*], and that
is the sensible world."[14] In this order of things, the humans were to

9. E.g., Chaucer's *Legend of Good Women*: "With a penne coude she nat wryte.
/ But letters can she weve to and fro" (2357–58). Cf. the *chanson de toile*, a "female"
genre, and the emphatically oral Alisoun of Bath on women and "spynnyng" (*Wife
of Bath's Prologue* III.401).

10. See Russell, *Satan*, pp. 83–84.

11. Gottschalk, *Opuscula de rebus grammaticis* 1.64; cited in *Mittellateinisches
Wörterbuch bis zum ausgehenden 13. Jahrhundert* (Munich, 1959–), s.v. *chirogra-
phum*, col. 536, lines 7–12. Cf. Col. 2.14.

12. E.g., Ambrose, *Epistola* 73.5; Vincent of Beauvais, *Speculum historiale* 1.42;
Hugh of St. Victor, *De sacramentis* 1.6.5; and Hugh of Folieto, as cited in Curtius,
European Literature, p. 320.

13. On Bonaventura and Augustine, see Pelikan, *The Christian Tradition* 3:270–
84.

14. Bonaventura, *Breviloquium* 2.11.2; ed. R. P. Aloysii a Parma, *Doctoris Seraphici S. Bonaventurae... Opera Omnia*, vol. 5 (Quaracchi, 1891), p. 229a; trans. José
de Vinck, *The Works of Bonaventure: Cardinal, Seraphic Doctor, and Saint*, vol. 2

understand God's outer writing, the Book of Creation, through the inner writing on their hearts or souls. But Adam and Eve instead "misread" the outer "book" by listening to a false exegesis. Bonaventura specifies that Eve was the first to misread God's original "written" word:

> Now, the woman, hearing in the external way the serpent's suggestion, failed to read the internal book that was open and quite legible to the right judgment of reason. She kept her mind on the external book instead, and began to be concerned with the external good. Because her mind was not upon infallible truth, her desire soon began to lean toward the perishable good. And so she set her heart upon what the devil promised, and agreed to do what he proposed.[15]

Having followed the Serpent's gloss, Eve in turn distracted Adam from the inner divine text: "The woman, led astray, beguiled the man. He, too, turned to the external book and to perishable good."[16] Thus Adam and Eve fell through a shared "misreading" of God's "Book," or through what Augustine had called "carnal" reading, a subjection to the flesh "in the pursuit of the letter."[17]

The notion that writing or books could elicit sin had appeared already in the Old Testament pseudepigrapha, and this ancient idea found new life in the medieval context, specifically within an Augustinian perspective on writing and the Fall.[18] As textual or literary glosses on the Fall moved from scholastic to more popular literature, metaphorical writing tended to become a literal, external text, and the primal sin took on obvious sexual implications, with authors emphasizing the role of the written word as a medium or mirror for desire between men and women. Abelard's story of his literary seduction of Heloise, which hints at the Fall, is exemplary of this transition; although written in Latin, it soon bore much vernacular fruit.

(Paterson, N.J., 1963), p. 101 (translator's brackets). Cf. Ezek. 2.10 (Vulg. = 2.9), Rev. 5.1.

15. *Breviloquium* 3.3.2, *Opera Omnia* 5:232b, trans. de Vinck, p. 115.

16. *Breviloquium* 3.3.3, *Opera Omnia* 5:233a, trans. de Vinck, p. 116. As one "led astray" (*illecta*, from *inlicio*, "to entice"), Eve is also "unread" (*illecta*, fem. of *inlectus*, from *in* "not" + *legere* "to read").

17. Augustine, *Doc* 3.5.9. On Augustine and carnal reading, see above, Chapter 2.3–4. On Bonaventura's gloss, see Curtius, *European Literature*, p. 321; and Gellrich, *The Idea of the Book*, pp. 157–58, with references.

18. See above, Chapter 2.2, esp. the reference to *Jubilees* 8.

Abelard attributes his sexual fall to his own pride and to Fortune, who "flattered me, as the saying goes, to bring me toppling down from my pedestal."[19] Insinuating himself into the household of Heloise's uncle and guardian expressly in order to seduce the girl, Abelard expected Heloise to consent more readily because of her "love of letters," and his account of their erotic tutorials confirms this expectation: "Her studies allowed us to withdraw in private, as love desired, and then with our books open before us, more words of love than of our reading passed between us, and more kissing than teaching. My hands strayed oftener to her bosom than to the pages; love drew our eyes to look on each other more than reading kept them on our texts."[20] Although here books are largely a pretext, the interleaving of the text with looks and caresses suggests that the written word aids in fulfilling a mutual desire. Moreover, in planning the seduction, Abelard anticipated that afterward, when separated, the lovers could "enjoy each other's presence by exchange of written messages" which would also allow them to "speak more openly than in person."[21] Ironically, Abelard's plans for "phallic" writing led to his own castration, and his letters were practically all that Heloise got of him. After their parting, she by chance sees one of his letters and then writes to him, "I saw at once from the heading that it was yours"—a glimpse of her lover's face (*frons*, "heading, brow") in his script, a textual mediation of him that stirs her desire anew.[22]

Abelard and Heloise's story, with its tragic ending, may have inspired Dante's equally famous story of Paolo and Francesca (*Inferno 5*), a literary seduction based even more directly on the Fall, and one whose typological echoes have often been noted.[23] In the

19. Abelard, *Historia calamitatum*, chap. 5, trans. Betty Radice, *The Story of His Misfortunes*, in *The Letters of Abelard and Heloise* (Harmondsworth, 1974), p. 66. Latin text, *PL* 178:113–82.

20. *Historia calamitatum*, chap. 6, trans. Radice, p. 67.

21. *Historia calamitatum*, chap. 6, trans. Radice, p. 66.

22. Trans. Radice, in *Letters*, no. 1, p. 109 ("superscription" modified to "heading"); Latin text, *PL* 178:181. See *OLD*, s.v. *frons* (n. 2). I am indebted to James Cain for calling this detail to my attention. The letter to which Heloise refers is Abelard's *Historia calamitatum*, written in epistolary form. For more on eros and writing in the cloister, including the letters of Abelard and Heloise, see Nichols, "An Intellectual Anthropology of Marriage," pp. 83–88.

23. The parallel is noted, and possible influence suggested, by Peter Dronke, "Francesca and Héloïse," *Comparative Literature* 27 (1975): 113–35 (see 130–35). On typology in *Inferno 5*, see references in Gellrich, *The Idea of the Book*, pp. 152–53. A perceptive reading of the canto is Susan Noakes, "The Double Misreading of Paolo

well-known story, Paolo and Francesca, wife of Paolo's brother, are reading together one day from a romance of Lancelot when, reading of a kiss conferred by the hero, they themselves kiss each other, reading no further that day.[24] Although Dante's version of the story is unverifiable, tradition records that the two lovers were slain for adultery by Francesca's jealous husband. The pilgrim hears the story from Francesca during a momentary lull in the windstorm that forever sweeps the lustful about their circle in hell. At Francesca's final words, which refer to the go-between in the Lancelot romance, *Galeotto fu 'l libro e chi lo scrisse* ("A Gallehault was the book and he who wrote it" [v. 137]), the pilgrim swoons and falls as if in death.

It is a critical commonplace that this episode "revolves around the question of desire mediated by literature."[25] Furthermore, various patterns and allusions suggest that Dante is here offering a literary version of the Fall, including mention of "the first root [*la prima radice*] of our love" (v. 124), the couple's embarrassed glances at each other, the emphasized orality of their kiss, the implied sexual sin, and of course the pilgrim's dying fall. Jesse Gellrich sees a parallel between this episode and "various medieval ideas about reading and the fall of man," particularly Augustine's:

> On the basis of the exegetical tradition that identified spiritual blindness and sense appetite with the femininity of Eve, Dante establishes a parallel between the carnal desire and fornication of the lovers and their response to the French text. The parallel makes use of the fundamental distinction, argued by Augustine in *De doctrina Christiana*, between "enjoying" a text "for its own sake" and "using" its literal sense in order to understand spiritual truth.[26]

In another Augustinian parallel, the lovers read "no further," apparently a reminiscence of Augustine's conversion, where, after he has perused the passage from Paul's letter, Augustine has "no wish to read further."[27] Within the context of Dante's poem, the palinode

and Francesca," *PQ* 62 (1983): 221–39; condensed in *Timely Reading: Between Exegesis and Interpretation* (Ithaca, N.Y., 1988), pp. 41–48.

24. *Inferno* 5.127–42. Unless otherwise noted, further citations are from *The Divine Comedy*, ed., trans., and comm. Singleton.

25. Mazzotta, *Dante, Poet of the Desert*, p. 165, referring to Renato Poggioli, "Paolo and Francesca," in *Dante: A Collection of Critical Essays*, ed. John Freccero (Englewood Cliffs, N.J., 1965), pp. 61–77 (orig. pub. *PMLA* 72 [1957]).

26. Gellrich, *The Idea of the Book*, p. 152, citing *Doc* 1.3.3, 3.5.9.

27. *Inferno* 5.138 ("quel giorno più non vi leggemmo avante"). *Conf* 8.12 ("nec ultra volui legere"). The parallel is noted by Mazzotta, *Dante, Poet of the Desert*, p. 166, with references to earlier scholarship.

anticipates Adam's later declaration to the pilgrim in the terrestrial paradise that the first sin lay in transgressing the sign (*il trapassar del segno*), the abuse of texts being a form of such trespass.[28] Finally, the fallen reading in *Inferno* 5 is figuratively redeemed in the last canto of the whole poem, where, likewise in a single moment (*punto*), the pilgrim glimpses a heavenly book bound together by divine love, an image of the transcendent Word.[29]

In dealing with desire and literature in this canto, critics have tended to dwell on the act of reading, or misreading, emphasizing the lovers' abuse of the text in hand. But clearly Dante implicates the writer, too, and the act of writing, in the question of desire and literature, and in the larger question of language and the Fall. This implication appears in the most famous line of the canto (*Galeotto fu 'l libro e chi lo scrisse*), which tellingly moves backward in time and causality from the book as pandering object to its genesis in the author's writerly act. Whatever the meaning of Francesca's much-discussed allegation, Dante here raises the question of both readerly and authorial responsibility, hinting that authors, including himself, might arouse the carnality of their readers not just accidentally, as with Paolo and Francesca, but even intentionally.

As a final precedent for textual abuses in the *Merchant's Tale*, it is worth glancing at Chaucer's early poem "Adam Scriveyn." Here the poet addresses a scribe named Adam, whom he faults for mis-writing his works, suggesting that the scribe be punished, like the first Adam, for his fallen writing:

Adam scriveyn, if ever it thee bifalle
Boece or Troylus for to wryten newe,
Under thy long lokkes thou most have the scalle,
But after my makyng thow wryte more trewe;
So ofte adaye I mot thy werk renewe,
It to correcte and eke to rubbe and scrape,
And al is thorugh thy negligence and rape.[30]

This famous little poem has been much discussed as a gloss on writing and the Fall. In his "Troylus," too, Chaucer worries that scribes will "myswrite" his poetry, so that "Adam Scriveyn" seems

28. *Paradiso* 26.117. See Shoaf, *Milton, Poet of Duality*, p. 33 ("the transgression of the sign").

29. *Inferno* 5.132 ("solo un punto"), *Paradiso* 33.94 ("un punto solo"); on this and other parallels, see Noakes, *Timely Reading*, pp. 51–53.

30. "Chaucers Wordes unto Adam, His Owne Scriveyn," in *The Riverside Chaucer*, p. 650.

to be a bit of witty authorial revenge on those who would mistake, miswrite, and thus mistransmit the letter of his text.[31] On this reading, Adam the scribe stands to Chaucer the poet as the first Adam stood to the divine Author, a copyist who bears the author's image but cannot write "after" his master without error or imperfection.[32]

Although ultimately a son of the first Adam, Chaucer's scribe descends more immediately from a scribe of the same name who appears in a twelfth-century Latin poem that begins, "Beneath a certain tree, Adam the clerk wrote of how the first Adam sinned by means of a certain tree."[33] This poem, too, draws on medieval ideas about the Fall as the genesis of writing, including what R.E. Kaske describes as "a tradition of Adam as the inventor of letters."[34] But the Latin poem goes on for the rest of its more than fifty lines to list the faults of women as daughters of Eve. This antifeminist theme in turn has recently drawn attention to the word "rape" which resoundingly concludes "Adam Scriveyn."[35] As used here, *rape* is usually rendered as "haste," but the violent or sexual sense of the term was already current in Chaucer's time.[36] Jane Chance, noting that stylus and parchment are standard medieval "symbols of the genitals," argues that in Chaucer's poem *rape* "also implies 'seizure,' 'stealing away,' and sexual rape, as with the pen of the page."[37] And Carolyn Dinshaw asserts that the poem's last word has "strong and assertively masculine associations [which] suggest the idea that writing is a masculine act, an act performed on a body construed as feminine."[38]

31. *Troilus and Criseyde* 5.1795 (p. 584).

32. Curtius, *European Literature*, p. 314, cites references to "God [as] the *dictator*, under whom holy men write."

33. Text in S. G. Owen, "A Medieval Latin Poem," *English Historical Review* 2 (1887): 525–26; trans. R. E. Kaske, "*Clericus Adam* and Chaucer's *Adam Scriveyn*," in *Chaucerian Problems and Perspectives: Essays Presented to Paul E. Beichner C. S. C.*, ed. Edward Vasta and Zacharias P. Thundy (Notre Dame, 1979), pp. 114–18 (p. 114).

34. Kaske, "*Clericus Adam*," p. 116.

35. See Jane Chance, "Chaucerian Irony in the Verse Epistles 'Wordes Unto Adam,' 'Lenvoy a Scogan,' and 'Lenvoy a Bukton,' " *PLL* 21 (1985): 115–28 (pp. 117–20); and Dinshaw, *Chaucer's Sexual Poetics*, pp. 3–14.

36. See *MED*, s.v. *rape*; and Dinshaw, *Chaucer's Sexual Poetics*, pp. 8–9.

37. Chance, "Chaucerian Irony," p. 119, citing Alan of Lille, *De planctu naturae* (prose 5.33–34). Dinshaw, *Chaucer's Sexual Poetics*, noting "the obvious and age-old association of the pen with the phallus," also cites Alan of Lille and *Le Roman de la Rose* (p. 7).

38. Dinshaw, *Chaucer's Sexual Poetics*, p. 9. On bodily tropes for texts, see Dinshaw, pp. 19–25; and above, Chapter 2, note 99.

On this reading, "Adam Scriveyn" links writing, sex, and the Fall in especially problematic ways, pointing toward an essentially masculine eros of inscription in which scribes violate texts and thereby authors themselves.[39] A similar masculine eros of writing appears throughout the *Merchant's Tale*, in both its action and narration. Texts there are continually mistaken and violated; and though the literary seduction is a mutual one, it begins with phallic writing and ends with sex as conceived solely from a male point of view. Finally, the Merchant's misogyny carries his own intrusive narrative close to committing a vicarious rape on the female target of his whole performance.

2. Literary Foreplay

The problems of language and the Fall in the *Merchant's Tale* are framed by its narrator, clearly a bitter man whose view of life seems to have been soured by just two months of marriage.[40] Apparently having abandoned all hope, the Merchant seems intent on showing in his tale that the alleged paradise of marriage is not so much a purgatory as a veritable hell. In his misery he loves company, and his tale, with its many opinionated asides, is shot through with *Schadenfreude*. Withal, most critics have found it a dark vision of marriage, of women, and of life in general—a kind of medieval "Kreutzer Sonata."[41] Recent criticism has stressed that the Merchant debases not only marriage and women but also signs, reducing practically everything to its face value in his own cash economy; and, furthermore, that as a redactor of diverse literary materials he mismanages the signs and texts that he appropriates as his literary property.[42]

39. Dinshaw, *Chaucer's Sexual Poetics*, pp. 9–10, indicates various textual violations suggested by "rape" in Chaucer's poem.

40. "I have ywedded bee / Thise monthes two, and moore nat" (IV.1233–34); further citations from the Merchant's *Prologue* and *Tale* omit the fragment number (IV), which is supplied for other citations from the *Canterbury Tales*.

41. The classic view appears in G. G. Sedgewick, "The Structure of *The Merchant's Tale*," *The University of Toronto Quarterly* 17 (1948): 337–45; and Donaldson, "The Effect of the *Merchant's Tale*," in *Speaking of Chaucer*, pp. 30–45.

42. See R. A. Shoaf, "The Merchant and the Parody of Creation," in *Dante, Chaucer, and the Currency of the Word: Money, Images, and Reference in Late Medieval Poetry* (Norman, Okla., 1983), pp. 185–209; and Robert R. Edwards, "Narration and Doctrine in the *Merchant's Tale*," *Speculum* 66 (1991): 342–67. Priscilla Martin, *Chaucer's Women: Nuns, Wives, and Amazons* (Iowa City, 1990), pp. 102–5, 116–21, argues that the tale mocks "sexual, financial and spiritual opportunism," reflexively condemning its teller's cynicism as well (p. 121). For Deborah S. Ellis,

An example of the Merchant's abusive way with women and texts appears already in his *Prologue*, a denunciation of marriage that heavily tilts the tale that follows toward confession or autobiography, despite his promise to tell "namoore" of his "owene soore" (1243–44). Bemoaning his unhappy marriage, he slanders his own wife in typological terms that set up his narrative as a personal gloss on the Fall. "I have a wyf," he complains, "the worste that may be; / For thogh the feend to hire ycoupled were, / She wolde hym overmacche, I dar wel swere" (1218–20). The Merchant's main point is that his redoubtable wife would prevail over the Devil himself; yet his remark also hints at the ancient libel about Eve's coupling with the Devil. The Merchant's nasty crack even alludes to the climax of the tale he is about to tell, which exposes a wife to view while she is literally "ycoupled" with her husband's rival, Damyan, a veritable devil of a fellow.

The tale itself opens with the old bachelor knight's decision to marry at sixty—in medieval times, a ripe old age attained only by a few—after having freely enjoyed the pleasures of the flesh out of wedlock for as long as has dared. The Merchant "kan nat seye" whether "this knyght" was marrying "for hoolynesse or for dotage," but "day and nyght he dooth al that he kan / T'espien where he myghte wedded be" (1253–57). January's attempt to "espien" an opportunity for marriage highlights his blindness, now spiritual and later physical ("love is blynd alday, and may nat see" [1598]), and it anticipates the carnal visions that soon he is entertaining every night in his mind's eye. Even the internal rhyme on "knyght"/"nyght" suggests that he lives in a darkness of his own making.

Several allusions to the original Garden establish the typology of the Fall for what is to follow.[43] As the Merchant mockingly re-

---

"The Merchant's Wife's Tale: Language, Sex, and Commerce in Margery Kempe and in Chaucer," *Exemplaria* 2 (1990): 595–626, both teller and characters inhabit a world of commerce based on "intrinsic instability and distrust" (p. 613). According to Lee Patterson, *Chaucer and the Subject of History* (London, 1991), pp. 333–44, the tale stages the teller's personal and social insecurity but finds "a moment of resolution" in the Pluto-Proserpina episode (p. 358). Although my treatment tends to reify the Merchant as the producer of his tale, I recognize that the tale reciprocally "produces" the teller. See H. Marshall Leicester, Jr., "The Art of Impersonation: A General Prologue to the *Canterbury Tales*," *PMLA* 95 (1980): 213–24: "The tales . . . concentrate not on the way preexisting people create language but on the way language creates people" (p. 217).

43. The tale's Genesis typology has been noted often. Besides Shoaf, as cited above, see Robertson, "The Doctrine of Charity in Mediaeval Literary Gardens," pp. 47–49; Kenneth A. Bleeth, "The Image of Paradise in the *Merchant's Tale*," in

counts, January prays that God will grant him to live happily "under that hooly boond / With which that first God man and womman bond" (1261–62), the old knight declaring that "wedlok is so esy and so clene, / That in this world it is a paradys" (1264–65). If these initial remarks on the Garden suggest an abuse of the scriptural letter in the service of carnal pleasure, January's marriage encomium takes this abuse much further by offering some very doubtful glosses on Eve, marriage, and women.

Most critics treat the lengthy encomium (1267–1392), an unattributed speech, as the Merchant's satirical reflection of January's thoughts.[44] January begins his gloss on Eve with a scriptural paraphrase and quotation from Genesis 2:

> The hye God, whan he hadde Adam maked,
> And saugh him al allone, bely-naked,
> God of his grete goodnesse seyde than,
> "Lat us now make an helpe unto this man
> Lyk to hymself"; and thanne he made him Eve.
>
> (1325–29)

Whereas the embedded quotation in itself is an accurate rendering of the Vulgate text, its paraphrased context is selective and distorted.[45] First of all, Scripture makes no mention of God having seen Adam "bely-naked," or naked in any other way, confining perceptions of nakedness to the humans themselves, both innocently before the sin (Gen. 2.25) and guiltily afterward (Gen. 3.7, etc.).[46] Scripture does show God asking Adam who has told him that he is naked, but only after the sin and then in response to Adam's own admission (Gen. 3.10–11). Taken as January's term for Adam, *bely-naked* is thus a prolepsis of the Fall that betrays a benighted conception of man's original state. Or, taken instead as the Merchant's

---

The Learned and the Lewed: Studies in Chaucer and Medieval Literature, ed. Larry D. Benson (Cambridge, Mass., 1974), pp. 45–60; and Wolfgang E. H. Rudat, "Chaucer's Spring of Comedy: The *Merchant's Tale* and Other 'Games' with Augustinian Theology," *AM* 21 (1981): 111–20.

44. See Edwards, "Narration and Doctrine," pp. 351–57, with references to earlier scholarship.

45. Gen. 2.18 ("faciamus ei adiutorium similem sui"). Chaucer's glosses on Genesis 2–3 are discussed by Fyler, "Man, Men, and Women in Chaucer's Poetry"; on *Merchant's Tale*, see pp. 159, 167.

46. Donaldson, "The Effect of the *Merchant's Tale*," pp. 38–40, discusses "bely-naked" as a sign of the Merchant's disgust for humans as God's handiwork.

cynical aside, the term betrays the narrator's attempt to taint with sin, or signs of sin, an otherwise innocent state. In either case, it is a carnal reading.

In paraphrasing Eve's creation, January also elides God's first, failed attempt to find Adam a helper: namely, the intervening creation of the animals, their being brought to Adam, and his naming them (Gen. 2.19–20). This omission may seem minor and inconsequential, except that January goes on to treat woman herself *like* an animal who must unquestioningly obey man's commands:

> Al that hire housbonde lust, hire liketh weel;
> She seith nat ones "nay," whan he seith "ye."
> "Do this," seith he; "Al redy, sire," seith she.
> (1344–46)

Nor is this all; later on January actually compares his future wife to various beasts: " 'Oold fissh and yong flessh wolde I have fayn. / Bet is,' quod he, 'a pyk than a pykerel, / And bet than old boef is the tendre veel' " (1418–20).

But January's worst mistaking of the scriptural letter may be his gloss on woman as man's marriage partner. With great certitude, he describes his prospective wife in various terms denoting her subordinate status, the first of which is grounded in biblical authority, but the last of which ends up in highly questionable terrain:

> Heere may ye se, and heerby may ye preve,
> That wyf is mannes *helpe* and his *confort*,
> His *paradys terrestre*, and his *disport*.
> (1330–32; emphasis added)

Here "Adam" names "Eve," but what he names her says more about *him*. Falling down the slippery slope from "helpe" to "confort," and from "confort" to "disport," January already anticipates his later behavior in his pleasure garden, where he sensually urges May, "Lat us taken oure disport" (2147). Not only does this gloss on woman as man's sexual servant or slave have no biblical authority; it runs in the face of church doctrine, which forbade using sexual intercourse for the purpose of pleasure, enjoining a strictly procreative intent.[47]

---

47. January acknowledges the sin of "avoutrye" (1435) and the duty of "leveful procreacioun" (1448), but he does not count his own marital lust or conjugal "disport" as sins.

In sum, January's glosses on Genesis constitute a serious misreading of Scripture, and the Merchant's sarcastic reportage implicates him, too, in the abuse of the letter. In the medieval context, any misconstruction of Scripture signals danger, but January's mistaking of passages related to the Fall is an especially serious (and ironic) error, for these misreadings determine his attitude toward the garden of marriage and his wifely "paradys." In the famous words of Chaucer's Summoner, "Glosynge is a glorious thyng, certeyn, / For lettre sleeth, so as we clerkes seyn" (III.1793–94).

The subsequent marriage debate between January's two brothers (1469–1576) contains further textual glosses, both biblical and classical, which are used solely to support their opposed views of marriage. Placebo, the sycophant, chimes in with January's marriage encomium, whereas Justinus, voicing the Merchant's own sour sentiments, warns against marriage. The counsel of neither has any real effect on January's predecided "purpos" (1571), and he picks the course that pleases him after going through the motions of taking advice.[48]

Regarding marriage and woman, January not only reads but also writes carnally. In the first place, his marriage to May—who is of humble rank, "of smal degree" (1625)—involves an abundance of "scrit and bond / By which that she was feffed in his lond" (1697–98). Documents ensuring property rights were a standard part of the marriage contract. But May's enfeoffment through writing emphasizes her own status as property, as the "paradys terrestre" and "disport" that January has designated her. Furthermore, this initial "scrit and bond" sets a precedent for the charters that January later promises May in his garden to ensure that she will remain his sexual property.

January also employs another sort of carnal writing, an inner writing on the soul or heart. Critics have noted that inward "impressions" are mentioned throughout the tale, and have discussed this motif in terms of psychology, sexuality, coinage, and the Pygmalion myth, but they have not stressed its significance as another form of the carnal letter.[49] The imagery of impressions first appears—in external form—when January is telling his friends that he wants a

---

48. Justinus also makes a further, conciliatory speech (1655–88). For a recent discussion of the debate, see Edwards, "Narration and Doctrine," pp. 357–60.

49. E.g., Alfred David, *The Strumpet Muse: Art and Morals in Chaucer's Poetry* (Bloomington, Ind., 1976), p. 177; and Shoaf, *Dante, Chaucer, and the Currency of the Word*, pp. 188–90.

young wife rather than an old one, for he will be able to mold a docile "yong thyng" to suit his will like "warm wex" in his hands:

> sondry scoles maken sotile clerkis;
> Womman of manye scoles half a clerk is.
> But certeynly, a yong thyng may men gye,
> Right as men may warm wex with handes plye.
>
> (1427–30)

This passage alludes to the Pygmalion myth, which January blindly reenacts, much as he ignorantly recapitulates the Fall. The concurrence of "warm wex" and "clerkis" is also significant, for wax tablets were used in "scoles" and also the counting house as a cheap, erasable substitute for expensive paper or parchment.

That wax tablets, an ancient form of "erasable" notebook, were still common in Chaucer's day is evidenced by their mention in the *Summoner's Tale.*[50] Medieval tradition also knew of wax tablets from Ovid's *Art of Love,* which cites them in connection with love letters, a precedent especially relevant to the *Merchant's Tale,* where writing, wax, and impressions are associated with sexual desire.[51] Furthermore, an ancient rhetorical tradition, passed down to the Middle Ages, invoked wax writing tablets as a figure for the impressions left in the memory by words or other experience.[52] A related notion is the Platonic "writing in the soul," with its analogue in the Pauline "tables of the heart," a metaphor that lived on variously in patristic and medieval tradition, including the notion of God's original "writing" in Adam's heart.[53] In medieval tradition, inner writing usually represents a natural, divine law, by comparison with external, "fallen" writing. In the *Merchant's Tale,* however, inner writing turns out to be as carnal as its external counterpart.

The metaphor of inner writing is first implied by the mention of impressions left on January's mind by the fantasies he entertains while seeking a wife:

50. *Summoner's Tale* III.1741–42, mentioning "a peyre of tables al of yvory, / And a poyntel polysshed fetisly" with which the friar writes the names of almsgivers, only to erase them later: "He planed awey the names everichon" (1758).

51. Ovid, *Ars amatoria* 1.437–38; 2.395–96, 543; 3.469, 495–96, 621.

52. For classical loci, see Yates, *The Art of Memory,* pp. 6–7, and other index entries, s.v. "wax imprints."

53. Ambrose, *Par* 8.39, refers to divine commands "impressed [*impressum*] in our hearts."

Heigh fantasye and curious bisynesse
Fro day to day gan in the soule impresse
Of Januarie aboute his mariage.
Many fair shap and many a fair visage
Ther passeth thurgh his herte nyght by nyght.

(1577–81)

The narrator also compares January's fantasies about women to figures reflected as they pass a "mirour" in a marketplace (1582–84),
but the primary image is one of impressions left in his "soule" or
"herte," a kind of inner writing.[54] A further hint of inner writing in
this passage occurs when January, finally deciding whom to marry,
"atte laste *apoynted* hym on oon" (1595; emphasis added), with
perhaps a glance at *point* ("a punctuation mark, period"), or *pointel*
("stylus").[55] January's stopping at this point, like Dante's fated readers at their particular *punto*, reveals him as a carnal reader and writer.

Into the "paradys" of January's marriage there creeps a serpent who
is rather more skilled at carnal reading and writing than the old
knight himself. January's "squyer, highte Damyan, / Which carf
biforn the knyght ful many a day," is a lone exception to the general
"joye and blisse" at January's wedding (1771–73); smitten with passion for May, he puts down his knife to take up his pen, another
phallic image for his carnal designs on his master's wife.[56]

   Damyan's role as the rival in the conventional marriage triangle
of the fabliau, and as the tempter in the original marriage triangle
of Eden, is manifest. In keeping with the established Garden typology, the Merchant likens Damyan to a "naddre," among other
things:

O perilous fyr, that in the bedstraw bredeth!
O famulier foo, that his servyce bedeth!

---

   54. See *MED*, s.v. *impressen* 1d ("to write"), and *impressioun* 1a ("the carving
or writing of symbols").
   55. *MED*, s.v. *pointe* (n. 1) 1a, citing *Canon's Yeoman's Tale* VIII.1480 ("Ther
a poynt, for ended is my tale"); and s.v. *pointel* 1a (see *Summoner's Tale* III.1742, as
cited above).
   56. January later assures May that "a man may do no synne with his wyf, / Ne
hurte hymselven with his owene knyf" (1839–40); and, in the garden, that he would
rather "dyen on a knyf" (2163) than offend her.

> O servant traytour, false hoomly hewe,
> *Lyk to the naddre in bosom sly untrewe.*
> (1783–86; emphasis added)

The phrase is proverbial, but *naddre* is a common Middle English term for the Serpent of Genesis 3 and is used as such elsewhere in the *Canterbury Tales*.[57] The snake in the "bosom," recalling patristic topoi about Satan or the Serpent "creeping" into the human heart, also foretells the internal dynamics of language in the seduction soon under way.[58] Physically, Damyan also resembles the Serpent in later going "lowe" (2013), in "stirt[ing]" through the garden gate (2153), and as "the lechour, in the tree" (2257), while January's unsuspecting praise of his squire as "wys, discreet, and...secree" (1909) suggests the character of the wise or subtle Serpent.

Unlike the serpent in the garden against whom Geoffrey de la Tour Landry warns his daughters, Damyan seems truly taken with his love object, as suggested by his state of extreme lovesickness: "He was so ravysshed on his lady May / That for the verray peyne he was ny wood" (1774–75). Of course, this remark may be more of the Merchant's sarcasm. In fact, although the squire's seduction of the knight's lady begins in essentially courtly terms, as the affair develops it turns out that neither of the two "lovers" has a trace of romantic idealism.

Damyan begins May's temptation and seduction not with a flattering speech but with an artful letter that opens a series of secret epistolary exchanges between the two lovers. Taken together, these exchanges dramatize in concrete form the central theme of the carnal letter, of the written sign as a locus of rhetorical and hermeneutical problems traditionally associated with the Fall.

The Merchant describes in detail the entire progress of the initial love letter (so to call it)—how it is written, hidden, delivered and received, hidden again, read, and finally destroyed, as well as how it is eventually answered, thus completing the readerly/writerly circuit. The various letters are shown to mediate desire between the two lovers, arousing that desire until the letters bear fruit in the form of carnal deeds. The fact that both lovers conceal and carry

---

57. E.g., *Parson's Tale* X.330 ("There may ye seen that deedly synne hath, first, suggestion of the feend, as sheweth heere by the naddre"). See also *MED*, s.v. *naddre* 1c.

58. E.g., Augustine, *Civ* 14.11 ("[Satan] sought...to work his way [*serpere*] into the heart of man"). See also *GenM* 2.14.20 ("intravit in cor").

letters near the "herte" or "bosom" stresses the relation of desire to reading and writing.

This amorous correspondence arises, as the Merchant explains, because Damyan "langwissheth for love" (1867) and yet hesitates to speak of his passion to May since he believes she will either refuse him or betray him: "How shaltow to thy lady, fresshe May, / Telle thy wo? She wole alwey seye nay. / Eek if thou speke, she wol thy wo biwreye" (1871–73). In raising and answering this "demaunde" (1870), the Merchant again mocks courtly ideals. At the same time, he supplies a cause for Damyan's displacement of desire from speech onto writing. As the Merchant further explains, Damyan finally writes a letter in order to alleviate his burning sexual passion:

This sike Damyan in Venus fyr
So brenneth that he dyeth for desyr,
For which he putte his lyf in aventure.
Ne lenger myghte he in this wise endure,
But prively a penner gan he borwe,
And in a lettre wroot he al his sorwe,
In manere of a compleynt or a lay,
Unto his faire, fresshe lady May.
(1875–82; emphasis added)

This first act of letter writing in the tale anticipates Damyan's later act of phallic inscription directly on May. As noted earlier, writing is a common medieval trope for sexual intercourse. R. A. Shoaf remarks that in the *Merchant's Tale* this trope is "almost literalized," and that signs and writings not only "anticipate" adultery but constitute its "early stages."[59] Damyan's—expressly phallic—writing initiates and symbolizes this adultery. In this scene, Damyan's "penner" (pen case) symbolizes the male prerogative of inscription. Instead of "penner," one manuscript has "penne," an even more directly phallic image.[60]

As a "naddre" in January's "paradys," and as a writer of seductive letters, Damyan points to Augustine's comparison of the Serpent to a pen or stylus, as well as to medieval folklore about the Devil as a

59. Shoaf, *Dante, Chaucer, and the Currency of the Word*, p. 198, emphasizing May's "extraordinary capacity for signification"; on writing tropes, see also pp. 194–96.

60. Vr. in *The Text of the Canterbury Tales, Studied on the Basis of All Known Manuscripts*, ed. John M. Manly and Edith Rickert, 8 vols. (Chicago, 1940), 6:449 (l. 1879). For semantics, see *MED*, s.v. *penner*.

scribe or writer, as in the legend of the Devil's Letter, a compendium of rhetorical art that actually circulated in Chaucer's time.[61] As a branch of rhetoric in general, the art of letter writing (*ars dictaminis*) was particularly associated with Bologna, not far from the setting of the tale in Lombardy.[62] Most important, Damyan's writing a seductive "lettre" foregrounds the Fall as a scene of persuasion through written rhetoric, among other things.

The rhetorical artifice embodied in Damyan's letter is enhanced by the mention of its style or genre, "a compleynt or a lay." These generic labels may indicate conventional poetic love epistles, of which several Middle English examples survive; in any case, *compleint* is a typical term for the rhetoric of courtly seduction, and it recalls, for example, the seducer's (spoken) *pleinte* in *Ancrene Wisse*.[63] The generic labels also betoken the letter's crafted, premeditated nature, hinting that its main purpose is to project rather than to express feeling (i.e., "al his sorwe") so as to elicit a certain desired response in its recipient. It is the seducer's written representation of feelings, not his sincerity, that is stressed here.

After finishing his letter, Damyon conceals it in a little pouch: "In a purs of sylk heng on his sherte / He hath it put, and leyde it at his herte" (1883–84). *Purs* ("scrotum") is a sexual emblem that furthers the theme of carnal writing.[64] At the same time, Damyan's keeping the yet undelivered letter near his "herte," just as May subsequently keeps it in her "bosom" before she has a chance to read it, suggests not only the theme of "inner writing" but also writing's deferral of voice, presence, and desire. Script, as opposed to speech, defers mediation by the temporal and spacial distance that separates writing from reading, making author and reader absent from each other and even, in a sense, absent from themselves. The carnality of the letter in the *Merchant's Tale* heightens this absence and deferral, which are symptoms of writing as a product of the Fall.

In his stricken state, Damyan has "hastily" taken to bed (1779), and January, out of concern for his squire's health, ingenuously orders May to visit him there with her ladies-in-waiting and to divert

61. Augustine, *GenL* 11.29.36. On the Devil as scribe, etc., see Jeffrey Burton Russell, *Lucifer: The Devil in the Middle Ages* (Ithaca, N.Y., 1984), pp. 87–89.

62. See Murphy, *Rhetoric in the Middle Ages*, pp. 211–15.

63. On semantics, see *MED*, s.v. *compleint* 3; and *lai* (n. 2) 1b. On poetic love epistles, see references in Davis, "The *Litera Troili*," p. 240. On *Ancrene Wisse*, see above, Chapter 5.2.

64. See *MED*, s.v. *purs(e* 4a, citing *Wife of Bath's Prologue* III.44b ("nether purs"). Cf. "The Complaint of Chaucer to His Purse," lines 1–2 ("purse" = "my lady dere").

or comfort him: "Alle ye go se this Damyan. / Dooth hym disport" (1923–24). When the visitors arrive, May herself sitting "doun by his beddes syde" (1934), Damyan watches for his chance and slips her the "purs" containing the letter, an overture to a kind of "disport" that January—like May herself, for now—scarcely suspects:

> This Damyan, whan that his tyme he say,
> In secree wise his purs and eek his bille,
> In which that he ywriten hadde his wille,
> Hath put into hire hand, withouten moore,
> Save that he siketh wonder depe and soore,
> And softely to hire right thus seyde he:
> "Mercy! And that ye nat discovere me,
> For I am deed if that this thyng be kyd."
>
> (1936–43)

In response, May quietly conceals the letter near her own heart and then departs: "This purs hath she inwith hir bosom hyd / And wente hire wey" (1944–45).

Not only must May wait to read the letter, she does not know for certain what the pouch contains, though unlike Francesca she can hardly "suspect nothing." In any case, the Merchant's added taunt, "ye gete namoore of me" (1945), conceals her inner state. Nonetheless, as an object received by her and concealed near her heart, the letter embodies the theme of writing as mediation, and May's gesture, whatever her state of mind, symbolizes that Damyan's letter, "in which that he ywriten hadde his wille," is now in a position to convey his heart's desire to hers.

In its new hiding place, the letter also embodies several other themes related to writing and the Fall. For example, in carrying the letter "inwith hir bosom," May figuratively conceals Damyan as a "naddre in bosom sly untrewe." Furthermore, like the letter at Damyan's "herte," the letter now in her "bosom" hints again at inner writing.[65] Finally, as a *bille* (cf. 1952, 1971), a term often meaning "document" or "contract," Damyan's letter rivals January's explicitly legal "scrit and bond" (and his later "chartres") as yet another

---

65. The embosomed letter leading to an inward "impression" appears to be an adaptation of an image from Ovid, *The Art of Love* 3.621–22 (in *The Art of Love and Other Poems*, ed. and trans. J. H. Mozley, 2d ed., rev. G. P. Goold, LCL [London, 1979]).

form of "fallen writing" used to secure May as sexual property.[66] Damyan's whispered plea to May as he hands her his letter hints also at the letter of the law, specifically the possibility of death at his lord's hands should he be exposed ("I am deed if that this thyng be kyd"). In a spiritual sense, of course, Damyan is already "deed" through his carnal use of writing.

In telling May to visit Damyan, January has sent her from his own "chambre" (1922), urging her to be quick about her errand, since he wants his own "disport" with her when she gets back: "And spede yow faste, for I wole abyde / Til that ye slepe faste by my syde" (1927–28). Indeed, when May returns, January "taketh hire, and kisseth hire ful ofte, / And leyde hym doun to slepe, and that anon" (1948–49). The implication is that May is to go to bed with him—for intercourse first, and then a nap.[67] But Damyan's letter is still hidden in her bosom, and to undress now before her husband would expose her (and the squire) to discovery. May, certainly suspecting that Damyan's "purs" contains something illicit, excuses herself by going to the privy to read the letter and dispose of it there, as I will discuss in a moment.

Clearly the exchange of the first letter, occurring when May and her husband are temporarily separated, is a symbolic rupture of January's marriage. And the break in the narrative sequence formed by May's visit to Damyan, with its interruption of her coupling with January, figures the impending break in the marriage itself, despite the verbal patching that smooths things over again after the crisis in January's garden. While both January and Damyan are separately abed, May moves between them, though mediating very little if anything at all. January has given her a message to convey to his squire—"telleth hym that I wol hym visite" (1925)—but there is no evidence that May does so; and the message she takes away from Damyan remains tightly in her bosom.

The Fall, of course, involves a good deal of domestic breakage; and gaps, interruptions, and fissures abound in this domestic version of the Fall, with its violated garden gate, its counterfeit key to January's "wedlok," and even its mention of Pyramus and Thisbe "rownynge thurgh a wal" (2128–30). January is named for not only the two-faced Roman god, Ianus (or Janus), and his eponymous month, signifying wintry old age, but also doorways and entrances

66. See *MED*, s.v. *bille*, where this instance (l. 1937) is oddly placed under sense 1a ("A formal document") rather than 6a ("A personal letter"), though it has documentary connotations, as indicated.

67. "Anon he preyde hire strepen hire al naked; / He wolde of hire, he seyde, han som plesaunce" (1958–59).

(*ianua*, "door"), as played out in his role as gatekeeper.[68] January guards the gate to his garden and death's door (*ianua*, "the gateway of death, of the underworld"), as well as the sensory "gate" to the soul (*ianua*, "the mouth, features, as the means of communication with the mind, etc."].[69] As such, this sleepy old Adam ought to be on the lookout for the Serpent, who, in Bernard of Clairvaux's tropology of the Fall, "finds the neglected opening in the wall of circumstance and enters the paradise of my mind unresisted, discovers me sleeping within the very retreat of evil, and creeping up to the little ear of my Eve and hissing into it the poison of evil persuasion, awakens her by the side of the sleeper and leads her away along the path of curiosity to the tree of the knowledge of good and evil."[70]

The "Serpent" in January's domestic paradise whispers a few words to "Eve," but he sends his main temptation in a letter, slipping it into the narrative gap formed by May's bedside visit. The letter thus figures the capacity of writing in general to create not only continuities but also ruptures—temporal, narrative, domestic, and so forth. Although January and Damyan both practice fallen writing, the latter's "love" letter threatens to destabilize the more legalistic writings of the former, as each lays claim to the same feminine "paradys" and the use of the same garden. In the passage specifying that May conceals Damyan's letter in her "bosom," one scribe mistook a couple of letters and instead wrote "body"—that is, "This purs hath she with in hir *body* hyd."[71] This case of misreading and miswriting, if such it is, brings out more fully the sexual implications of the letter exchanged here; it also spells out unequivocally the terrain contested by the two scribes in the tale itself. Of course, May can write, too, and in her own carnal letters she will sign over her body to Damyan.

Although Damyan's letter merely takes advantage of an initial narrative gap, it actually instigates a second gap, May's visit to the privy:

She feyned hire as that she moste gon
Ther as ye woot that every wight moot neede;

68. See *OLD*, s.v. *ianua* 1a–b, *ianitor*; and, for the further senses listed below, *ianua* 2a–b.

69. As gatekeeper, January is also associated with an "entrance" to knowledge (*ianua*, "a way of approach, initial stage [in achievement, learning, etc.]").

70. *Parabola de octo beatitudinibus*, in *Opera*, 6/2:299, as cited above, Chapter 5.1.

71. Manly and Rickert, eds., *The Text of the Canterbury Tales* 6:455–56, line 1944 (emphasis added).

And whan she of this bille hath taken heede,
She rente it al to cloutes atte laste,
And in the pryvee softely it caste.

(1950–54)

Apparently the medieval privy sometimes did serve as a retreat for reading; domestic architecture in Chaucer's time increasingly afforded privacy to well-to-do women, but even in January's spacious "palays" (2415) the privy offers May virtually her sole refuge from the common "halle," her husband's "chambre," and the company of "alle hir wommen."[72] At the same time, the privy is a fixture in fabliaux, and the Merchant, with his excremental vision of female sexuality, uses this place and its associations to point to the private ("privee") parts, to sexual intercourse, and the like.[73] The letter was written "prively" by Damyan (1879), and so is it read by May. The whole scene thus may show "superbly bad taste," as E. Talbot Donaldson remarked, but as a gloss on the carnal letter it is also superbly revealing.[74]

First, as part of a Fall typology, the privy scene replaces the usual tête-à-tête between the seducer and the "daughter of Eve" with an expressly written form of temptation.[75] As such, the scene plays out the Temptation as a "privation," whether inwardly among the faculties of the soul or outwardly in the sexual politics of Paradise. According to Augustine's tropology of the Fall, pleasurable stimulus (the Serpent) separates appetite (Eve) from reason (Adam), thus violating the "wedlock" (coniugio) within the soul.[76] When this inward separation occurs, "then, as it were, the serpent discourses with the woman. And to consent to this allurement, is to eat of the forbidden tree"—consent being either "the pleasure of thought" (cogitationis delectatio) or the deed itself. As part of the internal fall, pleasure tempts the soul or mind "to enjoy itself as if it were some private [privato] good of its own." May, in privily reading Damyan's letter, is seeking precisely "some private good"—not only the private pleasure of reading the letter itself but also the further private pleasure of her eventual tryst with Damyan. Of course, Jan-

---

72. The "chambre" and "halle" are mentioned at 1922, and May's "wommen" at 1921, 1933. On privies and reading, see Margaret Wood, *The English Mediaeval House* (London, 1965), pp. 384–85, with references.

73. See *MED*, s.v. *prive* (n.) 1c; *prive* (adj. 1) 4; and *privete* (n.) 1g.

74. Donaldson, "The Effect of the Merchant's Tale," p. 36.

75. On the feudalized Fall, see above, Chapter 5.2, 4.

76. *Trin* 12.12.17.

uary/Adam scarcely lives up to his role as "reason," giving May/Eve
an advantage in pursuing her appetite for pleasure.

The privy was a common medieval emblem for "foul" or dis-
honest language. It occurs as such in both *Ancrene Wisse*, which
evokes "the Devil's privy" in connection with flattery, and the *Livre
du Chevalier*, which tells of a nobleman who hides his nocturnal
trysts from his wife by saying that he has been at the privy.[77] May's
"feyned" need for the privy likewise covers one bodily function with
another; as R. Howard Bloch notes, the "cloaking of coitus behind
cloaca" is common in fabliaux.[78] Furthermore, May's cloacal feign-
ing in the privy inaugurates further "privee" exchanges with Damyan, which of course climax with their sexual union in the tree.

Significantly, the letter is not only read in the privy but also
disposed of there. Once May has "taken heede" of its content, she
treats the "bille" itself as superfluous and even dangerous, a scarlet
letter to be kept only at her peril, and Damyan's too. Heloise may
glimpse the face of her absent lover in Abelard's letters, as Troilus
does in Criseyde's; but May counts on getting more than just a
mediated presence, and, with her own lover not far from her in
another room of the palace, she unsentimentally destroys the letter
that now could only separate them more. By discarding the letter,
she actually improves her chances of possessing its author. Furthermore, it soon becomes clear that May gives up only the material
letter, saving its sense within herself, incorporated for good into her
"bosom"—a more secure and yet more private realm than the privy.

As for the letter itself, having entered through one narrative gap
and through one room hidden from January's sight, it now leaves
by another. Torn to "cloutes," where *clout* ("fragment, piece, piece
of cloth") links texts with textiles, Damyan's letter is reduced from
an artful composition of feelings, a rhetorical fabrication, to mere
scraps of paper or parchment.[79] Since the contents of medieval privies were usually carted into gardens and fields, it is tempting to
suppose that Damyan's composed letter ultimately ends up fertil-
izing January's pear tree.[80] But now reduced from linguistic order to
mere ordure, the letter as part of a load of dung would hardly com-
plement the sweet herbs and flowering trees typically cultivated in

---

77. *The English Text of the Ancrene Riwle*, Corpus MS., fol. 21b–22a, p. 45;
trans. Salu, p. 37. *Le Livre du Chevalier*, ed. Montaiglon, chap. 17, p. 37.

78. R. Howard Bloch, *The Scandal of the Fabliaux* (Chicago, 1986), p. 86.

79. *MED*, s.v. *clout* (n. 1) 4, 5. The term appears in *Ancrene Wisse* (as *bicluten*,
"to clothe") in connection with verbal "fig leaves," as cited above, Chapter 5.3.

80. Cf. *Nun's Priest's Tale* VII.3018–19, 3036.

medieval pleasure gardens. Moreover, as torn up and thrown into
the privy, the carnal letter here dies a kind of death. Chaucer elsewhere suggests that verbal signs, like humans themselves, are born
inter urinas et faeces: one bird in the *Parliament of Fowls* silences
another by sneering, "Out of the donghil cam that word ful right!"
(597); and the Pardoner, with an even fouler imagination than the
Merchant's, describes the stomach as a bag full "of dong and of
corrupcioun! / At either ende of thee foul is the soun" (VI.535–36).
In January's privy, however, the process is reversed, as words—here,
written ones—die and return to the ground and to silence. Thus are
signs reduced to mere things, a fate already foretold by their abuse
in the carnal letter.

May's inward reaction to Damyan's letter is deferred until the
"bille" itself has been disposed of, as if to stress the letter's permanent inward effects. Her first reaction is wonderment: "Who stu-
dieth now but faire fresshe May?" (1955). Next, after returning to
January's bedroom, she apparently finds her husband's insistence on
"som plesaunce" less than a pleasure herself: "How that he wroghte,
I dar nat to yow telle, / Or wheither hire thoughte it paradys or
helle" (1959, 1963–64). Finally, with a nod to astrology ("that tyme
fortunaat / Was for to putte a bille of Venus werkes" [1970–71]), her
feelings are divulged:

> this fresshe May
> Hath take swich impression that day
> Of pitee of this sike Damyan
> That from hire herte she ne dryve kan
> The remembrance for to doon hym ese.
> "Certeyn," thoghte she, "whom that this thyng displese
> I rekke noght, for heere I hym assure
> To love hym best of any creature,
> Though he namoore hadde than his sherte."
>
> (1977–85)

In standard medieval style, the Merchant specifies the letter's inward
results in terms of various psychological faculties: Damyan has
marked May's memory ("remembrance"), engendered sympathetic
feeling ("pitee"), and stirred her sexual appetite, her desire "for to
doon hym ese." Although May has seen, heard, and even touched
Damyan, her powerful emotional response occurs only after she
reads his letter, underscoring the role of the written word in stimulating and shaping her thoughts and feelings.

May's readerly response is figured as an inner writing ("impression") and as an internal monologue (" 'Certeyn,' thoghte she," etc.), both of which suggest that she internalizes the letter which at first she merely carries "inwith hir bosom hyd," its content still unknown to her. As part of a Fall typology, May's monologue figures a response to the tempter's "voice," recalling the traditional notion that seductive words remain dormant in the memory and can reawaken at any time to tempt the soul.[81]

The "impression" left by Damyan's letter on May's "herte" is erotic rather than spiritual "writing." In the *Merchant's Tale*, inner and outer writing are not signs of spiritual and material reality, respectively; rather, both become signs and instruments of the same carnal ends, with inward impressions (on heart, soul, or mind) serving as analogues for the letters and other documents outwardly exchanged by the characters to underwrite their carnal desires. At the same time, the inward impression left on May by Damyan's letter signifies the phallic writing that already has been figured by his "penner" and "purs," and that eventually takes the form of his more direct inscription directly on May's body.[82] May's heart is not, like some, "as hard as any stoon" (1990), and she takes an impression easily; nor does the commandment against adultery, written in stone by Moses, seem to be a stumbling block to her.[83]

Soon May herself is writing a letter of reply to Damyan, thus completing the written circuit and figuring "Eve's" active role in her own seduction. This time, rather than just offering generic labels, the Merchant paraphrases the letter's content:

> This gentil May, fulfilled of pitee,
> Right of hire hand a lettre made she,
> In which she graunteth hym hire verray grace.
> Ther lakketh noght oonly but day and place
> Wher that she myghte unto his lust suffise,
> For it shal be right as he wole devyse.
>
> (1995–2000)

In terms of Fall typology, May's letter represents Eve's reply to the Serpent and the traditional idea that the tempter's overture estab-

81. See references above, Chapter 5.2.

82. Ovid, *The Art of Love* 3.625–26, refers to love letters written on the back of a confidante.

83. On writing, the Law, and the stone tablets, see Vance, *Mervelous Signals*, pp. 8–9.

lished a discursive conduit that Eve kept open by her ill-advised
reply. May's writerly mood of "pitee" reflects the lingering effects
of Damyan's letter, as she now mediates back to him her own desire.
Although for now May submits to what Damyan "wole devyse,"
later she takes a more active role in planning and directing the
fulfillment of their desires. In any case, from this point on, with the
writerly circuit now established, both would-be lovers conspire in
writing the rest of the plot behind January's back, using their private
letters to undo his own more public "scrit and bond."

Now on her own initiative, though still in the company of her
attendants, May visits Damyan in order to deliver her letter, which
she does in a sexually suggestive manner:

> And whan she saugh hir tyme, upon a day
> To visite this Damyan gooth May,
> And sotilly this lettre doun she threste
> Under his pilwe; rede it if hym leste.
> She taketh hym by the hand and harde hym twiste
> So secrely that no wight of it wiste,
> And bad hym been al hool, and forth she wente
> To Januarie....
>
> (2001–8)

Rather than slipping her letter into Damyan's hand (as he had done
with her), May puts it under the pillow and secretly squeezes Damyan's hand, a furtive instance of bodily contact that foretells where
the letter will lead. Again, May is quick to put aside the body of the
letter for the body of her lover. Of course, May's "twiste" to Damyan's hand is also a secret sign, the first of many to come. It seems
intended to reassure him even before he reads her letter that she has
given herself to him. May's bidding Damyan to be "al hool" can be
taken as a further coded signal (i.e., that she will heal his "sickness").
Thus May's letter, in contrast with Damyan's, functions less as the
message in itself and more as a supplement to other signs.[84]

Nonetheless, May's letter has remarkable curative and aphrodisiac powers, as reflected by Damyan's immediate and vigorous
readerly response: "*Up riseth* Damyan the nexte morwe; / Al passed
was his siknesse and his sorwe" (2009–10; emphasis added). The
hint of phallic arousal replies to the content of May's letter, in which

---

84. The clause "rede it if hym leste" suggests that May's consent is evident
without Damyan's reading her letter.

"she graunteth hym hire verray grace," possibly a bawdy pun.[85] Damyan's sudden rising also befits his role as the phallic "naddre" equipped with "penner" and "purs," while pointing ahead to his rendezvous with May in the garden, where he experiences another resurrection of the flesh.[86] Damyan's response, both affective and bodily, also suggests how writing reflects desire back and forth between the two lovers. May and Damyan continue "writyng to and fro" (2104), a closed circuit in which each letter mirrors the previous one, creating a potentially infinite reflection of mimetic desire. For Augustine, the restless cycle of language and desire can only end in God. For the two lovers, it will end, at least temporarily, in the earthly consummation devoutly wished for by each.

3. A Literal Fornication

Not long after May and Damyan begin their private correspondence, January decides to build a private pleasure garden. In this garden January realizes most fully his marital "fantasye," and there also his marriage is most completely violated by his rival and his wife. January's garden is not just a moralized landscape but a typological ground for the reenacted Fall in which all three members of the marriage triangle are implicated. The transgression in January's garden, specifically in his pear tree, not only violates marriage vows through the theft of sexual fruit but also literalizes as fornication the abuse of signs and writing that has brought these "types" of Adam, Eve, and Serpent to the fruit tree in the first place. Augustine had described abuses of language—especially writing—as "fornication," and as such are they dramatized here.[87] Thus the climax of the tale in January's garden also culminates the abuse of the carnal letter that built the garden in the first place.

In building and using his garden, January does not seem to realize that he is treading on typological ground. As we have already seen, he cites and distorts Scripture to find precedents in the Garden of Eden for his debased notion of "paradys." He also knows that somewhere there grows a Tree of Sin, having "herd seyd, ful yoore ago," that man should not confuse heavenly with earthly bliss, and that he should "kepe hym fro the synnes sevene, / And eek from every

---

85. On *grace/gras* (i.e., "pubic hair"), see Thomas W. Ross, *Chaucer's Bawdy* (New York, 1972), pp. 96–98, s.v. *grace*.

86. Cf. "up he wente" (2211), as quoted below.

87. For Augustine on sign abuse as "fornication," see above, Chapter 2.4.

branche of thilke tree" (1637, 1640–41). But January defies this wisdom, insisting that he can have his "hevene in erthe heere," since marriage promises him "so parfit felicitee," as well as "ese" and "lust" (1647, 1642–43).[88] In equating sexual pleasure with heavenly bliss, January fails to understand metaphor. But there is more here than just a failure of imagination; in his "fantasye," he is convinced that there is nothing higher than his own good, as he sees it. In making sexual "ese" or "lust" an end in itself, January determines simply to enjoy (frui) pleasure for its own sake, a tendency that Augustine equated with the first sin of eating the forbidden fruit (fructus).[89] The Tree of Sin should remind January of certain dangers in his earthly paradise, but the meaning of this sign is completely lost on him.[90] He makes a garden, plants this tree, and even tastes its fruit, all without realizing it.

The Merchant alludes to typology by comparing January's garden to the one in the *Roman de la Rose*, but the narrator's sarcastic point is that January intends to use his garden as scenery for priapic adventures, for phallic writing like that featured in the *Roman* itself:

> He made a gardyn, walled al with stoon;
> So fair a gardyn woot I nowher noon.
> For, out of doute, I verraily suppose
> That he that wroot the Romance of the Rose
> Ne koude of it the beautee wel devyse;
> Ne Priapus ne myghte nat suffise,
> Though he be god of gardyns, for to telle
> The beautee of the gardyn and the welle,
> That stood under a laurer alwey grene.
>
> (2029–37)

In a further nod to classical gardens, the Merchant adds that Pluto and Proserpina would often "Disporten hem" near January's well (2040), a detail that prepares for the later intervention of these deities in the action. Still, the main precedents for January's garden are biblical and patristic ones, including the Garden of Eden, the *hortus conclusus* of the Canticle, and Augustine's gardens in the *Confes-*

---

88. "Lust" denotes pleasure rather than sexual desire per se; and "ese," enjoyment, as distinct from use ("office"); cf. *Wife of Bath's Prologue* III.127.

89. On *frui* and *fructus*, see above, Chapter 2.4.

90. On the Tree of Knowledge as a model for the medieval Tree of Sin, see Katzenellenbogen, *Allegories of the Virtues and Vices in Medieval Art*, pp. 63–68.

sions. As Shoaf aptly says, "Precisely because it is a garden, [it] is full of signification; it bristles with signs."[91]

Entirely oblivious to the signs that bristle there, January unlocks his garden for one thing only:

> whan he wolde paye his wyf hir dette
> In somer seson, thider wolde he go,
> And May his wyf, and no wight but they two;
> And thynges whiche that were nat doon abedde,
> He in the gardyn parfourned hem and spedde.
>
> (2048–52)

Although it follows on the mention of Priapus, this passage seems to be less a classical vision than one from the *Kamasutra*. In any case, the spry old knight scarcely imagines that a "naddre" more acrobatic than he will soon rival him in "thynges whiche that were nat doon abedde."

Not long after completing his garden, January, already blind to much of what is going on around him, is "sodeynly" bereft of his eyesight (2071). Rather than making things easier for the lovers, however, this development further obstructs their plans. In his blindness January is more "jalous" than ever of May (2086), and he "nolde suffre hire for to ryde or go, / But if that he had hond on hire alway" (2090–91). January's heavy hand on May embodies even more graphically her status as his sexual property, besides creating a new obstacle for the lovers. At this inconvenience, May weeps, thinking "hir herte wolde breste" (2096), for now Damyan cannot even approach her: "neither nyght ne day / Ne myghte he speke a word to fresshe May" (2099–2100). Damyan wants to speak to May specifically "As to his purpos," but "Januarie moste it heere, / That hadde an hand upon hire everemo" (2101–3).

But love will find a way, a ruse, a "sleighte" (2126), and the lovers overcome this new obstacle with further writings and a new mode of private communication:

> nathelees, by writyng to and fro
> And privee signes wiste he what she mente,
> And she knew eek the fyn of his entente.
>
> (2104–6)

Clearly these "privee signes" are hand signals; later, in the garden, the lovers use signs made with the "fynger" (2209). Manual signs

---

91. Shoaf, *Dante, Chaucer, and the Currency of the Word*, p. 199.

of a sort have already appeared with May's "twiste" to Damyan's hand while delivering her letter, but now the lovers begin using sign language in a major way to supplement the closed circuit of mediated desire originally established by their "writyng to and fro."

Sign language among lovers is a medieval literary commonplace, and it was a reality among monks, who used hand signals to keep their vow of silence.[92] But rather than signs of spiritual devotion that serve a contemplative silence, the signs used by the lovers serve a fleshly love and carry them further into corporeal language—a language of gesture that, by a kind of synecdoche, anticipates intercourse itself. At the same time, May and Damyan seem to regress to an infantile state (in-fans, "without speech"), recalling Augustine's description of infants wriggling with inarticulate desire.[93] Whereas January serves a carnal end by using his "hond" to enforce silence, the lovers serve their own equally carnal "fyn" by using their hands to make signs and letters, here conjoined as the products of two manual arts. As body language, and as language for the body, both arts point toward the pear tree.

In all this privy communication, the lovers share a private intention, understanding, or desire—an "entente."[94] January's own intent or purpose, as well as his limited understanding of things, is announced early in the tale, when he sends for his friends to announce his intention to marry—"th'effect of his entente" (1398). January's marital "entente" is of course to create a sexual paradise for himself, and his earlier rhetorical question reflects his certainty that his marriage will bear out this intention: "Who is so trewe, and eek so *ententyf* / To kepe hym, syk and hool, as is his make?" (1288–89; emphasis added). January's wife will offer an unexpected answer to this question; and his own squire, as the Merchant apostrophizes, "Entendeth for to do thee vileynye" (1791). But January simply assumes that his "entente" rules his household (1467) and that nothing there means anything more than he understands by it. Soon after

92. E.g., Andreas Capellanus, *De amore* 2.1; Ovid, *Metamorphoses* 4.63 (Pyramus and Thisbe; ed. and trans. Frank J. Miller, 2 vols., 3d ed., rev. G. P. Goold, LCL [London, 1977]). On monks, see Jean Umiker Sebeok and Thomas A. Sebeok, eds., *Monastic Sign Languages* (Berlin, 1987).

93. *Conf* 1.6. Cf. Brown, *Augustine of Hippo*: "Adam and Eve found that they could only communicate with one another by the clumsy artifice of language and gestures" (p. 261). Augustine discusses manual signs in *Mag* 10.34–35, as cited below.

94. See *MED*, s.v. *entente* 3a ("will, wish, desire"), 5b ("meaning, significance, import"); the term is applied to letters in *Clerk's Tale* IV.762, and *Troilus and Criseyde* 5.1630 ("Th'entente is al, and nat the lettres space").

January's marriage to May, Damyan fails to wait on him in the hall, and January asks, "how may this be, / That Damyan entendeth nat to me?" (1899–1900). When his other squires answer that Damyan has been taken abed with "siknesse" (1903), January takes appearance as the reality, never suspecting that his squire is attending to, and intending, something else.

In their private signs and writings, as also in their earlier coded speech, May and Damyan subvert the social function of language as a bond that forms humans into a community, and which presumes a certain shared "entente," a common understanding, intention, or purpose. Their pursuit of private pleasure involves a private "entente"—what Augustine calls an illicit mental intention (*intentio mentis*) in the tropology of the Fall cited above.[95] Elsewhere Augustine describes how speech, like language and signs in general, enables humans to be bound together (*sociari*) into a community, which would be impossible without words or names for things, corporeal media of exchange that allow humans to share their thoughts, to use language "almost as an interpreter to link them together [*sibi copulandos*]."[96] But by the same token, as Eugene Vance remarks, the language that underwrites or embodies the social order is also "a primal instrument of subversion for those who *will* it to be so."[97]

In the *Merchant's Tale*, January to some extent "privatizes" language for his own selfish motives (as in his carnal scriptural glosses), just as he keeps his garden as private property for his use alone. But it is May and Damyan especially who privatize language to serve their private intent, and who thereby subvert the social order. Their verbal and social subversions are in fact mirror images of each other. Besides separating them from the community in which they live, which is January's household, their private language also points ahead to their ultimate subversion of the social and the verbal order through their private intercourse or juncture (*copula*) in the pear tree.

As private signs and writings bring the lovers steadily closer to fulfilling their secret "entente," they together arrange to counterfeit the key to the gate of January's garden:

95. *Trin* 12.12.17. Augustine, *Mag* 10.34, also uses *intentio* in the sense of "pointing" (with the hand or finger), as discussed below.

96. *Ord* 2.12.35.

97. Vance, *Mervelous Signals*, p. 191 (original emphasis), citing the same passage from Augustine, *De ordine*.

> This fresshe May, that I spak of so yoore,
> In warm wex hath emprented the clyket
> That Januarie bar of the smale wyket,
> By which into his gardyn ofte he wente;
> And Damyan, that knew al hire entente,
> The cliket countrefeted pryvely.
> Ther nys namoore to seye....
>
> (2116–22)

Here the effects of Damyan's "writing" on May's heart are figured as an external, plastic impression. The "warm wex" also harks back to January's attempt to mold a "yong thyng" to his carnal designs, here foiled by May's own counterfeit image making, which involves shaping January himself to her own designs. At the same time, the scene alludes to Nature's sexual forge, a variant trope for phallic writing, with May creating the "female" mold and Damyan the "male" casting.[98] "Pryvely," by now an old joke, strikes the Merchant's sarcastic tone; "Ther nys namoore to seye," indeed.

Now that the lovers have the key to their problem, May herself urges January to visit his garden, "eggyng" him on (2135), a standard Middle English epithet for Eve.[99] January, his "wil" aroused, and eager "for to pleye / In his gardyn" with his wife (2134–36), coos to May in the language of the Canticle, "Rys up, my wyf, my love, my lady free! / The turtles voys is herd, my dowve sweete" (2138–39). Yet another one of January's glosses on a scriptural garden, this one betrays his literalism, ignoring the standard medieval interpretation of the Canticle as a hymn of praise to Christ's "wedding" with the church or the soul.[100] Another symptom of January's literalism is that he calls on the resources of metaphor without imagining that his words will come true in any other sense than he "entendeth." Little does he suspect that May will soon "rys up" into one of his trees and perch there like the turtledove, or the "columbyn" to which he also compares her (2141), for amorous "pleye" with someone other than himself. Although the Merchant's censure on January's "olde lewed wordes" (2149) is spiteful and verges on scorn for Scripture itself, January does abuse language in allowing his carnal "wil" to blind him in the imagination.

98. On Nature's forge in *Le Roman de la Rose* and earlier literature, see Shoaf, *Dante, Chaucer, and the Currency of the Word*, pp. 194–96.

99. See *MED*, s.v. *egging* (ger. 1) 1b, with attested application to Eve from as early as ca. 1200 ("eggunge of eue").

100. See above, Chapter 5.2.

With this instance of fallen "reading" as a prelude, January's garden now becomes a scene for fallen writing and the abuse of signs. After January concludes his speech, May signals Damyan, the first of a series of signs pointing the way to the pear tree:

> On Damyan a signe made she,
> That he sholde go biforn with his cliket.
> This Damyan thanne hath opened the wyket,
> And in he stirte, and that in swich manere
> That no wight myghte it se neither yheere,
> And stille he sit under a bussh anon.
>
> (2150–55)

Besides trespassing on January's private property, the "naddre" figuratively penetrates the "garden" of the mind or soul, as well as the "paradys terrestre" embodied in May herself. To "stirte" in and "sit under a bussh" are bawdy jokes, reminding that Damyan intends to steal forbidden sexual fruit; the concealing "bussh" also hints at Adam and Eve hiding their sexual shame among the trees in the first Garden.

Husband and wife pass through the gate close behind the rival, "Januarie, as blynd as is a stoon, / With Mayus in his hand" (2156–57), a variation on the blind leading the blind, and possibly a glance at Augustine's denial that Adam and Eve had blindly groped their way around the Garden, touching the forbidden tree in ignorance before their eyes were opened (Gen. 3.7).[101] Once inside his garden, January wants to conduct some business with May before getting down to "pleye." Making a windy speech, the gist of which is that he loves her and wants her in turn to be "trewe" (2169), he proposes that they draw up some documents to ensure her faithfulness, as if his hand (and hers) to a contract were better than his "hond on hire alway."

January's "chartres" further satirize his idolatry of the letter. According to him, these documents will confer on May all his earthly goods—"al myn heritage, toun and tour" (2172). Being blind, he puts the actual paperwork, so to speak, in her hands: "maketh chartres as yow leste; / This shal be doon to-morwe er sonne reste" (2173–74). The mention of sunset, apart from its notarial import (i.e., "by the end of the next business day"), echoes the Fall, for

---

101. *GenL* 11.31.40. Later May urges the blind January that he take the pear tree "inwith [his] armes" (2342).

Augustine and other exegetes made a great deal of the dying of the light after Adam and Eve had eaten of the forbidden Tree.[102] January's "chartres" also reflect the traditional notion that Adam and Eve had "sold" themselves to the Devil, along with all their progeny, by "signing" a contract of sin. January is willing to sign away not only his material wealth but also his soul in exchange for sexual bliss. In the medieval sexual politics of the Fall, this old Adam's willingness to consign his land to "Eve" represents a further abdication of his reason and responsibilities. In sum, January's attempt to underwrite his fantasies with additional contracts shows him to be truly enslaved to the letter.

This enslavement can also be seen in January's remark that May's "beautee" is "depe enprented in my thoght" (2178–79), another reference to the inner "writing" on the heart or soul. Though blind, January has been deepening the impression of May in his mind, an impression he has been tracing there ever since he finished shopping for a wife. Harking back to his premarital nocturnal fantasies about women, this passage transfers his illicit "pleasure of thought" (*delectatio cogitationis*) from his bed to the equally fertile ground of his garden. As such, it underscores that this ground represents not just the Garden of Eden but also the garden of the soul, an inner landscape where every sinful act recapitulates the Fall in tropological terms.

At January's talk of infidelity, May, her own mind deeply impressed by Damyan, begins to "wepe," answering her husband "benyngnely" that she values both body and soul (2186–87), and that she hopes to die should she ever shame him or "empeyre" her name through infidelity (2198–99). If she does so, he can strip her naked, put her in a sack, and drown her in the nearest river (drowning was a typical capital punishment for women). Within minutes, of course, May will allow Damyan to "strepe" her and "empeyre" her name, a pun on the pear tree ("pyrie") where this event will take place. May even goes on to chide January for suggesting that she might betray him when it is men themselves that "been evere untrewe," while always reproving women for the same (2203–4). With this cheeky reply May covers all the better her imminent infidelity.

At the very next instant May spots Damyan—"And with that word she saugh wher Damyan / Sat in the bussh" (2207–8)—and immediately signals him to climb a tree:

102. Augustine, *GenM* 2.16.24, *GenL* 11.33.43.

> coughen she bigan,
> And with hir fynger signes made she
> That Damyan sholde clymbe upon a tree,
> That charged was with fruyt, and up he wente.
> For verraily he knew al hire entente,
> And every signe that she koude make,
> Wel bet than Januarie, hir owene make,
> For in a lettre she hadde toold hym al
> Of this matere, how he werchen shal.
>
> (2208–16)

While setting the scene for the recapitulated Fall, this passage summarizes the itinerary that has brought the lovers to this point.

First of all, May's significant cough is a case of liminal speech that again marks the sign's bodily nature. For her to speak normally to Damyan would give away the game, but the cough is an ambiguous vocalization whose "entente" is clear to her lover while January does not even recognize it as a sign. May's cough harks back to January's cough in bed, and his reawakened sexual desire, and it may also allude to the famous cough at the first fault written of Guinevere (*al primo fallo scritto*), as cited by Dante from the same romance misread by Paolo and Francesca.[103]

The pear tree itself is of course a sign "charged" with far more than just its actual fruit, since it figures a long series of typological trees going back to the Tree of Knowledge in the first Garden. "Fruyt" likewise points variously to the forbidden fruit of Eden, to forbidden sexual fruit, and also to hermeneutical "fruit"—the sense or meaning of signs, as distinct from "leaves," the mere sound, letter, or material text. Damyan's suggested erection ("up he wente") is corollary with his climbing the tree toward its fruit, the tree itself being the central phallic symbol in the whole episode. Damyan "uses" the tree as a sign but in the wrong way, merely as a way of achieving carnal enjoyment. His action, soon to be repeated by May, who "climbs the tree" in a double sense, stresses that the lovers reduce words and signs to things.

Throughout his hasty erotic preparations, Damyan is guided not only by May's "signes" but also by a recollected "lettre," which harks back to their literary foreplay and puts writing at the center

103. January wakes himself with a "coughe" after May returns from the privy, commanding that she "strepen hire al naked" for his pleasure (1957–58). Dante, *Paradiso* 16.14–15.

of this recapitulated Fall. At the same time, this detail hints satirically at Augustine's conversion, where a letter likewise plays a central role.[104] Rather than an apostolic letter, Damyan relies on a love letter written by a woman. Both letters arouse their readers, but to very different ends: Augustine uses divine Scripture to defeat his carnal impulses, whereas Damyan uses an amorous scripture expressly to stimulate his. Finally, Damyan reverses the thrust of Paul's text, achieving its exact opposite as he strips May for carnal purposes instead of "putting on" Christ.[105]

Before Damyan does so, however, the narrative is interrupted by a classical interlude (2219–2319) in which Pluto and Proserpina enter "the ferther syde" (2226) of the garden, sit down, and open a debate about marriage that eventually leads to their intervention in the action at the pear tree. This marriage debate forms an analogue to the earlier one between Placebo and Justinus; though shorter, it too abounds in scriptural (and other) citations which show, once again, that glossing is a perilous thing. Its upshot is that the two deities take sides according to sex, Pluto vowing that January "shal have ayen his eyen syght" so as to see his wife's infidelity (2260), and Proserpina that May shall have "suffisant answere" to meet her husband's inevitable accusations (2266). By this deus ex machina is the tale's denouement arranged.

Narrative causality aside, scholars have found various links between this interlude and the tale at large. For example, there is a resemblance between January and Pluto as desirous old husbands, and between May and Proserpina as unwilling young wives.[106] Furthermore, the classical myth of Pluto and Proserpina forms an analogue to the biblical myth of Adam and Eve, as authors ranging from Clement of Alexandria to Sigmund Freud have noted, and as Chaucer himself certainly recognized.[107] Though without citing this critical tradition, Karl Wentersdorf has put the case well: "The leg-

---

104. On hermeneutics and rhetoric in Augustine's conversion, see above, Chapters 2.5, and 3.5.

105. *Conf* 8.12, quoting Rom. 13.14. Even Damyan's tree climbing, with his suggested erection, seems to mock Augustine's readerly resurrection in the garden: "[I] rose to my feet [*surrexi*]."

106. See Mortimer J. Donovan, "The Image of Pluto and Proserpine in the *Merchant's Tale*," PQ 36 (1957): 49–60.

107. Clement of Alexandria, *The Exhortation to the Greeks*, chap. 2, pp. 30–31 (see note), citing Demeter and Persephone (Ceres and Proserpina) directly after a gloss on Eve and the Serpent as figures for pagan orgiastic rites. Freud, letter to Carl Jung, 17 December 1911, in *The Freud/Jung Letters: The Correspondence Between Sigmund Freud and C. G. Jung*, ed. William McGuire (Princeton, 1974), no. 288F, p. 473.

end of Pluto constitutes a kind of pagan Fall: just as, according to
the Biblical story, death came into the world because of specific
sinful acts by Adam and Eve, so, in the classical legend, the death
of nature in the winter of each year is the result of an original
wrongdoing—Pluto's ravishment of Ceres' daughter."[108] Wentersdorf further argues that the classical myth near the end of the tale
replies to the Christian myth of Adam and Eve cited near its beginning, compensating for "the common medieval view" that blames
death, evil, and marital discord on woman (i.e., Eve) by shifting the
responsibility to man (i.e., Pluto).[109] In sum, the classical interlude
not only resolves the pear tree story but also extends the theme of
the carnal letter, deepens the mythical backdrop for the sexual politics of marriage, and helps balance out the misogyny of the medieval
myth of the Fall, especially as exploited by the Merchant.

Meanwhile, back at the pear tree, Damyan lurks on high like
the Serpent of old, awaiting his opportunity, while January and May
wander around the garden's apparently labyrinthine ways, "longe
aboute the aleyes" (2324), January singing all the while, "Til he was
come agaynes thilke pyrie / Where as this Damyan sitteth ful myrie
/ An heigh among the fresshe leves grene" (2325–27). At this point,
May feigns another need—this time for some fruit from the tree:

> This fresshe May, that is so bright and sheene,
> Gan for to syke, and seyde, "Allas, my syde!
> Now sire," quod she, "for aught that may bityde,
> I moste han of the peres that I see,
> Or I moot dye, so soore longeth me
> To eten of the smale peres grene.
> Help, for hir love that is of hevene queene!"
>
> (2328–34)

May's appetite recapitulates Eve's, of course, with the sexual
motif in the biblical myth here brought to the fore by May's clearly
erotic craving for "fruit." Although medieval tradition usually associated the forbidden fruit, typically an apple, with Eve's breasts,
here the "smale peres grene" desired by May suggest instead the

108. Karl P. Wentersdorf, "Theme and Structure in the *Merchant's Tale*: The
Function of the Pluto Episode," *PMLA* 80 (1965): 522–27 (p. 527).
109. Wentersdorf, "Theme and Structure," p. 527. See also Marcia A. Dalbey,
"The Devil in the Garden: Pluto and Proserpine in Chaucer's *Merchant's Tale*," *NM*
75 (1974): 408–15.

male sexual organs, a metaphor having precedent in medieval art.[110] In a further parody of the Fall, May's exaggerated appetite ("Or I moot dye") alludes to the deadly results of the first sin while hinting at her own spiritually perilous state. Finally, May's appeal to Mary, "hevene queene," points ironically to the traditional Eve/Mary typology of Fall and Redemption.[111]

At May's yearning for "peres," January, blind literalist that he is, and again swayed like Adam at Eve's urging, concludes that his wife wants some fruit to eat. But alas, he is blind and cannot climb the tree himself, and there is no servant or boy, no "knave," to be sent up it for the pears (2338). (A kind of "knave" of course has already climbed up there.) Yet May has an idea: she will fetch the fruit herself by climbing into the tree from January's back while he encircles the trunk with his arms, since "wel I woot that ye mystruste me" (2343–45).

January readily agrees, and the tale's climax quickly follows, the Merchant apologizing for his plain terms:

> He stoupeth doun, and on his bak she stood,
> And caughte hire by a twiste, and up she gooth—
> Ladyes, I prey yow that ye be nat wrooth;
> I kan nat glose, I am a rude man—
> And sodeynly anon this Damyan
> Gan pullen up the smok, and in he throng.
>
> (2348–53)

This passage is a catalog of typological gestures. For example, January's stooping under May figures Adam's loss of mastery to Eve; Damyan's lifting of May's smock, as discussed later, figures a carnal revelation; and Damyan's penetration of May figures the violation of "paradys" in its various senses (fig. 7).

Although it is not clear whether the lovers experience a sexual climax during their brief union in the tree, this moment is still the climax of their fall as sign abuse and literary "fornication." In the tree the two lovers commit a "transgression of the sign," but rather than tasting of the tree they use the tree to taste of each other. Heedlessly clambering up its trunk to fulfill their sexual desires

110. See Robertson, *Preface to Chaucer*, p. 328n; and also Ross, *Chaucer's Bawdy*, p. 173, s.v. *pyrie*. In sound, the "peres" also resemble Damyan's "purs," earlier used to enclose his letter.

111. On May and Mary, see Douglas Wurtele, "The Blasphemy of Chaucer's Merchant," *AM* 21 (1981): 91–110.

7. The climax of the pear tree story. Woodcut print, ca. 1481: Aesop, *Vita et Fabulae*, printed by Heinrich Knoblochtzer, Strassburg. The Pierpont Morgan Library, New York. PML 50.

among its leaves and branches, the lovers take pleasure literally *in* the sign rather than using it to understand higher things.

Apart from the tree as a sign, there is the sign made in the tree. Until now, in their speech, writings, and gestures, the lovers have been trying to overcome the distance between themselves, extending corporeal language toward its extreme limit in an anticipation of the ultimate bodily sign, sexual intercourse itself. In finally making this sign, for a moment at least, they come face-to-face, with nothing between them, their desires mediated only by their bodies. At the same time, this ultimate bodily sign is an act of "writing" as well. First, as Damyan's sexual inscription upon May's body, it fulfills the phallic intention of his first letter and reiterates his first "impression" upon her "herte." Second, it fulfills the "writyng to and fro" shared by the lovers in their private circuit of literary foreplay, now reifying as intercourse the carnal letter that hitherto has mediated their desire.

As a symbolic and typological site, the pear tree figures the ancient links between writing and trees, especially between writing and the Fall, a crisis viewed by medieval culture as the ultimate

genesis of script or letters.[112] Aptly, the carnal letter finds its cul-
mination among the shady leaves (*folia*) of the tree, traditional emblems for concealment, illicit desire, and spiritual death as embodied
in "fallen writing." Besides the Tree of Knowledge, the pear tree
points to other typological trees that serve as scenes for the letter—
from Augustine's fig tree to the generic one where Adam the clerk
writes about the fall of the first Adam.

Regarding Augustine's tree in particular, the lovers carnally re-
verse the inward and spiritual movement of signs as traced in the
garden at Milan. At the climax of his own story, Augustine retreats
within himself to a silent inner word, away from the progressively
more corporeal signs that are speech, writing, and gesture. By the
time they climb the tree, May and Damyan have already reduced
most forms of the sign to carnality, and with their sexual act they
arrive at the limit of the sign itself. Or rather, they arrive at the
limit of *their* signs, for here the desired signifier and the signified
desire become one, at least for a moment, as the lovers do themselves.

For Augustine, of course, what the lovers do in the tree is a
multiple abuse of signs and writing, a "fornication" in more than
one sense of the term. As earlier suggested, the lovers' private exchanges violate both the social and the verbal order, and these violations culminate in the tree. The lovers subvert not only the
spiritual function of language, which is to join the soul with God,
but also its social function, which is to join (*copulare*) people to one
another in communal bonds. Though the lovers join themselves to
each other, theirs is a brief, private, and illicit union—intercourse
in the most limited sense. As Shoaf puts it, their union is "a false
copula" that "looks like communication, but there is in fact little
community in it—at most, it is 'irreferent' exchange of sexual pleasure."[113] Whereas the signs leading to the tree point to intercourse,
the sign of intercourse itself—as performed by Damyan and May—
points to nothing. And even their prior signs are autotelic in the
sense described by Augustine when he says, of pointing with the
finger (*intentio digiti*), that "as a gesture it is a sign of something
being pointed out rather than of the object pointed out."[114] In other

112. On trees, writing, and the Fall, see above, Chapter 2.2.

113. Shoaf, *Dante, Chaucer, and the Currency of the Word*, p. 198.

114. *Mag* 10.34. See Markus, "St. Augustine on Signs," in *Augustine: A Collection of Critical Essays*, pp. 61–91, esp. 70–72. On gestures as signs, see also *Doc* Prol.
3, and 2.3.4.

words, it is a sign that points to itself as a sign. In the tree the lovers act out their entrapment in their own private circuit of signs, which refers to nothing outside of itself. All their pointing finally achieves its point, only to be revealed in the end as virtually pointless.

In sum, the lovers' chief violation is not trespassing, or lying, or even adultery, per se, but rather a flagrant abuse of the sign in all its forms. Like the pear tree in Augustine's *first* garden, what January's pear tree represents is mainly the erasure or disappearance of the sign. Chaucer's story of stolen sexual fruit surely amused nearly everyone in his audience; the more astute or spiritually minded, however, would have recognized in the tale's comic climax a complete collapse of the sign. That is, an eclipse of the necessary difference between sign and referent that is supposed to keep humans not only bound together in a community of mutual understanding but also on the road to the true, heavenly Paradise.

4. The Smock of Language

As soon as the lovers are sexually united in the pear tree, and as though they have thereby broken a spell, Pluto restores January's eyesight, and Proserpina equips May with ready words. The husband's restored sight is a stock feature of the pear tree story, but of course it also parallels the aftermath of the biblical Fall ("the eyes of both were opened" [Gen. 3.7]) as well as Dante's experience right before speaking with Adam in the terrestrial paradise, when the scales fall from his eyes to reveal a radiant Beatrice, of whom he inquires in amazement (*quasi stupefatto*) about spiritual things.[115]

In January's terrestrial paradise, too, a woman is revealed, prompting a question from the amazed observer, though about carnal rather than spiritual things, and in circumstances not sublime but ridiculous. His "thoght" (like till now his "hond") "everemo" on May (2359), January looks up into the tree, and what he sees there makes it hard for him to speak at all:

> up he yaf a roryng and a cry,
> As dooth the mooder when the child shal dye:

---

115. *Paradiso* 26.80, with imagery of reawakening and clothing: "sleep . . . broken by a piercing light" that goes "from tunic to tunic" (vv. 70, 72).

> "Out! Help! Allas! Harrow!" he gan to crye,
> "O stronge lady stoore, what dostow?"
>
> (2364–67)

His sight restored, but at a sudden loss for words, January can only "ror" like a beast for a moment; monosyllables follow, then polysyllables, and finally a short sentence in the form of a question.

"Out!" may be not only an exclamation of woe or shame but also an imperative pointing to coitus interruptus.[116] In any case, with great aplomb for a wife caught in flagrante under especially awkward circumstances, May replies to her apoplectic husband:

> Sire, what eyleth yow?
> Have pacience and resoun in youre mynde!
> I have yow holpe on bothe youre eyen blynde.
>
> (2368–70)

Swearing that she tells the truth, May explains that she learned ("As me was taught") that the only remedy for January's blindness was for her to "strugle" with a man in a tree, which she claims to have done just now "in ful good entente" (2371–75). January is beside himself:

> "Strugle?" quod he, "Ye, algate in it wente!
> God yeve yow bothe on shames deth to dyen!
> He swyved thee; I saugh it with myne yen,
> And elles be I hanged by the hals!"
>
> (2376–79)

Since January balks at semantics, May turns to optics, rejoining that he cannot yet see properly: "Ye han som glymsyng, and no parfit sighte" (2383). Now beginning to doubt his eyes, January begs her to come down, offering a halfhearted apology for having questioned her word: "Com doun, my lief, and if I have myssayd, / God helpe me so, as I am yvele apayd" (2391–92). He is still uncertain, however, about what he has actually seen: "But, by my fader soule, I *wende* han seyn / How that this Damyan hadde by thee leyn, / And that thy smok hadde leyn upon his brest" (2393–95; emphasis added). January's hesitation figures the conflict between his senses and his "fantasye," the mental faculty that he allows to function as

---

116. On the emotive sense, see *MED*, s.v. *out(e* (interj.).

his reason, and which May here skillfully manipulates through speech.

Evidently sensing January's lingering doubts, May decides to clinch her argument before climbing down. She has already told January that he has only partial vision, "glymsyng," and now, as if it were an everyday occurrence, she explains that a man just restored from blindness to sight is unable to see clearly, like one that "waketh out of his sleep" (2397); in a day or two, January will see just fine, but until then, "Ther may ful many a sighte yow bigile" (2406). Of course, it is not "sighte" at all that is beguiling him, but his wife's words and his own imagination.

January's eyes are just no match for May's mouth, nor his mind for hers. As soon as he has regained his sight, she pulls the smock of language over his eyes, plunging him back into darkness.[117] In typological terms, Eve thus prevails over Adam, outwitting and out-talking him, even ironically urging him to regain his "resoun." As retailed by the Merchant, May's actions confirm "the common medieval view" that Eve is consonant with evil—especially with an evil tongue. But even if January's "paradys" contains a devious wife and a clever rival, he is finally his own worst enemy. In the end, nearly tongue-tied in his gullible bemusement, he allows himself to be subdued in the knots of language, to be figuratively "hanged by the hals."

Having had the last word, May finally comes down: "with that word she leep doun fro the tree" (2411). May's "leep" suggests Eve's "leaping," a standard term for the first woman's fall.[118] May's leaping after her "word" also suggests fallen language, and she herself is a fallen woman, an embodiment of January's lost paradise. But with her "word" she has allayed her husband's last suspicions, and he is "glad" (2412) to have her back in his arms. He hugs and kisses her; and, in the tale's well-known concluding image of apparently restored marital harmony, "on hire wombe he stroketh hire ful softe" (2414). No more is said of Damyan, and the tale concludes with a prayer for Mary's blessing.

The pure Mary, as "mooder" of God (2418), contrasts sharply with the carnal May, of course. May earlier alludes to herself as a mother when asking for pears, typically craved by "a womman in my plit" (2335). It even has been suggested that May's brief inter-

---

117. David, *The Strumpet Muse*, p. 178, writes that "January is only too willing to let the truth be decently hidden once more under the smock of language."

118. Cf. *Ancrene Wisse*, as cited above, Chapter 5.2; and Kaske, "Eve's 'Leaps' in the *Ancrene Riwle*."

course with Damyan leaves her pregnant. Obstetric judgments are impossible here, but in symbolic terms May's intercourse with Damyan the "naddre" parallels a common typology of language and the Fall. According to this typology, Eve's "conception" of the Devil's word through the Serpent was reversed, as was Eve's name itself ("Eva"/"Ave"), by the Virgin's conception of the divine Word through the impregnating Holy Spirit.[119] But January's household, garden, and unacknowledged ménage à trois—a parody of the Holy Family—offers little hope for any redemption of language, being instead a fertile ground for further reproducing the language of the Fall.

At the end of the tale, all three members of the romantic triangle are still enveloped by the tree and its shade, which are traditional emblems for not only fallen writing but also fallen speech, particularly illicit persuasion and excuses as used in the original Garden.[120] In January's garden, the lovers especially are associated with foliage and shade, as when Damyan sits "among the fresshe leves grene," and "fresshe May" stands right below and is about to join him there (2327–28). Later, with Damyan at her side, May remains in the tree to offer her excuses, verbal "fig leaves" to cover the shame of nakedness and sin, "shady words" fabricated to hide her "shady pleasures."

Fittingly, the recapitulated Fall ends with a dispute about language. From the tree May defends herself in part by appealing to her "ful good entente," by putting a friendly interpretation on the deed itself so as to cover up her private "entente" with Damyan, which suddenly has gone public, in a limited sense. But the dispute between husband and wife is mainly about language itself—specifically, about which word best describes what has happened in the pear tree: *strugle* or *swyve*. May's term is obviously a euphemism, but it does not make January's cruder term any "truer," for the latter is equally loaded.

In linguistic terms, their dispute concerns language in its "paradigmatic" aspect. On a lexical level, this is essentially a matter of choosing a single term from a set of "synonyms" to fill one grammatical slot, with the chosen term excluding or displacing all others. Both parties to this dispute agree that *something* happened in the tree between a man and a woman, but they disagree about the linking verb, the copula. May chooses *struglen*, and January *swiven*, each

---

119. For examples, see Phillips, *Eve*, pp. 133–34.
120. On leaves, shade, and rhetorical artifice, see above, Chapter 3.4.

choice excluding the other. (The Merchant adds a third option, *thrin-gen*, discussed later in this section.) The two alternatives may pose a false dilemma, but, as a paired opposition, like old January and young May themselves, they represent the principle of difference on which language, sexuality, marriage, and society are founded, and whose founding was located by medieval culture in the Garden of Eden. When January and May argue about what happened in the pear tree, this exchange suggests Adam and Eve arguing about the Fall itself. Each has a different version of the story, and we have not yet heard the end of either.

As already suggested, fallen language is also figured by May's smock, a light piece of cloth with a weighty significance at the end of the tale. May's smock possibly is meant to evoke "Eve's smock," apparently a medieval commonplace for feminine deceit or sensuality. (The sole attestation in the *Middle English Dictionary*, from circa 1330, refers to the deceitful wife of a "Marchaunt.")[121] As worn by May and momentarily lifted from her, "Eve's smock" suggests not only deceit and sensuality but also revelation—sexual, moral, hermeneutical, and so forth. Damyan's climactic lifting of this garment or veil, with its carnal revelation of May's body, is instant with the revelation that January himself receives through his restored sight, and which provides him too with a view of May's body, his first in a long time.

The tale has long foreshadowed this ultimate revelation. The nuptials show May in bed with January, but the Merchant draws the curtain on all but their initial intimacies. In a later bedroom scene, January tells May to "strepen hire al naked" for his pleasure, since "hir clothes dide hym encombraunce," and May "obeyeth," but the Merchant "dar nat" say more lest he offend some listeners (1958–63). And just now in the garden May herself has urged January to "strepe" her if he finds her untrue (2200). Finally, in the pear tree, Damyan "Gan pullen up the smok," as reiterated a moment later by January in berating May—"thy smok hadde leyn upon his brest."[122]

These passages play peekaboo with May's naked body, reflecting the hermeneutic of masculine eros that patristic and medieval cul-

---

121. *MED*, s.v. *smok* 1d, citing *The Seven Sages of Rome (Southern Version)*, ed. Karl Brunner, EETS OS 191 (London, 1933), p. 100, lines 2195, 2198 ("[she] hadde a parti of Eue smok"). "Mary's smock" was also proverbial; see *MED*, s.v. *smok* 1b.

122. May loves Damyan though "he namoore hadde than his sherte" (1985), a detail that foreshadows his nakedness, too, though this nakedness is a comparatively minor motif in the tale.

ture founded on the Fall as the origin of the difference between nakedness and clothing and between the naked truth and the smock of language. According to this hermeneutic, the way to take pleasure in the text, and to test its truth, is to take off its "clothing." With biblical and classical texts alike, the veil of allegory was to be removed, a pleasurable act in itself that revealed the greater delights of wisdom or truth beneath. Thus Augustine learns from Ambrose to "draw aside the veil of mystery" from Scripture, as consummated later in the garden at Milan; this scriptural "veil" is of a piece with the garments of Paradise, the skin clothing provided for Adam and Eve after their sin.[123] In a related image, the divine Word appears in Scripture only as through a glass darkly; the "mirror" of language keeps the soul from coming face-to-face with God while yet on earth.[124]

In January's garden of perversion, unlike Augustine's garden of conversion, the carnal readers and writers mistake the metaphorical text for the reality, the image in the mirror for the reflected object. Rather than lifting the veil of the letter, Damyan lifts May's smock, exactly reversing Paul's injunction, "Make not provision for the flesh in concupiscence."[125] With her smock thus raised, May embodies what January and Damyan regard as the ultimate "naked text"—the unclothed female body. This is the naked truth which they most seek to know intimately. But January's "glymsyng" shows him only his reflected fantasies (both what he fears and what he wants to believe), whereas Damyan "transcends" language, including May's "lettre," only in a carnal sense as he comes face-to-face for a moment with his desired object. Augustine said that he desired to behold divine Wisdom in "an utterly untroubled gaze, a most clean embrace; to cling to Her naked, with no veil of bodily sensation between."[126] Augustine's ideal woman may be *Sapientia*, but Damyan and January want to cling to a woman of flesh and blood. Nor, having lifted May's smock, would either like to lift as well the "veil" of the senses, since this is principally where they take their pleasure.

123. *Conf* 6.4, 8.12, 13.15. See also Hugh of St. Victor, *De sacramentis* 2.9.7, on the temple curtain as a sign for the "veil" of the letter.

124. Augustine, *Conf* 13.15, cites both the veil ("skins") and the mirror ("glass"). Cf. the "mirour" of January's mind (1582), the scene of his carnal fantasies as he shops for a wife.

125. As he lifts the veil of the letter in the garden, Augustine is also restored to the "garment of grace," as suggested in Paul's injunction to "put on" (*induere*) Christ.

126. *Sol* 1.13.22; as cited in Brown, *The Body and Society*, p. 394.

Augustine's woman is just a lifeless trope to them, and their woman is just a living metaphor to Augustine.

All along, the Merchant himself has been implicated in the various problems of language and the Fall raised by his tale, as he signals most clearly in his warning to the "Ladyes" right before its climax. At that point, in declaring that "I kan nat glose" what is about to happen in the pear tree, the Merchant seems about to pull up the smock of language in order to offer a glimpse of the naked act. But in a narrative, any narrative, whether fictional or not, there is no such thing as a naked act; language always mediates the "reality." Furthermore, the particular version of "reality" offered by the Merchant exposes the fact that he, as much as any of his characters, is subject to the limits and ambiguities of fallen language and of his own nature as a fallen human.

   First of all, the Merchant's narrative "I" offers a strictly male perspective on what happens in the pear tree: "And sodeynly anon this Damyan / Gan pullen up the smok, and in he throng." Here Damyan is active, May passive; man is the subject, woman the object. This perspective is hardly surprising and certainly not incriminating; the Merchant's choice of verb is another matter, however. *Thringen* ("to thrust, press") stresses not only the penetrative nature of Damyan's act but also its haste and violence. The verb is rare in Chaucer, and it tends to occur in connection with weapons or wounds.[127] By comparison, May's term, *struggle with*, while suggesting conflict, also conveys the shared or mutual quality of the act. Even January's crude *swiven*, a term confined to Chaucer's fabliaux (all told by men), suggests more in the way of motion than violence, being akin to *swivel*.[128] (January, too, adopts the male viewpoint on the sex act, though here it is hard to separate his voice from the Merchant's.) Moral connotations aside, then, the Merchant's word is the most violent and physically graphic of all three terms and certainly the least suggestive of mutual activity, of consensual sex, which the act in question clearly is, judging by the lovers' literary foreplay. Indeed, the Merchant's phrasing is not so much "rude" as downright brutal, suggesting rape rather than an

127. E.g., *Romaunt of the Rose* 7417 ("in his sleve he gan to thringe / A rasour sharp"); *Anelida and Arcite* 55 ("[Mars] throng now her, now ther"). Ross, *Chaucer's Bawdy*, p. 221, cites the term's "connotation of violence and rudeness."

128. For usage, see *MED*, s.v. *swiven*, quotations. For etymology, see *OED*, s.v. *Swive*; and cf. *MED*, s.v. *swivel*.

amorous embrace. The Merchant's misogyny, as well as his violence
with texts, is nowhere clearer than here, where he specifically addresses the "Ladyes."

Shoaf compares the Merchant to Augustine as one who "writes"
a confessional autobiography.[129] Extending this point, we might say
that although the Merchant only *speaks* he is a fictional "author,"
and that as such he is "corrected" by his own characters, who despite
their own carnality sometimes offer better readings than his own of
his fictional world. The Merchant claims that he "kan nat glose,"
but of course he is glossing all the time. His avowedly "naked text"
is not only a fictional fabrication but also, as a gloss on the Fall, a
piece of rhetorical "clothing" after the fashion of the original garments of Paradise—coverings or excuses for his own faults.[130]
Dressed in "mottelee" (I.271), the Merchant early on shows his rhetorical colors and provides an early hint of the smock of language
that he tries to pull over his audience, and himself, in the course of
his confessional tale.[131]

5. Retracting the Letter

The *Merchant's Tale* shows writing at its most ambiguous, a mediation of presence that is ultimately founded on absence, a revelation that always conceals something, a product of "male"
inscription and yet an enveloping "female" body, a frangible material form that can last indefinitely. The tale especially highlights
the varied life expectancy of the dead letter. May destroys the first
of the letters she receives, and such would seem to be the fate of
the rest—ephemeral records of desire that must not fall into other
hands. Yet January's "scrit" and prospective "chartres," equally
records of desire, are meant to last permanently as legal documents
underwriting spoken agreements that would be imperiled without
them. As a trace that either persists indefinitely or suddenly dis-
appears, the letter marks the uncertainties of fallen writing as a
whole.

During the later Middle Ages, as literacy and the ability to write

129. Shoaf, *Dante, Chaucer, and the Currency of the Word*, p. 206.
130. Chaucer refers to the "naked text" in *Legend of Good Women*, Prologue
G.86; and *Romaunt of the Rose* 6556 ("nakid text"). For discussion, see Gellrich,
The Idea of the Book, pp. 214–20, 224–47; and Dinshaw, *Chaucer's Sexual Poetics*,
chap. 2.
131. MED, s.v. *motleid*, attests a later rhetorical application of the term.

were on the rise, written texts increasingly brought people face-to-face with these uncertainties, which in turn altered their own attitudes toward writing. For its part, monastic culture continued to value script as a priceless link with the past, as a vehicle for inherited knowledge that was to be transmitted with the utmost care, as may be seen from the copying rules that governed the scriptorium and from the curses against tampering that scribes added to their completed books.[132] Generally speaking, monks neither prized originality nor feared plagiarism; rather, they valued accuracy and feared its loss through error or malignity.

In vernacular letters, however, especially among lay authors, a somewhat different ethos came to prevail. Authors more freely altered or adapted their sources, as Chaucer himself did with the story of the Fall, the ancient pear tree story, and many other literary sources in the *Merchant's Tale*. Moreover, secular scribes evidently felt much freer to tamper with the texts entrusted to them for copying, as Chaucer's complaint to "Adam" his scribe suggests and as abundant documentary evidence attests. It is generally accepted that Dante even invented *terza rima* in part to prevent tampering with his text, so that his *Commedia*, though extant in hundreds of manuscripts, has one of most accurate textual traditions in all of medieval vernacular literature.[133]

As indicated earlier, the scribes responsible for Chaucer's works did not always respect the letter of the text. Textual scholarship is an inexact science and can never tell us with absolute certainty what belongs to the author and what to the scribe. Nonetheless, the scribe who wrote that May put Damyan's first letter in her "body," rather than in her "bosom," probably was departing from Chaucer's intention, though whether through error or conscious choice it is hard to say; it may just be a Freudian slip. In other cases, however, it is fairly clear that scribes purposely changed what Chaucer wrote, and sometimes even their motives can be guessed. A case in point is the remarkable textual history of *swiven* in Chaucer's works, which provoked many evasive euphemisms from squeamish scribes who evidently felt that it was part of their job to clean up Chaucer's text.[134] In the Merchant's *narrative*, January of course substitutes this term for May's. But in the written *text* of Chaucer's tale, the

132. The rules of the scriptorium go back to Cassiodorus, *Institutiones* 1.15. On book curses, see Marc Drogin, *Anathema! Medieval Scribes and the History of Book Curses* (Totowa, N.J., 1983).

133. See J. S. P. Tatlock, "Dante's *Terza Rima*," *PMLA* 51 (1936): 895–903.

134. For a compendium, see quotations in *MED*, s.v. *swiven*.

same term is also contested, one scribe substituting the euphemistic *dide*, so that January's protest becomes, "He dide thee so, I saugh it with myne yen."[135] (Another variant in this line, *dyght*, has writerly connotations.)[136] In a late Middle English poem satirizing Carmelite friars, one squeamish scribe used a simple code to retract the offending word: citing "fratres" who "swiven" men's wives, he transliterates *suuiuyt* ("swived") into *txxkxzv*.[137] Not that this veil over the carnal letter would have hidden the truth from the reader for long.

Several times in the *Canterbury Tales*, especially near its beginning and end, Chaucer directly addresses the fact that the letter of his text might cause offense. First, in the *General Prologue*, in the person of Geoffrey the pilgrim, he begs the audience to excuse him for "pleynly" or "proprely" reporting the words spoken by the other pilgrims:

> I pray yow, of youre curteisye,
> That ye n'arette it nat my vileynye,
> Thogh that I pleynly speke in this mateere,
> To telle yow hir wordes and hir cheere,
> Ne thogh I speke hir wordes proprely.
>
> (I.725–29)

Geoffrey himself has no evil intent and simply "speke[s]" again what others have spoken. A few lines later, he appeals to written precedents: "Crist spak hymself ful brode in hooly writ, / And wel ye woot no vileynye is it. / Eek Plato seith, whoso that kan hym rede" (I.739–41). Here *spak* and *seith* contrast with *writ*, whereas *rede* hovers between orality and literacy, as does Chaucer's text itself.[138] The bold way in which Chaucer's text here jostles into company with Plato's, and with Scripture itself, can be taken variously. Is it a jocular claim to similar authority as a written "record," or a subtle acknowledgment that its speeches, like those of Socrates and Jesus,

135. Manly and Rickert, eds., *Text of the Canterbury Tales*, 6:496 (l. 2378).

136. See *MED*, s.v. *dighten* 3a(b) ("to write"), 7b ("to have sexual intercourse"); the verb derives from Latin *dictare* ("to say, write").

137. "Carmina jocosa," ed. Thomas Wright and James O. Halliwell, in *Reliquiae Antiquae: Scraps from Ancient Manuscripts, Illustrating Chiefly Early English Literature and the English Language*, 2 vols. (1841–43; rpt. New York, 1966), 1:91 (l. 10); cited in *MED*, s.v. *swiven* 1b (quot. *Flen flyys*, reading "txxkxzv nfookt xxzxkt" as "suuiuyt mennis uuyuis").

138. The verb "read" still had heavily oral connotations during the Renaissance; see Ferry, *The Art of Naming*, chap. 1.

represent persons who left behind no writings of their own? In any case, Chaucer's ostensible point is that his "brode" language is in good company.

Chaucer returns to the problem of the offending letter in the head-link to the *Miller's Tale*, where a good deal of bawdy matter lies just ahead, including lots of "swivyng." But now, in his authorial persona, Chaucer invokes the text at hand in decisively literary terms, indeed as a book:

> every gentil wight I preye,
> For Goddes love, demeth nat that I seye
> Of yvel entente, but for I moot reherce
> Hir tales alle, be they bettre or werse,
> Or elles falsen som of my mateere.
> And therfore, whoso list it nat yheere,
> *Turne over the leef* and chese another tale.
> (I.3171–77; emphasis added)

Although the term *yheere* may allude to the practice of reading aloud, either alone or socially, the mention of turning the "leef," and the underlying assumption that one has any choice in the "mateere," suggests that Chaucer is here speaking—or, rather, writing—mainly as a literary author to a reading audience. Going on to assure his readers that there is God's plenty here, Chaucer adds a warning: "Blameth nat me if that ye chese amys" (I.3181). As a maker of tales, as the creator of a fictional world, Chaucer here seems to be absolving himself from any responsibility for readerly sins. The responsibility to "chese" wisely lies with the readers, and if they choose "amys," it is their fault alone. Paolo and Francesca, as it were, stand forewarned.

In the *Retraction* that ends the *Canterbury Tales*, Chaucer raises again, for the last time in his book and his oeuvre, the problem of the offending letter. But here, rather than trying to absolve himself, he takes full responsibility, even confessing various literary sins. Apparently speaking as author, and addressing both listeners *and* readers ("alle that herkne this litel tretys or rede"), Chaucer asks his audience to excuse him if anything in his work "displese[s]" them (X.1080–81). Then he asks God's forgiveness for "my giltes; and namely of my translacions and enditynges of worldly vanitees, the whiche I revoke in my retracciouns" (X.1083–84). Among these writings, Chaucer specifies "the tales of Caunterbury, thilke that sownen into synne"

(X.1085). With this remark, followed by a thankful *Te deum* for his religious writings, and the usual Latin formula for ending prayers, Chaucer closes his book.

Widely divergent interpretations have been evoked by Chaucer's *Retraction*, which follows the Parson's long penitential sermon and is clearly voiced, or written, as a confession.[139] Does this confession stand within the dramatic framework of the *Tales*, with the pilgrim answering the Parson's call for repentence? Or does it break the dramatic frame, dropping the pilgrim's mask to show the author's, whose literary confession and retraction hark back to Augustine's? Or, in a variation of this view, does it constitute mainly a final list of Chaucer's works, an attempt to establish his canon? Or does the confession further abandon fiction for documentation, offering us a transcript of Chaucer's supposed deathbed repentance?

These views are not mutually exclusive, and all of them may be true in part; if Chaucer's writings have multiple meanings throughout, there seems little reason to reduce his "final" words to a single sense. Yet with reference to the offending letter, the retraction carefully spells out a specific "entente." Quoting Romans (15.4), Chaucer writes, " 'Al that is writen is writen for oure doctrine,' and that is myn entente" (X.1082). This line clearly suggests that his literary works are meant to edify the reader, to inspire "moralitee, and devocioun" (X.1088), an aim consistent with the ostensible purpose of the Canterbury pilgimage itself.

In retracting or revoking the tales that "sownen into synne," Chaucer seems to mean primarily those tales that are "about" sin.[140] But *sounen* can also mean "to be in accord with" and, even more evocatively, "to cause, produce, lead to, incite, encourage," senses that accord with Chaucer's evident concern about his audience throughout the *Tales* and just now again at the head of his retraction.[141] Thus Chaucer may be asking forgiveness not only for his literary "giltes" as finished works but also for any sinful readerly responses that his writings might provoke, especially among the carnally minded.

Sounen has various hermeneutical senses ("to mean, intend," etc.) as well as numerous rhetorical ones; derived from Old French

139. For a survey of critical views, see Douglas Wurtele, "The Penitence of Geoffrey Chaucer," *Viator* 11 (1980): 335–59.

140. This passage is cited as an example by the *MED*, s.v. *sounen* 7a ("to concern").

141. *MED*, s.v. *sounen* 7, subsenses (b) and (d), respectively.

soner (and ultimately Latin *sonare*, "to sound"), it can mean to speak, declare, pronounce, and even to read aloud.[142] Thus the Merchant is "Sownynge alwey th'encrees of his wynnyng" (I.275), though his tale sounds more like a record of his personal losses. In one instance, a Wycliffite tract written around 1400, *sounen* is used of the Devil speaking through the Serpent.[143] On a rhetorical level, Chaucer's concern about writings that "sounen" into sin may allude to his own art of literary impersonation (*per-sonare*, "to sound through"); after all, the *Canterbury Tales* resound throughout with persuasive voices urging numerous moral and imaginative possibilities. In reading his works aloud at court, in publicly "sounding" such voices, Chaucer would have been made especially aware of the ethical and social implications of his literary art.

A manuscript of Chaucer's *Troilus*, one of the works he retracts, contains a painted miniature generally thought to show the poet reciting his poem at court.[144] In the audience, one elegant couple is dallying in the foreground, and farther back another couple eyes each other—painterly hints that books can prompt mimetic desire. Much as the carnal letter in the *Merchant's Tale* parallels the seductive romance text in Dante's story of Paolo and Francesca, Chaucer's retraction at the end of his book resembles Dante's dying fall at the end of the canto, suggesting the author's awareness of his complicity in readerly sins, as if to say, "*Goffredo fu 'l libro e chi lo scrisse.*" In sum, Chaucer's concluding retraction of the letter seems to reflect an awareness that, however high-minded his "entente," his own writings can sound the tempter's voice.

6. Conclusion

The *Merchant's Tale* uses the carnal letter as an emblem for the literary text of which it forms a part, implicating the *Canterbury Tales*, Chaucer's writings as a whole, even all of literature, in the problems of language and the Fall. What Giuseppe Mazzotta says of *The Divine Comedy*, with its palinode in the Paolo and Francesca episode, is equally true of Chaucer's human comedy: "[It] does not simply claim the privileged position of demystifying 'romantic' lies;

142. See *MED*, s.v. *sounen* 3a–c, 4a–b, 5–6.
143. See *MED*, s.v. *sounen* 3a (quot. *Wycl.Elucid.*).
144. Cambridge, Corpus Christi College, MS. 61. A color reproduction appears in David, *The Strumpet Muse*, frontispiece.

it acknowledges itself as part of the unavoidable ambiguities of the language of desire."[145] One might add that Chaucer's text, like Dante's, acknowledges itself as part of the syndrome of fallen language in general.

Although Chaucer follows Dante's lead in certain respects, there are also some important differences. For one thing, Dante's palinode concerns an accidental arousal in which author and reader(s) are only unwitting collaborators, and where the text in question drifts out of context or away from its original intent. The *Merchant's Tale*, on the other hand, depicts an active collaboration between two lovers who knowingly read and write each other into adultery, and where the jealous husband remains blind to this betrayal even after he has seen it with his own eyes. Furthermore, the pandering text is not a courtly romance but a private love letter, which, along with January's more impersonal and public "scrit" and "chartres," situates the problems of language and the Fall in the everyday life of the literate medieval household.

On the other hand, what May and Damyan find in their amorous scripture differs little in its essentials from what Paolo and Francesca find mirrored in their romance book. As Frank Kermode remarks, "Carnal readings are much the same. Spiritual readings are all different."[146] Multiple transgressions of the sign take place in January's house and garden, yet they all serve the same fleshly end. Despite their differences, even January and Damyan seem like younger and older versions of each other. The phallic rivalry between Adam and the Serpent for Eve's body had long been a subtext of patristic typology, and Chaucer, in turning the Fall into a fabliau, simply brings to the surface this aspect of the ancient combat myth. Of course, January's pen is no match for Damyan's.

As for May, the Eve figure, she is smart, sensual, and devious like Alisoun of Bath; she, too, yields her "bele chose" for a good "glose" and through sex gains control of "hous and lond," though apparently without Alisoun's ambitions to "maistrie."[147] Furthermore, May is literate, which gives her advantages over Alisoun, who is locked out of the male world of letters and has only her capable tongue to reply to men's libels on women, whether these libels are scriptural glosses or stories of wicked wives. Able to read and write her own desire, May avenges Eve on the letter, authoring her own

145. Mazzotta, *Dante, Poet of the Desert*, p. 169.
146. Kermode, *The Genesis of Secrecy*, p. 9.
147. *Wife of Bath's Prologue* III.509–10 ("glose"/"bele chose"), 814 ("hous and lond"), 818 ("maistrie").

script and even directing Damyan as they collaborate on a plot or narrative that subversively revises her husband's assuming glosses on the Garden.

But what is it that May desires most? Apart from what she gets in the pear tree, this question remains something of a mystery. Our only glimpse into her mind occurs after she receives Damyan's first letter, and here her thoughts are conventional. For the rest, the Merchant pulls the curtain on her inward life, as in her procrustean marriage bed: "God woot what that May thoughte in hir herte" (1851). This silence is not the Merchant's modesty but his ignorance; Chaucer, who could create a Criseyde, or an Alisoun, a feat of the male imagination that rivals Joyce's creation of Molly Bloom, deliberately makes this misogynist blind to the "feminine soul." As a result, despite May's writing, little of the story of Eve emerges after all.[148] Like January, the Merchant regards woman as only "half a clerk" (1428).

If the action of the pear tree story ends by fulfilling a desire as ephemeral as the paper or parchment on which it was first written, what of Chaucer's text itself and the desired end or fulfillment of its action? The avowed end of the Canterbury pilgrimage is a spiritual one, "The hooly blisful martir for to seke" (I.17), with all that this quest implies, but before long we learn that Chaucer's "sondry folk" (I.25) have very mixed motives for undertaking their journey. And while the Merchant may tell an especially carnal tale, the *Canterbury Tales* as a whole moves continually between the fundament and the firmament, between scatology and eschatology. The pilgrims may be journeying to the shrine in Canterbury, and ultimately to the heavenly City of Jerusalem (X.49–51), but to get to either place they have to plod along a road full of mud and mire, by which some of them are splattered and into which one or two of the more carnal pilgrims actually fall along the way.[149] Chaucer's book is located in the same fallen space, whether as a perishable artifact grounded in a bodily order of things or as a "tretys" making claims for transcendence in the manner of "hooly writ" itself. Like all written

148. Edwards says of January that he "cannot recognize even the possibility of May's appetite, much less the probability that it might be constructed differently from his own" ("Narration and Doctrine," p. 360). As for the Merchant, he can recognize for May only a crude appetite identical to Damyan's or to his own.

149. Near the outset the Miller is so drunk that "unnethe upon his hors he sat" (*Miller's Prologue* I.3121); and, near the end of the *Tales*, the Cook, in a fit of anger at the Manciple, pitches off his horse into the road (*Manciple's Prologue* IX.48–49) and must be hoisted back into the saddle by the other pilgrims.

texts, Chaucer's book partakes of the "fallen" writing whose ultimate origin lies in the Garden.

It is true that January's garden contains not only a typological
fruit tree but also a "laurer" whose leaves are "alwey grene" (2037).
With this traditional emblem of poetry, Chaucer may be suggesting
that the leaves of his book also embody a secular afterlife of fame,
that the Fall engendered both the gift of divine Scripture and that
of human poetry. Like his great Italian predecessors, Chaucer apparently sought an earthly immortality, and like Petrarch in particular he may have felt torn between Augustine's penitential fig tree
and the laurel of poetic self-creation.[150] Yet the last tree mentioned
in the *Canterbury Tales* is not the poetic laurel but the Tree of
Penitence (X.110), which bears among its leaves the "fruyt of pen-
aunce" (X.1075), and which points not to literary self-creation and
self-advancement but rather back to the Garden and to the divine
beginning and end of all language. Chaucer may chastise his scribe
for miswriting the letter, but ultimately he recognizes his own af-
finity with "Adam" as one who equally labors in the shadow of the
Fall.

In his literary works, Chaucer figures the condition of fallen
language most fully under the sign of the "lettre." As far as we
know, Chaucer, unlike other poets of his age, left no "personal"
letters, no letters to posterity, but only the letters written by his
characters—letters sent to us indirectly, as it were. On the other
hand, more letters appear in Chaucer's literary works than in those
of any earlier medieval poet. In many cases, Chaucer gives us not
only their contents but also the details of their writing, transmission,
and reception. Thus situated within poetic fictions as the products
of imaginary personae, and as subject to the usual contingencies,
these fictional letters represent Chaucer's own literary corpus as
well as the written word in general, the "lettre," as a locus of a
myriad problems and possibilities. Like other texts, these letters are
a scene of interpretive ambiguity and of unforeseen or unrealized
rhetorical effects. They are a mysterious nexus of soul and body, of
spirit and matter, of the inner and the outer. They are an occasion
for pleasure or pain, for joy or sorrow. They are a place to find or
lose God, to sign away or redeem one's soul. And, finally, for Chaucer
and for us, the author and his literary audience as separated by time,
space, and much more, they are a sign of the eternal absence of
writer and reader from each other.

150. See Freccero, "The Fig Tree and the Laurel."

Epilogue

Signs of the Fall:
From the Middle Ages to Postmodernism

> If Adam had remained in innocence, [God's] preaching
> would have been like a Bible for him and for all of us; and
> we would have had no need for paper, ink, pens, and that
> endless multitude of books which we require today,
> although we do not attain a thousandth part of that wisdom
> which Adam had in Paradise.
> —*Martin Luther*

THE CHRISTIAN Middle Ages turned the Fall into a comprehensive myth for language, literature, and verbal culture at large. According to patristic and medieval tradition, the transgression in the Garden of Eden had upset not only the created order of things (*res*) but also the order of language itself (*verba*). Moreover, the Fall was held to represent not just a primal crisis of language but also the perennial problems of discourse that confronted—and even threatened—the order of medieval culture, particularly in the areas of doctrine, hermeneutics, and eloquence. The medieval myth of the Fall thus embodied the imagined shape of an archaic past as well as the ideals and realities of a distinct, if evolving, historical present.

In the first place, the Fall represented a crisis in the mediation of teaching, knowledge, or truth from God to humankind. God's command to Adam, as conveyed in turn by Adam to Eve, was a "precept" representing all sacred doctrine, and at the same time a "text" to be preserved in its original form, and thus a model for sacred tradition itself. With the Fall, this original text, teaching, or tradition had been corrupted, along with the hierarchy of authority whereby it had been disseminated. In the theological sphere, the

Fall thus represented the perennial conflict between truth and false-hood, doctrine and heresy. In the political sphere, the Fall embodied a crisis of authority whose implications extended from church affairs to secular life at large, especially the feudal hierarchies that struc-tured European society during the Middle Ages. In the sphere of sexual politics particularly, the Fall represented a challenge to the self-claimed right of men to teach and govern women, whether in religious, social, or domestic matters. In sum, medieval readings of the Fall reflect a keen awareness that knowledge implies power and that in the Fall both of these were inseparably at stake.

Second, medieval culture used the Fall as a paradigm for her-meneutics—for sign theory, notions about writing, and problems of interpretation in general. Adam and Eve had abused God's command by "enjoying" the forbidden fruit as a thing rather than "using" it as a sign; therefore, they had been exiled from the Garden into a world of toil and error where bodily needs and desires beset the soul in the search for spiritual food. Exiled from God's speaking presence, as well as from the knowledge that hitherto they had enjoyed through an inner, unmediated vision, humans were exiled also into the realm of writing, which inherently signified the absence of God. Although God's written word partly compensated humans for their lost paradise of knowledge, the scriptural truth was often veiled in allegory, a figurative extension of the leaf and skin coverings worn by Adam and Eve after their sin. Indeed, the "letter" in general, sacred or secular, could occasion further hermeneutical error among Adam and Eve's descendants. In the primal scene of hermeneutics, Eve had seduced Adam; likewise, the fleshly "feminine" text could tempt the "masculine" reader into an abuse of signs that Augustine described as "carnal" reading or "fornication." Yet the Fall had also brought about a rebirth of the Sign in the Person of the Word, who fulfilled the scriptural promises and paradoxically redeemed the fallen sign in his own flesh.

Finally, the Fall had hinged on the persuasions of eloquence, so that it also served medieval culture as a paradigm for the art of rhetoric. Whereas God's speech about the Tree of Knowledge was a precedent for the eloquence of truth, the Serpent's seductive speech to Eve, and Eve's supposedly similar speech to Adam, embodied a corruption of rhetoric and exemplified all subsequent abuses of that art. Furthermore, the common belief that Satan had spoken *through* the Serpent turned the Fall into an adaptable exemplum for decep-tion in general—fiction, theater, illusion, and the like. In sum, the

Fall had left eloquence in a moral middle ground—like the Tree of Knowledge itself, planted in the middle of the Garden. On the one hand, the art of rhetoric offered a dangerous sweetness (*suavitas*) as well as deceptive coverings for sin. On the other hand, rhetoric was a valuable tool in the service of the good, and medieval culture followed Augustine in idealizing a redeemed eloquence that could flavor the wholesome food of truth, and that could teach, move, and delight an audience in proclaiming God's word. At the same time, however, the Fall served as the foremost seduction scenario in medieval moral literature, a vivid cautionary tale for the sons of Adam and the daughters of Eve about the role of language in sexual politics and in the dynamics of fleshly temptation.

It is often imagined that medieval culture died in giving birth to modernity, and that the myth of the Fall passed away at the same time. The end of the Middle Ages, however, was not accompanied by anything like a comparable waning of this myth, despite the great sundering of Christendom in the sixteenth century with the Reformation. Indeed, Luther, the seminal Protestant theologian and exegete, emphatically reasserted Augustine's theology and general theory of signs. Moreover, he reaffirmed the Fall as a comprehensive paradigm for verbal culture, repeating and even improving on many medieval glosses on the school of paradise, the genesis of hermeneutics, and the garden of eloquence, including the crucial notion that the Fall had exiled humans from an immediate knowledge of God into a world of indirect and ambiguous signs.[1]

The same preoccupation with the Fall as a crisis of language and a paradigm of verbal culture appears in Milton's great poem, which, among other things, is a summa of patristic, medieval, and Protestant glosses on language and the Fall. For example, Milton's version of the speech in which Adam conveys the prohibition to Eve—Adam having already received the command from God—bespeaks a close conjunction between original sin and sign abuse:

God hath pronounc't it death to taste that Tree,
The only *sign* of our obedience left

1. Martin Luther, *Lectures on Genesis, Chapters 1–5*, trans. Jaroslav Pelikan, *Luther's Works*, vol. 1 (St. Louis, 1958), p. 105, as quoted above in the epigraph to this Epilogue.

> Among so many *signs* of power and rule
> Conferr'd upon us. . . .[2]

Here echoing the familiar Augustinian notion that abusing signs leads to death, Milton suggests that the Fall as semiosis extends outwardly from the fruit, a thing that is also a sign, to the system of verbal signs that conjoins Adam with Eve, and the humans with God. Later, Milton's Serpent, as false teacher, exegete, and "Orator" (9.670), plays out with Eve the further implications of language and the Fall in this scene. As one of Milton's contemporaries put it, the Fall was the fruit of language itself: "Original sin came first out of the mouth by speaking, before it entered in by eating."[3]

It is true that already by Milton's time the doctrine of the historical Fall had been weakened by the new science of biblical criticism as well as by a growing religious skepticism among learned Europeans. The demise of the historical Fall is usually dated to the Enlightenment, though on the eve of the eighteenth century John Locke could still devote a whole treatise to Genesis 1–3 as a set of *historical* precedents for law, authority, and property.[4] Even during that century, as the Fall dwindled in many minds from a historical reality into a metaphor or trope, leading *philosophes* such as Condillac and Rousseau persisted in founding theories of language on this primeval site. And theological residue concerning language and the Fall appears in major works of philosophy, linguistics, and anthropology written during the past century and a half. In even the most secular modern contexts, writes Jacques Derrida, "the sign is always a sign of the Fall. Absence always relates to distancing from God."[5]

Many modern authors, critics, and theorists have returned to the Fall as a paradigm for matters of language—for poetics, rhetoric, hermeneutics, and the like. For example, in his well-known poem "Adam's Curse," W. B. Yeats turns the Fall into a Protestant work ethic for *poesis*: "It's certain there is no fine thing / Since Adam's

2. Milton, *Paradise Lost* 4.427–30; my emphasis.

3. Richard Allestree, *The Government of the Tongue* (1667; Fifth Printing, Oxford, 1675), p. 7 (*entred* altered to *entered*); cited in Robert L. Entzminger, *Divine Word: Milton and the Redemption of Language* (Pittsburgh, 1985), p. 69. Recent work on language and the Fall in Milton also includes R. A. Shoaf, *Milton, Poet of Duality*.

4. John Locke, *Two Treatises of Government* (London, 1698), First Treatise.

5. Derrida, *Of Grammatology*, p. 283, referring to Hegel and Husserl, among others. On Condillac and Rousseau, see pp. 280–95.

fall but needs much labouring."⁶ Even as an object of demytholo-
gizing, the Fall has provided authors with a creative impulse. Thus
Stéphane Mallarmé's avant-garde manifesto "The Book: A Spiritual
Instrument" grounds its formalist poetics in a reprise of Augustine's
readerly epiphany in the garden ("Seated on a garden bench where
a recent book is lying, I like to watch a passing gust half open it and
breathe life into many of its outer aspects"), idealizing a purely
material book in place of the spiritual one exalted by the Middle
Ages, and thus eclipsing an older theological poetics that held earthly
books to be merely images of higher, spiritual realities.⁷ Again, James
Joyce repeatedly invokes the Fall in *Finnegans Wake*, as in its "opening" lines—"riverrun, past Eve and Adam's, from swerve of shore
to bend of bay"—which recall Augustine's reflections on how the
human race, history, and language itself ultimately flow out of the
Garden of Eden.⁸ At the same time, however, Joyce deconstructs
this traditional myth of origins, while subverting the Western myth
of linear narrative itself.⁹

In the domain of contemporary literary theory, Kenneth Burke
and Paul Ricoeur have glossed the Fall extensively as an originary
scene for rhetoric and hermeneutics, respectively.¹⁰ Another influential critic in our time, Harold Bloom, has made the Fall—via the
Romantic poets and Freud—central to his theory of poetic genesis.
Interpreting Genesis 3 in oedipal and Gnostic terms, Bloom invokes
a repressive Creator/Father against whom the filial poet heroically
rebels—not like Adam but like that earlier transgressor, Satan. The
"strong" poet resembles Satan insofar as he rebelliously falls away
from "God"—that is, from "cultural history, the dead poets, the
embarrassments of a tradition grown too wealthy to need anything
more."¹¹ Again, the Fall also serves as a paradigm for contemporary

6. William Butler Yeats, "Adam's Curse" (1904), in *The Collected Poems of W. B. Yeats*, def. ed. (New York, 1956), pp. 78–79, lines 21–22.

7. Stéphane Mallarmé, "Le Livre, instrument spirituel" (1895), trans. Bradford Cook, in *Critical Theory since Plato*, ed. Hazard Adams (New York, 1971), pp. 690–92 (p. 691).

8. Joyce, *Finnegans Wake*, p. 3. Augustine, *Conf* 1.16.

9. On the Fall in the *Wake*, see Kimberly J. Devlin, *Wandering and Return in Finnegans Wake: An Integrative Approach to Joyce's Fictions* (Princeton, 1991), pp. 87–92.

10. Burke, *The Rhetoric of Religion*, pp. 172–272. Ricoeur, *The Symbolism of Evil*, pp. 232–78.

11. Harold Bloom, *The Anxiety of Influence: A Theory of Poetry* (London, 1973), p. 21. On this model, "poetry begins with our awareness, not of a Fall, but that *we are falling*" (p. 20; orig. emphasis), Milton's Satan being "archetype of the modern poet at his strongest" (p. 19).

debates about orality and literacy. Some critics evoke "the medieval myth of a pristine orality prior to the Fall into linguistic confusion," whereas others insist that "there is no edenic world of speech that has been corrupted by a serpent in the guise of a stylus."[12]

Vestiges of the medieval myth about language and the Fall survive not only in critical theory and the literary canon but also in the mass media of popular culture. Advertisers use the myth and symbols of the Fall to sell everything from apples to underwear; after all, the Serpent was the first fast-talking salesman and Adam and Eve the first gullible "consumers."[13] The Fall even shows up in popular music, a modern oral tradition. For example, in the lyrics of one recent song, styled as an ersatz Caribbean tale, a couple lives happily together on an island until a walking, talking snake appears and enchants the woman:

> There was a little fire inside his mouth and the flame
> would come dancing out of his mouth.
> And the woman liked this very much.
> And after that, she was bored with the man.[14]

Here again are the sexual seduction and social alienation that have been part of the Fall myth for centuries. The Fall also continues to color the sexual politics of everyday life, as evidenced by a recent *New York Times* news commentary that reported, in reference to the wife of a presidential candidate, that "Republicans are busy mining fears as old as Adam and Eve about the dangers of an assertive, ambitious woman speaking into the ear of her man."[15] The application is contemporary, but the topos—Eve speaking into Adam's ear—goes right back to the Middle Ages and the church fathers.

In a postmodern landscape still littered with signs of the Fall, critics have raised questions about the cumulative cultural influence of

12. Jesse Gellrich, "Orality, Literacy, and Crisis in the Later Middle Ages," p. 466, discussing Derrida. Myron C. Tuman, rev. of Walter Ong, *Orality and Literacy* (1982), in *College English* 45 (1983): 769–79 (p. 777).

13. For an especially witty example, see *The New York Times Book Review*, 11 August 1991, p. 27 (ad for book club).

14. Laurie Anderson, "Langue d'Amour," *Mister Heartbreak* album (Difficult Music / BMI, 1984). In her filmed performance of this song, Anderson wears a snake outfit, recalling the snake/woman of medieval legend (*The Home of the Brave*, prod. Paula Mazur [Cinecom International Films, 1986]).

15. Maureen Dowd, "Hillary Clinton as Aspiring First Lady: Role Model, or a 'Hall Monitor' Type?" *The New York Times*, 18 May 1992, p. A15, col. 1.

this myth. For example, although debate continues about whether the antifeminism traditionally associated with the Fall is inherent in the text or mainly a result of misreading by a patriarchal tradition, clearly the *received* myth of the Fall has been used against women during most of its history.[16] Nor are concerns about the possibly malign effects of the Fall myth limited to feminist critics. Derrida alleges that the myth of the Fall, as part of a Western "logocentrism," has both encouraged phallocentric attitudes and fostered illusions about language and the human subject, while upholding an ancient hegemony of speech over writing. On such a view, the myth of the Fall, with its central image of the fatal fruit, is itself a kind of drug or potion—a *pharmakon*—that has had ill effects on the discourse of an entire culture or civilization.[17]

What future generations will make of the myth of the Fall is impossible to say. But clearly the story of Adam, Eve, and the Serpent still fascinates us, as do all stories that ultimately are about ourselves. And however old and fractured the mirror of this myth becomes, it will likely continue to reflect back to us bits of what we recognize as ourselves, our human condition, and our enigmatic significance. For, as one of our oldest and most enduring myths, the Fall not only troubles and enchants us but even tempts us to suspend our disbelief, as though we still think of ourselves as exiles from the Garden.

16. See Meyers, *Discovering Eve*, esp. chap. 4.
17. On deconstructing the Fall, see also Taylor, *Erring*, pp. 61–68, 151–54.

Bibliography

Abbetmeyer, Charles. *Old English Poetical Motives Derived from the Doctrine of Sin.* Minneapolis: Wilson, 1903.

Abelard, Peter (and Heloise). *The Letters of Abelard and Heloise.* Trans. Betty Radice. Harmondsworth: Penguin, 1974.

Aelfric. "Aelfric's Version of *Alcuini Interrogationes Sigeuulfi in Genesin.*" (Old English version of Alcuin's *Interrogationes.*) Ed. George E. MacLean. *Anglia* 7 (1884): 1–59.

———. *Homilies of Aelfric: A Supplementary Collection.* Ed. John C. Pope. 2 vols. EETS OS 259–60. London: Oxford University Press, 1967–68.

Aelred of Rievaulx. *De institutione inclusarum.* Ed. C. H. Talbot. *Corpus Christianorum, continuatio medievalis* 1:635–82. Turnholt: Brepols, 1971. Trans. Mary Paul Macpherson as *A Rule of Life for a Recluse.* In *The Works of Aelred of Rievaulx* 1:43–102. Spencer, Mass.: Cistercian Publications, 1971.

Alan of Lille. *De planctu naturae.* Ed. N. M. Häring, *Studi Medievali,* 3d ser., 19 (1978): 797–879. Trans. James J. Sheridan as *The Plaint of Nature.* Toronto: Pontifical Institute of Mediaeval Studies, 1980.

———. *Liber poenitentialis (On penance).* PL 210:279–304.

Alcuin. *Adversus Elipandum Toletanum (Against Elipandus).* PL 101:243–300.

———. *Carmina (Poems).* Ed. Ernest Dümmler. *Poetae latini aevi Carolini* 1:169–351. MGH. Berlin, 1881.

———. *Commentaria in S. Johannis evangelium (Commentary on the Gospel of John).* PL 100:743–1008.

———. *Epistolae (Letters).* Ed. Ernest Dümmler. *Epistolae Karolini Aevi* 2:18–481. MGH. Berlin, 1895.

———. *Interrogationes et responsiones in Genesin (Questions and Answers on Genesis).* PL 100:517–66.

Alford, John A. "Scriptural Testament in *The Canterbury Tales*: The Letter Takes Its Revenge." In *Chaucer and Scriptural Tradition,* ed. David Lyle Jeffrey, pp. 197–203. Ottawa: University of Ottawa Press, 1984.

Alfred (the Great). *King Alfred's Version of St. Augustine's Soliloquies.* Ed. Thomas A. Carnicelli. Cambridge: Harvard University Press, 1969.

———. *König Alfreds Übersetzung von Bedas Kirchengeschichte.* (Alfred's Old English version of Bede's *Ecclesiastical History.*) Ed. Jacob Schipper. Bibliothek der angelsächsischen Prosa, vol. 4. Leipzig: Wigand, 1899.

Ambrose. *De Paradiso. PL* 14:275–314. Trans. John J. Savage as *Paradise.* In *Saint Ambrose: Hexameron, Paradise, and Cain and Abel,* pp. 285–356. FOC, no. 42. New York: Fathers of the Church, 1961.

——. *Epistolae. PL* 16:849–1286. Selections trans. Mary M. Beyenka as *Saint Ambrose, Letters.* FOC, no. 26. New York: Fathers of the Church, 1954.

Ancrene Wisse (British Library, MS. Cotton Cleopatra C.vi). *The English Text of the Ancrene Riwle.* Ed. Eric J. Dobson. EETS OS 267. London: Oxford University Press, 1972.

—— (British Library, MS. Cotton Nero A.xiv). *The English Text of the Ancrene Riwle.* Ed. Mabel Day. EETS OS 225. London: Oxford University Press, 1952.

—— (British Library, MS. Cotton Vitellius F.vii). *The French Text of the Ancrene Riwle.* Ed. J. A. Herbert. EETS OS 219. London: Oxford University Press, 1944.

—— (Corpus Christi College, Cambridge, MS. 402). *The English Text of the Ancrene Riwle: Ancrene Wisse.* Ed. J. R. R. Tolkien. EETS OS 249. London: Oxford University Press, 1962.

—— (Magdalene College, Cambridge, MS. Pepys 2498). *The English Text of the Ancrene Riwle.* Ed. Arne Zettersten. EETS OS 274. London: Early English Text Society, 1976.

—— (Merton College MS. 44; British Library, MS. Cotton Vitellius E.vii). *The Latin Text of the Ancrene Riwle.* Ed. Charlotte D'Evelyn. EETS OS 216. London: Oxford University Press, 1944.

—— (Trinity College, Cambridge, MS. R.14.7). *The French Text of the Ancrene Riwle.* Ed. W. H. Trethewey. EETS OS 240. London: Oxford University Press, 1958.

Anderson, Laurie. "Langue d'Amour." *Mister Heartbreak* album. Difficult Music / BMI, 1984.

Andreas Capellanus. *De amore libri tres.* Ed. E. Trojel. Copenhagen, 1892. Trans. John Jay Parry as *The Art of Courtly Love.* 1941. Rpt. New York: Norton, 1969.

The Anglo-Saxon Poetic Records: A Collective Edition. Ed. George Philip Krapp and Elliott Van Kirk Dobbie. 6 vols. New York: Columbia University Press, 1931–53.

Arbery, Glenn C. "Adam's First Word and the Failure of Language in *Paradiso* xxxiii." In Wasserman and Roney, eds., pp. 31–44.

Ariès, Philippe, and Georges Duby, gen. eds. *A History of Private Life.* 5 vols. Trans. Arthur Goldhammer. Cambridge: Harvard University Press, 1987–91.

Astell, Ann W. "Holofernes's Head: *Tacen* and Teaching in the Old English *Judith.*" *ASE* 18 (1989): 117–33.

Auerbach, Erich. *Literary Language and Its Public in Late Latin Antiquity and in the Middle Ages.* Trans. Ralph Manheim. New York: Pantheon, 1965.

——. *Mimesis: The Representation of Reality in Western Literature.* Trans. Willard R. Trask. Princeton: Princeton University Press, 1953.

——. *Scenes from the Drama of European Literature: Six Essays.* Trans.

Ralph Manheim and Catherine Garvin. 1959. Rpt. Gloucester, Mass.: Peter Smith, 1973.

Augustine. *Confessionum libri xiii*. Ed. Martinus Skutella, rev. H. Juergens and W. Schaub. Stuttgart: Teubner, 1981. Trans. Rex Warner as *The Confessions of St. Augustine*. New York: New American Library, 1963.

——. *De catechizandis rudibus*. Ed. I. B. Bauer. *CCSL* 46:115–78. Trans. S. D. F. Salmond as *On the Catechising of the Uninstructed*. NPNF, ser. 1, vol. 3. 1887. Rpt. Grand Rapids: Eerdmans, 1980.

——. *De civitate Dei*. Ed. and trans. George E. McCracken et al. as *The City of God against the Pagans*. 7 vols. LCL. London: Heinemann, 1957–72.

——. *De doctrina Christiana*. Ed. H. J. Vogels, *Florilegium patristicum* 24 (1930): 1–103. Trans. D. W. Robertson, Jr., as *On Christian Doctrine*. Indianapolis: Bobbs-Merrill, 1958.

——. *De Genesi ad litteram*. PL 34:245–486. Trans. John H. Taylor as *The Literal Meaning of Genesis*. ACW, nos. 41–42. New York: Newman Press, 1982.

——. *De Genesi contra Manichaeos*. PL 34:173–220. Trans. Roland J. Teske as *Two Books on Genesis against the Manichees*. In *Saint Augustine on Genesis*, pp. 45–141. FOC, no. 84. Washington: Catholic University of America Press, 1991.

——. *De libero arbitrio*. Ed. W. M. Green. *CCSL* 29:205–321. Trans. John H. S. Burleigh as *On Free Will*. In *Augustine: Earlier Writings*, pp. 102–217. Philadelphia: Westminster, 1953.

——. *De magistro*. Ed. Klaus-Detlef Daur. *CCSL* 29:139–203. Trans. John H. S. Burleigh as *The Teacher*. In *Augustine: Earlier Writings*, pp. 64–101. Philadelphia: Westminster, 1953.

——. *De nuptiis et concupiscentia*. Ed. Charles F. Urba and Joseph Zycha. *Corpus Scriptorum Ecclesiasticorum Latinorum* 42:209–319. Vienna: Tempsky, 1902. Trans. Philip Schaff as *On Marriage and Concupiscence*. NPNF, ser. 1, vol. 5. 1887. Rpt. Grand Rapids: Eerdmans, 1980.

——. *De ordine*. Ed. W. M. Green. *CCSL* 29:87–137. Trans. Robert P. Russell as *Divine Providence and the Problem of Evil*. In FOC, no. 5. New York: Fathers of the Church, 1948.

——. *De sermone Domini in monte*. Ed. Almut Mutzenbecher. *CCSL* 35. Trans. William Findlay as *Our Lord's Sermon on the Mount*. NPNF, ser. 1, vol. 6. 1887. Rpt. Grand Rapids: Eerdmans, 1980.

——. *De spiritu et littera*. PL 44:201–46. Trans. Peter Holmes as *On the Spirit and the Letter*. NPNF, ser. 1, vol. 5. 1887. Rpt. Grand Rapids: Eerdmans, 1980.

——. *De Trinitate*. Ed. W. J. Mountain and Fr. Glorie. *CCSL* 50 (2 pts.). Trans. Arthur W. Haddan and W. G. T. Shedd as *On the Holy Trinity*. NPNF, ser. 1, vol. 3. 1887. Rpt. Grand Rapids: Eerdmans, 1980.

——. *De vera religione*. Ed. Klaus-Detlef Daur. *CCSL* 32:169–260. Trans. John H. S. Burleigh as *Of True Religion*. In *Augustine: Earlier Writings*, pp. 218–83. Philadelphia: Westminster, 1953.

——. *Enarrationes in Psalmos*. Ed. Eligius Dekkers and Johannes Fraipont.

CCSL 38–40. Trans. as *Expositions on the Book of Psalms.* 6 vols. LOF, vols. 24, 25, 30, 32, 37, 39. Oxford, 1847–57.

——. *Enchiridion.* Ed. E. Evans. *CCSL* 46:21–114. Trans. J. F. Shaw as *The Enchiridion.* In NPNF, ser. 1, vol. 3. 1887. Rpt. Grand Rapids: Eerdmans, 1980.

——. *Epistolae. PL* 33:61–1162. Trans. Wilfrid Parsons as *St. Augustine, Letters.* 5 vols. FOC, nos. 12, 18, 20, 30, 32. New York: Fathers of the Church, 1951–56.

——. *Soliloquia. PL* 32:869–904. Trans. John H. S. Burleigh as *The Soliloquies.* In *Augustine: Earlier Writings,* pp. 17–63. Philadelphia: Westminster, 1953.

Avitus, Alcimus Ecdicius. *Epistolae. PL* 59:198–290, 381–86.

——. *Poematum de spiritalis historiae gestis.* Ed. Daniel J. Nodes. *Avitus, The Fall of Man.* Toronto: Pontifical Institute of Mediaeval Studies, 1985.

Baldwin, Charles S. *Medieval Rhetoric and Poetic to 1400: Interpreted from Representative Works.* New York: Macmillan, 1928.

Barratt, Alexandra. "The Five Wits and Their Structural Significance in Part II of *Ancrene Wisse." MAE* 56 (1987): 12–24.

Barthes, Roland. *Mythologies.* Paris: Seuil, 1957. Trans. Annette Lavers as *Mythologies.* New York: Hill and Wang, 1972.

——. *Le Plaisir du texte.* Paris: Seuil, 1973. Trans. Richard Miller as *The Pleasure of the Text.* 1973. New York: Hill and Wang, 1975.

Bede. *Historia ecclesiastica gentis anglorum (Ecclesiastical History of the English Nation).* Ed. and trans. J. E. King in *Baedae opera historica.* 2 vols. LCL. London: Heinemann, 1930.

——. *In Pentateuchum commentarii (Commentary on the Pentateuch). PL* 91:189–394.

Belanoff, Pat. "The Fall(?) of the Old English Female Poetic Image." *PMLA* 104 (1989): 822–31.

Bell, Susan Groag. "Medieval Women Book Owners: Arbiters of Lay Piety and Ambassadors of Culture." In *Women and Power in the Middle Ages,* ed. Mary Erler and Maryanne Kowaleski, pp. 149–87. Athens, Ga.: University of Georgia Press, 1988.

Benedict. *Sancti Benedicti regula.* Ed. and trans. Justin McCann. *The Rule of Saint Benedict in Latin and English.* London: Burns and Oates, 1941.

Beowulf and the Fight at Finnsburg. Ed. Friedrich Klaeber. 3d ed. Boston: Heath, 1950. Trans. E. Talbot Donaldson as *Beowulf: A New Prose Translation.* New York: Norton, 1966.

Bernard of Clairvaux. *Sancti Bernardi Opera.* Ed. Jean Leclercq, C. H. Talbot, and H. M. Rochais. 8 vols. in 9 pts. Rome: Editiones Cistercienses, 1957–77. Translated as *The Works of Bernard of Clairvaux.* Spencer, Mass., and Washington, D.C.: Cistercian Publications, 1970–.

Bersuire, Pierre (Petrus Berchorius). *Opera omnia.* 3 vols. Antwerp, 1609.

Bible (Old Latin). *Vetus latina: Die Reste der altlateinischen Bibel.* Vol. 2 (Genesis). Ed. Bonifatius Fischer. Freiburg: Herder, 1951.

—— (Revised Standard Version). *The New Oxford Annotated Bible with the Apocrypha, Expanded Edition.* Ed. Herbert G. May, Bruce M. Metzger. New York: Oxford University Press, 1977.

—— (Septuagint). *Septuaginta, id est Vetus Testamentum Graece iuxta LXX interpretes.* Ed. Alfred Rahlfs. 2 vols. Stuttgart: Privilegierte, 1935.

—— (Vulgate). *Biblia sacra iuxta vulgatam versionem.* 3d ed. Ed. Robertus Weber, Bonifatius Fischer, et al. Stuttgart: Deutsche Bibelgesellschaft, 1983.

Birch, Walter de Gray, ed. *Cartularium Saxonicum: A Collection of Charters Relating to Anglo-Saxon History.* 3 vols. London, 1885–93. Rpt. New York: Johnson, 1964.

Bleeth, Kenneth A. "The Image of Paradise in the *Merchant's Tale.*" In *The Learned and the Lewed: Studies in Chaucer and Medieval Literature,* ed. Larry D. Benson, pp. 45–60. Cambridge: Harvard University Press, 1974.

Bloch, R. Howard. *Etymologies and Genealogies: A Literary Anthropology of the French Middle Ages.* Chicago: University of Chicago Press, 1983.

——. *The Scandal of the Fabliaux.* Chicago: University of Chicago Press, 1986.

Bloom, Harold. *The Anxiety of Influence: A Theory of Poetry.* London: Oxford University Press, 1973.

Boethius. *De consolatione philosophiae (The Consolation of Philosophy).* Ed. and trans. S. J. Tester. In *Boethius: The Theological Tractates, The Consolation of Philosophy.* Rev ed. LCL. London: Heinemann, 1973.

Bolton, Whitney F. *Alcuin and Beowulf: An Eighth-Century View.* New Brunswick, N.J.: Rutgers University Press, 1978.

Bonaventura. *Breviloquium.* Ed. R. P. Aloysii a Parma. In *Doctoris Seraphici S. Bonaventurae... Opera Omnia* 5:199–291. Quaracchi, 1891. Trans. José de Vinck. In *The Works of Bonaventure: Cardinal, Seraphic Doctor, and Saint,* vol. 2. Paterson, N.J.: St. Anthony Guild, 1963.

The Book of the Knight of La Tour-Landry, Compiled for the Instruction of His Daughters. Ed. Thomas Wright. Rev. ed. EETS OS 33. 1906. Rpt. New York: Greenwood, 1969.

Bornstein, Diane. *The Lady in the Tower: Medieval Courtesy Literature for Women.* Hamden, Conn.: Archon Books, 1983.

Bosworth, Joseph, and T. Northcote Toller, eds. *An Anglo-Saxon Dictionary.* Oxford: Oxford University Press, 1898. *Supplement,* ed. T. Northcote Toller, 1921. *Enlarged Addenda and Corrigenda to the Supplement,* ed. Alistair Campbell, 1972.

Bradof, Carol A. "*Genesis B,* Carolingian History, and the Germanic Heroic Tradition." Columbia University dissertation, 1990.

Bright, James W. "The Relation of the Caedmonian *Exodus* to the Liturgy." *MLN* 27 (1912): 97–103.

Brown, Peter. *Augustine of Hippo: A Biography.* Berkeley: University of California Press, 1967.

——. *The Body and Society: Men, Women, and Sexual Renunciation in Early Christianity*. New York: Columbia University Press, 1988.

Burchmore, Susan. "Traditional Exegesis and the Question of Guilt in the Old English *Genesis B*." *Traditio* 41 (1985): 117–44.

Burke, Kenneth. *The Rhetoric of Religion: Studies in Logology*. Boston: Beacon, 1961.

Bynum, Caroline Walker. *Holy Feast and Holy Fast: The Religious Significance of Food to Medieval Women*. Berkeley: University of California Press, 1987.

The Cambridge History of the Bible. Ed. P. R. Ackroyd, C. F. Evans, et al. 3 vols. Cambridge: Cambridge University Press, 1963–70.

Camille, Michael. *The Gothic Idol: Ideology and Image-making in Medieval Art*. Cambridge: Cambridge University Press, 1989.

Capek, Michael J. "The Nationality of a Translator: Some Notes on the Syntax of *Genesis B*." *Neophilologus* 55 (1971): 89–96.

Carlson, Paula J. "The Grammar of God: Grammatical Metaphor in *Piers Plowman* and *Pearl*." Columbia University dissertation, 1983.

Cassiodorus Senator. *Institutiones divinarum et humanarum lectionum*. Ed. Roger A. B. Mynors. *Cassiodori Senatoris Institutiones*. Oxford: Clarendon Press, 1937. Trans. Leslie W. Jones as *An Introduction to Divine and Human Readings*. 1946. Rpt. New York: Norton, 1969.

Cayré, Fulbert. *Manual of Patrology and History of Theology*. Trans. H. Howitt. 2 vols. Paris: Desclée, 1935.

Chadwick, Henry. *The Early Church*. The Pelican History of the Church, vol. 1. Harmondsworth: Penguin, 1967.

Chance, Jane. "Chaucerian Irony in the Verse Epistles 'Wordes Unto Adam,' 'Lenvoy a Scogan,' and 'Lenvoy a Bukton.' " *PLL* 21 (1985): 115–28.

——. *Woman as Hero in Old English Literature*. Syracuse, N.Y.: Syracuse University Press, 1986.

Chaucer, Geoffrey. *The Riverside Chaucer*. 3d ed. Ed. Larry D. Benson. Boston: Houghton Mifflin, 1987.

Cherewatuk, Karen. "Standing, Turning, Twisting, Falling: Posture and Moral Stance in *Genesis B*." *NM* 87 (1986): 537–44.

Cherniss, Michael D. "Heroic Ideals and the Moral Climate of *Genesis B*." *MLQ* 30 (1969): 479–97.

Christine de Pizan. *Le Livre de la cité des dames*. Trans. Earl Jeffrey Richards as *The Book of the City of Ladies*. New York: Persea, 1982.

Cicero. *Orator*. Ed. and trans. H. M. Hubbell. In *Cicero: Brutus, Orator*. Rev. ed. LCL. London: Heinemann, 1962.

(Pseudo-) Cicero. *Ad C. Herennium de ratione dicendi (Rhetorica ad Herennium)*. Ed. and trans. Harry Caplan. LCL. London: Heinemann, 1954.

Clanchy, Michael T. *From Memory to Written Record, England, 1066–1307*. Cambridge: Harvard University Press, 1979.

Clark, Donald L. *Rhetoric in Greco-Roman Education*. New York: Columbia University Press, 1957.

Claudius Marius Victor. *Alethia.* Ed. P. F. Hovingh. *CCSL* 128:125–93.
Clement of Alexandria. *The Exhortation to the Greeks.* Ed. and trans. G. W. Butterworth. In *Clement of Alexandria.* LCL. London: Heinemann, 1953.
Colish, Marcia L. *The Mirror of Language: A Study in the Medieval Theory of Knowledge.* Rev. ed. Lincoln, Nebr.: University of Nebraska Press, 1983.
——. "St. Augustine's Rhetoric of Silence Revisited." *AS* 9 (1978): 15–24.
Corpus Christianorum, series latina. Turnholt: Brepols, 1953–.
Couffignal, Robert. *Le Drame de l'Éden: Le récit de la Genèse et sa fortune littéraire.* Toulouse: Association des publications de l'Université de Toulouse-Le Mirail, 1980.
Curtius, Ernst Robert. *European Literature and the Latin Middle Ages.* Trans. Willard R. Trask. Princeton: Princeton University Press, 1953.
Cyprian of Gaul (Cyprianus Gallus). *Heptateuchos.* Ed. Rudolfus Peiper. *Corpus Scriptorum Ecclesiasticorum Latinorum* 23:1–208. Vienna, 1881.
Dahlberg, Charles. *The Literature of Unlikeness.* Hanover, N.H.: University Press of New England, 1988.
Dahood, Roger. "*Ancrene Wisse,* the Katherine Group, and the *Wohunge* Group." In *Middle English Prose: A Critical Guide to Major Authors and Genres,* ed. A. S. G. Edwards, pp. 1–33. New Brunswick, N.J.: Rutgers University Press, 1984.
Dalbey, Marcia A. "The Devil in the Garden: Pluto and Proserpine in Chaucer's *Merchant's Tale.*" *NM* 75 (1974): 408–15.
Damrosch, David. *The Narrative Covenant: Transformations of Genre in the Growth of Biblical Literature.* New York: Harper and Row, 1987.
Dante Alighieri. *De vulgari eloquentia.* Ed. Aristide Marigo. In *Opere di Dante,* ed. Michele Barbi, vol. 6. Florence: Le Monnier, 1938. Trans. Robert S. Haller as *On Eloquence in the Vernacular.* In *Literary Criticism of Dante Alighieri,* pp. 3–60. Lincoln, Nebr.: University of Nebraska Press, 1973.
——. *The Divine Comedy.* Ed., trans., and comm. Charles S. Singleton. 3 vols. in 6 pts. Princeton: Princeton University Press, 1970–75.
David, Alfred. *The Strumpet Muse: Art and Morals in Chaucer's Poetry.* Bloomington: Indiana University Press, 1976.
Davis, Norman. "The *Litera Troili* and English Letters." *RES* n.s. 16 (1965): 233–44.
De Hamel, Christopher F. R. *Glossed Books of the Bible and the Origins of the Paris Booktrade.* Woodbridge, Suffolk: D. S. Brewer, 1984.
Derrida, Jacques. *Of Grammatology.* Trans. Gayatri C. Spivak. (Orig. *De la Grammatologie,* 1967.) Baltimore: Johns Hopkins University Press, 1976.
——. *Writing and Difference.* Trans. and ed. Alan Bass. Chicago: University of Chicago Press, 1978.

Devlin, Kimberly J. *Wandering and Return in Finnegans Wake: An Integrative Approach to Joyce's Fictions.* Princeton: Princeton University Press, 1991.

Dictionary of Old English. Ed. Angus Cameron et al. Toronto: Pontifical Institute of Mediaeval Studies, 1986– (microfiche).

Dinshaw, Carolyn. *Chaucer's Sexual Poetics.* Madison: University of Wisconsin Press, 1989.

Doane, Alger N., ed. and comm. *The Saxon Genesis: An Edition of the West Saxon "Genesis B" and the Old Saxon Vatican Genesis.* Madison: University of Wisconsin Press, 1991.

Dobson, Eric J. *Moralities on the Gospels: A New Source of "Ancrene Wisse."* Oxford: Clarendon Press, 1975.

——. *The Origins of "Ancrene Wisse."* Oxford: Clarendon Press, 1976.

Donaldson, E. Talbot. *Speaking of Chaucer.* 1970. Rpt. New York: Norton, 1972.

Donovan, Mortimer J. "The Image of Pluto and Proserpine in the *Merchant's Tale.*" *PQ* 36 (1957): 49–60.

Dowd, Maureen. "Hillary Clinton as Aspiring First Lady: Role Model, or a 'Hall Monitor' Type?" *The New York Times.* 18 May 1992. A15.

Dracontius. *De laudibus Dei* (or *Carmen de Deo*). Ed. F. Vollmer. *Auctores Antiquissimi* 14:23–113. MGH. Berlin: Weidmann, 1905.

Drogin, Marc. *Anathema! Medieval Scribes and the History of Book Curses.* Totowa, N.J.: Allanheld and Schram, 1983.

Dronke, Peter. "Francesca and Héloïse." *Comparative Literature* 27 (1975): 113–35.

Duby, Georges. *Medieval Marriage: Two Models from Twelfth-Century France.* Trans. Elborg Forster. Baltimore: Johns Hopkins University Press, 1978.

Duchrow, Ulrich. "*Signum* und *superbia* beim jungen Augustin (386–390)." *REA* 7 (1961): 369–72.

Eden, Kathy. "The Rhetorical Tradition and Augustinian Hermeneutics in *De doctrina christiana.*" *Rhetorica* 8 (1990): 45–63.

Edwards, Robert R. "Narration and Doctrine in the *Merchant's Tale.*" *Speculum* 66 (1991): 342–67.

Ehrhart, Margaret J. "Tempter as Teacher: Some Observations on the Vocabulary of the Old English *Genesis B.*" *Neophilologus* 59 (1975): 435–46.

Eliade, Mircea. *Myth and Reality.* Trans. Willard R. Trask. New York: Harper and Row, 1963.

Elliott, Ralph W. V. *Runes: An Introduction.* 2d ed. Manchester: Manchester University Press, 1989.

Ellis, Deborah S. "The Merchant's Wife's Tale: Language, Sex, and Commerce in Margery Kempe and in Chaucer." *Exemplaria* 2 (1990): 595–626.

Entzminger, Robert L. *Divine Word: Milton and the Redemption of Language.* Pittsburgh: Duquesne University Press, 1985.

Evans, John M. *"Genesis B* and Its Background." *RES* n.s. 14 (1963): 1–16, 113–23.

——. *Paradise Lost and the Genesis Tradition.* Oxford: Clarendon Press, 1968.

Ferguson, Margaret W. "Saint Augustine's Region of Unlikeness: The Crossing of Exile and Language." *Georgia Review* 29 (1975): 842–64.

Ferrante, Joan M. *Woman as Image in Medieval Literature, From the Twelfth Century to Dante.* New York: Columbia University Press, 1975.

Ferrari, Leo C. "The 'Food of Truth' in Augustine's *Confessions." AS* 9 (1978): 1–14.

Ferry, Anne. *The Art of Naming.* Chicago: University of Chicago Press, 1988.

Fiero, Gloria K., Wendy Pfeffer, and Mathé Allain, eds. *Three Medieval Views of Women: La Contenance des Fames, Le Bien des Fames, Le Blasme des Fames.* New Haven: Yale University Press, 1989.

Finnegan, Robert E. "Eve and 'Vincible Ignorance' in *Genesis B." Texas Studies in Literature and Language* 18 (1976–77): 329–39.

Fish, Stanley E. *Self-Consuming Artifacts: The Experience of Seventeenth-Century Literature.* Berkeley: University of California Press, 1972.

Fleming, John V. *The Roman de la Rose: A Study in Allegory and Iconography.* Princeton: Princeton University Press, 1969.

Forsyth, Neil. *The Old Enemy: Satan and the Combat Myth.* Princeton: Princeton University Press, 1987.

Foucault, Michel. *The Order of Things: An Archaeology of the Human Sciences.* (Orig. *Les Mots et les choses,* 1966.) 1971. Rpt. New York: Vintage, 1973.

Freccero, John. "The Fig Tree and the Laurel: Petrarch's Poetics." *Diacritics* 5 (1975): 34–40.

Freud, Sigmund. *The Freud/Jung Letters: The Correspondence between Sigmund Freud and C. G. Jung.* Ed. William McGuire. Trans. Ralph Manheim and R. F. C. Hull. Princeton: Princeton University Press, 1974.

Fulgentius. *De aetatibus mundi et hominis.* Ed. R. Helm. In *Fabii Planciadis Fulgentii opera,* pp. 129–79. Leipzig, 1898. Trans. Leslie G. Whitbread as *On the Ages of the World and of Man.* In *Fulgentius the Mythographer,* pp. 177–231. Columbus: Ohio State University Press, 1971.

Fyler, John M. "Man, Men, and Women in Chaucer's Poetry." In *The Olde Daunce: Love, Friendship, Sex, and Marriage in the Medieval World,* ed. Robert R. Edwards and Stephen Spector, pp. 154–76. Albany: SUNY Press, 1991.

Gellrich, Jesse M. *The Idea of the Book in the Middle Ages: Language Theory, Mythology, and Fiction.* Ithaca, N.Y.: Cornell University Press, 1985.

——. "Orality, Literacy, and Crisis in the Later Middle Ages." *PQ* 67 (1988): 461–73.

Gendt, Anne-Marie de. " 'Por ce a cy bon exemple': Morale et récit dans *Le*

Livre du Chevalier de la Tour Landry." In *Non Nova, Sed Nove: Mélanges de civilisation médiévale, dédiés à Willem Noomen,* ed. Martin Gosman and Jaap van Os, pp. 67–79. Groningen: Bouma, 1984.

Gollancz, Israel, ed. *The Caedmon Manuscript of Anglo-Saxon Biblical Poetry.* Oxford: Oxford University Press, 1927.

Grayson, Janet. *Structure and Imagery in Ancrene Wisse.* Hanover, N.H.: University Press of New England, 1974.

Greenfield, Stanley B., Daniel G. Calder, and Michael Lapidge. *A New Critical History of Old English Literature.* New York: New York University Press, 1986.

Gregory the Great (Pope). *Moralia in Iob (Commentary on Job). PL* 75:499–76:782.

——. *Regula pastoralis. PL* 77:13–128. Trans. Henry Davis as *St. Gregory the Great: Pastoral Care.* ACW, no. 11. New York: Newman Press, 1950.

Grigsby, John L. "A New Source of the *Livre du Chevalier de la Tour Landry.*" *Romania* 84 (1963): 171–208.

Guillaume de Lorris and Jean de Meun. *Le Roman de la Rose.* Ed. Ernest Langlois. 5 vols. Paris: Société des anciens textes français, 1914–24.

Hall, J. R. "Duality and the Dual Pronoun in *Genesis B.*" *PLL* 17 (1981): 139–45.

——. "The Old English Epic of Redemption: The Theological Unity of MS. Junius 11." *Traditio* 32 (1976): 185–208.

Hanning, Robert W. "From *Eva* and *Ave* to Eglentyne and Alisoun: Chaucer's Insight into the Roles Women Play." *Signs* 2 (1977): 580–99.

Hartman, Geoffrey H. *Saving the Text: Literature/Derrida/Philosophy.* Baltimore: Johns Hopkins University Press, 1981.

Hieatt, A. Kent. "Eve as Reason in a Tradition of Allegorical Interpretation of the Fall." *Journal of the Warburg and Courtauld Institutes* 43 (1980): 221–26.

Hill, Thomas D. "Notes on the Old English 'Maxims' I and II." *N&Q* 215, n.s. 17 (1970): 445–47.

Horace. *Ars poetica.* Ed. and trans. H. Rushton Fairclough. In *Horace: Satires, Epistles, and Ars Poetica.* Rev. ed. LCL. London: Heinemann, 1929.

Houvet, Étienne. *Cathédrale de Chartres.* 5 vols. in 7. Chelles: Faucheux, 1919–21.

Howard, Donald R. *The Three Temptations: Medieval Man in Search of the World.* Princeton: Princeton University Press, 1966.

Hrabanus Maurus. *De universo. PL* 111:9–614.

Hugh of St. Victor. *De sacramentis christianae fidei. PL* 176:173–618. Trans. Roy J. Deferrari as *On the Sacraments of the Christian Faith.* Cambridge, Mass.: Medieval Academy of America, 1951.

Huppé, Bernard F. *Doctrine and Poetry: Augustine's Influence on Old English Poetry.* Albany: SUNY Press, 1959.

Isidore of Seville. *Etymologiae.* Ed. W. M. Lindsay. 2 vols. OCT. Oxford: Clarendon Press, 1911.

Jackson, B. Darrell. "The Theory of Signs in St. Augustine's *De Doctrina Christiana*." *REA* 15 (1969): 9–49. Rpt. in Markus, ed., pp. 92–147.

Jager, Eric. "Invoking/Revoking God's Word: The *Vox Dei* in *Genesis B*." *ES* 71 (1990): 307–21.

———. "Speech and the Chest in Old English Poetry: Orality or Pectorality?" *Speculum* 65 (1990): 845–59.

———. "Tempter as Rhetoric Teacher: The Fall of Language in the Old English *Genesis B*." *Neophilologus* 72 (1988): 434–48.

———. "The Word in the 'Breost': Interiority and the Fall in *Genesis B*." *Neophilologus* 75 (1991): 279–90.

Jerome. *Contra Jovinianum*. PL 23:211–338.

———. *Epistolae*. Ed. I. Hilberg. *Corpus Scriptorum Ecclesiasticorum Latinorum*, vols. 54–56. Trans. Charles C. Mierow as *Letters*. ACW, no. 33. Westminster, Md.: Newman Press, 1963.

Le Jeu d'Adam (Ordo representacionis Ade). Ed. Willem Noomen. Paris: Champion, 1971. Trans. Richard Axton and John Stevens. In *Medieval French Plays*, pp. 1–44. New York: Barnes and Noble, 1971.

Johannot, Yvonne. *Tourner la page: Livre, rites, et symboles*. Aubenas d'Ardèche: Millon, 1988.

John Scotus Erigena. *De praedestinatione (On predestination)*. PL 122:347–440.

Josephus. *Jewish Antiquities*. Ed. and trans. H. St. J. Thackeray et al. 7 vols. LCL. London: Heinemann, 1930.

Joyce, James. *Finnegans Wake*. 1939. Rpt. Harmondsworth: Penguin, 1976.

Kaske, R. E. "*Clericus Adam* and Chaucer's *Adam Scriveyn*." In *Chaucerian Problems and Perspectives: Essays Presented to Paul E. Beichner C. S. C.*, ed. Edward Vasta and Zacharias P. Thundy, pp. 114–18. Notre Dame, Ind.: University of Notre Dame Press, 1979.

———. "Eve's 'Leaps' in the *Ancrene Riwle*." *MAE* 29 (1960): 22–24.

Katzenellenbogen, Adolf. *Allegories of the Virtues and Vices in Medieval Art from Early Christian Times to the Thirteenth Century*. Trans. Alan J. P. Crick. 1939. Rpt. Toronto: University of Toronto Press, 1989.

Kelly, Henry A. "The Metamorphoses of the Eden Serpent during the Middle Ages and Renaissance." *Viator* 2 (1971): 301–28.

Kelly, John N. D. *Early Christian Doctrines*. 5th ed. New York: Harper, 1978.

Kelly, Louis G. "Saint Augustine and Saussurean Linguistics." *AS* 6 (1975): 45–64.

Kennedy, Charles W., trans. and comm. *Early English Christian Poetry Translated into Alliterative Verse*. New York: Oxford University Press, 1952.

Ker, Neil R. *Catalogue of Manuscripts Containing Anglo-Saxon*. Oxford: Clarendon, 1957. Rpt., with *Supplement*, 1990.

Kermode, Frank. *The Genesis of Secrecy: On the Interpretation of Narrative*. Cambridge: Harvard University Press, 1979.

Kirkconnell, Watson, comp. and trans. *The Celestial Cycle: The Theme of*

Paradise Lost in World Literature, with Translations of the Major Analogues. 1952. Rpt. New York: Gordian, 1967.

Klaeber, Friedrich, ed. *The Later Genesis and Other Old English and Old Saxon Texts Relating to the Fall of Man*. Englische Textbibliothek, no. 15. Heidelberg: Winter, 1913.

Kliman, Bernice W. "Women in Early English Literature, *Beowulf* to the *Ancrene Wisse*." *Nottingham Mediaeval Studies* 21 (1977): 32–49.

Laistner, M. L. W. *Thought and Letters in Western Europe, A.D. 500 to 900*. Rev. ed. 1957. Rpt. Ithaca, N.Y.: Cornell University Press, 1966.

La Tour Landry, Geoffroy de. *Le Livre du Chevalier de La Tour Landry pour l'enseignement de ses filles*. Ed. Anatole de Montaiglon. Paris: Jannet, 1854.

Leclercq, Jean. *The Love of Learning and the Desire for God: A Study of Monastic Culture*. Trans. Catharine Misrahi. 2d ed. New York: Fordham University Press, 1977.

Leicester, H. Marshall, Jr. "The Art of Impersonation: A General Prologue to the *Canterbury Tales*." *PMLA* 95 (1980): 213–24.

Lerer, Seth. *Literacy and Power in Anglo-Saxon Literature*. Lincoln, Nebr.: University of Nebraska Press, 1991.

Lesky, Albin. *A History of Greek Literature*. Trans. James Willis and Cornelis de Heer. New York: Crowell, 1966.

Levy, Bernard S., ed. *The Bible in the Middle Ages: Its Influence on Literature and Art*. Binghamton, N.Y.: Medieval and Renaissance Texts and Studies, 1992.

Locke, John. *Two Treatises of Government*. London, 1698. Ed. Peter Laslett. Cambridge: Cambridge University Press, 1988.

Lubac, Henri de. *Exégèse médiévale: Les quatres sens de l'Écriture*. 4 vols. Paris: Aubier, 1959–64.

Lucas, Peter J. "Manuscript Junius 11 and Malmesbury." *Scriptorium* 34 (1980): 197–220; 35 (1981): 3–22.

Luther, Martin. *Lectures on Genesis, Chapters 1–5*. Trans. Jaroslav Pelikan. *Luther's Works*, vol. 1. St. Louis: Concordia, 1958.

McHugh, Michael P. "Satan and Saint Ambrose." *Classical Folia* 26 (1972): 94–106.

McMahon, Robert. *Augustine's Prayerful Ascent: An Essay on the Literary Form of the Confessions*. Athens, Ga.: University of Georgia Press, 1989.

Mallarmé, Stéphane. "Le Livre, instrument spirituel." Trans. Bradford Cook as "The Book: A Spiritual Instrument." In *Critical Theory since Plato*, ed. Hazard Adams, pp. 690–92. New York: Harcourt, Brace, Jovanovich, 1971.

Manly, John M., and Edith Rickert, eds. *The Text of the Canterbury Tales, Studied on the Basis of All Known Manuscripts*. 8 vols. Chicago: University of Chicago Press, 1940. Rpt. 1967.

Markus, R. A., ed. *Augustine: A Collection of Critical Essays*. New York: Anchor/Doubleday, 1972.

——. "St. Augustine on Signs." *Phronesis* 2 (1957): 60–83. Rpt. in Markus, ed., pp. 61–91.

Martin, Priscilla. *Chaucer's Women: Nuns, Wives, and Amazons.* Iowa City: University of Iowa Press, 1990.

Mazzeo, Joseph A. "St. Augustine's Rhetoric of Silence." *JHI* 23 (1962): 175–96.

Mazzotta, Giuseppe. *Dante, Poet of the Desert: History and Allegory in the Divine Comedy.* Princeton: Princeton University Press, 1979.

Mediae Latinitatis Lexicon Minus. Ed. J. F. Niermeyer. Leiden: Brill, 1976. Rpt. 1984.

Melitus. *Clavis cum variorum commentariis.* Ed. Jean Baptiste Pitra. In *Spicilegium solesmense, complectens sanctorum patrum scriptorum-que ecclesiasticorum anecdota hactenus opera,* vols. 2–3. Paris, 1855.

Meyers, Carol. *Discovering Eve: Ancient Israelite Women in Context.* New York: Oxford University Press, 1988.

A Microfiche Concordance to Old English. Comp. Antonette diPaolo Healey and Richard L. Venezky. Toronto: Pontifical Institute of Mediaeval Studies, 1980. Rev rpt. 1985.

Middle English Dictionary. Ed. Hans Kurath, Sherman M. Kuhn, Robert E. Lewis. Ann Arbor: University of Michigan Press, 1952–.

The Middle English Genesis and Exodus. Ed. Olof Arngart. Lund: Gleerup, 1968.

Milton, John. *John Milton: Complete Poems and Major Prose.* Ed. Merritt Y. Hughes. Indianapolis: Bobbs-Merrill, 1957.

Mittellateinisches Wörterbuch bis zum ausgehenden 13. Jahrhundert. Munich: Beck'sche, 1959–.

Moi, Toril. "Desire in Language: Andreas Capellanus and the Controversy of Courtly Love." In *Medieval Literature: Criticism, Ideology, and History,* ed. David Aers, pp. 11–33. New York: St. Martin's, 1986.

Murdoch, Brian O. *The Recapitulated Fall: A Comparative Study in Mediaeval Literature.* Amsterdamer Publikationen zur Sprache und Literatur 11. Amsterdam: RUDOPI N.V., 1974.

Murphy, James J. *Rhetoric in the Middle Ages: A History of Rhetorical Theory from Saint Augustine to the Renaissance.* Berkeley: University of California Press, 1974.

Nichols, Stephen G., Jr. "An Intellectual Anthropology of Marriage in the Middle Ages." In *The New Medievalism,* ed. Marina S. Brownlee, Kevin Brownlee, and Stephen G. Nichols, pp. 70–95. Baltimore: Johns Hopkins University Press, 1991.

——. *Romanesque Signs: Early Medieval Narrative and Iconography.* New Haven: Yale University Press, 1983.

——. "Solomon's Wife: Deceit, Desire, and the Genealogy of Romance." In *Space, Time, Image, Sign: Essays on Literature and the Visual Arts,* ed. James A. W. Heffernan, pp. 19–37. New York: Peter Lang, 1987.

Noakes, Susan. "The Double Misreading of Paolo and Francesca." *PQ* 62 (1983): 221–39.

——. *Timely Reading: Between Exegesis and Interpretation.* Ithaca, N.Y.: Cornell University Press, 1988.

O'Connell, Robert J. *Art and the Christian Intelligence in St. Augustine.* Cambridge: Harvard University Press, 1978.

The Old Testament Pseudepigrapha. Ed. James H. Charlesworth. 2 vols. Garden City, N.Y.: Doubleday, 1983–85.

Ong, Walter J. *Orality and Literacy: The Technologizing of the Word.* London: Methuen, 1982.

Opland, Jeff. *Anglo-Saxon Oral Poetry: A Study of the Traditions.* New Haven: Yale University Press, 1980.

Overing, Gillian R. "On Reading Eve: *Genesis B* and the Readers' Desire." In *Speaking Two Languages: Traditional Disciplines and Contemporary Theory in Medieval Studies,* ed. Allen J. Frantzen, pp. 35–63. Albany: SUNY Press, 1991.

Ovid. *The Art of Love and Other Poems.* Ed. and trans. J. H. Mozley. 2d ed. Rev. G. P. Goold. LCL. London: Heinemann, 1979.

——. *Metamorphoses.* Ed. and trans. Frank J. Miller. 2 vols. 3d ed. Rev. G. P. Goold. LCL. London: Heinemann, 1977.

Owen, S. G. "A Medieval Latin Poem." *English Historical Review* 2 (1887): 525–26.

The Oxford English Dictionary. 1st ed. 13 vols. Oxford: Clarendon Press, 1933. *Supplement,* 1986.

Oxford Latin Dictionary. Ed. P. G. W. Glare. Oxford: Clarendon Press, 1982.

Pächt, Otto, C. R. Dodwell, and Francis Wormald, eds. *The St. Albans Psalter (Albani Psalter).* London: Warburg Institute, 1960.

Pagels, Elaine. *Adam, Eve, and the Serpent.* New York: Random House, 1988.

Panofsky, Erwin. *Studies in Iconology: Humanistic Themes in the Art of the Renaissance.* 1939. Rpt. New York: Harper and Row, 1972.

Parkes, M. B. "The Literacy of the Laity." In *The Mediaeval World,* ed. David Daiches and Anthony Thorlby, pp. 555–77. *Literature and Western Civilization,* vol. 2. London: Aldous Books, 1973.

Patrologia Latina. Ed. J.-P. Migne. 221 vols. Paris, 1841–1905.

Patterson, Lee. *Chaucer and the Subject of History.* London: Routledge, 1991.

——. *Negotiating the Past: The Historical Understanding of Medieval Literature.* Madison: University of Wisconsin Press, 1987.

Pelikan, Jaroslav. *The Christian Tradition: A History of the Development of Doctrine.* 5 vols. Chicago: University of Chicago Press, 1971–89.

Peter Comestor. *Historia scholastica.* PL 198:1053–1722.

Peter Lombard. *Sententiae.* PL 192:519–962.

Phillips, John A. *Eve: The History of an Idea.* 1984. Rpt. San Francisco: Harper and Row, 1985.

Philo of Alexandria. *Legum allegoria.* Ed. and trans. G. H. Whitaker as *Allegorical Interpretation of Genesis 2–3.* In *Philo* 1:140–473. LCL. London: Heinemann, 1929.

Plato. *The Collected Dialogues of Plato, Including the Letters.* Trans. Lane

Cooper et al. Ed. Edith Hamilton and Huntington Cairns. 1961. Rpt. Princeton: Princeton University Press, 1963.

Poggioli, Renato. "Paolo and Francesca." In *Dante: A Collection of Critical Essays*, ed. John Freccero, pp. 61–77. Englewood Cliffs, N.J.: Prentice-Hall, 1965. (Orig. pub. *PMLA* 72 [1957]).

Pollard, Graham. "The Pecia System in the Medieval Universities." In *Medieval Scribes, Manuscripts, and Libraries: Essays Presented to N. R. Ker*, ed. M. B. Parkes and Andrew G. Watson, pp. 145–61. London: Scolar, 1978.

Preus, James S. *From Shadow to Promise: Old Testament Interpretation from Augustine to Young Luther*. Cambridge: Harvard University Press, 1969.

Pulsiano, Phillip. "Redeemed Language and the Ending of *Troilus and Criseyde*." In Wasserman and Roney, eds., pp. 153–74.

Quasten, Johannes. *Patrology*. 4 vols. Utrecht and Westminster, Md.: Spectrum and Christian Classics, 1950–86.

Quintilian. *The Institutio Oratoria of Quintilian*. Ed. and trans. H. E. Butler. 4 vols. LCL. London: Heinemann, 1920–22.

Ratramnus. *Liber de nativitate Christi (On the Parturition of Saint Mary)*. PL 121:81–102.

Réau, Louis. *Iconographie de l'art Chrétien*. 3 vols. Paris: Presses Universitaires de France, 1955–59.

Renoir, Alain. "Eve's I.Q. Rating: Two Sexist Views of *Genesis B*." In *New Readings on Women in Old English Literature*, ed. Helen Damico and Alexandra Hennessey Olsen, pp. 262–72. Bloomington: Indiana University Press, 1990.

Ricoeur, Paul. *The Symbolism of Evil*. Trans. Emerson Buchanan. (Orig. *La Symbolique du mal*, 1960.) 1967. Rpt. Boston: Beacon, 1969.

Riga, Peter. *Aurora: Petri Rigae Biblia versificata: A Verse Commentary on the Bible*. Ed. Paul E. Beichner. 2 vols. Notre Dame: University of Notre Dame Press, 1965.

Robbins, Gregory A., ed. *Genesis 1–3 in the History of Exegesis: Intrigue in the Garden*. Lewiston, N.Y.: Mellen, 1988.

Robert of Basevorn. *Forma praedicandi*. Trans. Leopold Krul as *The Form of Preaching*. In *Three Medieval Rhetorical Arts*, ed. James J. Murphy, pp. 109–215. Berkeley: University of California Press, 1971.

Roberts, Colin H., and T. C. Skeat. *The Birth of the Codex*. London: Oxford University Press, 1987.

Roberts, Michael. "The Prologue to Avitus' *De spiritalis historiae gestis*: Christian Poetry and Poetic License." *Traditio* 36 (1980): 399–407.

Robertson, D. W., Jr. *Essays in Medieval Culture*. Princeton: Princeton University Press, 1980.

———. *A Preface to Chaucer: Studies in Medieval Perspectives*. Princeton: Princeton University Press, 1962.

Rosenberg, David, trans., and Harold Bloom, comm. *The Book of J*. New York: Grove Weidenfeld, 1990.

Ross, Thomas W. *Chaucer's Bawdy*. New York: Dutton, 1972.

Rudat, Wolfgang E. H. "Chaucer's Spring of Comedy: The *Merchant's Tale* and Other 'Games' with Augustinian Theology." *AM* 21 (1981): 111–20.

Russell, Jeffrey B. *Lucifer: The Devil in the Middle Ages*. Ithaca, N.Y.: Cornell University Press, 1984.

——. *Satan: The Early Christian Tradition*. Ithaca, N.Y.: Cornell University Press, 1981.

Salu, Mary B., trans. *The Ancrene Riwle: The Corpus MS.: Ancrene Wisse*. London: Burns and Oates, 1955.

Sayers, Dorothy L., trans. *The Song of Roland*. Harmondsworth: Penguin, 1937.

Schiller, Gertrud. *Iconography of Christian Art*. Trans. Janet Seligman. 2 vols. Greenwich, Conn.: New York Graphic Society, 1971–72.

Sebeok, Jean Umiker, and Thomas A. Sebeok, eds. *Monastic Sign Languages*. Berlin: Mouton de Gruyter, 1987.

Sedgewick, G. G. "The Structure of *The Merchant's Tale*." *The University of Toronto Quarterly* 17 (1948): 337–45.

The Seven Sages of Rome (Southern Version). Ed. Karl Brunner. EETS OS 191. London: Oxford University Press, 1933.

Shoaf, Richard A. *Dante, Chaucer, and the Currency of the Word: Money, Images, and Reference in Late Medieval Poetry*. Norman, Okla.: Pilgrim Books, 1983.

——. "Medieval Studies after Derrida after Heidegger." In Wasserman and Roney, eds., pp. 9–30.

——. *Milton, Poet of Duality: A Study of Semiosis in the Poetry and the Prose*. New Haven: Yale University Press, 1985.

Smalley, Beryl. *The Study of the Bible in the Middle Ages*. 1952. Rpt. Notre Dame, Ind.: University of Notre Dame Press, 1964.

Solignac, A., comm. *Oeuvres de Saint Augustin: Les Confessions*. Bibliothèque augustinienne, 2d ser., vols. 13–14. Paris: Desclée, 1962.

Steiner, George. *After Babel: Aspects of Language and Translation*. London: Oxford University Press, 1975.

Stenton, Frank M. *Anglo-Saxon England*. 3d ed. The Oxford History of England, vol 2. Oxford: Clarendon Press, 1971.

Tatlock, J. S. P. "Dante's *Terza Rima*." *PMLA* 51 (1936): 895–903.

Taylor, Mark C. *Erring: A Postmodern A/theology*. Chicago: University of Chicago Press, 1984.

Tentler, Thomas N. *Sin and Confession on the Eve of the Reformation*. Princeton: Princeton University Press, 1977.

Tertullian. *De anima (On the Soul)*. PL 2:646–752.

——. *De carne Christi (On the Body of Christ)*. PL 2:751–92.

Thesaurus Linguae Latinae. Leipzig: Teubner, 1900–.

Thornley, G. C. "The Accents and Points of MS. Junius 11." *Transactions of the Philological Society* (1954): 178–205.

Timmer, Benno J. *The Later Genesis*. Rev. ed. Oxford: Scrivner, 1954.

Trible, Phyllis. "Depatriarchalizing in Biblical Interpretation." *Journal of the American Academy of Religion* 41 (1973): 30–48.

Tuman, Myron C. Rev. of Walter Ong, *Orality and Literacy* (1982). *College English* 45 (1983): 769–79.

Vance, Eugene. *Mervelous Signals: Poetics and Sign Theory in the Middle Ages.* Lincoln, Nebr.: University of Nebraska Press, 1986.

Vickrey, John F. "*Genesis B*: A New Analysis and Edition." University of Indiana dissertation, 1960.

——. "On *Genesis* 623–5." *ES* 70 (1989): 97–106.

——. "The Vision of Eve in *Genesis B.*" *Speculum* 44 (1969): 86–102.

Vincent of Beauvais. *Speculum quadruplex, sive Speculum maius: naturale, doctrinale, morale, historiale.* Douai, 1624. 4 vols. Rpt. Graz, Austria: Akademische Druck-u. Verlagsanstalt, 1964–65.

Virgil. *Aeneid.* Ed. and trans. H. Rushton Fairclough. *Virgil.* 2 vols. Rev. ed. LCL. London: Heinemann, 1934.

Warner, Marina. *Monuments and Maidens: The Allegory of the Female Form.* New York: Atheneum, 1985.

Warren, Ann K. *Anchorites and Their Patrons in Medieval England.* Berkeley: University of California Press, 1985.

Wasserman, Julian N., and Lois Roney, eds. *Sign, Sentence, Discourse: Language in Medieval Thought and Literature.* Syracuse, N.Y.: Syracuse University Press, 1989.

Watkins, Calvert, comp. "Indo-European Roots." In *The American Heritage Dictionary of the English Language,* pp. 1505–50. Boston: Houghton Mifflin, 1969.

Wentersdorf, Karl P. "Theme and Structure in the *Merchant's Tale*: The Function of the Pluto Episode." *PMLA* 80 (1965): 522–27.

Williams, Norman P. *The Ideas of the Fall and of Original Sin: A Historical and Critical Study.* London: Longmans, 1927.

Wood, Margaret. *The English Mediaeval House.* London: Phoenix House, 1965.

Woolf, Rosemary. "The Fall of Man in *Genesis B* and The *Mystère d'Adam.*" In *Studies in Old English Literature in Honor of Arthur G. Brodeur,* ed. Stanley B. Greenfield, pp. 187–99. Eugene: University of Oregon Books, 1963.

Wright, Thomas, and James O. Halliwell, eds. *Reliquiae Antiquae: Scraps from Ancient Manuscripts, Illustrating Chiefly Early English Literature and the English Language.* 2 vols. 1841–43. Rpt. New York: AMS Press, 1966.

Wurtele, Douglas. "The Blasphemy of Chaucer's Merchant." *AM* 21 (1981): 91–110.

——. "The Penitence of Geoffrey Chaucer." *Viator* 11 (1980): 335–59.

Yates, Frances A. *The Art of Memory.* Chicago: University of Chicago Press, 1966.

Yeats, William Butler. *The Collected Poems of W. B. Yeats.* Def. ed. New York: Macmillan, 1956.

INDEX

Library of Congress Cataloging-in-Publication Data

Jager, Eric, 1957–
    The tempter's voice : language and the fall in Medieval litera-
ture / Eric Jager.
        p. cm.
    Includes bibliographical references and index.
    ISBN 0-8014-2753-3 (cloth). — ISBN 0-8014-8036-1 (pbk.)
    1. Fall of man in literature. 2. Literature, Medieval—History
and criticism. 3. Bible. O.T. Genesis III—Criticism and
interpretation, etc.—History—Early church, ca. 30–600. 4. Bible.
Middle Ages, 600–1500. I. Title.
PN56.F29J34 1993
809'.93382—dc20   93-11811